大使讲中英关系

On China-UK Relations

Volume II

刘晓明著有：

1. 《大使讲中国故事》(2022年，中信出版集团)，被全国千家实体书店推选为第五届"全民阅读·书店之选"主题出版类"十佳"作品。

2. 《尖锐对话》(2022年，北京出版集团)，被人民日报图书馆"金台好书榜"列为"十大好书"，入选《出版业"十四五"时期发展规划》，2024年被评为第二十三届输出版优秀图书。

3. 《有问必答》(2024年，北京出版集团)，被"探照灯好书"评为"人文社科原创佳作"，多次登上京东政治图书热卖榜。

大使讲中英关系

我们需要什么样的中英关系？

下卷

刘晓明 著

On China-UK Relations

Volume II

Liu Xiaoming

中信出版集团 | 北京

图书在版编目（CIP）数据

大使讲中英关系：全2册/刘晓明著. -- 北京：
中信出版社, 2024. 8. -- ISBN 978-7-5217-6813-8
Ⅰ.D829.561
中国国家版本馆CIP数据核字第2024XR4456号

大使讲中英关系
著者：   刘晓明
出版发行：中信出版集团股份有限公司
　　　　　（北京市朝阳区东三环北路27号嘉铭中心　邮编　100020）
承印者：　北京盛通印刷股份有限公司

开本：787mm×1092mm 1/16　　印张：66.5　插页：16　字数：980千字
版次：2024年8月第1版　　　　　印次：2024年8月第1次印刷
书号：ISBN 978-7-5217-6813-8
定价：198.00元（全2册）

版权所有·侵权必究
如有印刷、装订问题，本公司负责调换。
服务热线：400-600-8099
投稿邮箱：author@citicpub.com

目 录
Contents

第一章　文化交流
PART I　Cultural Exchanges

增进了解，促进友谊 ································· 005

Promote Understanding and Strengthen Friendship ············· 007

语言是文化的重要载体 ······························ 009

Language Is an Important Carrier of Culture ················ 011

文化的表征，思想的形象 ···························· 013

Garments Are Cultural Symbols ························ 015

仁者乐山，智者乐水 ································ 017

Enjoy Mountains and Water ·························· 019

增进中西方了解，扩大中西方合作 ···················· 021

Increase Mutual Understanding and Cooperation ············· 023

中国时装业，扬帆出海正当时 ························ 027

China's Fashion Industry: Time for Going Global ············· 031

东方和西方的完美结合 ······························ 037

Unite the East and the West ·························· 039

精彩的"故乡行" ··································· 043

An Amazing "Home Trip" ···························· 045

中英旅游合作天时、地利、人和 049
Enjoy Three Favorables 051
续写辉煌 055
Create New Splendour 057
为中英文化交流增光添彩 059
A Highly Acclaimed Achievement in China-UK Cultural Exchanges 062
中国文化季恰逢其时 067
A Timely China Cultural Season 070
海纳百川，有容乃大 075
The Vast Sea Admits Hundreds of Rivers 077
为中英人文交流插上智慧的翅膀 081
Give Wings of Wisdom to China-UK Cultural Exchanges 083
深化中英体育合作，共创世界美好未来 085
Deepen China-UK Sports Cooperation for a Better World 090
为中英关系贡献更多创意，注入更多活力 097
Contribute More Creativity and Dynamism to China-UK Relations 100
编织梦想，共创中英互利合作美好明天 105
Weave the Dream of China-UK Cooperation 107
传承历史文明，践行未来梦想 111
Pass on the Torch of Civilizations to Realize the Dream for the Future 114
感受中国之美，共建友谊合作之桥 119
Enjoy the Beauty of China and Build a Bridge of Friendship and Cooperation 121
文物交流传佳话，中英友好续新篇 125
A Beautiful Story of China-UK Cultural Exchanges and Friendship 127

第二章　春节庆典
PART II　Spring Festival Celebrations

生生不息，和谐长久 ······ 135

Longevity and Harmony ······ 137

趣品中国味，厚植中英情 ······ 141

A Delightful Taste of China, a Closer China-UK Bond ······ 143

品尝中西交融美味，迎接互利共赢未来 ······ 147

Fusion of Flavours for a Fruitful Future ······ 150

共同建设美好世界大家庭 ······ 153

Build a Big Global Family Together ······ 156

第三章　教育交流
PART III　Educational Exchanges

记忆中国，难忘母校 ······ 167

Share Experiences of Studying in China ······ 170

从相识到相知，从相知到相通 ······ 173

From Acquaintance to Understanding, from Understanding to Connection ······ 176

中英教育合作未来更美好 ······ 179

A Brighter Future for China-UK Educational Cooperation ······ 184

春华秋实结硕果，交流互鉴促发展 ······ 193

Develop Together through Exchanges and Mutual Learning ······ 196

共谋中英关系百年大计 ······ 201

Plan for One Hundred Years of China-UK Relations ······ 204

凝聚智慧，共建世界和平与繁荣 ······ 209

Build World Peace and Prosperity on Wisdom ······ 213

携手谱写中英教育交流与合作的"华彩乐章" ······ 221

A Symphony of China-UK Educational Exchanges and Cooperation ······ 224

激扬青春梦想，共促中英合作 ·· 229

Devote Your Youthful Vigour to China-UK Cooperation ················ 232

为中英教育交流合作增光添彩 ··· 237

Make Greater Contribution to China-UK Educational Exchanges
and Cooperation ··· 240

第四章　孔子学院
PART Ⅳ　Confucius Institutes

学习语言，传承友谊 ·· 249

Study Language, Promote Friendship ·· 251

为"汉语热"助阵 ··· 253

Add to the Momentum of Rising Demand for Mandarin ············· 256

中英、中欧合作结硕果 ·· 261

Fruits of China-UK and China-Europe Cooperation ···················· 263

拿起手中"魔法棒"，谱写中英关系新篇章 ···································· 267

Wave Your Magic Wand to Contribute a New Chapter to
China-UK Relations ·· 270

秉持交流初心，共建理解之桥 ·· 275

Build a Bridge of Exchanges and Understanding ······················· 278

第五章　军事往来
PART Ⅴ　Military Exchanges

威武之师，和平之师，友谊之师 ··· 287

A Valiant Force for Peace and Friendship ·································· 289

忠诚、使命、奉献 ·· 293

把握时刻，开启新程 ··· 295

Seize the Moment and Start a New Journey ································· 297

为中英关系增彩，为世界和平担当 ································· 301

For World Peace and More Splendid China-UK Relations ················ 304

捍卫和平，促进发展 ································· 307

Safeguard Peace and Promote Development ································· 310

第六章 华侨华人
PART Ⅵ Chinese Community

众人拾柴火焰高 ································· 319

虽有智慧，不如乘势 ································· 323

越是民族的就越是世界的 ································· 327

What Is Unique to a Nation Is Precious for the World ················ 329

秉持"石头精神"，推进中英合作 ································· 333

牢记共同的血脉，开创共赢的未来 ································· 337

Our Common Roots, Our Shared Future ································· 339

共庆新春佳节，共筑复兴伟业 ································· 343

第七章 英国友人
PART Ⅶ British Friends

研究历史，关注当代 ································· 351

Study History and Focus on the Present ································· 353

友谊的记忆永不褪色 ································· 357

The Memory of Friendship Never Fades ································· 360

老骥伏枥，志在千里 ································· 365

A Steed Aspires to Gallop a Thousand Miles ································· 367

踏遍青山人未老，前路更加美好 ································· 371

A Better View Further down the Road ································· 374

改革促发展，合作促友谊 ·· 379
Reform Promotes Development and Cooperation Enhances
Friendship ·· 382

第八章　中英认知
PART VIII　Understanding between China and the UK

筷子与刀叉，中西方文明共存互鉴 ··· 391
Chopsticks vs Knives and Forks ································· 395
相互尊重，同舟共济 ·· 401
Respect Each Other and Stand Together through Thick and Thin ········· 406
兼听则明，偏信则暗 ·· 411
A Clear Head Comes from an Open Mind ······························ 416
共促合作，共同发展 ·· 423
Collaborate and Grow Together ·· 427
构建新型中西方关系 ·· 435
Build a New Type of Relationship between China and the West ········ 443
弘扬严复精神，加强中西互鉴 ·· 455
Carry Forward Yan Fu's Spirit ··· 458

后　记 ··· 463
Afterword ··· 465

第一章 文化交流
PART I Cultural Exchanges

英国历史悠久，文化底蕴深厚，是世界文化大国之一。全国约有 2500 家博物馆和展览馆，其中大英博物馆、国家美术馆等闻名于世。英国皇家芭蕾舞团、伦敦交响乐团等艺术团体具有世界一流水准。英国每年举办 500 多个专业艺术节，其中爱丁堡国际艺术节是世界上规模最大的艺术节之一。英国传媒业在世界上有较大影响，人均报纸销量居世界首位。英语是国际信息传播的主要语言，世界上约 80% 的信息以英语传播。英国还是欧洲最大的电视节目出口国，拥有英国广播公司、天空电视台等世界知名广播和电视媒体。

中英文化交流源远流长。在我担任驻英大使期间，两国建立了高级别人文交流机制。2012 年 4 月，中国首次作为主宾国出席伦敦书展。2013 年，两国续签《中英两国政府 2013 至 2018 年文化交流计划》。2015 年，两国举办"中英文化交流年"活动，其间双方在对方国家举办以"新世代"为主题的"英国文化季"和以"创意中国"为主题的"中国文化季"。2016 年，两国举办"纪念汤显祖、莎士比亚逝世 400 周年"系列活动。两国每年都有各种文化团体互访，从文学、语言、戏剧、音乐、舞蹈、电影、动漫，到旅游、体育、时装、设计、建筑、绘画、展览，再到新媒体、数字文化、创意产业，双方交流广泛而深入，取得了丰硕成果，惠及两国人民。

本章收录了我的 20 篇演讲，内容涵盖图书、语言、文学、戏剧、歌舞、服饰、书展、旅游、体育、影视、文物、手工艺、"中国文化季"等，读者可以从中领略中英文化交流的广度与深度。

The United Kingdom, with its long history and rich heritage, is one of the world leaders in cultural strength. The country boasts approximately 2,500 museums and galleries, including the world-renowned British Museum and National Gallery. The Royal Ballet and the London Symphony Orchestra are among the world's top art groups. Each year, the UK hosts over 500 professional art festivals, including the Edinburgh International Festival, one of the biggest in the world. The British media has global influence and the industry has the highest per capita newspaper circulation in the world. English is the primary language in international information dissemination, with about 80% of global information conveyed in English. The UK is also Europe's largest exporter of television programmes. It is home to internationally recognized broadcasters such as the BBC and Sky TV.

China-UK cultural exchanges have a long history. During my tenure as the Chinese Ambassador to the UK, the two countries established a High-Level People-to-People Exchange Mechanism. In April 2012, China participated as the Guest of Honour at the London Book Fair for the first time. In 2013, the two countries renewed the "China-UK Cultural Exchange Programme 2013—2018". 2015 witnessed the "Year of Cultural Exchanges". The two countries held the "UK Cultural Season" in China with the theme "New Generation" and "China Cultural Season" in the UK with the theme "Creative China". In 2016, the two countries commemorated the 400th anniversary of the passing of Tang Xianzu and Shakespeare with a series of events. Various cultural groups from the two countries visited each other annually, covering literature, language, theatre, music, dance, film, animation, tourism, sports, fashion, design, architecture, painting, exhibitions, new media, digital culture, and creative industries. These exchanges are extensive and deep, yielding fruitful results and benefiting the peoples of both countries.

This chapter includes 20 of my speeches, covering books, language, literature, theatre, music, dance, costumes, book fairs, tourism, sports, film and television, cultural relics, handicrafts, and the "China Cultural Season", showcasing the breadth and depth of China-UK cultural exchanges.

增进了解，促进友谊 *

尊敬的大英图书馆董事会主席科林·卢卡斯爵士，

大英图书馆馆长林恩·布林德利女士，

女士们、先生们：

很高兴今晚出席大英图书馆举办的答谢"中国之窗"赠书项目招待会。

我抵英时间不长，今天是我第一次来到大英图书馆，我却有一种似曾相识的感觉。我想，一个原因是大英图书馆作为世界上最大的图书馆之一久负盛名，而且它与马克思的渊源在中国众所周知。另一个更重要的原因是无论我走到哪里，促进双方图书馆之间的合作都是我工作的一部分。我在担任驻埃及大使时，曾多次造访有"人类文明世界的太阳"之称的亚历山大图书馆，并积极促成在亚历山大图书馆举办"中国汉字展"；在出任驻朝鲜大使后，我代表中国政府向朝鲜国家图书馆——人民大学习堂赠书。现在我担任驻英大使，推动中英图书馆之间的交流与合作仍将是我工作的重要一环。

我很高兴得知大英图书馆和中国国家图书馆保持着长期良好的合作关系。双方的交流与互访非常密切，2009年下半年，布林德利馆长应邀参加了中国国家图书馆百年馆庆纪念活动。谈到两馆合作，不能不提及"国际敦煌项目"。由于我曾在甘肃省担任省长助理，因此对敦煌有着特殊的感情。敦煌文献是人类文明的珍贵遗产，它不仅属于中国，也属于世界。两馆合作9

---

* 在大英图书馆举办的答谢"中国之窗"赠书项目招待会上的讲话。2010年5月11日，大英图书馆。

年来，将敦煌文献数字化，不仅推动了文献保护修复与研究的国际合作，而且是对世界文献研究的一大贡献。

自 2006 年起，大英图书馆开始接受中国国家图书馆的"中国之窗"赠书项目，迄今为止接受赠书约 3500 册。这些图书成为英国读者了解中国发展、感知中国文化的重要资源。

图书是记录人类文明的载体，图书馆是人类文明成果的集散地。各国图书馆之间加强交流与合作，有利于实现全球文明成果的共享，增进人民之间的理解和友谊，促进各国的共同进步和发展。

我祝愿中英两国图书馆在图书交换、学术研究、技术研发等领域的交流与合作能取得更多丰硕成果，为两国公众开启更多认识和了解彼此的窗口，为促进两国人民之间的友谊做出更大贡献。

谢谢大家！

Promote Understanding and Strengthen Friendship*

Sir Colin Lucas,

Dame Lynne Brindley,

Ladies and Gentlemen,

It's a great pleasure to join you at tonight's reception to celebrate the "Window to China".

This is my first visit to the British Library. But I do not feel as if I was a stranger here. For one thing, the British Library has a long-standing reputation as one of the world's leading libraries. It is particularly well-known in China because of its association with Karl Marx. As Ambassador, I see it as an important part of my mission to strengthen knowledge and understanding between China and my host countries, an inherent part of which is to facilitate exchanges and cooperation between libraries.

When I was Ambassador to Egypt, I visited the Library of Alexandria many times, which is known as the sun of the civilized world. I have also worked to bring an exhibition of Chinese Characters to the library. During my ambassadorship in the DPRK, I donated books to the Korean national library on behalf of the Chinese government. Here as Ambassador to the UK, I am even more enthusiastic about facilitating exchanges between libraries as a vehicle for spreading knowledge, understanding and friendship among the people.

I am glad to learn that the British Library and the National Library of China have

---

* Remarks at the Reception Hosted by the British Library to Celebrate the "Window to China". British Library, 11 May 2010.

developed a sound partnership based on close communication and regular exchanges. Last year, Chief Executive Dame Brindley attended the centennial celebration of the National Library of China. Any mention of the cooperation between the two libraries will not be complete without reference to the International Dunhuang Project. Dunhuang has a special place in my heart, as I worked as Assistant Governor of Gansu Province, the home province of Dunhuang. The Dunhuang manuscripts are precious legacies of human civilization that belong not just to China, but also to the world. The digitalization of the Dunhuang manuscripts as part of the 9-year cooperation between the two libraries is not only conducive to international protection and restoration of ancient manuscripts, but also contributes immensely to global research in this area.

From 2006 on, the British Library became a beneficiary of the "Window to China" project sponsored by the National Library of China and has received about 3,500 books by far. These books have become an important resource for British readers to understand China and appreciate Chinese culture.

Books are the written records of human civilization, and libraries are the hubs that accumulate and spread human achievements. Strengthening exchanges and cooperation between libraries of various countries enables the sharing of the fruits of global civilization, enhances the understanding and friendship between people, promotes the common progress and development of all countries.

While celebrating the "Window to China", I hope libraries of our two countries will work together to open up more windows for people to better understand each other and contribute more to strengthening the friendship between our two peoples.

Thank you!

语言是文化的重要载体 *

尊敬的英中协会名誉主席杰弗里·豪勋爵，
尊敬的牛津大学校长汉密尔顿教授，
女士们、先生们：

我很高兴出席《牛津英汉汉英词典》的发行仪式。这一词典的出版发行，对于广大学习英语的中国人，以及日益增多的正在学习汉语的英语母语者来说，无疑是一个大好消息。因此，我要致以热烈的祝贺。

在中国，英语是大中小学的必修课，许多幼儿园也开设了英语课。数据显示，目前中国有 4 亿多人在学习英语，约占中国总人口的 1/3。甚至有专家预测，再过几年，中国学习英语的人数将超过英语母语国家的总人口数。而在英国，目前也正兴起"汉语热"，开设汉语的大中小学越来越多，孔子学院和孔子课堂遍布英国。无论是学习英语还是汉语，一本词典都必不可少。

自 100 多年前《牛津英语词典》这一"词典之帝"出版以来，可以说牛津大学出版社一直执全球词典出版界之牛耳。"牛津"二字几乎成了高质量英文工具书的代名词。据称，世界上每分钟就有 6 个人购买牛津大学出版社出版的词典。

牛津大学出版社是与中方合作最多的外国出版社之一。牛津大学出版社的系列英语词典是中国人学习英语的必备工具书，也是许多人的首选工具书。我还记得我年轻时就拥有一部《精选英汉汉英词典》，这是 20 世纪 70

---

* 在《牛津英汉汉英词典》发行仪式上的讲话。2010 年 9 月 9 日，伦敦英中协会。

年代末牛津大学出版社和中国现代历史最悠久的出版社——商务印书馆最早合作的产物。而两家在20世纪80年代推出的《牛津高阶英汉双解词典》则更是风靡一时、长盛不衰，被英语学习者奉为圭臬。

现在牛津大学出版社与中国规模最大的大学出版社——外语教学与研究出版社强强携手，与时俱进，合作编写出版了词汇更庞大全面的、翻译更准确权威的《牛津英汉汉英词典》，我相信这必会广受读者欢迎和好评，并成为英汉词典的又一座重要里程碑。

编纂词典是一项费心劳力的经年苦役，塞缪尔·约翰逊曾在其成名巨著《约翰逊英语词典》中对"词典编纂者"下了这样一个定义——"无害的苦工"。这一自嘲既是幽默，也道出了实情。但是，编纂词典又何尝不是一种"甜美的苦役"？其甜美在于它将成为无数使用者的学海明灯。感谢《牛津英汉汉英词典》编纂者的辛勤努力，由于你们的付出，我们在学习英语的漫漫长路上又多了一位良师益友。

语言是文化的载体。学习一个国家语言的过程，也是了解一个国家文化的过程。因此，《牛津英汉汉英词典》的出版，其意义不仅在于为读者提供高质量的语言工具书，更在于为促进中英文化交流做出新的贡献。

最后，我祝愿《牛津英汉汉英词典》的发行取得佳绩，也祝愿牛津大学出版社与中国出版界的合作蒸蒸日上。

谢谢！

Language Is an Important Carrier of Culture*

Lord Howe,

Professor Hamilton,

Ladies and Gentlemen,

It is my great pleasure to join you at the launching ceremony of the *Oxford Chinese Dictionary*. I offer my warmest congratulations on the dictionary, as there is no doubt that its launch will be great news for the many people learning English in China and the increasing number of mandarin-learning native English speakers.

Today English is a compulsory course in Chinese universities, as well as in primary and secondary schools and is even taught in many kindergartens. It is estimated that one in three people in China or over 400 million people are learning English. And it is predicted that in a few years, the English learning population in China will exceed the combined total population of all native English-speaking countries. We are also seeing an emerging "Mandarin fever" in the UK, with more and more schools at all levels putting mandarin in their curriculum. This is in addition to the many Confucius Institutes and Classrooms to be found across the country. Needless to say, a good dictionary is a must for all language students.

Since the classic *Oxford English Dictionary* was published more than a century ago, Oxford University Press (OUP) has been the most prestigious dictionary publisher in the world. Even the name "Oxford" represents a quality guarantee for English

---

* Remarks at the Launching Ceremony of the *Oxford Chinese Dictionary*. Great Britain-China Centre, 9 September 2010.

reference books, and if proof was needed, it is said that 6 Oxford dictionaries are sold every minute.

OUP is one of the largest foreign publishing partners of China, with Oxford English dictionaries being the must-have dictionaries for students learning English and, for many others, their first choice as a reference book. When I was a young diplomat, I used to have a *Concise English-Chinese Chinese-English Dictionary*, which was the result of the early cooperation between OUP and the Commercial Press back in the late 1970's. The two later worked together again to produce another immensely popular dictionary, the *Oxford Advanced Learner's English-Chinese Dictionary*, which many Chinese students believe is the leading English-Chinese dictionary.

Now OUP, in cooperation with FLTRP, the largest university press in China, have launched the *Oxford FLTRP English-Chinese Chinese-English Dictionary*, which has a larger vocabulary and more accurate and authoritative translations. I am sure it will be well received and become another milestone for OUP in its evolution of the English-Chinese dictionary.

It takes years of hard work to compile a dictionary. No wonder Samuel Johnson defined "lexicographer" with some humour in his dictionary as "a harmless drudge". But I would argue that tedious and painstaking as it is, the job may also be enriching, as dictionaries offer their users valuable knowledge and understanding. So, I would like to thank the lexicographers for the time and energy they have devoted to this dictionary and for their dedication and professionalism which will make learning English easier for many.

Language is an important carrier of any culture and when you learn a foreign language, you get to know aspects of the culture you would otherwise miss. That is why the publication of this dictionary will not only help users to develop their language skills, but also improve their understanding and contribute to improving China-UK cultural exchanges.

To conclude, I wish this dictionary every success and may OUP and the Chinese publishing industries enjoy closer cooperation!

Thank you!

文化的表征，思想的形象 *

尊敬的维多利亚与阿尔伯特博物馆董事会主席保罗·拉多克先生，
尊敬的维多利亚与阿尔伯特博物馆馆长马克·琼斯爵士，
各位来宾，
女士们、先生们：

很高兴今晚参加"紫禁城皇家服饰展"开幕式。首先我要对中国故宫博物院和维多利亚与阿尔伯特博物馆联合举办此次展览表示热烈的祝贺。

此次展览将向英国公众展示故宫博物院收藏的中国明清时期的皇家服饰。这些服饰精工巧作，处处显示皇家的雍容与典雅，无论是丝绸锦缎的流光溢彩还是刺绣文饰的精美绝伦，都达到了中国古代宫廷服饰水平的巅峰。

"衣裳是文化的表征，衣裳是思想的形象。"当我们欣赏这些巧夺天工的中国古代服饰精品时，或许应多一些了解和认识中国的角度。

一是由表及里。中国古人将日常生活分为衣食住行四个方面，其中衣服居于首位。中国的服饰体现着中国不同时期的生产力发展水平，体现着社会制度、宗教信仰、生活习俗及审美情趣，在物质文化和精神文化双重层面上折射出中华民族的成长发展史。因此，服饰是"穿在身上的历史"。今天，我们从明清时期的皇家服饰中，既可以看到当时中国人的聪明才智和精湛技艺，又可以看到明礼仪、讲服饰、重举止的社会习俗与风尚。可以说，今天

---

* 在"紫禁城皇家服饰展"开幕式上的讲话。2010 年 12 月 6 日，伦敦维多利亚与阿尔伯特博物馆。

的展览为我们打开了了解中国传统文化的一扇重要窗口。

二是由古及今。服饰是时代的镜子,反映时代的风貌,随时代而变迁。今天的中国与数百年前相比,变化可谓"沧海桑田",政治、经济和社会制度都发生了巨大变革,因而服饰也经历了脱胎换骨式的转型。即使是与改革开放前的30多年相比,中国人的服装也完成了从"蓝色一片"到五彩缤纷的蝶变。希望大家既能从此次展览了解到曾经创造辉煌文化的古代中国,也能看到一个正在追求进步和繁荣的现代中国。

三是由点及面。近年来,"盛世华章——中国:1662—1795"故宫文物展、"中国秦代兵马俑展"等先后在伦敦举办,吸引了众多英国民众参观,此次"紫禁城皇家服饰展"是中英两大顶级博物馆之间又一次精诚合作的结晶。文化是人们心灵沟通最好的桥梁。中英两国历史背景、社会制度和价值观念不同,但这并不是也不应当是两国文化交流的障碍。中国古人说:"和实生物,同则不继。"中英文化有差异,但正因为差异,才相互吸引,才需要相互了解。中英文化交流的成果也充分说明,不同文化只有相互借鉴和学习,才会共同发展和繁荣。

当前,中英两国关系正处在新的起点,面临着新的发展机遇,我衷心地期望中英两国文化界共同努力,不断加强文化交流与合作,增进两国民众之间的了解和友谊,为中英关系的不断发展做出积极贡献。

最后,我预祝此次"紫禁城皇家服饰展"取得圆满成功。

谢谢!

Garments Are Cultural Symbols[*]

Mr Paul Ruddock,

Sir Mark Jones,

Distinguished guests,

Ladies and Gentlemen,

It gives me great pleasure to attend the opening of the Imperial Chinese Robes from the Forbidden City Exhibition. Let me offer my warm congratulations to the Palace Museum and the Victoria & Albert Museum for co-hosting this event.

This exhibition gives the British public a rare view of royal robes from Ming and Qing Dynasties, which are part of the treasured collections of the Palace Museum. The shiny silk brocade, exquisite embroidery and elaborate craftsmanship of these robes obviously put them at the very top in elegance and artistry among the imperial robes in Chinese history.

Garments are cultural symbols and give shape to our thought and creativity. They bring us artistic enjoyment and provide an opportunity to learn more about China.

First, this exhibition tells much deeper stories about Chinese culture. In the eyes of ancient Chinese, life was all about "clothing, food, housing and travels". Clothing came first. What people wore at different times in history directly reflects the level of development, social system, religious belief, cultural traditions and aesthetic values of their times. In short, they offer both material and spiritual clues to Chinese life. It is a lesson about Chinese history that one can wear. The Qing and Ming imperial robes on

---

[*] Remarks at the Opening of the Imperial Chinese Robes from the Forbidden City Exhibition. Victoria & Albert Museum, London, 6 December 2010.

display not only speak to the talent and ingenuity of the Chinese people in the 14th to 19th centuries, but also shed much light on the social life and etiquette of that period. In this sense, today's exhibition is a window on traditional Chinese culture.

Second, this exhibition provides a historical perspective on the development of China. Garments evolve with the times. The enormous political, economic and social changes in China in the past centuries were also reflected in the changes in people's clothing. Over 30 years ago, you saw dark blue wherever you went in China, but now there is an explosion of colours on the streets of China. I hope that when you get a sense of an ancient China and its cultural splendor from this exhibition, you will also appreciate a modern China in pursuit of progress and prosperity.

Third, this exhibition helps with mutual understanding between China and the UK. This event is yet another example of close cooperation between first-class museums of the two countries. It comes close on the heels of the successes of China: The Three Emperors, 1662—1795 and the First Emperor: China's Terracotta Army exhibitions held in London in the past few years. Culture is a bridge that reaches into the hearts of people and brings them closer. Our differences in historic values and social system should not stand in the way of cultural exchanges. Just as an ancient Chinese sage said, "harmony creates many, while uniformity none." Cultural diversity can draw us closer and encourage greater effort at mutual understanding. The dynamic cultural exchanges between our two countries are a good example of how mutual learning between different cultures leads to common development and prosperity.

China-UK relations now stand at a new starting point and with new opportunities. I sincerely hope that the Chinese and British cultural communities will work together for more robust cultural exchanges and cooperation, and deepen mutual understanding and friendship between our peoples. This will make a positive contribution to a prosperous China-UK relationship.

I wish the Imperial Chinese Robes from the Forbidden City Exhibition a great success.

Thank you!

仁者乐山，智者乐水 *

尊敬的英国外交国务大臣豪威尔勋爵，
尊敬的英国文化教育协会首席执行官马丁·戴维信先生，
女士们、先生们、朋友们：

首先，我热烈欢迎大家参加中国驻英国大使馆主办的这场别开生面的时尚活动。

今晚，我们的主题是时装，我们的主角是依文和例外这两个中国著名时装品牌，我们的主旨是感受东方之美。

时装是地域的标志，是各个民族、不同文化的外在特征。透过时装，人们领略到不同民族文化的魅力；通过时装，不同文明得以交流。早在两千多年前，东西方之间就因丝绸这一华丽的时装半成品开辟了"丝绸之路"，打开了文明交往的大门。

时装是时代的产物，是每个时代的符号和脉搏。中国历朝历代的服饰都各不相同，可以说每个朝代都有其特定的"时装"。在中国改革开放前，中国的时装不是绿色的军装就是蓝色的中山装，且不分男女老少。今天，中国早已告别那个着装单调的年代，人们要求穿出个性风采，希望穿出时尚潮流。因此，在中国这个当今世界第一大服装生产国和消费国，各种品牌和时尚款式如雨后春笋般层出不穷。

---

* 在中国驻英国大使馆举办的"山水·2012 中国时装秀"上的讲话。2012 年 2 月 17 日，中国驻英国大使馆。

依文和例外就是当今中国比较有代表性的两个时尚品牌。它们今年来到了英国，参加伦敦时装周期间的国际时装展示，展现中国时装产业的新水平。它们今晚也应邀来到了中国驻英国大使馆，为大家展现中国时尚与东方审美的有机结合。

孔子说："仁者乐山，智者乐水。"山和水，一静一动，一阴一阳，是东方审美的永恒主题。今晚，依文和例外，其一如山之沉稳，其一如水之灵动。每一根细丝、每一缕粗麻，都仿佛生命般具有灵性；每一个图案、每一个款式，都在表达设计师心中的东方之美。我衷心希望各位朋友也能从中发现美、感受美。

中国驻英国大使馆举办今晚的活动，既是庆贺中英建立大使级外交关系40周年的系列活动之一，也是促进两国文化交流的一次积极尝试。我要感谢《艺术与设计》杂志社、英国文化委员会和英国时装协会对此次活动的大力支持。

最后，祝大家度过一个赏心悦目的夜晚！

谢谢！

Enjoy Mountains and Water[*]

Lord Howell,

Mr Martin Davidson,

Ladies and Gentlemen,

Dear Friends,

First, my warm welcome to you all to this Chinese Fashion Show at our Embassy.

The fashion show tonight features two Chinese fashion brands, EVE and EXCEPTION. What they bring us today is a wonderful opportunity to feel the creativity and charm of Chinese fashion.

Fashion carries much geographic symbolism. It's a good showcase of the cultural identity and artistic appeal of a nation.

These attributes have given fashion a unique value as a bridge for cross-cultural exchange.

One brilliant example was how the Silk Road served as a bridge between China and Europe over two millennia ago.

It began with the overland "silk routes" and then the maritime "silk routes". Trade was the driver but the exchange of ideas that traveled along profoundly changed the world.

Fashion also bears the hallmark of its time.

China's 5,000-year history is a witness of how our dressing styles have evolved over time.

Before the reform and opening-up in the late 1970s, the most popular dress in China

---

[*] Speech at the "Mountain · Water" Chinese Fashion Show Hosted by the Chinese Embassy in the UK. The Chinese Embassy, 17 February 2012.

was either a dark green army style uniform or a deep blue Chinese tunic suit.

This has become a thing of the past. Today, dressing style is more of a personal choice. It's diverse and fashionable.

Also China has established itself as the world's number one garment producer and consumer. In turn, more of Chinese designers and fashion brands have established their presence on the world fashion arena.

In the spotlight today are EVE and EXCEPTION. They are two of the better known brands in China's fashion industry. They are here as part of the International Fashion Showcase activities.

Their presence at the London Fashion Week displays what China's fashion industry can offer to the world. And their show tonight provides a wonderful presentation of the Chinese fashion and artistic standards.

Confucius famously remarked:

"The benevolent enjoy the mountains, the wise enjoy the water."

In Chinese culture mountains and water represent firmness and flexibility. These are ancient themes in Chinese culture and art.

Tonight, EVE and EXCEPTION will interpret the theme of "mountains and water" with their unique collections.

Everything in these collections is meant to show the best of Chinese fashion and art. These range from the choice of materials to the design of garments.

It's my sincere hope that all of you will feel the beauty that comes through these designer collections!

The fashion show tonight is part of the series of events to mark 40 years of China-UK full diplomatic relations.

It's also a brilliant platform to strengthen the cross-cultural understanding between our two nations.

I must thank *Art and Design*, the British Council and the British Fashion Council for their strong support to this event.

In closing, I wish all of you an enjoyable evening!

Thank you!

增进中西方了解，扩大中西方合作 *

各位媒体朋友：

欢迎大家出席 2012 年伦敦书展"市场焦点"中国主宾国活动的首场新闻发布会！

千百年来书籍一直在我们的生活中占有举足轻重的地位。我想大家都知道古罗马政治家西塞罗的名言："没有书籍的房间就像没有灵魂的躯体。"在过去的两千多年里，中国本身就是一部内容丰富的书，中国人最早发明了纸张和活字印刷术。

中国高度重视一年一度的伦敦书展。这是享誉 41 年的全球出版业盛会，也是世界第二大国际图书版权交易会。更让我们高兴的是，中国将成为本届伦敦书展的"市场焦点"。中国出版业将会带着新视角和新概念在本次书展中亮相。

伦敦书展"市场焦点"中国主宾国活动时间为 4 月 16 日至 18 日。主会场在伯爵宫，同时各场活动将遍布伦敦甚至全英国。中国许多作家、小说家、剧作家、记者、艺术家、演奏家、制作人和出版商将云集伦敦，他们都是活动的主角，同时中国领导人将出席活动开幕式及相关活动。

中方将组织 300 多场各种类型的活动，内容涉及文化、出版、文学、艺术、教育、经济等领域，形式包括高端对话、出版交流活动、作家学者交

---

* 在 2012 年伦敦书展"市场焦点"中国主宾国活动新闻发布会上的讲话。2012 年 3 月 7 日，伦敦朗廷酒店。

流、图书展示和文化艺术展览等。

伦敦书展"市场焦点"中国主宾国活动是中国出版业与英国及国际同行的一次深度交流机会。中国出版业组成了"国家队"，阵容整齐强大，展品丰富精美，立足于充分展示中国出版业的最新水平，借鉴并吸取国外同行的发展经验，促进中国出版业进一步走向世界。

伦敦书展"市场焦点"中国主宾国活动是中英两国庆祝建立大使级外交关系40周年的一项重要活动。我们高兴地看到，40年来中英关系持续发展，两国政治互信在不断增加，经贸合作在不断拓展，人文交流在不断深化。伦敦书展"市场焦点"中国主宾国活动既是2012年中英关系中的一大盛事，也是促进中英人文领域交流与合作的一大契机。

伦敦书展"市场焦点"中国主宾国活动是展现中国文化事业繁荣和各项事业全面发展的一个重要平台。中国的发展是全面的发展，我们不仅大力发展经济，在短短30多年内使中国成为世界第二大经济体，而且高度重视文化建设，努力满足人民群众日益增长的文化和精神需求。中国不仅是经济大国，而且是文化大国。我相信，具有5000年深厚文化底蕴和不断改革创新、与时俱进的中国能为世界文明发展做出更大贡献。

我诚挚地邀请各位英国媒体界的朋友关注伦敦书展中国主宾国，了解中国出版业的发展壮大，了解中国文化事业的繁荣兴旺，了解当代中国的全面进步，了解中英关系的全面发展，并将你们了解到的信息介绍给英国乃至世界公众。

中国有句俗语："一回生，二回熟。"中国首次以主宾国身份参与伦敦书展，希望能结识很多新朋友，也希望今后通过不断参加伦敦书展使我们成为老朋友。

让我们共同努力，以新视角和新概念加强中西方交流，增进中西方了解，扩大中西方合作。

谢谢！

Increase Mutual Understanding and Cooperation[*]

Ladies and Gentlemen,

Welcome to this press conference on China Market Focus at the London Book Fair.

Books have been an important part of our lives for centuries. I am sure you are familiar with this quote from that very famous Roman called Cicero:

"A room without books is like a body without a soul."

For the past two thousand years and more, China has always been a book of rich culture. Indeed, the first printed book was made in China.

So this history of books in China means that we very warmly welcome the London Book Fair. But even more so we are delighted China will be the market focus country at the London Book Fair this year.

The London Book Fair is a global market place for the publishing industry with a history of 41 years. So as a guest China will showcase its publishing sector at the London Book Fair with the theme of "New Perspectives and New Concepts".

The China-related events will take place on April 16th–18th for the London Book Fair with the main venue at Earls Court. There will also be related activities across London and around the UK.

I am happy to tell you that many writers, novelists, playwrights, journalists, artists, performers, producers and publishers will be coming from China to London for this Book Fair. Apart from that there will be Chinese leaders attending the opening

---

[*] Speech at the Press Conference on China Market Focus. London Book Fair 2012, Langham Hotel, London, 7 March 2012.

ceremony and related activities.

Chinese organizers are planning more than 300 activities covering culture, publishing, literature, art, education and economics. These activities will take place in diverse forms, such as high-level dialogue, publishers' meetings, seminar for writers and researchers. In addition there will be exhibitions on books, literature and arts.

The London Book Fair brings together publishing professionals from around the world. So this China Market Focus event offers a rare opportunity. It will enable the Chinese publishing sector to interact with their counterparts in the UK and other countries.

Representing China at the London Book Fair will be a strong team—indeed it is very much a National Team. They will display the finest products of China's publishing sector. They will introduce to the world the latest trends and developments in China. They will also take this opportunity to draw on useful experience from other countries. This will help China's publishing sector with its go-global efforts.

China Market Focus at the London Book Fair has another objective. It is an important part of the series of events celebrating the 40th anniversary of the full diplomatic relations between China and the UK.

Over the past 40 years, China-UK relations have moved from strength to strength:

- There has been growing political mutual trust.
- There has been expanding economic cooperation.
- There has been deepening cultural exchanges.

This means China's participation at the London Book Fair is also of much importance for the overall China-UK relationship.

China Market Focus at the London Book Fair is an important platform for presenting China's achievements in culture and other fields. There is a need for the breadth and depth of China's development to be better understood worldwide.

On the one hand there is the need to grasp how China has grown into the second largest economy of the world over the past 30 years and more. But just as important is the need to communicate the richness of its culture.

What we are doing now in China is to meet the ever rising cultural needs of our people. China aims to celebrate the richness of its thousands of years of history and culture. But at the same time create a China that keeps pace with a fast changing world.

In this way I believe China will make an even greater contribution to world civilization.

I warmly invite all of you to cover China Market Focus at the London Book Fair. If you do this, I have no doubt you will gain a better understanding of China.

You will win a full grasp of the growing Chinese publishing sector. Through that you will observe a thriving Chinese culture and the progress on all fronts in today's China. We will help you share your experience with the British public and people around the world. We look forward to working with you to increase mutual understanding and cooperation between China and the rest of the world from new perspectives and with new concepts.

To conclude, let me quote an old Chinese saying:

"To read a book for the first time is to make an acquaintance with a new friend; to read it for a second time is to meet an old one."

As this is the first time China is the guest of honour at the London Book Fair, I hope many new friendships are formed.

Over time may the London Book Fair be the means to create many old friends.

Thank you!

中国时装业，扬帆出海正当时 *

女士们、先生们：

非常高兴出席第十二届中国（深圳）国际品牌服装服饰交易会。

今天是我作为中国驻英国大使第三次参加中国时装活动。第一次是2011年9月，深圳市经济贸易和信息化委员会及深圳市服装行业协会主办的"时尚深圳"系列活动第四次亮相世界著名的伦敦时装周，我到场祝贺并予以支持。第二次是2012年2月，也是在伦敦时装周期间，我将依文和例外两个中国本土时装品牌请进了中国驻英国大使馆，合作举办了一场别开生面的时装走秀。后来一些英国朋友对我说，他们曾经多次到中国驻英国大使馆参加活动，但那次的时装秀最令人难忘。

交易会主办方希望我今天谈谈中国服装业在当今世界新形势下所面临的机遇和挑战。这个题目很大，也非常具有挑战性，应当由整个中国服装界和在座的各位专业人士来共同思考和回答。今天，我愿结合个人的一些观察和体会谈谈当前中国时装业如何"走出去"，希望能起到一些建言献策的作用。

众所周知，中国的纺织服装业是中国市场化最早、开放程度最高、国际竞争力最强的产业之一，是传统出口支柱，而且一直是中国出口产业中最耀眼的一环。现在，中国出口的纺织服装产品占到世界市场1/3的份额。过去常说，"我们的朋友遍天下"。今天可以说，"我们的服装遍天下"。世界上无

---

* 在第十二届中国（深圳）国际品牌服装服饰交易会上的主旨演讲。2012年7月9日，深圳。

论哪里的人，可能身上或多或少都穿着中国生产的服装。我在英国演讲时引用过这样一句话："中国用8亿件衬衫才能换回一架空客飞机。"这本意是指中国产品的附加值不高，但也从另一个角度说明服装业是中国的拳头出口产品，是中国经济与外贸发展的"历史功臣"。

但我们也必须看到，经过改革开放30多年的发展，虽然中国服装产品"走出去"了，但中国时装企业还没有"走出去"。我们还没有世人皆知的国际服装品牌，以及遍布全球的品牌服装营销网络。一个简单的事实是，在伦敦著名的购物街牛津街和摄政王街上，目前还没有一家中国品牌时装专卖店，而法国、意大利和美国品牌服装店却比比皆是，尽管这些品牌服装的标签上可能印着"中国制造"。这就是我们必须正视的现实。

当前，世界经济形势总体处于复苏阶段，但仍存在许多不稳定性和不确定性。美国经济增长的乏力及欧债危机的反复都很让人担忧。危机还没有过去，中国时装业所处的外部环境并不乐观。订单、成本、资金这些问题可能会继续困扰许多中国企业。但俗话说，"大浪淘沙"，只有这样，真正有规模、有实力的时装企业才能脱颖而出，获取市场优势地位。常言道：危机危机，危中有机。我们有困难，但别人的困难可能比我们更大。比如，一些国际大牌时装企业出现了资金链紧张甚至断裂问题。我认为，有资金、有品牌、有创新的中国时装企业只要抓住机遇、趋势而上，就能打入国际时装高端市场。

今天，我们常说中国要转变发展方式，中国经济要转型升级。但经济如何转型升级？我认为首先就是中国企业要转型升级，也就是说我们的企业不仅要会"中国制造"——制造产品，保持我们的传统优势，也要会"中国创造"——创造形象、风格和效益，实现自我超越。

我认为，当前中国时装企业"走出去"就是实现自身转型升级的必要步骤和重要工程。中国时装企业应当勇于扬帆起航，进军国际市场，走国际化发展道路，从而将自己做大做强。为此，中国企业应当顺应国际时装产业的发展规律，牢牢抓住三个重要环节。

第一个重要环节是品牌。品牌是企业的生命。这些年，中国时装企业在品牌建设上下了不少功夫，创建了不少知名品牌，如依文、鄂尔多斯、雅戈尔等，我就不一一列举了，它们在国内市场上已经具有相当的知名度。深圳市服装行业协会就素有品牌发展"助推器"之称。中国时装企业也收购了一些国外的品牌。

如何在世界上成功塑造中国自己的国际品牌，我认为有两个因素必不可少。

一是历史积淀。国际知名的时装品牌都具有相当长的历史积淀，不少都是百年经典。比如，博柏利是英国的一个百年品牌，创办于1856年。156年来，博柏利以经典的格子图案、独特的布料功能和大方优雅的剪裁历久不衰，从而成为最能代表英国气质的品牌。中国企业在培育品牌的过程中，要借鉴国外经验，学会耐得下心，沉得住气，制定长远战略，构筑百年大计，厚积而薄发。

二是文化内涵。企业品牌的生命力在于它总是与特定文化、历史事件或某一众人皆知的故事联系在一起。博柏利与英国历史上最令人怀旧的一场战争——第一次世界大战密不可分，它的风雨衣在一战中成为英军的军衣。今天，人们每当看到一战影片中英军穿着的风雨衣，就会想到博柏利。在英语字典里，Burberry甚至被用来代表风雨衣。中国企业也要学会给自己的品牌赋予"中国故事"，并且相信随着中国的发展，"中国故事"迟早也会成为"世界故事"。

中国时装业"走出去"，第二个重要环节是设计。时装不同于一般的服装，它的价值主要来自设计。但长期以来，设计恰恰是中国时装企业普遍的软肋。要解决这个问题，我认为应加强两点。

一是中国时装企业要建设自己一流的设计团队。将优秀的时装设计师收归麾下，创立附属于企业的设计工作室，为设计师创造一个充分展现才华的空间。可以说，中国时装企业的强大，首先是设计团队的强大；中国时装企业"走出去"，首先是中国的时装设计师"走出去"，成为世界一流的设计师。

二是中国时装企业必须紧跟世界时尚潮流。中国优秀的时装企业应当走进伦敦、米兰、巴黎和纽约这样的国际著名时装周，去直接和及时了解、掌握世界时尚的最新信息动态和流行元素，同时也带去作品，交流切磋。

我高兴地看到，近年来，中国时装设计师不断出现在伦敦时装周这样的国际著名时装舞台，将他们的作品展现给世界。英国时装协会主席哈罗德·蒂尔曼曾对我说："中国时装设计师已经达到了世界一流水平，他们应当在国际舞台上有更多的精彩展示。"英国文化协会首席执行官马丁·戴维信也对我说："以前常说英国向中国出口高端时装，现在看来中国也可以向英国出口高端服饰。"

我也高兴地看到，深圳市服装行业协会发挥了龙头作用，联合深圳各大时装企业有效整合资源，在深圳市人民政府的支持下，近年来连续参加伦敦时装周，共同出海，集体亮相，实现了中国时装企业的突破。

中国时装业"走出去"，第三个重要环节是营销。就产业价值链来说，这与设计、研发可谓旗鼓相当，都属于高附加值环节。同时，企业只有掌握了营销，才能在市场中及时了解顾客需求，获悉市场对产品的反馈。

可能在座的大多数人都知道西班牙时装企业 ZARA 所创造的"ZARA 模式"。"ZARA 模式"作为工商管理中的一个经典案例，最为人称道的就是产品从需求、设计、生产、物流到上架销售只需要两个星期，就能实现为顾客提供"买得起的快速时装"。ZARA 公司是怎么做到这一点的呢？很重要的一点就是公司坚持自己拥有和运营几乎所有的连锁店网络，从而实现了出色的全程供应链管理，也实现了市场信息的快速收集和反馈。

中国时装企业"走出去"，就是企业实现国际化的过程。一个单纯的生产型企业，谈不上成为国际化企业。一个国际化企业，必须掌握全球营销渠道。

综上所述，我认为中国时装业在"走出去"的过程中，如果牢牢抓住品牌、设计和营销三大重要环节，实际上就是完整掌握了服装产业的价值链高端部分，也就是利润最大、效益最好的三个环节，而这三个环节恰恰是中国时装企业多年来没有迈过的一道发展门槛。这道门槛的确很高，不容易跨越，但是我们只要跨过去，就将进入一片新天地，前途一片光明。现在是跨越它的时候了！

最后，我衷心祝愿中国时装业越做越大，越做越强！也预祝第十二届中国（深圳）国际品牌服装服饰交易会圆满成功。

谢谢！

China's Fashion Industry: Time for Going Global*

Ladies and Gentlemen,

It is a great pleasure for me to join you at the 12th China (Shenzhen) International Brand Clothing & Accessories Fair.

This is the third Chinese fashion event I have ever attended as the Chinese Ambassador in the UK. The first was the fourth "Fashion Shenzhen" event during the world famous London Fashion Week in September 2011. The event was co-organized by Commission of Science, Industry, Trade and Information Industry of Shenzhen Municipality and Shenzhen Garment Industry Association. I attended the event to offer congratulations and support. The second was a special fashion show in the Chinese Embassy this February, also during the London Fashion Week. It was presented in collaboration with our domestic fashion brands EVE and EXCEPTION. Some of my British friends told me later that the fashion show was the most memorable one among the numerous events they attended in the Chinese Embassy.

The organizer of this forum asked me to talk about the "opportunities and challenges facing the Chinese garment industry in the new international situation". This is quite a general topic, and also very challenging. I think it is what should be thought about and addressed by the Chinese garment industry as a whole and by all of you presented here. Today, I want to say something about how the Chinese garment industry can "go global" according to my own observations and experience. I hope this will be of some

---

* Keynote Speech at the 12th China (Shenzhen) International Brand Clothing & Accessories Fair. Shenzhen, 9 July 2012.

help to you.

As we all know, the textile and garment industry is among the first market-oriented industries in China. It is also one of our most open and internationally competitive industries. It is always a pillar and the brightest part in China's export sector. Today, the textile and garment products exported from China have a share of 1/3 of the global market. In the past we often say that "our friends are all over the world". Today we can say that "our garments are all over the world". People around the world, no matter where they are, may wear more or less the garments produced in China. When I make speeches in the UK, I sometimes quote such a sentence: "China has to sell 800 million shirts in order to buy one Airbus plane." This is originally meant to indicate the low added value of the Chinese products. But we can also see from it that garment products are China's key exports, and the garment industry is the historical contributor to China's economic and foreign trade development.

But we must also be aware of one thing: It is true that the Chinese garment products are "going global" after the past 30-odd years of development, but our garment enterprises are not doing so. We have no well-known international clothing brands. Nor do we have any global marketing network for brand clothing. This is evidenced by a simple fact. Oxford Street and Regent Street are the famous shopping streets in London. But along these streets there is not even a single fashion boutique for Chinese brands. In comparison, the boutiques for the French, Italian and American brands are seen everywhere, though the cloths of these brands may have the mark "made in China" on their labels. This is the fact that we must face squarely.

Generally speaking, the world economy is recovering. But there are still many factors of instability and uncertainty. For example, the weak economic growth in the US and the persistent European debt crisis are both the issues of great concerns. We should say that the crisis is not over yet. So we have no reason to be optimistic about the external environment of the Chinese fashion industry. The issues of orders, costs and capital may continuously plague many Chinese enterprises. But as the saying goes, "the great waves wash away the sands to display the gold." Only in crisis can the large and strong fashion enterprises stand out and become market leaders. We Chinese often see the opportunities in crisis. It is true that we are in difficulties. But others are likely to be in greater difficulties. Some international big-name fashion enterprises are suffering from the tense or even broken capital chain. From my point of view, the Chinese fashion enterprises have their capital, brands and innovative mind. They can enter into the high-end international market if only they can seize the opportunity and make good use of it.

Today, we often say that China needs to change its mode of development and to transform and upgrade its economy. How to transform and upgrade the economy? I think the Chinese enterprises should be transformed and upgraded first. That is to say, our enterprises should be able to both make and create. We need the products "made in China" to maintain our traditional strengths. At the same time, we also need the image, style and benefits "created in China" to achieve self-transcendence.

In my opinion, "going global" is now an important and necessary step for the Chinese fashion enterprises to realize their own transformation and upgrading. These enterprises should have the courage to set sail into the international market and develop internationally. This will help them to become bigger and stronger. To this end, the Chinese enterprises should follow the law of development of the international fashion industry and firmly focus on the following three important aspects:

The first aspect is brand. Brand is the lifeline of an enterprise. The Chinese fashion enterprises have made great efforts on brand building these years and have created a lot of well-known brands in the domestic market, such as EVE, ERDOS and YOUNGOR, to name but a few. Shenzhen Garment Industry Association has long been known as the "booster" of brand building. Moreover, the Chinese fashion companies have also acquired some foreign brands.

Then how to build our own international brands? I think there are two essential factors. The first factor is the historical accumulation. All the world renowned fashion brands have a long history. Many of them are "century classics". For example, BURBERRY is a century-old British brand founded in 1856. Over the past 156 years, BURBERRY has maintained its popularity with its classic plaid patterns, unique fabrics and elegant tailoring. It becomes the most representative brand of the British style. In the process of brand building, the Chinese enterprises should learn from the foreign experience and be patient. They need to develop a long-term strategy, set a long-term goal and lay a solid foundation for success.

The second factor for building an international brand is cultural content. A vibrant brand is always linked with a specific cultural or historical event or a well-known story. Let's still take BURBERRY as an example. The brand is inseparable from the World War I, the most memorable war in the British history. Its raincoat was the military uniform of the British Army in that war. Today, people will think of BURBERRY once they see the British officers wearing raincoats in the films about the World War I. The word "Burberry" is even a synonym of raincoat in English dictionaries. The Chinese enterprises should learn to give "Chinese stories" to their own brands. I believe that with the development of China, the "Chinese stories" will sooner or later become "world stories".

The second aspect for the Chinese fashion industry to "go global" is design. Unlike general garments, fashion clothes realize their value primarily from the design. But it is precisely the design that has long been a common weakness of the Chinese fashion companies. To address this weakness, I think we have to make more efforts in two ways:

First, the Chinese fashion companies need to build their own first-class design teams. They should attract the excellent fashion designers and establish subsidiary design studios for the designers to allow them to fully demonstrate their talent. It is reasonable to say that for our fashion enterprises to become powerful, the design teams should first become powerful, and for the fashion enterprises to "go global", the Chinese fashion designers should first "go global" and become world-class designers.

Second, the Chinese fashion companies must closely follow the world fashion trend. The excellent fashion companies in China should go to the famous fashion weeks in London, Milan, Paris and New York. There, they can directly get the latest information on the world fashion dynamics and the popular elements, and they can also bring their own works for exchange of views.

I'm pleased to see more and more Chinese fashion designers at the well-known international fashion stages such as the London Fashion Week in recent years, presenting their works to the world. Mr Harold Tillman, Chairman of the British Fashion Council, told me that "the Chinese designers are world-class ones. They should have more dazzling shows in the international arena". Mr Martin Davidson, Chief Executive of the British Council, also said to me that "In the past, Britain often exported the high-end fashion clothes to China. It now appears that China can also export these clothes to Britain".

I'm also pleased to see that the Shenzhen Garment Industry Association is playing a leading role. With the support of the Shenzhen Municipal People's Government, the Association has effectively integrated resources and organized the major fashion enterprises in Shenzhen to attend the London Fashion Week for several consecutive years. This collective debut abroad is a breakthrough among the Chinese fashion enterprises.

The third important aspect for the Chinese fashion industry to "go global" is marketing. This is an equally important and high value-added part in the value chain compared with design and R&D. At the same time, only the enterprises with the strength in market can keep abreast of the customer demand in the market and the market feedback.

Perhaps most of you know the "ZARA mode" created by the Spanish fashion company ZARA. This is a typical case of business administration. The most impressive thing of the "ZARA mode" is: it takes just two weeks for the whole process from demand, design, production, logistics through to the shelves. With this mode, the ZARA company achieves the goal of providing customers with "affordable fast fashion". How does ZARA do this? I think it is important that the company owns and operates almost all of its chain stores. This enables an excellent, complete supply chain management and a rapid market information collection and response.

To the Chinese fashion enterprises, "going global" is a process of internationalization. A simple production-oriented enterprise cannot be an international one. It should have its global marketing channels.

In summary, I think if the Chinese fashion industry firmly focuses on brand, design and marketing in the process of "going global", it will in fact completely grasp the high-end part of the value chain of the garment industry, that is, the three most profitable and beneficial sectors. These sectors are exactly a threshold that the Chinese fashion enterprises have not crossed for many years. Indeed, this threshold is high and not easy to cross. But as long as we cross it, we will enter a new world and face a bright future. Now it is time to cross it!

I sincerely hope that the Chinese fashion industry will become bigger and stronger!

I wish the 12th China (Shenzhen) International Brand Clothing & Accessories Fair a great success.

Thank you!

东方和西方的完美结合 *

各位来宾：

欢迎大家出席今晚我为现代芭蕾舞剧《简·爱》在英国首演举行的招待会。

我相信，此时此刻很多来宾与我一样，心绪仍沉浸在感人至深的爱情故事中，脑海中仍不断萦绕着华丽优美的舞步、舞姿。

让我们一起热烈祝贺来自上海芭蕾舞团的舞蹈家们，他们今晚在英国国家歌剧院的精彩演出证明了他们高超的艺术水准，也给我们带来了无穷的艺术享受。

今晚的演出有太多值得称颂的地方，我想特别提出三点。

第一，它是文学和舞台的完美结合。《简·爱》是英国文学的经典，是笔尖下的不朽名篇。它以一种不可抗拒的力量吸引了全世界无数的读者。记得我在少年时代，就仔细阅读过这本英语学习者的必读书籍，为此还查过无数次字典，在书上做过许多标注。我也看过英国拍摄于20世纪70年代初的电影《简·爱》，这部电影曾在中国公映，流传很广。现代芭蕾舞剧《简·爱》则是艺术的再创造，是对文学的形象再现，是脚尖跳跃和旋转出的舞台新作。它表现出的大胆追求平等幸福的勇气和不屈不挠的精神，同样令人深深感动和震撼。

第二，它是古典和现代的完美结合。《简·爱》诞生于19世纪，它展现

---

* 在上海芭蕾舞团现代芭蕾舞剧《简·爱》于英国首场演出招待会上的讲话。2013年8月14日，英国国家歌剧院。

出华丽、优雅、考究和精致，是当时英国社会生态的真实写照。现代芭蕾舞剧《简·爱》无论是从故事情节上还是服装、布景和音乐上，均体现了浓浓的英格兰风情，充满怀旧的味道。但它的舞蹈编排、肢体语言无疑又是现代的，充满着速度和力量，畅若流水，自由奔放。它带给我们的不仅是熟悉，更多的是惊喜。

第三，它是东方和西方的完美结合。就在2013年7月，英国新诞生了一位"王室宝宝"——乔治王子。而现代芭蕾舞剧《简·爱》则是一个"跨国宝宝"，它有着英国的文学原创、德国的编导、法国的舞美服装设计，以及大家耳熟能详的英国、德国音乐家的著名作品，上海芭蕾舞团的改编创意，中国舞蹈家的肢体表现……这完全是中西方艺术合作的结晶。

此次演出，上海芭蕾舞团称之为"故乡行"。其实，中英之间这样的"故乡行"还有很多，我记得2012年中国国家话剧院就曾在莎士比亚环球剧场上演《理查三世》，2011年上海京剧院在爱丁堡国际艺术节奉献新编京剧《王子复仇记》。不久之后，北京人民艺术剧院将为2013年的爱丁堡国际艺术节献上根据莎士比亚剧作改编的话剧《大将军寇流兰》。

所有这些说明，中英都是文化大国，两国的文化是开放包容的，都在借鉴和吸纳对方的优秀文化，从而进一步丰富本国的思想和艺术。近年来，中英人文交流日趋活跃，领域不断拓宽，合作日益深入。

我衷心希望中英两国艺术家、文艺团体、文化机构今后能够不断加强相互交流与合作，更多借鉴对方的优秀文化和作品，在对方国家举办更多高水准的演出和展览，共同创作更多思想共通的艺术作品，进一步增进两国人民之间的了解、信任和友谊，从而促进中英关系更加稳定健康地发展。

最后，让我们共同举杯，再次对上海芭蕾舞团的精彩首演表示祝贺，预祝他们在今后几天的演出继续取得圆满成功！

谢谢！

Unite the East and the West*

Distinguished Guests,

Warmly welcome all of you to this reception.

We are gathered to celebrate the premiere of the ballet production of *Jane Eyre*.

I am sure all of you share my feelings and are still enchanted by the wonderful performance we all enjoyed this evening.

Please join me in congratulating all the dancers from the Shanghai Ballet Company!

The superb performance tonight from the Shanghai Ballet Company has given us all a great artistic treat. It also attests to their attainments in the art of ballet.

There are many credits to this performance. But I want to highlight three points.

First, it is a perfect match of the pen and the stage.

Jane Eyre is world famous as a masterpiece of writing by Charlotte Bronte. Around the globe, and across China, the book has a large passionate following. It is also a must-read for English language learners.

When I was young I read the novel with great interest. I consulted a dictionary many times and made profuse quantities of notes. I also watched the film *Jane Eyre* produced in the early 1970s. This film was shown in China and was immensely popular.

The Ballet production of *Jane Eyre* is a re-interpretation of this literary classic. It transfers the story from the book to the stage. It portrayed characters through dancing rather than writing. Yet, what remains unchanged and equally powerful is the message: equality, courage and the pursuit of love.

---

* Speech at the Reception of the Premiere of *Jane Eyre* by the Shanghai Ballet Company. The London Coliseum, 14 August 2013.

Second, it is the combination of the classic and the contemporary.

The book *Jane Eyre* was written in the 19th century. It records the elegance and subtlety of the English social life at that time.

The interpretation by the ballet retains the authentic English style in storyline, costume, scenery and music; but, this ballet production also has taken on bold modern choreography.

The body language underlines speed and strength. At the same time, the dancers move smoothly with effortless grace. For me the ballet has brought not only familiarity of the original story but also provides surprise that gives added pleasure.

The third point I want to highlight is how the ballet unites the East and the West.

Last month the whole of Britain was on "baby watch". Indeed, people were thrilled by the arrival of His Royal Highness the Prince George of Cambridge.

This ballet production of *Jane Eyre* is a multinational "baby". It is a marriage of English literature, German choreography, French costume and prop design. Then there is the original adaptation of the Shanghai Ballet Company and performance by Chinese dancers. Of course, there is also music by British and German composers. So this ballet work is in every measure a new "baby" created by Chinese and Western artists.

The Shanghai Ballet Company has called this show a "home trip". It brings a Chinese interpretation of *Jane Eyre* back to the home country where the book was written.

In fact there have been many other "home trips" in recent China-UK exchanges.

Last year, the National Theatre Company of China performed *Richard III* at Shakespeare's Globe Theatre.

During the Edinburgh International Festival, the Shanghai Peking Opera troupe performed *The Revenge of the Prince* which was adapted from *Hamlet*.

Next week, Beijing People's Art Theatre will stage *The Tragedy of Coriolanus* during this year's Edinburgh International Festival. This is another Chinese production of Shakespeare's work.

All these show that China and Britain both have rich cultures and our cultures are open and inclusive. Through mutual learning we have enriched our own thinking and art. These are also examples of ever expanding and deepening cultural exchanges between our two countries.

I do hope that artists, cultural groups and agencies will enhance exchanges and cooperation and draw on each other's strengths. I hope we will put on more high quality shows and exhibitions in each other's country. Through collaboration we should aim to jointly produce more works reflecting our common values and feelings.

Joint efforts as such will contribute to greater understanding, trust and friendship between Chinese and British people. In turn that will create a more stable and healthy China-UK relationship.

In conclusion, I propose a toast to the excellent debut of the Shanghai Ballet Company with *Jane Eyre*!

I wish them great success for many performances!

Thank you!

精彩的"故乡行" *

爱丁堡国际艺术节总监乔纳森·米尔斯先生，

拿督黄纪达基金会主席黄铃玳爵士夫人，

北京人民艺术剧院的各位艺术家，

各位来宾：

欢迎大家出席中国驻爱丁堡总领事馆为北京人民艺术剧院《大将军寇流兰》在英国演出举办的招待会。首先，我对《大将军寇流兰》在爱丁堡国际艺术节赢得满堂喝彩、取得圆满成功表示热烈祝贺。这是我担任中国驻英大使以来第一次出席爱丁堡国际艺术节的活动，幸运的是，第一次出席我就欣赏到了中国艺术家的精湛表演。

看了昨晚北京人民艺术剧院《大将军寇流兰》成功亮相爱丁堡国际艺术节，我有三点感言。

第一，这是又一次精彩的"故乡行"。2011年，上海京剧院在爱丁堡国际艺术节奉献了新编京剧《王子复仇记》。2012年，中国国家话剧院在莎士比亚环球剧场上演了《理查三世》。就在上周三，我出席了上海芭蕾舞团现代芭蕾舞剧《简·爱》在伦敦的首演。这次，北京人民艺术剧院将莎士比亚的晚期作品《大将军寇流兰》的中文版本带到了莎翁的故乡，带到了全球历史最久、规模最大的文化艺术盛会——爱丁堡国际艺术节。如濮存昕先生

---

* 在中国驻爱丁堡总领事馆为北京人民艺术剧院《大将军寇流兰》于英国演出招待会上的致辞。2013年8月21日，中国驻爱丁堡总领事馆。

所说，这是对莎翁的崇高"致敬"、是"圆梦之旅"，我想这也是一次最好的"回乡之旅"。

第二，这场演出代表了中国话剧的最高水平。首先，北京人民艺术剧院是中国话剧的一面旗帜，是国宝级的艺术明珠，在中国话剧史上创造过许多辉煌，同时它也是中国话剧的希望所在。其次，这部作品凝聚了许多艺术大师的心血。英若诚先生的翻译，林兆华先生的导演，易立明先生的设计，濮存昕先生的表演等，诸多艺术大师的共同锤炼造就了此剧的气势恢宏、非同凡响。正如苏格兰议会副议长约翰·斯科特昨晚对我所说："此剧令人震撼。"

第三，这是一部令人耳目一新的"新话剧"。许多英国朋友对我说，此剧的音乐给他们留下了深刻印象。的确，此剧不仅让我们感受到传统话剧的实力，而且让我们感受到重金属摇滚带来的冲击。我认为，这部作品实现了话剧与摇滚的"跨界联姻"，是两种艺术的有力结合，具有强烈的舞台魅力。中国艺术家这种大胆尝试和先锋探索进一步照亮了爱丁堡国际艺术节这一多姿多彩的舞台。

正因上述三点，我要感谢北京人民艺术剧院的杰出艺术家们，感谢支持此次演出的爱丁堡国际艺术节组委会和拿督黄纪达基金会，你们不仅给我们带来了完美的视觉和听觉享受，你们还正在用自己的行动促进中英之间的艺术文化交流，增进两国人民之间的相互了解。我也期待着中英双方的文化界人士以此次携手合作为契机，共同规划、设计、推出更多的高水准交流项目，使中英文化交流更加频繁密切，使两国人民的友谊更加深入人心。

最后，再次祝贺北京人民艺术剧院《大将军寇流兰》在爱丁堡国际艺术节的成功演出，我也期待着你们今后带来更多展现中国文化的优秀作品！

谢谢！

An Amazing "Home Trip" *

Sir Jonathan Mills,

Lady Davies,

Artists from the Beijing People's Art Theatre,

Distinguished Guests,

Welcome to the reception of the European Premiere of *The Tragedy of Coriolanus* hosted by Chinese Consulate-General in Edinburgh. I warmly congratulate the stunning success of *The Tragedy of Coriolanus* at the Edinburgh International Festival!

This is the first time that I have attended the Edinburgh International Art Festival since I took office as Chinese Ambassador to the UK. I am delighted to observe the increasing participation of Chinese cultural entities over recent years in Edinburgh. On my first visit to the Edinburgh International Festival I feel very fortunate that I have enjoyed such a superb performance by Chinese artists.

I have three thoughts to share with you about the successful European Premiere of *The Tragedy of Coriolanus* by Beijing People's Art Theatre.

First, this is another amazing "home trip".

Two years ago, during the Edinburgh International Festival, the Shanghai Peking Opera troupe performed *The Revenge of the Prince* which was adapted from *Hamlet*.

Last year, the National Theatre Company of China performed *Richard III* at Shakespeare's Globe Theatre.

Only last Wednesday, I watched the premiere of *Jane Eyre* by Shanghai Ballet

---

* Speech at the Reception of the European Premiere of *The Tragedy of Coriolanus* by Beijing People's Art Theatre. Chinese Consulate-General in Edinburgh, 21 August 2013.

Company at the London Coliseum.

Now, Beijing People's Art Theatre has brought a Chinese production of *The Tragedy of Coriolanus* to the home country of Shakespeare, and to the Edinburgh International Festival, the world's most time-honored and largest arts and cultural celebrations.

The Tragedy of Coriolanus is a tragedy believed to have been written in Shakespeare's late years. As Mr Pu Cunxin said, this Chinese adaptation is a tribute to Shakespeare. This performance is a dream fulfilled and a home-coming.

Second, this performance is the quintessence of Chinese stage play acting. Beijing People's Art Theatre has long been the standard setter of Chinese theatrics. It is our national treasure. It set many records in Chinese dramatic history. At the same time it is where the future of Chinese theatre lies.

This production has pooled together the talents of many great artists. These include Mr Ying Ruocheng the translator, Mr Lin Zhaohua the director, Mr Yi Liming the lighting and set designer, and Mr Pu Cunxin, who plays the title role. The collaboration of so many virtuosos has made this play truly glorious and exceptional. As Deputy Presiding Officer of the Scottish Parliament Mr John Scott observed last night, "This production is very powerful."

Third, this is an original interpretation. Many British friends have told me that they were deeply impressed by the music of the show. Indeed, the performance has overwhelmed us by not only brilliant acting but also live rock music. This unconventional marriage of the drama and rock music has given this performance extra vigour. This bold and implausible exploration by Chinese artists has added to the appeal of the Edinburgh International Festival.

For all the above mentioned, I want to thank the outstanding artists from Beijing People's Art Theatre. I am also grateful for the support of Edinburgh International Festival and the KT WONG Foundation. You have blessed us with a visual and auditory feast. Moreover, you are promoting China-UK arts and cultural exchanges. In this way you are increasing mutual understanding between Chinese and British people with your own actions.

I hope in the years ahead Chinese and British cultural circles will build on this performance, and put together more high quality joint cultural projects. They will contribute to closer cultural links between our countries and stronger friendship between our people.

In conclusion, I once again congratulate on the success of *The Tragedy of Coriolanus* at the Edinburgh International Festival by Beijing People's Art Theatre.

I look forward to you bringing to Britain more fine works of Chinese culture!

Thank you!

中英旅游合作天时、地利、人和 *

尊敬的英国旅游局代理首席执行官凯斯·比查姆先生，
尊敬的世界旅游旅行理事会总裁大卫·斯考希尔先生，
各位来宾，
女士们、先生们：
大家晚上好！

首先，我对"中国旅游之夜"活动的举办表示热烈祝贺。

"中国旅游之夜"活动的主题是"美丽中国，古老长城"。这让我回想起不久前由中国中央电视台和英国广播公司联合摄制的纪录片《美丽中国》，该片所呈现的中国自然、人文和历史之美，想必给大家留下了深刻的印象。

最近，我们在英国中小学做了一个关于中国认知的调查，师生们都认为长城是中国最具代表性的景点，也是他们最想参观的中国景点。今天，我们在这里举办以"美丽中国，古老长城"为主题的"中国旅游之夜"活动，可谓"天时、地利、人和"。

第一，深化中英旅游合作蓄势待发，是谓"天时"。2014年6月，李克强总理成功访问英国，中英双方共同宣布2015年为"中英文化交流年"，届时将共同举办丰富多彩的文化交流活动。"国之交在于民相亲"，旅游业已成为促进中英两国人民交往的桥梁，是两国文化交流活动的重要内容。我相信乘着"中英文化交流年"的东风，中英两国旅游合作将更上一层楼，两国人民

---

* 在"中国旅游之夜"活动上的讲话。2014年8月21日，英国伦敦千禧年饭店。

的友谊将不断深化。

第二，中国旅游条件日益完善，是谓"地利"。中国正积极推动以改革开放增强旅游业发展动力，优化旅游发展环境，提升旅游产品品质和内涵，推动旅游业转型升级。2013年中国旅游总收入达2.9万亿元，国内旅游人数达32.5亿人次，出境旅游人数约9730万人次。联合国世界旅游组织统计，2013年中国出境旅游支出居世界第一，入境旅游人数和收入排名世界第四。可以预见，随着中国旅游、基础设施及社会公共服务体系的不断建设和完善，中国将为包括英国在内的各国游客提供更优质的服务、更美好的环境和更令人满意的旅游经历。

第三，中英人民之间怀有深厚的感情，两国公众对彼此文化的兴趣与日俱增，是谓"人和"。中英两国都是旅游大国，互为客源地，旅游资源互补性很强。皮尤研究中心2014年7月调查报告显示，英国是对中国好感度最高的欧洲国家。中国国家旅游局统计，2013年英国访华人数达63万人次。英国同样是最受中国公民欢迎的旅游目的地之一。2014年上半年中国公民赴英人数同比增长了7.4%，达20.52万人次。随着两国人员交往逐渐频繁和深入，相信两国旅游管理部门的合作也会齐头并进，水涨船高，为旅游者提供更多、更便捷的服务，在产业融合、旅游装备制作、旅游支付系统、旅游保险和建立双方旅游主管部门合作对话机制等方面的交流与合作也会进一步加强。

历史上，长城是抵御外来侵略的军事防御工事。如今，长城已经成为中国的一张国际名片，是现代中国敞开胸怀迎接各国人民的象征。事实上，中国幅员辽阔、旅游资源十分丰富，长城只是其中之一。"上有天堂、下有苏杭""桂林山水甲天下"……这些都是对中国锦绣河山的赞美。

关于长城，毛泽东主席有句名言："不到长城非好汉。"4年前，我陪同卡梅伦首相登长城时，曾向他介绍了这句名言。他兴奋地说："今天我可以当好汉了！"我欢迎更多的英国朋友以后也到长城争当好汉，同时希望你们去中国各地走一走、看一看，亲身感受中国的秀美山川和多彩文化，为增进中英之间的相互了解和人民之间的友谊做出贡献。

最后，我祝"中国旅游之夜"活动圆满成功！

谢谢！

Enjoy Three Favorables*

Mr Keith Beecham,
Mr David Scowsill,
Distinguished Guests,
Ladies and Gentlemen,
Good evening!

I warmly congratulate China Tourism Night 2014!

The theme of this evening is "Beautiful China—Journey along the Great Wall". This reminds me of the widely acclaimed documentary *Wild China*. This co-production of BBC and China Central Television was an exceptional exploration of the beauty of China's nature, history and culture.

The recent survey on perception of China in British primary and middle schools shows that the Great Wall is the most recognized and most desired tourist destination in China. So the organizers of this evening have made a wise choice!

The event tonight enjoys three favourables.

First, favourable timing. Now, China-UK tourism cooperation is advancing by "leaps and bounds". When Chinese Premier Li Keqiang visited Britain in June, the two governments designated 2015 as the year of China-UK cultural exchanges. A great variety of cultural activities will be staged in the year.

Friendship between peoples is the foundation of state-to-state relations. Tourism is an essential part of our cultural exchanges and has become a bridge strengthening links between Chinese and British people. I believe that China-UK cultural exchanges year

---

* Speech at China Tourism Night. Millennium Hotel, London, 21 August 2014.

is an excellent opportunity to raise our tourism cooperation to a higher level. This will in turn further deepen friendship between our people.

The second favourable is the improved tourist conditions and capabilities in China. China's appeal to tourists is significantly advancing. China is pressing ahead with reform and opening-up in its tourist industry. The aim is to improve the offering to foreign tourists by raising the quality of products and promote all round improvements.

Statistics show that in 2013 China's revenues from its tourism sector totaled 2.9 trillion RMB with 3.25 billion domestic tourists. This made China the world's largest domestic tourist market. The number of China's outbound tourists stood at 97.3 million, leading all other nations in the world.

According to World Tourism Organization, in 2013 outbound Chinese tourists spent more than others in the world. The number of inbound tourists and the income thereof both ranked the fourth in the world.

I am sure that with better tourist infrastructure and public services, China will offer tourists from the UK and around the world improved services, a better environment and more satisfying experience.

The third favourable is the fast growth of people-to-people exchanges. The Chinese and British people are developing a deeper affection for each other. They also have a growing interest in each other's culture. Both China and the UK have a large tourist sector. We are each other's main source of inbound tourists. Therefore we have a lot to offer each other.

The Pew Research Centre report in July shows that Britain is the friendliest European country to China. Records of China National Tourism Administration show that in 2013, British people made 630,000 visits to China. Likewise, Britain is one of the most popular destinations for Chinese tourists.

In the first six month of this year, the number of Chinese tourists visiting the UK increased by 7.4% and exceeded 205,000. With a growth of people-to-people exchanges, our tourist authorities will also work more closely together to provide better and speedier service for tourists from both countries. This will boost China-UK cooperation across the whole tourism sector with:

- Upgrading facilities.

- Advancing support systems.
- Creating the most convenient means for tourist payments.
- And providing appropriate tourism insurance.

All these aims can be secured through deepening cooperation between our tourist sectors.

In history, the Great Wall used to be a military defence work to guard China from foreign invaders. Today, the Great Wall has become a name card introducing China to people around the world.

The exciting reality for foreign tourists visiting China is that they discover a treasure trove of tourist resources. The Great Wall is just one shining pearl of this rich treasure.

Some tourist sites in China are so well known that they have become eponyms of century-old Chinese sayings. For example:

- "Paradise in heaven, Suzhou and Hangzhou on earth."
- And "Rivers and mountains in Guilin have no rivals in the world."

All these speak volumes about China's natural marvels.

About the Great Wall, there is also a famous quote by Chairman Mao Zedong. It reads: "He who does not reach the Great Wall is not a hero."

Four years ago I accompanied Prime Minister David Cameron to the Great Wall. When I explained this quote to him, Prime Minister Cameron was thrilled. He said:

"So I am a hero today!"

I welcome more British friends to the Great Wall to become heroes.

I also suggest you visit other parts of China and experience for yourselves China's natural beauty and the richness of its culture.

I am sure that visiting China will enable you to contribute to better mutual understanding between China and the UK.

In turn, this will deepen friendship between Chinese and British people.

In conclusion, I wish China Tourism Night 2014 a complete success!

Thank you!

续写辉煌 *

各位来宾,

女士们、先生们:

欢迎大家出席中国驻英国大使馆举办的"明:盛世皇朝 50 年"展览早餐会。

2014 年英国举办了两场关于中国明代的展览,第一场是 2014 年 6 月至 10 月在苏格兰国家博物馆举行的"明代王朝:黄金帝国"展,第二场则是在大英博物馆举办的"明:盛世皇朝 50 年"展览。

人们不禁要问,为什么英国的两大博物馆会不约而同地举办大型明代主题展呢?

我想,这两个展览的名称已回答这个问题。明朝是中国历史上的一个黄金时代,政治稳定,经济发达,文化繁荣。就对外关系而言,明朝开启了中国与世界前所未有的交往局面。1405—1433 年,中国版的达伽马与哥伦布——郑和,带领由 200 多艘船只组成的庞大舰队七下西洋,开展和平之旅,发展友好关系,促进了中外经济文化的交流融合。

今天的中国处在一个新的黄金时代。中国与世界的关系也在发生更加深刻的变化,中国同世界的互联互动变得空前紧密,中国对世界的依靠、对国际事务的参与日益深化,世界对中国的依靠、对中国的影响也在不断加深。

因此,我认为大英博物馆此次展览,不仅是在"谈古",让大家欣赏瓷

---

* 在"明:盛世皇朝 50 年"展览早餐会上的讲话。2014 年 12 月 16 日,大英博物馆。

器、金器、珠宝、绘画、雕塑以及服饰等精美绝伦的中国文物，感受600多年前的中国社会风貌，也是在"论今"，启发大家如何认识今天的中国及其发展道路。

习近平主席提出"中国梦"，这是中华民族伟大复兴之梦。历史上中国曾经辉煌，今天的中国就是要续写辉煌，要走复兴之路，重现国家繁荣昌盛、人民幸福安康之盛世。中国坚持走和平发展道路，"中国梦"是和平、发展、合作、共赢的梦，我们追求的既是中国人民的福祉，也是世界各国人民共同的福祉。历史上，中国曾对世界文明发展和人类进步做出重要贡献，今天的中国将继续为世界的和平与繁荣贡献力量。

在此，我要感谢大英博物馆为举办"明：盛世皇朝50年"展览付出的辛勤努力，更要感谢大英博物馆长期以来为促进中英文化交流和两国人民相互了解做出的积极贡献。

最后，祝大家观展愉快！

谢谢！

Create New Splendour*

Distinguished Guests,

Ladies and Gentlemen,

Welcome to the Chinese Embassy breakfast for the exhibition Ming: 50 Years that Changed China.

This Ming exhibition is the second of its kind in the UK this year. The first was Ming: the Golden Empire at the National Museum of Scotland from June to October.

Two great museums, two major exhibitions, one and the same subject. One can't help asking what has caused such coincidence. I think perhaps the answer is in the names of the two exhibitions: Ming was a golden age in Chinese history. It was a period of political stability, advanced economy and prosperous culture.

In terms of external relations, China during the Ming Dynasty embarked on unprecedented exchanges with the world.

Zheng He, the Chinese explorer before Vasco da Gama and Christopher Columbus, led his great fleet of more than 200 ships on seven voyages down the western seas between 1405 and 1433. Those were missions of peace. They sowed seeds of friendship, promoted economic and cultural exchanges and fostered harmony between China and the world.

Today, China is in a new golden age. China's relationship with the rest of the world is undergoing more profound changes. Its close connection and interaction with the world is unprecedented.

---

* Remarks at a Breakfast for Ming: 50 Years that Changed China. British Museum, 16 December 2014.

As China becomes increasingly dependent on the world and deepens its participation in world affairs, the world's dependence and influence on China is also deepening.

So, I believe this exhibition at the British Museum is not only about the past. It is not merely an opportunity to appreciate the exquisite Chinese porcelain, gold ornaments, jewelry, paintings, statues and garments as well as life in China over six hundred years ago.

It is also about today. It inspires understanding of today's China and its development path to achieve the Chinese Dream.

The Chinese Dream advocated by President Xi Jinping is about the great renewal of the Chinese nation. China had its glories in the past. China is creating new splendour today. It has embarked on a road to national rejuvenation. This is a road that leads to prosperity of the country and better life for the people.

What China follows is a path of peaceful development.

What the Chinese Dream advocates are peace, development and win-win cooperation.

What we pursue is both the wellbeing of the Chinese people and the common good for people of all countries in the world.

China had made important contribution to world civilization and human progress in history. Today, China will continue to do its utmost for world peace and prosperity.

Before I conclude, I wish to express my hearty thanks to the British Museum. I thank you for the hard work in presenting Ming: 50 Years that Changed China. And more than that, I thank you for your continuous efforts over the years to promote China-UK cultural exchanges and to enhance mutual understanding between the people of our two countries.

In conclusion, I wish you all an enjoyable tour of the exhibition.

Thank you!

为中英文化交流增光添彩 *

尊敬的约翰逊故居基金会主席哈姆斯沃斯勋爵，
尊敬的伦敦金融城司法长官阿德莱女士，
各位来宾，
女士们、先生们：

我和我的夫人胡平华很高兴应邀出席约翰逊故居中文导览发布仪式。

首先，我要感谢哈姆斯沃斯勋爵和家族保护约翰逊故居这一充满感召力的义举。早在1911年，哈姆斯沃斯家族就着手保护这座故居。在这里，约翰逊博士撰写了著名的《约翰逊英语词典》。

来英工作5年多来，我时常听到英国各界人士提及约翰逊博士，讨论他的作品，引用他充满智慧的妙语，谈论起他的逸事。约翰逊博士堪称18世纪英国文坛的"一代盟主"，今天有机会到他的故居访问，我们深感荣幸。

刚才在流畅、清晰、准确的中文导览的陪伴下，我们参观了故居。整个故居小巧而精致，各展室布置得简约又古朴。我不禁想象着两百多年前，约翰逊博士在这里伏案工作，历经8年时间，终于编撰成了大词典。约翰逊博士曾经说，"伟大的工作不是用力量而是用耐心去完成的"。他正是以超乎常人的耐心和毅力，战胜困扰多年的疾病，克服生活上的拮据，忘却失去爱妻的痛苦，完成了《约翰逊英语词典》这部巨作。《约翰逊英语词典》在出版后引起轰动，成为当时最具权威的英文词典，雄霸英语世界一个半世纪之

---

* 在约翰逊故居中文导览发布仪式上的讲话。2015年6月16日，约翰逊故居纪念馆。

久，对英语的发展做出了重大贡献，使英语成为世界通用语言之一。

约翰逊博士之所以声名远扬，为后人津津乐道，不仅在于他编撰的大词典意义重大，也因为他独特的个性和人生经历，以及关于他的许多故事。《牛津国家人物传记大辞典》称约翰逊博士是"英国历史上最杰出的文人"。他思想敏锐，博闻强识。他的朋友、《约翰逊传》的作者包斯威尔一直疑惑他怎么有时间创作。约翰逊博士十分热衷于与各种人物会面，高谈阔论，并与美食美酒相伴。约翰逊博士还是一个风趣幽默的谈话大师，舌辩滔滔，总是能用出其不意的警句，给予伦敦社交圈和思想界以启示，也给后人留下一笔宝贵财富。时至今日约翰逊博士仍是英国被引用最多的人。比如，每当人们谈到伦敦就会引用他的名句："如果一个人厌倦了伦敦，他就厌倦了生活。"

约翰逊博士与中国有很深的渊源。他生前非常喜爱中国的茶，每天都会饮用。在其有生之年，他很想去中国看看，尤其想登上长城，他还一直鼓励他的朋友包斯威尔去中国。虽然约翰逊博士访华未能如愿以偿，但231年后的今天，中国或者说中国人和中文来到了他的故居。要知道，至情至性的约翰逊博士是一个"在坟墓中都盼望着能收到信件的人"，而且他的朋友包斯威尔多次提道，"约翰逊很喜欢接受别人的称赞"。他如果知道自己的故居不仅每年接待不少中国游客，而且现在还有了中文导览，知道我们在此用英文或者中文赞颂他，想必他一定会非常高兴。

女士们、先生们，

中文导览的发布，充分说明了约翰逊故居基金会对中国访客的重视。我还记得20世纪70年代我首次出国时，当时无论在欧美还是非洲，旅游景点既没有多少中国游客，更不会有中文介绍。而如今，中国每年出境游客近1亿人次。随着中国与世界的接触不断增多，中国民众日益走出国门，包括英国在内的越来越多的国家开始在景点和参观场所提供中文服务。每年中国访英游客大约23万人，并且在逐年递增。他们当中有许多英国文学、历史和语言爱好者，对约翰逊博士怀有浓厚兴趣，慕名来到这里参观。中文导览可以帮助他们跨越语言障碍，更直观、生动、全面地了解这位英国文坛的杰出人物，了解英国的历史，了解英国的文化。

女士们、先生们：

中英两国都是文化大国，具有深厚绚烂的文化，以各自文明交流互鉴为荣。丰富的文化交往将进一步增进中英两国人民之间的了解和认知，拉近距离，让中英友好的理念更加深植人心。今天约翰逊故居中文导览的正式启用就是为中英友好的大厦添砖加瓦，为中英文化交流增光添彩！

谢谢！

A Highly Acclaimed Achievement in China-UK Cultural Exchanges*

Lord Harmsworth,

Sheriff Fiona Adler,

Distinguished Guests,

Ladies and Gentlemen,

My wife Hu Pinghua and I greatly appreciate the invitation to be with you this morning.

It is a real pleasure for us to witness the launch of the Chinese language audio tour of Dr Johnson's House.

I also wish to congratulate Lord Harmsworth and his family for their inspired initiative of preserving Dr Johnson's House. I understand that back in 1911 the Harmsworth family took steps to preserve this historic house where Dr Johnson compiled his famous dictionary.

Since I came to London five years ago, I have heard many British people talking about the influence of Dr Johnson:

- They discuss his works.
- They quote his words of wisdom.
- They tell famous anecdotes about this 18th century British literary giant.

---

* Remarks at the Launch of the Chinese Language Audio Tour of Dr Johnson's House. Dr Johnson's House, 16 June 2015.

We are deeply honoured to have this opportunity of visiting the house Dr Johnson used to live in.

Just now, I toured the house accompanied by the newly commissioned digital Chinese language guide. I am delighted to tell you about the guide.

The guide was fluent, clear and accurate—a job well done!

As I walked around the house, I found the cozy, exquisite, minimal yet classic decoration of the house most impressive.

In my mind I could imagine Dr Johnson, over 200 years ago, working at his desk for eight long years before finishing his Dictionary.

Dr Johnson once said:

"Great works are performed not by strength but by perseverance."

Wise words indeed!

It was with extraordinary perserverence and willpower that Dr Johnson has won such fame. He faced chronic illness, financial challenges and the heart wrenching loss of his beloved wife.

Despite all these hurdles, Dr Johnson wrote his master piece—*A Dictionary of the English Language*:

- Its publication was received with great enthusiasm and appreciation.
- Its authority and influence in the English speaking world for over a century and a half that followed is undeniable.
- And its contribution to the development of the English language cannot be overstated. English went on to become a "world language".

The significance of the Dictionary is only one of many contributions to Dr Johnson's fame and the public interest in him over the years.

There were also his unique character, personal experience and the many stories about him.

According to the *Oxford Dictionary of National Biography*, Dr Johnson was:

"Arguably the most distinguished man of letters in English history."

His sharp wit and encyclopedic knowledge never failed to puzzle his friend and biographer James Boswell.

Boswell always wondered how Johnson managed to find time to write. We learn from Boswell how Johnson thrived on meeting people accompanied by eating, drinking and talking.

Dr Johnson was also a humourous and eloquent orator. He was always able to surprise his audience with epigrams of his creation. These words of wisdom not only brought light to London society and scholars of his time but also left a rich legacy to future generations.

Even today, Dr Johnson is still the most quoted Briton. For example, when people talk about London, they will always quote Dr Johnson:

"When a man is tired of London, he is tired of life."

Dr Johnson had a strong interest in China. He loved Chinese tea and is said to have drunk it every day. We know from Boswell that Johnson wished to visit China and especially to walk the Great Wall. He had been urging his friend Boswell to visit China. Although Dr Johnson did not get his wish, 231 years after his death, China, both its people and its language, come to him.

I believe that man of Dr Johnson's disposition would have loved to learn of his immense influence after he died. His friend Boswell mentioned a number of times that he always enjoyed praise.

But I wonder what the reaction of Dr Johnson would have been had he known that his old house is now receiving many visitors from China every year. What would Dr Johnson have made of this newly installed Chinese language audio tour? I feel sure he would have been delighted if he heard our words of praise either in English or in Chinese.

Ladies and Gentlemen,

The launch of the Chinese language audio tour clearly shows that Dr Johnson's House Trust values Chinese visitors.

When I first travelled outside China in the mid 1970s, there were no Chinese tourists in Europe, the Americas or Africa, let alone Chinese language tours.

Today, Chinese tourists make 100 million overseas trips every year. As China and the world come closer, and as more and more Chinese set out for overseas destinations, Chinese language services have become more available. At tourist attractions, increasing number of countries, including the UK, are providing Chinese language services.

Every year about 230,000 Chinese tourists visit the UK. And the numbers are increasing. Among these Chinese tourists are fans of English literature, history and language. For them an obvious place to visit is Dr Johnson's House. The Chinese language audio tour will help them get over the language barrier. This will allow them to appreciate more directly, vividly and comprehensively what they will see here. In this way they can gain a deep appreciation of the life and accomplishments of Dr Johnson. He was truly a man of great eminence in English literature as well as the British history and culture.

Ladies and Gentlemen,

Both China and the UK have a rich and splendid culture. Each of our nations takes pride in sharing knowledge about each of our civilizations:

- Sharing and appreciating each other's culture will enhance mutual understanding and recognition between the people of our countries.
- Sharing will bring our people closer.
- And sharing will allow China-UK friendship to take deeper roots.

Today's launch of Chinese language audio tour of Dr Johnson's House will further enable that sharing. It will add one more brick to the edifice of China-UK friendship. It is a highly acclaimed achievement in China-UK cultural exchanges.

Thank you!

中国文化季恰逢其时 *

女士们、先生们、朋友们：

欢迎各位出席中国驻英国大使馆举办的"中英文化交流年"中国文化季新闻发布会。

2014年6月，李克强总理访问英国期间，中英两国政府发表联合声明，宣布2015年为中英文化交流年，上半年在中国举办英国文化季，下半年在英国举办中国文化季。

2015年3月，英国剑桥公爵威廉王子在访华期间，为英国著名动画形象"小羊肖恩"雕塑点睛，拉开了英国文化季的序幕。英国文化季的系列活动成功展示了英国文化创意产业的精华，受到了中国公众的热烈欢迎。

当前中国文化季的各项精彩活动正在陆续登陆英伦，中国国家话剧院、中国人民解放军军乐团等知名演出团体一一亮相，将给英国人民带来更多的惊喜和高质量的艺术享受。

女士们、先生们，

"中英文化交流年"的开启，特别是中国文化季的举办，凸显了三个意义。

第一，凸显共同的辉煌。中英两国同为文化大国，都曾创造了辉煌灿烂的历史和文化，都有着厚重的文化底蕴，都重视传统文化的传承和创新发

---

* 在"中英文化交流年"中国文化季新闻发布会上的讲话。2015年8月4日，中国驻英国大使馆。

展，也都以各自独特的智慧和创造为人类的文明进步做出了卓越的贡献。中国有五千年未曾中断的悠久文明，孕育了博大精深、举世闻名的东方智慧，成为世界文明殿堂的不朽瑰宝。英国是启蒙运动和工业革命的重要发源地，所创造的科学技术、市场经济、金融制度、法律体系和工商业文化，对近代以来的世界发展产生了重大影响。威廉王子在英国文化季开幕式上谈道，"作为两个具有辉煌古老历史的国家，中国和英国有着共同的经历"。对此，我不仅深表赞同，而且坚信未来两国还将共同为人类文明做出更大的贡献。

第二，凸显文化的融通。文化没有国界，交流没有终点，距离的遥远挡不住中英文化交流的步伐。在长期交往中，中英两国人民始终相互欣赏彼此优秀的文明成果。中国古代儒家思想和科举制度在传播到欧洲后，受到了英国启蒙思想家的推崇。文艺复兴后英国涌现一批杰出的哲学家、文学家、艺术家，他们在中国同样家喻户晓。早在100多年前，莎士比亚的作品就在中国出版，并陆续以话剧、京剧等形式登上舞台，受到中国人民的喜爱。中国的曹禺、巴金等戏剧大师的作品也深受英国观众的喜爱。就在两周前，作为中国文化季的首场重要演出，中国国家话剧院在伦敦上演了中文版《理查三世》，对这部莎翁的经典作品进行了中国式的诠释，受到了英国朋友的热烈推崇。我相信，"中英文化交流年"丰富多彩的活动将为两国文化创意产业搭建更加广阔的合作平台，为两国人民共享彼此文学艺术的精华和交流互鉴的成果创造更多的机会。

第三，凸显文化助力中英关系持续深入发展。人文交流是国家之间关系的基础，正如中国古语所说："国之交在于民相亲。"2011年，中英两国政府达成重要共识，决定将中英人文交流提升到双边关系的战略层面，使之与中英战略对话、中英经济财金对话一道，共同构成中英全面战略伙伴关系的三大支柱。中英人文交流以两国民众之间的相知和理解培育两国友好的深厚土壤，使全面战略伙伴关系更加稳固、更具活力。近年来，在双方共同努力下，中英人文交流空前活跃。在中国，有超过3亿人学习英语，有数以亿计的英格兰足球超级联赛球迷。在英国，建立了27所孔子学院和113间孔子课堂，数量高居欧洲国家之首，500多所中小学开设了汉语课。51对中英省郡、城市缔结了友好关系，来英的中国游客每年以两位数字递增。加强人文交流，扩大文化合作，促进文明互鉴已成为两国政府和人民的广泛共识，为中英关系更加深入、持久的发展打下坚实的民意基础。

女士们、先生们，

2015年是中英关系的"大年"。2015年10月，习近平主席将应伊丽莎白女王陛下的邀请对英国进行国事访问。这次访问将成为两国关系新的里程碑。中英双方都在为这一重要访问进行积极准备。9月，中英高级别人文交流机制第三次会议将在英国举行。此时在英国举办中国文化季，可谓恰逢其时。我相信，中国文化季的一系列活动将推动中英文化交流与合作迈上新台阶，为两国关系发展注入新动力。

最后，我衷心祝愿"中英文化交流年"中国文化季取得圆满成功！

谢谢！

A Timely China Cultural Season*

Ladies and Gentlemen,

Friends,

Welcome to the Chinese Embassy.

It is a pleasure to have you with us to launch the China Season of the 2015 China-UK Year of Cultural Exchanges.

During Premier Li Keqiang's visit to the UK in June last year, the governments of China and the UK issued a joint statement, in which 2015 was designated as the Year of Cultural Exchanges between the two countries. The UK Season lasted from January to June. The China Season began in July.

In March this year, The Duke of Cambridge visited China. By painting the eye of a Shaun the Sheep model, he launched the UK Season. The series of cultural activities that followed were a successful display of the best of British creative industry. They were hugely popular with the Chinese public.

Right now, it is the China Season. A rich variety of cultural events are arriving in the UK and lighting up the stages here. Among them are the National Theatre Company of China and Military Band of the Chinese People's Liberation Army. The British audience is guaranteed to be wowed by top-notch artistic delight.

Ladies and Gentlemen,

It is of special significance that we are here today to launch the China Season of the China-UK Year of Cultural Exchanges. I want to summarize the significance of the

---

* Remarks at the Launch of the China Season of the 2015 China-UK Year of Cultural Exchanges. Chinese Embassy, London, 4 August 2015.

China Season with three "highlights".

First, the China Season highlights the proud history and culture of China and the UK.

Culturally, China and the UK are both influential countries who have contributed enormously to human civilization. Both countries have created a splendid history and culture. Both are proud of their cultural tradition, yet both are keen on innovation and creation.

China boasts a five-thousand-year uninterrupted civilization. It is the birthplace of the profound oriental wisdom that is forever a treasure in the palace of world civilizations.

Britain is where the Age of Enlightenment and the Industrial Revolution began. Its scientific and technological achievements, its economic, financial and legal systems, and its industrial and commercial culture have had a huge impact on the world development since modern times.

At the opening of the UK Season earlier in the year, the Duke of Cambridge said, "China and Britain are united in our experience as countries with a proud and ancient history." I cannot agree with him more. And I firmly believe that China and the UK are capable of making even greater contribution to human civilization in the future.

Second, the China Season highlights the cultural exchanges between China and the UK. Culture knows no border. Exchange sees no finish line. The geological distance is not a barrier to cultural exchanges between China and the UK. Throughout many years of mutual exchange, the people of China and the people of the UK have all along admired and appreciated the culture and civilization of each other.

When Confucianism and China's imperial examination system were first introduced to Europe, they were held in esteem by British enlightenment thinkers. Likewise, the British Renaissance philosophers, writers and artists became household names in China.

Shakespeare's works were published in China as early as a hundred years ago. Many of his plays have appeared on Chinese stage and sometimes in the form of Peking Opera. In China, people simply love Shakespeare. In Britain, the works of Chinese playwrights Cao Yu and Ba Jin take the fancy of local audience.

Two weeks ago, the National Theatre Company of China brought the Chinese version of *Richard III to* London. This was the first important performance of the China

Season. This Chinese interpretation of Shakespeare's classic was warmly applauded by the British audience.

It is therefore my firm belief that the colourful events of the China-UK Year of Cultural Exchanges will help build a broad platform for cooperation between the cultural and creative industries of our two countries. These events will open up windows for the Chinese and British people to share the best of their literature and art, and to enjoy the fruits of mutual learning.

Third, the China Season highlights the strength of cultural exchanges in promoting sustained and in-depth development of China-UK relations. People-to-people exchange is the foundation for state-to-state relations. As an old Chinese motto goes, "Affinity between the people holds the key to relations between countries."

In 2011, the governments of China and the UK reached an important consensus. We decided to make people-to-people exchange one of the three strategic pillars of our bilateral relations. The other two are China-UK Strategic Dialogue and China-UK Economic and Financial Dialogue.

People-to-people exchange will foster amiable sentiments and mutual understanding between the people of China and the UK. This will in turn provide rich soil for friendly ties between our two countries to grow even stronger. It will enable us to make China-UK comprehensive strategic partnership more solid and more energetic.

Thanks to the concerted efforts of both sides, China-UK people-to-people exchange has been more active in recent years than ever before.

- In China, over 300 million people are learning English and hundreds of millions of football fans identify with Premier League clubs.
- In the UK, there are 27 Confucius Institute and 113 Confucius Classrooms, more than any other European countries.
- Over 500 secondary and primary schools have Chinese language courses.
- 51 pairs of provinces, counties and cities have entered into sister relationship.
- And the number of Chinese tourists coming to the UK is increasing by double digits.

China and the UK must strengthen people-to-people exchange. We must expand cultural cooperation. And we must promote mutual learning. This is a definite consensus of both the governments and the people of our two countries. And this consensus will reinforce the popular support for deeper and sustained development of China-UK relations.

Ladies and Gentlemen,

2015 is a big year for China-UK relations. In October, at the invitation of Her Majesty The Queen, President Xi Jinping will pay a state visit to the UK. This visit is expected to mark a new milestone in China-UK relationship. Right now, both China and the UK are working hard to get ready for this important visit.

Next month, the Third Meeting of the China-UK High-Level People-to-People Exchange will be held in London. Against this backdrop, today's launch of the China Season in the UK cannot be more timely.

I am confident that the events of the China Season will bring our cultural exchanges and cooperation to a new and higher level. They will in turn give new impetus to the development of China-UK relationship.

In conclusion, I wish the China Season of the China-UK Year of Cultural Exchanges complete success.

Thank you!

海纳百川，有容乃大*

女士们、先生们：

很高兴出席皇家莎士比亚剧团为庆贺中国合作项目成功举办的招待会。

莎士比亚与中国渊源久远。1839年中国编译的《四洲志》第一次提到了莎士比亚。据考证，最早的舞台演出是1889年上海学生表演的《威尼斯商人》。特别值得一提的是，第一个向中国正式介绍莎士比亚的中国人是我的一位前任，19世纪70年代中国第一位外交使节、驻英公使郭嵩焘。时至今日，莎士比亚在中国可谓家喻户晓，我想可以用四个"最"来说明。

第一，莎士比亚被中国人认为是英国文化最突出的象征。中国有4亿多英语学习者，可以说，学英语的人没有不知道莎士比亚的。英国文化教育协会的一项国际调查结果显示，25%的中国受访者将莎士比亚排在英国名人榜的首位，超过了伊丽莎白女王陛下。

第二，在中国对外国作家的研究方面，有关莎士比亚的著述最多。中国学者出版了百余部莎士比亚研究专著、5部莎士比亚研究辞典。在中国，莎士比亚是外国文学研究领域的持久热点。

第三，莎士比亚是对中国现代戏剧发展最具影响力的外国人。中国现代戏剧的主要奠基人，如曹禺、田汉等，几乎都深受莎士比亚戏剧的影响。

第四，莎士比亚"中国化"成果最为显著。据统计，中国的话剧、京

---

* 在英国皇家莎士比亚剧团为庆贺中国合作项目成功举办招待会上的讲话。2017年1月24日，伦敦"中国站"。

剧、昆曲、越剧、川剧等 24 个剧种都排演过莎士比亚的作品，其中许多作品还多次应邀参加国际重要的艺术节，如英国爱丁堡国际艺术节。2016 年，在伦敦就上演了越剧版的《寇流兰与杜丽娘》。

"海纳百川，有容乃大。"莎士比亚在中国深受欢迎，既是因为莎士比亚伟大的艺术成就，更源于中国文化的开放与包容。我们一贯认为文化多样性是世界的基本特征。

正如习近平主席最近在联合国日内瓦总部的演讲中所说，"每种文明都有其独特魅力和深厚底蕴，都是人类的精神瑰宝。不同文明要取长补短、共同进步，让文明交流互鉴成为推动人类社会进步的动力、维护世界和平的纽带"。

习近平主席 2015 年在对英进行国事访问时，亲自提议两国在 2016 年共同纪念汤显祖和莎士比亚这两位中英文学巨匠逝世 400 周年，这一提议得到中英各界热烈响应。

莎士比亚曾说："要收获谷实，还得等待我们去播种。"皇家莎士比亚剧团作为中英文化交流的播种者，积极参与了 2016 年"纪念汤显祖和莎士比亚逝世 400 周年"系列活动。该剧团携莎士比亚"王与国"三部曲访华，还与中国国家大剧院、中国国家话剧院和上海话剧艺术中心等开展莎士比亚和中国古典戏剧互译项目，并陆续将翻译成果搬上中英两国的舞台。我相信，这些合作对中英文化的互鉴共融，对加深两国人民之间的了解和友谊，对促进中英关系深入发展，都具有重要意义。在此我表示衷心祝贺，也将在今后继续予以鼎力支持。

中国春节马上就要到了，2017 年是丁酉鸡年。鸡在中国文化中象征着勤劳、光明和吉祥。我祝大家在鸡年闻鸡起舞，吉祥如意！

祝皇家莎士比亚剧团取得更多、更大的成就！

祝中英文化交流不断结出更多成果！

谢谢！

The Vast Sea Admits Hundreds of Rivers[*]

Ladies and Gentlemen,

It gives me great delight to join you for this reception to celebrate the Royal Shakespeare Company's cultural exchanges with China.

William Shakespeare has a historical relationship with China. The name of Shakespeare first appeared in a Chinese book published in 1839, which is called the *Encyclopedia of Geography*. Shakespeare's play first met its Chinese audience in 1889, when a group of students staged *The Merchant of Venice* in Shanghai in 1889. Interestingly, the first Chinese who officially introduced Shakespeare to China was one of my predecessors Guo Songtao in the 1870s. Mr Guo was China's very first diplomatic envoy and the first Minister to Britain. More than a century later, in today's China, Shakespeare is now a household name.

I would like to use four "No.1's" to show you why Shakespeare is so popular in China.

First, Shakespeare is listed by the Chinese people as the No.1 recognizable British culture icon. In China, there are more than 400 million English language students. And there is no English language student who does not know Shakespeare. According to a survey by the British Council, 25% of the Chinese people put Shakespeare at the top of the list of best-known British historical and contemporary personalities. He certainly has a higher name recognition than Her Majesty The Queen.

Second, Shakespeare ranks No.1 among all foreign writers studied and researched by Chinese scholars and experts. So far Chinese scholars have published more than

---

[*] Remarks at the Reception of Celebrating the Royal Shakespeare Company's Cultural Exchanges with China. China Exchange, 24 January 2017.

100 monographs on Shakespeare's works and 5 dictionaries devoted to Shakespeare studies. Time may have changed but the enthusiasm for Shakespeare studies has always remained high in China.

Third, if we look at the influence of foreign playwrights on modern drama in China, Shakespeare is again No.1. Among the founders of China's modern drama, such as Cao Yu, Tian Han, etc, you could hardly name anyone who had not been deeply influenced by Shakespeare's works.

Fourth, in terms of local theatre adaptation of foreign plays in China, Shakespeare is also No.1. Shakespeare's plays have been staged in China in all 24 Chinese drama genres, including the modern drama, the Peking Opera, the Kunqu Opera, the Yue Opera and the Sichuan Opera. Many of them have been repeatedly invited to some of the world's most prestigious international art festivals, such as Edinburgh International Festival. Last year, a Yue Opera adaptation of one of Shakespeare's famous works, *Coriolanus and Du Liniang*, was performed on London's stage.

There is an old saying in China: "The sea is vast because it admits hundreds of rivers." While Shakespeare's popularity in China is undeniably attributed to his unprecedented artistic achievements, it would not have been possible without the openness and inclusiveness of the Chinese culture. We Chinese believe that cultural diversity is a fundamental feature of this world.

President Xi Jinping said during his visit to the UN Office at Geneva recently: "Every civilization, with its own appeal or root, is a human treasure. Diverse civilizations should draw on each other to achieve common progress. We should make exchanges among civilizations a source of inspiration for advancing human society and a bond that keeps the world in peace."

During his 2015 state visit to the UK, President Xi Jinping made a proposal for China and the UK to jointly commemorate the 400th anniversary of the passing of China's Tang Xianzu and Britain's Shakespeare in 2016. This proposal received enthusiastic responses from both countries.

Shakespeare wrote in his play *Measure for Measure*: "Our corn's to reap, for yet our tithe's to sow." The Royal Shakespeare Company (RSC) has worked tirelessly to sow the seeds of closer China-UK cultural exchanges. Last year, the RSC played an active role in the events to commemorate Tang and Shakespeare. This includes the "King and Country Trilogy" tour to China. The RSC also worked closely with its Chinese partners, including the National Centre for the Performing Arts, the National Theatre Company of China, and the Shanghai Dramatic Arts Centre. They are now engaged in the Shakespeare Folio Project and the Chinese Classics Project, which respectively aims at translating Shakespeare's works into Chinese and Chinese drama classics into English. Also on their agenda is the plan to present the translated works in both China and the UK on stage.

Such cooperation, I firmly believe, is highly significant. It helps promote mutual learning and interaction between the Chinese culture and the British culture. It helps deepen mutual understanding and cement stronger friendship between the Chinese people and the British people. It helps deepen China-UK relationship. Here I would like to extend my sincere congratulations to the RSC, and I pledge my continued and strong support in the days ahead.

In less than four days' time, we will ring in the Chinese New Year of the Rooster. The rooster in the Chinese culture is a symbol of hardwork, good luck and bright future.

May I wish everyone a happy and prosperous Year of the Rooster!

May I wish the RSC greater success and achievements!

May I wish more fruits in China-UK cultural exchanges!

Thank you!

为中英人文交流插上智慧的翅膀 *

尊敬的大英图书馆首席执行官基廷先生,

女士们、先生们:

很高兴出席大英图书馆举办的"大英图书馆在中国:共享知识与文化"招待会。这是近年来两国间的又一次大型文化交流项目,也是落实2016年底中英高级别人文交流机制会议成果的重要举措。此项目的重头戏"从莎士比亚到福尔摩斯:大英图书馆的珍宝"展览即将在北京开幕。我谨对此表示热烈祝贺。

我认为,这个项目创造了至少三个"第一"。

第一,这是大英图书馆经典藏品第一次进入中国。刚才,基廷先生告诉我,这也是大英图书馆第一次把这么多的珍品送到国外展出。莎士比亚、拜伦、勃朗特、狄更斯等英国文学巨匠的手稿原件和早期珍贵印本将首次在中国展出,中国公众对此充满期待,他们将有机会饱览英国文学的瑰宝。

第二,这是中国国家图书馆馆藏第一次与大英图书馆珍贵馆藏同时展出。包括朱生豪先生翻译莎士比亚作品手稿在内的诸多中国著名译作、改编及评论书籍和稿件将集中展出,彰显中英人文交流的悠久历史和辉煌成就。

第三,这是大英图书馆在华持续时间最长、举办地点最多的活动。整个"大英图书馆在中国:共享知识与文化"项目将持续3年,足迹遍及北京、

---

* 在"大英图书馆在中国:共享知识与文化"招待会上的讲话。2017年4月20日,大英图书馆。

上海、乌镇和香港等地，成为一次跨越时空、跨越地域的文化交流盛宴。

图书馆是人类智慧的宝库，记录着人类文明的发展脉络。两国图书馆之间的合作，是中英人文交流的重要组成部分，也是中西方文明交融互鉴的生动写照。此次活动以"共享知识与文化"为主题，非常恰当。我们不仅将分享知识、欣赏文化，还将加深了解、拓展合作、增进友谊。

2017年恰逢中英建立大使级外交关系45周年。我希望并相信，此次活动将为建交纪念活动增光添彩。

莎士比亚曾说，"生活里没有书籍，就好像没有阳光；智慧里没有书籍，就好像鸟儿没有翅膀"。中国著名美术教育家李苦禅也讲过，"鸟欲高飞先振翅，人求上进先读书"。

我衷心祝愿"大英图书馆在中国：共享知识与文化"项目取得圆满成功，为两国人文交流与合作插上智慧的翅膀，迎着中英关系灿烂的阳光，飞得更高、更远！

谢谢！

Give Wings of Wisdom to China-UK Cultural Exchanges*

Mr Roly Keating,

Ladies and Gentlemen,

I am delighted to join you here at the British Library to mark the project The British Library in China: Connecting through culture and learning.

This project is not only one of the major cultural events between China and the UK that we have seen in recent years. It is also a key follow-up to last year's China-UK High-Level People-to-People Dialogue.

A heavyweight component of this project is the exhibition entitled "Shakespeare to Sherlock: Treasures of the British Library". This exhibition will soon open in Beijing. Let me offer my warm congratulations!

This exhibition, The British Library in China, is a record-breaking event. It has made three "first's".

This is the first time that the British Library sent its treasured collections to China. I just learnt from Mr Keating that this is also the first time that the British Library sent so many of its collections overseas.

The original manuscripts and early printed copies of Shakespeare, Byron, Bronte and Dickens will be on display in China for the very first time. Chinese viewers are eagerly looking forward to this opportunity to appreciate the gems of British literature.

This is the first time that the treasures of the Chinese National Library and the collections of the British Library were on display side by side.

---

* Remarks at The British Library in China:Connecting through culture and learning Reception. The British Library, 20 April 2017.

The Chinese masterpieces of translations, adaptations and literary critics, including the manuscripts of Mr Zhu Shenghao's translation of Shakespeare's works, will all be part of the exhibition. This exhibition is a showcase of the history and achievements of China-UK people-to-people exchanges.

This is also the longest-lasting exhibition in China by the British Library that will visit more cities than before. It will stay in China for three years and tour Beijing, Shanghai, Wuzhen and Hong Kong. What a splendid cultural feast that transcends time and space and connects different countries and peoples!

A library is a treasure house of human wisdom. It is the temple of the development of civilization. The cooperation between the libraries of our two countries is an important part of China-UK cultural relations. It is also a vivid example of the exchanges and mutual learning between Chinese and Western civilizations.

The theme of The British Library in China is connecting through culture and learning. What a perfect theme!

This project will enable us to share knowledge and admire the jewels of culture.

This project will also help us to deepen understanding, expand cooperation and strengthen friendship.

This year marks the 45th anniversary of China-UK ambassadorial diplomatic ties. I hope and believe that the British Library exhibition will be a significant part of our commemorative activities.

Shakespeare once wrote, "A life without books is like a life without sunlight, and wisdom without books is like a wingless bird."

Li Kuchan, renowned Chinese art educator, also said this:

"A bird stretches its wings to fly high. A man reads books to be a better person."

With these words in mind, let me offer my sincere wishes to the exhibition The British Library in China:

I wish this exhibition will give wings to the people-to-people exchanges and cultural cooperation between China and the UK.

I wish that on these wings of wisdom, such exchanges and cooperation will fly high and far in the brilliant sunlight of China-UK relations.

And finally, I wish the exhibition a great success!

Thank you!

深化中英体育合作，共创世界美好未来 *

尊敬的大会主席怀特先生，
女士们、先生们：

很高兴出席由英国电讯传媒集团举办的第三届年度体育商业大会。本次大会以促进英国体育产业发展、合作与创新为主题，会聚了众多体育、商业、媒体和文化界精英人士，搭建了一个交流经验、分享机遇、促进合作的重要平台。

大会主席怀特先生希望我谈谈中国体育发展，以及中英两国在体育领域面临的合作机遇。这是一个内容丰富的题目，也是一个非常重要的题目。今天，我愿借此机会，谈谈我的一些看法。

中国是世界上人口最多的国家，也是一个体育大国，我们高度重视体育事业和体育产业的发展。因为体育是社会发展和人类进步的重要标志，也是综合国力和社会文明程度的重要体现。体育运动不仅提高了人们的健康水平，还体现了人类战胜自然、超越自我、追求卓越的精神。新中国成立60多年特别是改革开放以来，中国体育事业走过了不平凡的历程，取得了举世瞩目的成就，主要体现在5个方面。

第一，全民健身运动达到"新水平"。新中国成立前，中国人被称为"东亚病夫"，人均寿命仅有35岁。今天，中国人民生活和健康水平大幅提高，全民健身蔚然成风，人均寿命达到76岁，早已甩掉了"东亚病夫"的

---

* 在英国第三届年度体育商业大会上的主旨演讲。2017年5月9日，伦敦英国电信中心。

帽子。据统计，中国人民喜爱的体育健身项目多达60种，经常参加体育锻炼的人口比例超过总人口的1/3，远超出发展中国家平均水平。全国体育场地数量超过170万个，全国一半以上的市县建有全民健身中心，人均体育场地面积比10年前翻了一番。

第二，竞技体育实力勇攀"新高峰"。从1952年新中国首次参加奥运会，仅有1名运动员参加男子100米仰泳决赛，到1984年中国实现奥运金牌零的突破，再到2008年北京举办奥运会，实现百年奥运梦，中国竞技体育取得了长足发展。中国体育代表团在伦敦奥运会上取得境外参赛最好成绩，在2016年里约奥运会上保持既有运动项目优势，在2014年索契冬奥会上实现冬奥会基础大项金牌"零的突破"。2010—2015年，中国运动员共获得596个世界冠军，创造了57个世界纪录，为世界体育发展做出了贡献。

第三，体育机制改革迈出"新步伐"。中国实行改革开放近40年，体育机制也经历了深度改革。现在，我们引入更多竞争机制，大力促进体育职业化、专业化和商业化发展，致力于打造现代体育治理体系。以足球为例，我们采取了50多项改革措施，鼓励多元资本投入，通过资本市场发展壮大足球俱乐部。下一步我们还将继续深化全国综合性和单项体育赛事管理制度改革，向市场和社会释放更多体育资源。

第四，体育产业发展成为"新亮点"。中国体育产业规模逐步扩大，体育消费明显增加。据统计，中国体育及相关产业总产出从2013年末的1650亿美元增加到2014年的2025亿美元，2015年达到2550亿美元，每年增加值占国内生产总值的比重约为0.7%，较以往大幅提升。体育产业与文化、旅游、医疗、养老、互联网等领域的互动融合日益加深，产生积极的乘数效应，呈现井喷式发展态势。

第五，体育对外合作开拓"新格局"。20世纪70年代"乒乓外交"促进中美关系改善，成为中国外交史上的一段佳话。如今，体育进一步拉近了中国与世界的距离。2008年北京奥运会、2010年广州亚运会、2014年南京青奥会等体育盛会，搭建起中国与世界各国交流的新窗口。2022年中国将举办北京冬奥会，北京将成为世界上第一个既举办夏季奥运会又举办冬季奥运会的城市。所有这些都彰显了中国对世界体育事业的担当，促进了中国与世界各国的人文交流与合作。

当然，我们也清醒地认识到，中国虽然是体育大国，但还不是体育强国。中国体育事业仍面临发展不平衡、管理体制滞后等问题与挑战。但这些问题与挑战更多是中国体育事业"成长中的烦恼"。从长远来看，中国体育事业发展前景广阔，市场潜力巨大。不少人把中国体育产业比作一座"金矿"。我认为这个比喻十分恰当，主要有三方面原因，我将其称为"三大红利"。

一是庞大的"人口红利"。据不完全统计，目前中国的运动人群达 3.8 亿，泛户外运动人群达 1.3 亿，户外运动人群达 0.6 亿。这为体育产业发展奠定了数量庞大的群众基础，其中也蕴藏着巨大的消费需求。

二是稳定的"经济红利"。中国经济保持稳中向好的良好势头，体育作为经济新增长点的作用日益显现，成为带动力强、资源消耗低、附加值高的"绿色产业""朝阳产业"。预计到 2020 年，全国体育产业总规模将超过 4500 亿美元，体育服务业增加值占比超过 30%，体育消费额占人均居民可支配收入比例超过 2.5%。

三是良好的"改革红利"。中国发展体育产业已上升到国家战略层面。早在 2014 年，中国政府就提出实现体育产业 2025 年总规模达 7500 亿美元的目标。可以预见，随着体育商业化、产业化步伐加快，体育供给侧产业链资源将进一步对外放开，体育经济将逐步向消费型经济转型，中方在体育领域对国内外资本的需求也将持续上升。

女士们、先生们，

英国在发展体育事业和体育产业方面底蕴深厚、经验丰富、优势突出。英国是现代体育和体育产业的诞生地，迄今已举办了三届现代奥林匹克运动会。2014 年英国政府提出"运动越多，生活越好"倡议，2015 年制定了"体育的未来：充满活力的国家新战略"。英国奥运代表团在里约奥运会上取得的骄人成绩让人记忆犹新。英超联赛、温布尔登网球锦标赛、橄榄球世界杯赛、高尔夫英国公开赛、环英自行车赛等重大赛事蜚声世界，其中，英超联赛是影响最大、经营最成功的职业联赛之一。体育运动不仅是英国民众日常生活不可或缺的内容，也成为英国经济发展的一项重要支柱产业。

近年来，中英体育合作成果丰硕，势头良好。两国体育合作面临难得的发展机遇，双方应抓住机遇，顺势而上，推动中英体育合作迈上新台阶。我认为，双方应抓住"四大机遇"。

一是中英关系的机遇。2015年，习近平主席成功对英进行国事访问。访问期间，习近平主席专程参观曼彻斯特城市足球学院，希望双方加强包括足球在内的体育交流合作，提高两国人民健康水平，促进中英友好，为中英关系的未来绘就了美好蓝图，也为双方深化体育等人文领域合作指明了方向。

二是中英深化人文交流的机遇。在中英高级别人文交流机制下，双方就体育合作保持战略沟通，加强顶层设计。机制启动5年多来，双方在教育、科技、文化、卫生、媒体、体育等诸多领域开展了务实合作，有力地促进了中英两国民相亲、心相通。2016年12月，英国文化、媒体和体育大臣布拉德利女士赴华出席第四次会议期间，双方就加强体育合作达成多项重要共识。第五次会议将于2017年底在英国举办。双方要充分利用好这一机制平台，进一步拓展体育合作的广度和深度，尤其需要加强青少年体育交流，为促进两国友谊注入新活力。

三是中英体育界优势互补的机遇。中国体育产业方兴未艾，群众体育人群持续扩大，亟须引入先进的体育管理经验和技术。英方在体育设施管理、体育医疗与卫生服务、运动医学等领域经验丰富，双方可就此加强对接与合作。两国企业还可加强竞技体育产业合作，共同探索融合传媒、文化、科技产业与体育产业的合作新途径，实现互利共赢。

四是冬奥会等重大体育盛会的机遇。中英双方在2008年北京奥运会、2012年伦敦奥运会期间开展了卓有成效的合作。北京冬奥会将再次为中英合作提供重要机遇。中英双方已签署了关于冬奥会合作的谅解备忘录，双方应加强交流、深化合作，推动两国体育产业合作不断取得新成果。

女士们、先生们，

现代奥运之父顾拜旦说过，"体育运动是提高人内在素质的途径，人内在素质的提升将带来一个更美好的世界"。我衷心希望，中英两国体育、商业、媒体和文化界人士能抓住当前难得的机遇，不断推进两国体育交流与合作，使两国人民的内在素质不断提升，使我们的世界更加美好！

最后，预祝本次大会取得圆满成功！

谢谢！

Deepen China-UK Sports Cooperation for a Better World*

Chairman Jim White,

Ladies and Gentlemen,

It is a great pleasure to join you at the Telegraph Media Group's third Business of Sport Conference.

This is a premium annual event that aims to steer the UK sports industry to growth, innovation and collaboration. I am sure it is well positioned to unite sports, business, media and cultural leaders under one roof for a unique forum of learning, networking and cooperation.

Jim asked me to talk about the development of sports in China and the cooperation opportunities for China and Britain in the field of sports. This is a big topic as well as an important one.

Let me take this opportunity to share with you some of my thoughts.

With the world's largest population, China is a big sports nation. We attach high importance to sports and the development of the sports industry.

The sports excellence and level of participation is a significant indicator of social progress and human achievements. It is a reflection of a nation's overall strength and cultural advancement.

- Sports improves health.

---

* Keynote Speech at the third Business of Sport Conference. The BT Centre, London, 9 May 2017.

- Sports builds characters.
- Sports embodies the human spirit of ever striving to overcome difficulties, to reach for the limit, to be faster, higher and stronger.

For well over 60 years since the founding of New China, in particular during the nearly 4 decades of reform and opening-up, China has traveled an extraordinary journey in the development of sports. Remarkable achievements have been made in the following five aspects.

First, nationwide sports and fitness fervour has reached a "new high".

Before the founding of New China, the Chinese were labeled the "Sick Man of the East". The average life expectancy was only 35 years. Today, the standard of living and public health in China have been tremendously improved. The average life expectancy has reached 76 years, much higher than the average in developing countries. The label of the "Sick Man of the East" has long gone. There is a nationwide enthusiasm for sports and fitness exercise.

According to statistics, there are about 60 most popular sports and fitness exercises in China. More than a third of China's population take part in sports and exercise frequently. Again, that is way higher than the average in developing nations. There are more than 1.7 million sports venues nationwide. More than half of all cities and counties have sports centres. In the past decade, the area of sports ground per person has doubled.

Second, China's achievements in competitive sports have set "new records".

The past decades have recorded progress by leaps and bounds. The journey began in 1952 when New China sent its first ever delegation to the Olympic Games. Only one swimmer managed to take part in the 100-metre backstroke event. Fast-forward to 1984, China achieved a historical breakthrough in its Olympic gold medal count, that is, from zero to 15. In 2008, China hosted the Olympic Games in Beijing. It was a dream come true. Here in London in 2012, Chinese sportsmen and women achieved the best results of all the overseas events where they have ever competed. In Rio last year, Chinese athletes excelled in events where they have traditionally maintained a competitive edge. Then came Sochi and a major breakthrough for China once again—the first gold medal in a key winter event. From 2010 to 2015, Chinese athletes won a total of 596 world champions and set 57 new world records. That was an important contribution to world sports.

Third, the reforms of China's sports administration have taken "new steps".

For nearly four decades since reform and opening-up policies were adopted, China's sports administration has undergone profound reforms. Today, competition is introduced into the administration of sports, as we promote professional and commercial sports and build a modern sports governance.

Take football for example. We have taken more than 50 reform initiatives. We encourage diversified sources of investment in football. We hope that the capital market will help the football clubs grow.

Going forward, China will continue to reform the administrative system of both multi-sport and single-sport events. This will aim at opening up the sports sector to the market and non-public sectors.

Fourth, China's sports industry has become a "new economic highlight".

The past few years have witnessed a continuous expansion in China's sports industry. Sports-related consumption has notably increased.

The total output of China's sports and related industries increased from 165 billion US dollars in 2013 to 202.5 billion US dollars in 2014 and 255 billion US dollars in 2015. This translates into a much higher annual increment of 0.7% of GDP than in previous years.

Moreover, there is an increasing integration between sports industry and other sectors such as culture, tourism, public health, elderly care and IT. This has created a multiplying effect in the sports industry and led to a growth surge.

Fifth, China's sports collaboration with the world has entered into a "new era".

The Ping-Pong Diplomacy of the 1970s has been a much told story. It shows how sports played a significant role in China's diplomacy, especially the rapprochement between China and the United States.

Today, sports have continued to draw China and the world closer. China has hosted a number of major sports events, including the 2008 Olympic Games in Beijing, the 2010 Asian Games in Guangzhou and the 2014 Youth Olympic Games in Nanjing. These events have brought the world to the doorsteps of China and built the platform for exchanges between China and the world.

In 2022, China is going to host the Winter Olympics in Beijing. By then, Beijing will become the first city in the world to have hosted both the Summer and Winter Olympic Games.

All these have demonstrated China's commitment to world sports. They have also facilitated China's exchanges and cooperation with the world.

There is no doubt that China is a big sports nation. But we are fully aware that despite our progress, China is not yet a strong sports nation. There are still problems and challenges in the form of uneven development and inadequate administrative capability.

But these problems and challenges are more like the "growing pain". In the long run, China's sports sector has a broad prospect and a huge market potential to offer.

That's why many would compare China's sports sector to a "gold mine". I think such a comparison could not be more accurate for mainly three reasons. I call them "Three Bonuses".

First, China has huge "population bonus". Statistics show that 380 million people in China participate in sports regularly. Among these people, 130 million engage in general outdoor exercises and 60 million in outdoor sports. This huge number is important in two ways. It means a solid foundation for sports. And it signifies a huge market.

Second, China has reliable "economic bonus". For years the Chinese economy has maintained steady growth. The sports sector is fast emerging as a new growth point. This green and sunrise industry is characterized by its ability to drive affiliated sectors, its low energy consumption and its high added values. By 2020, the total output of China's sports industry will have exceeded 450 billion US dollars. The sports service industry will account for over 30% of the added values. Consumption on sports will account for over 2.5% of the per capita disposable income.

Third, China has significant "reform bonus". The development of sports is already part of China's national strategy. In 2014, the Chinese government set the target for sports to grow into an industry of 750 billion US dollar by 2025. In the foreseeable future, the commercialization and industrialization of sports in China will take a quicker pace. In turn, this will make the supply side of the sports industrial chain more accessible. This will also gradually make the sports sector more consumption-driven.

All these indicate a growing demand for domestic and foreign investment.

Ladies and Gentlemen,

When we talk about sports and the sports industry, we can never forget Britain.

Britain is the birthplace of modern sports and sports industry. It has hosted three modern Olympic Games and boasts a long-standing tradition, rich experience and unmatched advantages.

The British government attaches importance to sports. This is clearly manifested in its "moving more, living more" initiative of 2014 and its "Sporting Future—A New Strategy for an Active Nation" of 2015.

In addition to the tradition and strategy, the British athletes have made impressive achievements. Their performance in Rio was outstanding.

Britain is also not short of world renowned events, from The Premier League and the Wimbledon Championships to the Rugby World Cup, the Open Championship and the Tour of Britain. The Premier League, among others, is one of the most influential and successful professional leagues.

It is fair to say that sports are indispensable for the British people. Sports have become a pillar industry for the British economy.

In recent years, China-UK sports cooperation has produced fruitful results and gained a strong momentum. More opportunities for even greater cooperation lie ahead. It is time to seize the opportunities and achieve new success in China-UK sports cooperation.

What are the opportunities? I believe there are four major opportunities.

First and foremost, the opportunity provided by China-UK relations. President Xi Jinping paid a successful state visit to the UK in 2015. During his visit, President Xi visited the Manchester City Football Academy. His visit is a strong endorsement of closer China-UK exchanges and cooperation in football and other sports. This is in the interest of improving the fitness of our two peoples and strengthening the friendship between our two nations. Our shared commitment maps out the future of China-UK bilateral ties. This shared commitment charts the course for our cooperation in sports and in all the other fields of cultural and people-to-people exchanges.

Second, the opportunity of deepening China-UK cooperation in cultural and people-to-people exchanges. Within the framework of China-UK High-Level People-to-People Exchange Mechanism, China and the UK have maintained strategic communication and worked jointly to provide top-level design for sports cooperation. Five years on since the Mechanism was launched, China and the UK have had tangible cooperation in a wide range of areas of education, science and technology, culture, health, media and sports. Such cooperation has vigorously promoted the friendship and mutual understanding between the Chinese and British people. Mrs Karen Bradley, Secretary for Culture, Media and Sports, visited to China last December for the fourth meeting of the Mechanism. That meeting led to a series of important agreements on how to strengthen bilateral sports cooperation.

The fifth round of meeting will be held in the UK at the end of this year. Both China and the UK should make good use of this platform to expand sports cooperation both in width and depth. We should enhance in particular the sports exchanges between our young people. This will inject fresh dynamics into China-UK friendship.

Third, the opportunity of matching Chinese and British strengths in sports. The sports industry in China is booming, attracting an ever-growing number of the population. There is an urgent need for advanced expertise and techniques in sports management. The UK is experienced in running sports facilities, sports health services, sports medicine and other related undertakings. These are the areas where China and the UK can match up our needs and engage in closer cooperation. The business sectors could also step up cooperation in the field of competitive sports. They can work with one another and explore ways to integrate sports with media, culture, science and technology for win-win results.

Fourth, the opportunity provided by the Winter Olympics and other major sporting events. China and Britain had effective cooperation in the run-up to and during the 2008 Beijing Olympic Games and the 2012 London Olympic Games. The upcoming Winter Olympics in Beijing will again be a great opportunity for China-UK cooperation. Our two countries have already signed an MOU in this regard. We should continue to strengthen our commitment to closer exchanges and deepen our cooperation in order to produce new outcomes.

Ladies and Gentlemen,

Pierre de Coubertin, the founding father of the Modern Olympics, said this:

"For each individual, sport is a possible source for inner improvement. A better world could be brought about only by better individuals."

It is my sincere hope that leaders of sports, business, media and culture from both China and Britain will seize the valuable opportunities before you.

I hope you will join hands to advance sports exchanges and cooperation.

This will enable continuous inner improvement of our people and make our world a better place.

In conclusion, I wish this year's Business of Sport Conference a complete success!

Thank you!

为中英关系贡献更多创意，注入更多活力*

尊敬的英国国际贸易部管理总监乔麦克先生，

女士们、先生们、朋友们：

今天是英国全国哀悼日，我提议对在3天前伦敦恐袭中的遇难者表示深切的哀悼，对伤者和遇难者家属表示诚挚的慰问。我已代表中国政府和中国领导人向英方强调，在此艰难时刻，中国人民同英国人民坚定地站在一起。

现在，请允许我对"北京优秀影视剧海外展播季·英国"的正式开播表示热烈的祝贺。在今后3个月里，英国公众将不仅有机会享受来自北京的影视盛宴，而且可以感受中国博大精深的传统文化，体验日新月异的当代中国。

我认为，2017年在伦敦举办"北京优秀影视剧海外展播季·英国"活动可谓恰逢其时。它不仅为中英建立大使级外交关系45周年和北京与伦敦结好11周年献上大礼，也将为推动两国人文交流合作做出积极贡献。

一是加强影视交流，培育合作新亮点。英国是世界影视业先驱，也是影视强国。早在1894年，伦敦就建立了活动电影放映厅，世界首台电视机就是英国人约翰·贝尔德发明的。英国影视业年产值已达100亿英镑，年出口额近50亿英镑。"007"系列、《唐顿庄园》等佳片在全球热播，在中国也有众多影迷，影视业已经成为英国在世界上的一张独特名片。

中国影视业虽较英国起步晚，但近年来发展迅速，可谓后来者居上。

---

* 在"北京优秀影视剧海外展播季·英国"开播仪式上的讲话。2017年6月6日，伦敦乔治大街一号。

2016年，中国广播影视业创收800亿美元，广播电视节目制作经营机构达1.4万多家。特别是电影方面，全国有近8000家影院，2016年新增1612家，日均增加4.4家；全国有4万余块银幕，2016年新增9552块，日均增添26块。北京是中国影视业的领头羊，在产值产能、制作技术、基础设施和消费市场等方面均居全国前列。伦敦和北京加强影视合作潜力巨大，前景广阔。

二是借力文化大国，助推创意产业新发展。中英都是文化大国，两国创意产业合作基础扎实、优势互补。"创意产业"概念是由英国首先提出的，该产业已成为英国仅次于金融业的第二大产业。近年来，英国编创能力、制片水准、艺术人才，以及成熟的国际化发行运作体系，与中国创意产业的快速发展势头、资金渠道和市场规模相结合，取得丰硕成果。双方于2014年、2016年分别签署了电影、电视合拍协议，英国成为西方第一个与中国签署影视"双合拍"协议的国家。2016年，双方合拍了6部电影。可以说，影视合作已成为双方创意产业合作的新增长点。

习近平主席在2015年对英进行国事访问期间强调，中英应在创意产业领域加强交流互鉴，通过文化产品增进两国相互了解，实现共同发展。2016年12月，中英高级别人文交流机制第四次会议期间，双方举办了中英创意产业论坛，两国创意产业界约150名代表参加，签署了多项合作协议，为中英加强创意产业合作奠定了坚实的基础。

三是增进人文交流，建设沟通新桥梁。文明交流互鉴，既是推动人类文明进步的强大动力，也是中英关系行稳致远的重要基础。2015年，两国成功互办"中英文化交流年"活动。2016年，两国共同纪念汤显祖和莎士比亚逝世400周年，进一步拉近了两国人民之间的距离。今后数年，双方还将互办一系列重要展览，例如，英国国家海事博物馆拟于2020年举办"一带一路"主题特展，诠释中国"一带一路"倡议的重要意义。

在新媒体迅猛发展的时代，我们要不断创新文明交流互鉴的新形式、新渠道，影视交流与合作将为中英人文交流打造新平台、新桥梁。我们要利用好这些平台和桥梁，不断增进中英两国人民的相互了解与友谊。

女士们、先生们：

当前中英关系正处于历史最好时期，各领域的交流合作空前活跃。创意产业特别是影视业，正在成为双方务实合作新亮点，"北京优秀影视剧海外展播季·英国"登陆英伦就是最好的例证。为进一步推进双方在这一领域的合作，我想提三点建议。

一是把握机遇，促进合作。中英双方应抓住"一带一路"建设契机，加强创意产业交流，增进两国民意相通，夯实两国民意基础，不断探索合作新切入点和利益汇合点，为两国关系发展添砖加瓦。

二是完善机制，搭建平台。机制框架是双方合作的保障。近年来，中英在影视、时尚、设计、演艺、出版等创意产业领域积极互动，相关合作正在逐步深化。双方应以影视合作为样板，进一步加强机制建设，搭建合作平台，夯实创意产业合作基础。

三是加强对接，实现共赢。近年来，中英发挥地方优势，积极加大创意产业交流力度，为促进中英合作做出了重要贡献。北京市就是它们中的杰出代表。今后，双方可将创意产业合作与双方国家发展战略和地方发展规划更紧密地结合起来，推动创意产业合作取得更大发展，带动中英务实合作再上新台阶。

女士们、先生们：

影视是时间和空间的艺术，也是人类艺术史上最年轻的艺术形式之一。我衷心希望，中英影视合作能够跨越时间和空间，不断开拓创新、推陈出新，为中英关系贡献更多创意，注入更多活力。

最后，预祝"北京优秀影视剧海外展播季·英国"活动取得圆满成功！

谢谢大家！

Contribute More Creativity and Dynamism to China-UK Relations *

Managing Director Michael Charlton,

Ladies and Gentlemen,

Dear Friends,

A few hours ago, the UK just observed a minute's silence across the country. I would like to begin by calling on everyone to join me in expressing our deepest condolences on the victims who lost their lives in the terrorist attacks three days ago in London and extending our sincere sympathy to their families and those injured.

On behalf of the Chinese government and Chinese leaders, I have told my British colleagues that at this time of difficulties, the Chinese people stand firmly with the British people.

Now, please allow me to express warm congratulations on the opening of the 2017 China-UK Film and TV Conference.

In the coming three months, films and TV series from Beijing will bring to the British summer season a wonderful feast of Chinese culture. This will give the British audience a taste of the long history and rich culture of the Chinese civilization. It will also take viewers on a journey to experience the rapid changes taking place in China today.

Today's event cannot be held at a better time. This year marks the 45th anniversary of China-UK ambassadorial diplomatic relations and the 11th anniversary of the twin-

---

* Speech at the London Ceremony of 2017 China-UK Film and TV Conference. One Great George Street, London, 6 June 2017.

city relationship between Beijing and London. Today's event is not only a celebration of the ties between our two nations and the two great cities. It is also a contribution to our bilateral cooperation on cultural and people-to-people exchange in the following three ways.

First, film and TV exchanges between China and Britain have become a new highlight of China-UK cooperation.

In film and TV making, the UK has been a pioneer and a world leader. As early as 1894, London opened its own kinetoscope parlour. British engineer John Baird invented the world's first television. Today, British film and television industry has a GVA of 10 billion pounds and an annual export of nearly 5 billion pounds. It has become the best British brand in the world. Films and television dramas, such as the James Bond series and *Downton Abbey*, are international blockbusters. They have a large number of fans in China as well.

Compared to the UK, China is a latecomer. But in recent years, China is catching up quickly and becoming a leading producer of films and TV series. In 2016, China's radio broadcasting, film and television sector is valued at 80 billion US dollars. There are over 14,000 radio and television producing and operating companies. In films, there are nearly 8,000 cinemas in China, with 1,612 new ones added last year alone. That means an average of four or more cinemas added per day. There are now more than 40,000 screens in China. The number of increase last year was 9,552, which means 26 new screens were added each day.

Beijing is a leader in China's film and television industry in terms of total output, production standard, infrastructure and market. If London and Beijing could join hands and forge closer cooperation in this field, there is a huge potential to be tapped and broad prospects to be embraced.

Second, the rich cultural resources of China and Britain could be leveraged to step up the development of our creative industries.

Both China and Britain have a rich culture heritage. Both are cultural giants. Our respective strengths in the creative industries have much to offer to each other and our cooperation has a solid foundation.

Britain is the first to put forward the concept of creative industries. Now creative industries have become the second largest sector in this country only after the financial industry. Recent years have seen the combination of British strengths in creation, production, professional training and international marketing with the creative sector boom, strong financing capability and huge market potential in China.

The match up of these strengths has yielded fruitful outcomes. In 2014 and 2016, China and Britain signed film and television co-production treaties respectively. The UK is the first major Western country to sign both treaties with China. Last year, China and Britain co-produced six films. I would say that our cooperation on film and television has become a new growth point in our cooperation on creative industries.

President Xi Jinping said, during his state visit to the UK in 2015, that China and Britain should enhance exchange and mutual learning in the field of creative industries. Jointly made cultural products could help increase mutual understanding and enable common development.

In December last year, our two countries co-hosted the China-UK Creative Industries Forum during the fourth meeting of China-UK High-Level People-to-People Dialogue. That Forum brought together around 150 industry representatives from both countries and witnessed the signing of several cooperation agreements. That was a solid step toward closer cooperation on creative industries between China and the UK.

Third, enhanced cultural exchanges build a new bridge of communication.

Exchange and mutual learning between different civilizations have always been a strong driving force of human progress. This is also key to building a solid foundation for enduring China-UK relations.

In 2015, China and Britain successfully co-hosted the Year of Culture Exchange. Last year, we jointly commemorated the 400th anniversary of the passing of Tang Xianzu and William Shakespeare. The commemorative events helped bring our two nations closer together. In the coming years, China and Britain will co-host a number of exhibitions. These include an exhibition by the National Maritime Museum in 2020 that aims to explain to viewers the significance of China's Belt and Road Initiative.

We are living in a time of new media. It calls upon us to adopt new forms and open new channels of inter-civilizational exchanges and mutual learning. Clearly, enhancing exchange and cooperation in the field of film and television will create a new platform and build a new bridge for the cultural exchanges between our two countries. They can play a significant role in deepening the mutual understanding and friendship between

China and Britain.

Ladies and Gentlemen,

China-UK relationship is now at its best time in history, as evidenced by the ever-vibrant cooperation in all fields. The creative industries, the film and TV industry in particular, are fast becoming a new growth point in China-UK cooperation. This China-UK Film and TV Conference is one of the best examples.

We need to work harder to promote further cooperation. I would like to make three suggestions in this regard.

First, we should seize the opportunities. The opportunities are in the Belt and Road Initiative, and they are up for grabs. We should enhance exchange between our creative industries. We should increase mutual understanding between our people and build up public support for China-UK relations. We should dare to blaze new trails. We should explore to find common interests. These efforts will contribute to the growth of our overall relations.

Second, we should improve the mechanisms of cooperation and build new platforms. China-UK cooperation cannot progress without sound cooperation mechanism and framework. In recent years, China and the UK have had proactive interactions in film and TV, fashion, design, performing art and publication. These interactions have led to deeper cooperation. Of all these, cooperation in the film and TV industries have played a leading role. I hope other creative fields will follow suit by strengthening the mechanism, building the platform and laying a solid groundwork for cooperation.

Third, we should match up our strengths for win-win results. In recent years, different regions in China and Britain have been working together to leverage their respective strengths and boost the exchange between our creative industries. This has effectively contributed to the overall cooperation between our two countries. Beijing is an outstanding example. Going forward, we should work together to incorporate such efforts into our respective national and regional development strategies. This will help advance the cooperation between our creative industries and bring China-UK practical cooperation to a new high.

Ladies and Gentlemen,

Film and TV are arts of time and space. They are the youngest member in the family of art.

It is my sincere hope that China-UK cooperation on film and TV will defy the distance of time and space.

I look forward to more innovative efforts and new success in the cooperation between Chinese and British creative industries.

And I am sure such efforts and success will contribute more creativity and dynamism to China-UK relations.

In conclusion, I wish the London Ceremony of the 2017 China-UK Film and TV Conference a complete success!

Thank you!

编织梦想,共创中英互利合作美好明天 *

女士们、先生们、朋友们:

欢迎大家出席"编织梦想——中国手工艺文化时装秀"活动。

这是时隔 5 年,中国驻英国大使馆第二次举办文化时装秀活动。时装秀是最接近生活的舞台艺术,取之于生活,忠于生活,也高于生活。今天,来自中国西部贵州省黔西南布依族苗族自治州(以下简称黔西南州)的手工艺术家们,将为大家呈现一场独具特色的文化盛宴,更重要的是,她们将用时装的语言讲述心中的"梦想"。

第一,这是中国少数民族文化传承与发展的梦想。贵州省素以丰富多彩的民族文化而著称,黔西南布依族人的民族服饰历史悠久、独具特色,堪称中国少数民族服饰文化的瑰宝。近年来,在经济高速发展及外来文化冲击的背景下,如何传承和发展布依族传统服饰文化成为一个重要课题。在当地政府、企业和社会各界的大力支持下,在年青一代绣娘的不懈努力下,布依族服饰技艺、民俗文化和民族产业重新焕发生机,并走出国门、走向世界,向世人展示中国少数民族文化的独特魅力和风采。

第二,这是中国西部民众脱贫致富的梦想。中国还是一个发展中国家,仍面临脱贫问题。改革开放以来,我们用了 30 多年的时间使 7 亿多人口摆脱贫困。近 3 年来,我们每年减少贫困人口 1000 万以上,并计划到 2020 年

---

* 在"编织梦想——中国手工艺文化时装秀"活动上的致辞。2017 年 9 月 11 日,中国驻英国大使馆。

消除绝对贫困。贵州省黔西南州有 7 个国家贫困县，脱贫任务十分艰巨。中国有句古话："授人以鱼，不如授人以渔。"贵州省积极落实"精准扶贫"政策，在依文集团等企业的帮助下，因地制宜，通过大力发展少数民族服饰等传统产业，创新性地解决了黔西南地区特别是偏远山区少数民族女性就业问题，帮助她们走上自力更生、脱贫致富之路。2016 年，贵州省黔西南全州 3 个贫困乡镇摘帽，132 个贫困村退贫，10 万贫困人口脱贫，交出了一份亮眼的成绩单。这也使我们完全有信心在全国实现完全脱贫的目标。

第三，这是推动东西方文明交融共鉴的梦想。贵州省虽然地处中国西部内陆，但早在两千多年前就是中国同世界互联互通的重要通道。穿越云贵高原的"茶马古道""南方丝绸之路"，将产自中国的丝绸、茶叶源源不断地输往南亚大陆。今天，随着"一带一路"倡议的实施，贵州省凭借其自身区位优势，日益成为推动东西方文明交融、民心相通、合作共赢的排头兵和生力军。今晚，我们将欣赏贵州绣娘亲手编织的锦缎在时尚舞台上大放异彩，领略到东西方文化在华服美锦之间碰撞出璀璨的火花。

第四，这是深化中英人文交流合作的梦想。2017 年是中英建立大使级外交关系 45 周年。伦敦是世界时尚和创意之都，越来越多的中国时尚企业走进英伦，依文集团就是它们中的杰出代表。我高兴地看到，中英时尚企业家相互交流切磋，共同探索合作机遇，这不仅促进了中英文化创意企业之间的交流与合作，也增进了中英两国人民之间的了解与友谊。

英国著名诗人济慈曾说，"美的事物是永恒的喜悦"。我衷心希望各位朋友在中国驻英国大使馆度过一个美好和喜悦的夜晚，共同感受时尚创意之美、东方文化之美，共同编织中英互利合作的美好梦想！

谢谢！

Weave the Dream of China-UK Cooperation[*]

Ladies and Gentlemen,

Dear Friends,

First of all, a most warm welcome to the Chinese Embassy!

It is such a pleasure to have you all with us today for the "Weaving a Dream" Fashion Show.

This is the second fashion show that the Chinese Embassy is hosting in the past five years. I am sure this time it will be just as fascinating and inspiring as the last one.

Fashion show as a form of stage art is most closely related to the real life of the people. However sumptuous, fashion designs are always based on and reflect our everyday life.

Tonight, it is a great pleasure to have with us the seamstresses from Qianxinan in China's Guizhou Province. They will share with us their folk art in the form of a very unique fashion show. But most importantly, in the language of fashion, they will share with us their dream.

First of all, this is a dream to carry forward the culture heritage of the ethnic minorities in the mountains of Guizhou.

Guizhou Province is known for its diverse ethnic cultures. Qianxinan Prefecture in Guizhou Province is home to the Bouyei nationality. The traditional costume of the Bouyei nationality is highly appreciated for its long history and distinctive features.

In recent years, the rapid economic development and the influence of modern life

---

[*] Remarks at the "Weaving a Dream" Fashion Show. Chinese Embassy, 11 September 2017.

have posed a challenge to preserving and promoting the Bouyei nationality's costume culture.

Fortunately, the local government, the business community and people of many different backgrounds have come together to lend their support. The younger generation of seamstresses are working hard to keep the Bouyei nationality's traditions alive, including unique embroidery techniques, folk crafts and costumes making. Tonight, they are here to demonstrate the beauty and appeal of their very unique culture.

Second, the seamstresses' dream represents the aspiration and efforts of the people in western China to shake off poverty and build a better life.

Since China began its reform and opening-up, over 700 million people have been lifted out of poverty in 30 years and more. In the past three years, at least 10 million people per year were helped out of poverty and our goal is to eradicate abject poverty by 2020.

China is still a developing nation, where poverty is still a problem especially in remote mountains. In Qianxinan Prefecture where the seamstresses come from, poverty reduction remains a daunting task. There are seven poor counties in the Prefecture, where people, especially women, are still living below the national poverty line.

But we Chinese believe that "Rather than handing out fish to the needy, it is better to teach them how to fish". Thanks to the government policy of targeted poverty alleviation and the helping hand from enterprises like the EVE Fashion Group, we now have a creative way to "teach people how to fish".

Efforts to revive the craft skills and to create a contemporary commercial model for the traditional designs gave the women of the Qianxinan mountains new livelihood opportunities. With a stable job, they can now depend on themselves for a better life.

Last year in Qianxinan, three of the seven poor counties, 132 villages and 100,000 people were out of poverty. This was a remarkable achievement and such a strong boost to our confidence in accomplishing our poverty reduction goal by 2020.

The third dream the seamstresses from the mountains of southwest China are able to weave in London is a great accomplishment of the exchanges and mutual learning between Eastern and Western civilizations.

Guizhou is a landlocked province in southwest China. But for 2,000 years and more it has been on a major passageway linking China and the world. That was the "Tea

Horse Ancient Road" and "Southern Silk Road" over China's Yunnan-Guizhou Plateau. Via this route, silk and tea from China reached as far as South Asia.

Today, as China advances the building of the Belt and Road, Guizhou is again showing its geographical advantage. It is becoming a leader in facilitating win-win cooperation, cultural exchanges and friendship between the East and the West. Tonight, let us be amazed by the beauty of Bouyei nationality brocade and the splendour of the fusion between Eastern motifs and Western fashion.

Last but not least, the dream is about deepening China-UK cultural cooperation and people-to-people exchange.

This year marks the 45th anniversary of ambassadorial diplomatic relations between China and the UK. London is an international city of fashion and creativity. More and more Chinese fashion companies are coming here. The EVE Fashion Group is a fine representative.

I am most pleased to see that both Chinese and British business leaders from the fashion industry are gathered here to exchange ideas and explore opportunities. This will not only help build stronger ties between the cultural and creative sectors of our two countries. It will also contribute to the mutual understanding and friendship between our two peoples.

John Keats once said, "A thing of beauty is a joy forever."

I sincerely hope everyone present will cherish this night at the Chinese Embassy. I hope you will enjoy the beauty of fashion and the beauty of the Chinese culture. I hope we can all work together to weave the dream of closer and more fruitful China-UK cooperation.

Thank you!

传承历史文明，践行未来梦想*

尊敬的默西塞德郡女王代表布伦德尔先生，
尊敬的英国数字、文化、媒体、体育部政务次官埃利斯先生，
尊敬的利物浦市市长马尔科姆·肯尼迪先生，
尊敬的利物浦世界博物馆董事会主席大卫·亨肖先生，
女士们、先生们：
大家下午好！

很高兴来到著名的利物浦世界博物馆出席"秦始皇和兵马俑"展览开幕式。

秦兵马俑是中国的国宝，被誉为"世界第八大奇迹"。2007年"秦始皇帝——中国兵马俑"文物展在大英博物馆成功举办，吸引了85万名观众，盛况空前。时隔11年，兵马俑再次穿越时光、跨越重洋、登陆英伦，成为2018年中英人文交流的又一件盛事。我谨对为此展付出辛劳的两国各界人士表示衷心感谢。我认为，此次"秦始皇和兵马俑"展恰逢其时，具有三重意义。

第一，架起了一座中英相互了解与友谊之桥。上周，我有幸陪同梅首相首次正式访华。访问期间，两国领导人就推进中英各领域交流合作达成重要共识，为中英人文交流发展注入了新动力。梅首相还特意向习近平主席介绍了利物浦世界博物馆的"秦始皇和兵马俑"展览。我想，这不仅是因为利物

---

* 在英国利物浦世界博物馆"秦始皇和兵马俑"展览开幕式上的讲话。2018年2月8日，英国利物浦世界博物馆。

浦是梅首相丈夫的故乡，更因为利物浦文化多元、活力四射，被称为"欧洲文化之都"。利物浦与中国渊源深厚，拥有欧洲最古老的中国社区，利物浦大学也是最受中国留学生青睐的英国大学之一。相信利物浦将借力此次"秦始皇和兵马俑"展，为增进中英两国人民之间的了解与友谊、推动两国人文交流与合作发挥独特作用。

第二，讲述了一堂生动的中国历史课。中国是四大文明古国中唯一不间断传承5000年文明的国家，重要原因之一就是公元前221年，秦朝完成统一大业，使中国成为一个多民族统一的国家。从那以后，对统一与稳定的追求、对和平与繁荣的向往，就深深烙入中华民族的基因，流淌在中华民族的血液中代代相传。历史照进现实，2017年10月召开的中共十九大绘制了中国发展的宏伟蓝图，明确提出推进祖国和平统一进程，推动构建相互尊重、公平正义、合作共赢的新型国际关系，构建人类命运共同体，这正是对中国传统文化的最好传承与弘扬。希望英国民众在徜徉中国历史、领略中国古代文化魅力的同时，也能加深对中国传统思想和文明底蕴的了解。

第三，打开了一扇了解"一带一路"的窗户。兵马俑埋藏之地古称长安，今为西安，是历史上"丝绸之路"的东部起点。抚今追昔，我们不仅感受到"丝绸之路"曾经的辉煌兴盛，更体会到"新丝绸之路"焕发的勃勃生机。"一带一路"倡议开创的"新丝绸之路"，为欧亚大陆发展注入了新动力，也给世界发展提供了新机遇。自"一带一路"倡议提出4年多来，中国对"一带一路"共建国家投资累计超过500亿美元。中国企业已经在20多个国家建设了56个经贸合作区，为有关国家创造了近11亿美元税收和20万个就业岗位。中英作为"一带一路"的东西两端，应抓住"一带一路"带来的新机遇。

女士们、先生们，

中英都是拥有悠久历史和灿烂文化的伟大国家，两国人民都是执着追求、自强不息的伟大人民。习近平主席提出了"中国梦"，梅首相提出了"英国梦"，两个梦想都将各自发展与世界发展紧密融合，都将本国"梦想"与促进人类和平发展的"世界梦"紧密相连。出生在利物浦的甲壳虫乐队主唱约翰·列侬曾说，"一个人的梦只是一个梦，而一群人怀揣着同一个梦想，便会梦想成真"。让我们一起从两国优秀传统文化中汲取营养，从历史深处书写未来的光荣与梦想，共同为实现人类命运共同体的"世界梦"贡献力量！

再过8天就是中国农历新年狗年。在中国文化中，狗象征着忠诚、勇敢、勤劳、吉祥。我祝大家狗年吉祥如意、梦想成真！祝此次"秦始皇和兵马俑"展取得圆满成功！

谢谢！

Pass on the Torch of Civilizations to Realize the Dream for the Future*

Lord Lieutenant Mark Blundell,
Parliamentary Under Secretary Michael Ellis,
Lord Mayor Malcolm Kennedy,
Sir David Henshaw,
Ladies and Gentlemen,
Good afternoon!

It is a real delight to join you at the famous World Museum Liverpool to open the exhibition China's First Emperor and the Terracotta Warriors.

The terracotta warriors are China's national treasures. They are also the Eighth Wonder of the World.

This is not their first visit to Britain. Eleven years ago in 2007, the British Museum hosted them. The First Emperor: China's Terracotta Army attracted 850 thousand visitors and was a resounding success.

Now, once again, these ancient warriors have come through thousands of years and crossed boundless oceans to reach the shores of the British Isles. This exhibition is a definite highlight of the cultural and people-to-people links between China and the UK in 2018.

Please allow me to express my heartfelt thanks to everyone from both our countries

---

* Remarks at the Opening Ceremony of the Exhibition China's First Emperor and the Terracotta Warriors at the World Museum Liverpool. World Museum Liverpool, the UK, 8 February 2018.

who have worked so hard for so long to make this exhibition possible.

I believe this exhibition is well-timed and significant in the following three ways.

First, this exhibition serves as a bridge of understanding and friendship between China and the UK.

Last week, I had the honour to accompany Prime Minister May on her first official visit to China.

During this visit, the leaders of our two countries reached important agreement on exchanges and cooperation across the board. This has injected new impetus to China-UK cultural and people-to-people exchanges.

In their meeting, the Prime Minister specifically mentioned to President Xi this exhibition in Liverpool. Why is it? I think the reason is more than that Liverpool is the hometown of Mr May.

- Being a culturally diverse and vibrant city, Liverpool is well known as European Capital of Culture.
- Liverpool's historic connection with China has given the city the oldest Chinese community in Europe.
- It is also home to one of the favorite British universities for Chinese students— the University of Liverpool.

I am sure this exhibition of terracotta warriors will be a good opportunity for Liverpool to continue its special connection with China. With this connection, Liverpool will play a unique role in advancing cultural and people-to-people links between China and the UK, which is key to understanding and friendship between the people of our two countries.

Second, this exhibition is a vivid lesson on Chinese history.

Of the four ancient civilizations in the world, the Chinese civilization has the longest continuous history of 5,000 years. One important reason for this is that China has basically remained a united nation.

The First Emperor of Qin Dynasty, who ordered the creation of the terracotta army, brought different ethnic groups under a united China in 221 BC.

Since then, the yearning for unity and stability, and the pursuit of peace and prosperity have been deep in the vein of generations of Chinese nation.

Today, the best expression of this aspiration is the blueprint for China's future development outlined at the 19th National Congress of the Communist Party of China last October.

According to the blueprint,

- China will strive to achieve peaceful reunification of the country.
- China will work for a new type of international relations featuring mutual respect, fairness, justice and win-win cooperation.
- China will join hands with other countries to build a community with a shared future for mankind.

These goals reflect China's determination to carry forward our fine heritage.

I hope the exhibition of the terracotta warriors will offer a glimpse into the Chinese history and heritage. As you appreciate the charm of ancient China, I hope you could have a deeper understanding of the Chinese philosophy and civilization.

Third, this exhibition isn't just about history. It opens a window on today's Belt and Road Initiative.

The terracotta warriors were unearthed in Xi'an, the current name for Chang'an, which was the eastern starting point of the ancient Silk Road.

The relics from the past remind us of the glory of the ancient Silk Road. Their display here in Liverpool, thousands of miles away from home, is a fresh testament to the vitality of the new Silk Road.

This new Silk Road opened under the Belt and Road Initiative has become a source of driving force for the development of countries from Asia to Europe. It has also created new opportunities for the whole world.

- Since this Initiative was proposed 4 years ago, China has invested over 50 billion dollars in countries along the route.
- Chinese companies have set up 56 economic and trade cooperation zones in over 20 countries.
- This has generated some 1.1 billion dollars of tax revenue and created 200 thousand jobs locally.

China at the eastern end of the Belt and Road, and the UK at the Western end should seize the new opportunities created by this Initiative.

Ladies and Gentlemen,

China and the UK are both great nations. We both have time-honoured history and splendid culture.

The great people of our two countries are in persistent pursuit of self-improvement.

President Xi proposed the Chinese Dream, and Prime Minister May expounded a lot on the British Dream.

- Both dreams see the development of our respective countries in the larger picture of global development.
- Both align our national dreams with the world dream of peace and development.

John Lennon, who was born in this city, once said, "A dream you dream alone is only a dream. A dream you dream together is reality."

If we draw strength from our splendid past, we can write a glorious chapter of the future.

If we dream together the World Dream of a community with a shared future, we can make it a reality.

In eight days time, it will be the Chinese New Year, the Year of the Dog. In Chinese culture, the dog stands for loyalty, courage, diligence and good fortune.

I would like to take this opportunity to wish all of you good fortune in the Year of the Dog!

I wish all your dreams come true!

In conclusion, I wish the exhibition China's First Emperor and the Terracotta Warriors a complete success!

Thank you!

感受中国之美，共建友谊合作之桥 *

尊敬的英国数字、文化、媒体、体育部政务次官沃特利女士，

尊敬的英国议会上院议员贝茨勋爵，

女士们、先生们：

大家上午好！

很高兴出席"2019世界旅游交易会（伦敦）·中国展区"启动仪式。

在全球化深入发展的今天，旅游已成为不同国家、不同文化交流互鉴的重要渠道。2019年是中华人民共和国成立70周年。70年来，中国文化旅游业从小到大、从弱到强，如今迎来了大发展、大繁荣时代。2019年也是中英建立代办级外交关系65周年。65年来，中英文化旅游合作从无到有，不断走深走实。展望未来，中英旅游合作潜力巨大，前景广阔。

第一，旅游为体验人类文化魅力提供载体。旅游集物质消费和精神享受于一体，是修身养性之道，与文化密不可分。中华民族自古就把旅游和读书结合在一起，崇尚"读万卷书，行万里路"。中国既有深厚的5000年文化积淀，又有蓬勃发展的现代旅游产业，吸引着世界各地游客纷至沓来。同样，依托优秀人文资源发展旅游也是英国旅游业的一大特色。从大英博物馆到爱丁堡国际艺术节，从牛津大学、剑桥大学到莎士比亚故居，这些既是英国传统和现代文化的代表，也是重要的旅游名片。一切美好的事物都是相通的。

---

* 在"2019世界旅游交易会（伦敦）·中国展区"启动仪式上的讲话。2019年11月4日，伦敦会展中心。

中英两国虽然传统各异，但都把历史文化和现代文明融入旅游经济发展，致力打造更多体现文化内涵、人文精神的旅游亮点。

第二，旅游为提高人民福祉注入动力。旅游是发展经济、增加就业的有效手段。一方面，旅游减贫成为全球减贫的关键领域。改革开放40多年来，中国7亿多贫困人口摆脱了贫困，其中旅游业成为偏远乡村地区脱贫的重要途径。本次中国展区就讲述了旅游扶贫的成功故事。另一方面，中国已成为全球最大出境游市场。2017年中国出境旅游人数达1.43亿人次，出境旅游支出额达2577亿美元，均位居世界第一，不仅为世界旅游业发展做出了贡献，也为世界经济提供了中国力量。2018年，中国首次进入英国最具价值的十大入境游客市场行列，来英中国游客每人次平均花费超过1600英镑，是赴英旅游全球游客平均水平的2.8倍。

第三，旅游为增进东西方文明交流互鉴搭建桥梁。中英是东西方文明的代表，都拥有悠久历史、灿烂文化、壮美山川、多样风情，都是旅游大国。目前，中英之间的航班每周有168个班次，每天人员互访超过4000人次。旅游使两国民众深深感受到彼此的热情和好客，也增进了对彼此文明的了解和理解。文明因交流而多彩，因互鉴而发展。随着经济的发展和人民生活水平的提高，求新、求奇、求知、求乐日益成为旅游者的共同愿望。两国政府和业界可在旅游政策和实践上加强互学互鉴，增进民众友谊，进一步夯实两国关系的民意基础，为促进东西方人文交流发挥表率作用。

女士们、先生们，

人们常说：旅行开阔眼界。我期望，通过本次活动，大家能进一步开阔眼界，不仅感受中国之美，更看好中英文化旅游合作。让我们携起手来，为建设中英友谊之桥、合作之桥，为推动两国旅游业取得更大发展共同做出努力！

谢谢！

Enjoy the Beauty of China and Build a Bridge of Friendship and Cooperation *

Parliamentary Under Secretary Helen Whately,

Lord Bates,

Ladies and Gentlemen,

Good morning!

It is a real delight to join you at the Opening Ceremony of the China Pavilion at WTM (London).

In a deeply globalized world, tourism has become an important channel of exchanges and mutual learning between different countries and different cultures.

This year marks the 70th anniversary of the founding of the People's Republic of China. In the past 70 years, the cultural and travel industry in China has achieved much progress, turning the country into a major player in world tourism. China's tourism industry has entered an era of rapid development and great prosperity.

This year is also the 65th anniversary of China-UK diplomatic relationship at the chargé d'affaires level. The past 65 years have seen China-UK cooperation on culture and tourism starting from scratch and becoming deeper and more substantial.

Going forward, China-UK cooperation on tourism enjoys enormous potential and promising prospects.

First, travelling is an important way to experience the charm of different cultures.

People travel for spiritual well-being as well as leisure consumption. Travel is

---

* Remarks at the Opening Ceremony of the China Pavilion at WTM (London). ExCeL, London, 4 November 2019.

always regarded as a way to cultivate the mind and therefore is closely connected with culture.

The Chinese people have always regarded travel as part of culture, placing equal value on "reading ten thousand books" and " travelling ten thousand miles".

With a profound civilisation of 5,000 years and thriving modern tourism industry, China has attracted tourists from all over the world.

Likewise, an important feature of the UK's tourism industry is that it is rooted in Britain's rich cultural resources. "Must-see" destinations, such as the British Museum, the Edinburgh International Festival, the University of Oxford, the University of Cambridge and Shakespeare's Family Homes, all represent Britain's traditional and modern culture.

All beautiful things are similar. China and the UK, though with different traditions, have both integrated their traditional and modern cultures into the tourism industry. Both countries are committed to fostering tourism highlights that embody the essence and spirit of their cultures.

Second, travel industry provides an effective driving force for improving people's life.

The travel industry is an effective way to grow the economy and increase employment.

Reducing poverty through developing the tourism industry has played a key role in advancing the global cause of poverty reduction. Take China for example. In the past 40 plus years since the beginning of reform and opening-up, China has lifted more than 700 million people out of poverty. The development of tourism in remote rural areas played an important role in this success. Here at the China Pavilion, you could get to know some typical cases of poverty reduction through tourism.

China is now the largest market for outbound tourism. In 2017, China topped the world both in the number of people travelling abroad, which was 143 million, and in tourist expenditure overseas, which was 257.7 billion dollars. This was an important contribution not only to the global tourism industry, but also to the world economy as a whole.

In 2018, China became one of the UK's top ten most valuable sources of tourists. On average, Chinese tourists spent more than 1,600 pounds in Britain per person, which was 2.8 times the average tourist spending in this country.

Third, travelling helps build a bridge for exchanges and mutual learning between the Chinese and Western civilisations.

Both China and the UK are great civilisations. With profound history, splendid culture, magnificent landscape and diverse customs, both countries have rich tourism resources.

There are now 168 flights between China and the UK per week, facilitating more than 4,000 mutual visits every day. By visiting each other's country, our people could enjoy each other's hospitality and enhance understanding of each other's culture. Such exchanges and mutual learning in turn enrich civilisations.

As our economies continue to grow and people's life continues to improve, today's tourists aspire for new, unique, informative and entertaining experience. This requires the governments and tourism industry of our two countries to enhance mutual learning both in policies and in practice.

Closer exchange and cooperation will deepen the friendship between our peoples and cement the public support for our bilateral relations. It will also set an example for cultural exchanges between the East and the West.

Ladies and Gentlemen,

As people often say, "Travel broadens the mind." I hope today's event will give you a glimpse of the beauty of China and display the promising future of China-UK cooperation on culture and tourism.

Let's join hands to build a bridge of friendship and cooperation between our two countries and achieve greater success in our tourism industry!

Thank you!

文物交流传佳话，中英友好续新篇 *

尊敬的伦敦大都会警察局副总督察马丁先生，

尊敬的英国数字、文化、媒体、体育部创意产业国际战略政策顾问里德利先生，

尊敬的海斯探员，

女士们、先生们：

大家上午好！

很高兴出席中国文物返还移交仪式。这是我出使英国十多年来，第二次迎接中国文物"回家"。首先，我谨代表中国驻英国大使馆，对英国政府和伦敦大都会警察局提供的鼎力支持表示衷心感谢！

文物是历史的见证，是文明的传承，是穿越时空、超越国度的重要文化桥梁。在中英双方的共同努力下，这批文物即将回到祖国的怀抱，我认为具有三重重要意义。

一是为中英文物保护合作提供新动力。保护文物，功在当代，利在千秋。中英在文物保护、修护、联合考古等领域开展了良好合作。两年前，我在使馆见证了公元前 1000 年西周青铜"虎鎣"的捐赠接收仪式，目睹了流失海外百余年的圆明园青铜器踏上回家的旅程。昨天是圆明园罹难 160 周年。前事不忘，后事之师。今天，又一批中国海外流失文物回归，这将使人们铭记历史，避免圆明园的悲剧再次发生，也将进一步促进中英文物保护合作，

---

* 在中国文物返还移交仪式上的致辞。2020 年 10 月 19 日，中国驻英国大使馆。

使更多漂泊在海外的文物，包括圆明园珍宝陆续"回家"。

二是为中英联合打击文物走私树立新典范。中英同为联合国教科文组织《关于禁止和防止非法进出口文化财产和非法转让其所有权的方法的公约》缔约国，两国在公约框架下密切合作，有力打击文化财产的非法进出口和流通。1995—1998 年，中国国家文物局、中国驻英国大使馆与伦敦大都会警察局、英国富而德律师行合作，历经艰辛，克服困难，促成 3000 件走私文物回归中国，成为新中国历史上最大规模的文物回归。20 多年后的今天，一批遗留文物再次被返还，为两国通过外交、警务和司法合作打击文物走私积累了宝贵经验，也为流失文物返还国际合作贡献了中英智慧和中英方案。

三是为中英友好交往注入正能量。中英都拥有悠久历史和灿烂文明，都是具有全球影响力的大国。良好的中英关系，不仅有利于两国，也有利于世界。推动不同文明相互尊重、和谐共处，加强不同文明对话、交流与互鉴，是发展中英关系的基础。在当前新冠疫情肆虐的背景下，中英双方克服困难，促成此批文物返还，尤为不易，它必将为增进中英了解与友谊、促进中英文化交流与互鉴、推动两国关系行稳致远注入正能量。

中国有句古训，"乘众人之智，则无不任也；用众人之力，则无不胜也"。让我们共同努力，促成更多流失文物回归，共同书写文化遗产保护的新篇章！

最后，祝愿此批文物"回家之旅"顺利平安！

谢谢！

A Beautiful Story of China-UK Cultural Exchanges and Friendship*

Mr Martin,

Mr Ridley,

DC Hayes,

Ladies and Gentlemen,

Good morning!

It is a real delight to join you at the Handover Ceremony for Repatriation of Chinese Cultural Objects.

In my more than 10 years as Chinese Ambassador to the UK, this is the second time I have the honour to witness the homecoming of Chinese cultural objects.

On behalf of the Chinese Embassy, I would like to extend heartfelt thanks to the UK government and Metropolitan Police for your all-out support.

Cultural objects bear witness to the history and symbolize the continuation of civilisation. They are the link between the past and the present. They are also an important bridge connecting different countries and cultures.

Thanks to the concerted efforts of both the Chinese and the UK sides, these cultural objects will soon be on their way home.

I think today's event has three-fold significance.

First, it will give new impetus to China-UK cooperation on the protection of cultural objects.

---

* Remarks at the Handover Ceremony for Repatriation of Chinese Cultural Objects. Chinese Embassy, 19 October 2020.

China and the UK have engaged in sound cooperation in the protection and preservation of cultural objects and archaeology. By taking care of cultural objects, we are contributing to the long-term, greater good of both our countries.

Two years ago, I had the honour to attend the handover ceremony of Tiger Ying, a bronze ware dating back to the Western Zhou Dynasty of 1,000 BC. It was part of the collection of the Old Summer Palace in Beijing in late 19th century. I witnessed this cultural object, which had been away from China for over a century, embarking on its journey back home.

Yesterday happened to be the 160th anniversary of the ransacking of the Old Summer Palace. Past events, if not forgotten, serve as lessons for the future.

Today, we are witnessing again the handover of lost Chinese cultural objects. This is a reminder that history must not be forgotten and similar tragedies must never happen again. This is also a productive outcome of China-UK joint efforts to protect cultural objects so that more lost relics, including the treasures of the Old Summer Palace, can "find their way home".

Second, this event is a vivid example of China-UK joint efforts in cracking down on smuggling of cultural artifacts.

China and the UK are both contracting parties to the UNESCO Convention on the Means of Prohibiting and Preventing the Illicit Import, Export and Transfer of Ownership of Cultural Property. Our two countries have worked closely together under the framework of the Convention. We have both taken vigorous measures to crack down on the illicit activities prohibited by the Convention.

From 1995 to 1998, with the help of National Cultural Heritage Administration, the UK Metropolitan Police Service and Freshfields Bruckhaus Deringer, we realized the handover of 3,000 pieces of cultural objects to China against all the difficulties. That was the biggest repatriation since the founding of New China.

Today's repatriation, after more than 20 years, offers valuable experience in diplomatic, police and judicial collaboration against the smuggling of cultural objects. It is also a contribution of China-UK wisdom and solution to international cooperation on repatriation of lost cultural objects.

Third, today's event will inject positive energy into China-UK friendly exchanges.

Both China and the UK have time-honoured history and splendid civilizations. We are both major global players. A sound China-UK relationship serves the interests of both our two countries and the rest of the world.

Mutual respect, harmonious coexistence, dialogue, exchanges and mutual learning between the Chinese and the British civilizations constitute the solid foundation for the development of China-UK relations.

Despite the challenges of the Covid-19 pandemic, China and the UK have overcome various difficulties and ensured the handover of these cultural objects. Such hard-won achievements will go a long way towards enhancing the mutual understanding and friendship between our peoples, and cultural exchanges and mutual learning between our two countries. They will also inject positive energy into the steady and sustained development of China-UK relationship.

As an ancient Chinese saying goes,

"Pool the wisdom of everyone and there is nothing you cannot achieve. Gather the strength of everyone and there is no victory you cannot win."

Let's work together to help more cultural objects find their way home. Let's join hands to write a new chapter on protecting world cultural relics!

Thank you!

●**2011年2月10日**
在会见英国"百校组织"师生代表活动上发表讲话：《从相识到相知，从相知到相通》

●**2011年3月1日**
与英国王储查尔斯共同为威尔士兰德福瑞公学孔子课堂揭牌并在仪式上发表讲话：《学习语言，传承友谊》

●2011年11月23日
在香港中文大学发表演讲：《构建新型中西方关系》

●2012年3月7日
在2012年伦敦书展"市场焦点"中国主宾国活动新闻发布会上发表讲话：《增进中西方了解，扩大中西方合作》

2012 年 6 月 6 日
在 2012 年欧洲地区部分孔子学院联席会议开幕式上发表讲话：《中英、中欧合作结硕果》

2013 年 2 月 7 日
在英国布里斯托大学发表演讲：《中英教育合作未来更美好》

●2013 年 8 月 14 日

在上海芭蕾舞团现代芭蕾舞剧《简·爱》于英国首场演出招待会上发表讲话：《东方和西方的完美结合》

●2013 年 10 月 18 日

向英国剑桥大学李约瑟研究所赠书并发表讲话：《研究历史，关注当代》

2014年8月21日

在"中国旅游之夜"活动上发表讲话：《中英旅游合作天时、地利、人和》

2014年11月21日

在"中英留学交流四十年论坛"开幕式上发表讲话：《春华秋实结硕果，交流互鉴促发展》

2015年1月12日
登舰看望中国海军第十八批护航编队

2015年6月16日
在约翰逊故居中文导览发布仪式上发表讲话：《为中英文化交流增光添彩》

2015年8月4日
在"中英文化交流年"中国文化季新闻发布会上发表讲话:《中国文化季恰逢其时》

2015年10月20日
陪同英国王储查尔斯夫妇观看中国艺术品

● **2016年2月26日**
在"英国未来计划——留学中国同学会"启动仪式上发表讲话:《共谋中英关系百年大计》

● **2016年7月25日**
在伦敦华埠新牌楼落成仪式上致辞:《越是民族的就越是世界的》。左三为英国约克公爵安德鲁王子

第二章　春节庆典
PART Ⅱ　Spring Festival Celebrations

我担任驻英大使11年，其间出席了近百场春节庆典活动，春节已日益成为中英两国人民共同的节日。每到春节，一些英国朋友总会问我，"刘大使，你可以好好休息几天了吧？"我说，"每年春节都是我最忙的时候"。的确，从首相府到议会，从主要政党到各地方政府，从高等院校到公司企业，从博物馆到图书馆，从友好团体到华人社团，每年都有十几场甚至几十场春节庆典活动，我都要挤时间参加，有时一个晚上要跑两个地方。最有代表性的春庆活动是在伦敦特拉法加广场举办的庆典，每年都有70余万人次民众参加，这堪称是亚洲之外规模最大的春节庆典活动。每年我都到场讲话，伦敦市长、议会领袖、侨社代表、各界精英都悉数出席，英国女王和首相也会发来贺词。

　　本章收录了我的4篇演讲，其中一篇就是在特拉法加广场向几十万民众讲述中国春节的故事。

During my 11-year tenure as the Chinese Ambassador to the UK, I attended nearly a hundred Spring Festival celebration events. The Spring Festival increasingly became a festival for the people of both China and the UK. When Spring Festival came, my British friends would ask me, "Ambassador Liu, can you take a few days off?" I would reply, "Spring Festival is my busiest time of the year." Indeed, from 10 Downing Street to the Parliament, from major political parties to local governments, from universities to companies, from museums to libraries, from organizations of China-UK friendship to Chinese communities, there were always dozens of Spring Festival celebrations every year that I needed to attend, sometimes two events on one evening. The most representative celebration was the one held at Trafalgar Square in London which attracted over 700,000 spectators annually, making it the largest Spring Festival celebration outside Asia. Every year, I delivered a speech there, joined by the Mayor of London, parliamentary leaders, community representatives, and elites from various sectors. The Queen and the Prime Minister also sent their greetings.

This chapter includes 4 of my speeches, one of which was delivered to hundreds of thousands of people at Trafalgar Square, in which I told the story of the Chinese Spring Festival.

生生不息，和谐长久 *

尊敬的伦敦市市长约翰逊先生，
尊敬的西敏寺市市长伯布里奇女士，
尊敬的伦敦华埠商会主席邓柱廷先生，
各位来宾，
女士们、先生们、朋友们：

首先，我谨代表中国驻英国大使馆向各位嘉宾和朋友拜年！

春节是中华民族最重要的传统节日，已有2000多年的历史，它是辞旧迎新、家庭团聚、憧憬未来的美好时刻。

今天，春节已经走出中国，越来越受到世界各国人民的喜爱。人们喜爱春节，因为春节预示着欣欣向荣的春天即将来临，寄寓着人们对幸福生活的向往；人们喜爱春节，因为春节包含着中国文化的深厚积淀，体现着中国人"天人合一"的思想理念；人们喜爱春节，因为春节热闹非凡，丰富多彩，人们在喜气洋洋的氛围中感受快乐，同时把好运带回家。

今天，春节再次来到特拉法加广场，这已经是连续第11年了。如期而至的还有远道而来的中国艺术团体——"文化中国、四海同春"艺术团和"欢乐春节"艺术团，他们将与当地华人艺术团体联袂为我们奉献精彩的节目。同样如期而至的还有你们——来自四面八方的广大观众朋友，你们的热情参与是我们最大的期待。

---

* 在伦敦春节庆典活动上的讲话。2012年1月29日，伦敦特拉法加广场。

我真诚希望，通过特拉法加广场和遍布英伦的春节欢庆，越来越多的英国民众能了解中国文化的博大精深，了解中国人民的真诚友善，了解当代中国的发展进步。

2012年，中英将迎来建立大使级外交关系40周年，同时伦敦将举办第30届夏季奥运会，我期待着中英两国在新的一年里增强交流互信，扩大合作共赢，使双边关系取得新发展。

感谢大伦敦市政府、西敏寺市政府和伦敦华埠商会，感谢你们11年的坚持不懈和热情投入，也感谢你们为增进中英文化交流和人民友谊做出的重要贡献。

2012年是龙年，在中国，龙是吉祥如意、风调雨顺的象征。龙的汉语拼音（lóng）也恰好与英文（long，长久的）的拼写相同，喻示生生不息、和谐长久。

在这里，我衷心祝愿大家龙年兴隆发达，身体健康！

祝中英两国国泰民安，繁荣昌盛！

祝中英关系龙腾虎跃，人民友谊地久天长！

谢谢！

Longevity and Harmony[*]

Mayor Boris Johnson,

Lord Mayor Susie Burbridge,

Mr Chu Ting Tang,

Distinguished Guests,

Ladies and Gentlemen,

Dear Friends,

I extend very warm Chinese New Year greetings to you all on behalf of the Chinese Embassy.

The Chinese New Year or Spring Festival has been the most important time in the Chinese calendar for over two thousand years.

In the past decade the celebration of Spring Festival has spread far beyond China's borders.

This means that what matters so much to the Chinese people is gaining wider popularity around the world.

That is happening as the Chinese values of Spring Festival have universal appeal:

- Spring Festival is when we reunite with our families.
- It is in our nature to mark the end of one year and the beginning of another.
- From the cold and dark of winter it is natural to anticipate the light, warmth and blooming of spring.
- It is a time to look to the future with joy and optimism.

---

[*] Remarks at the Chinese New Year Celebrations. Trafalgar Square, London, 29 January 2012.

- For us Chinese people it is also a time when our culture celebrates the harmony between man and nature.
- And for all people of the world there is a strong eagerness for a happy celebration and for great personal fortune in the New Year.

With these shared values of Spring Festival, it is my strong wish that this will help the British people gain deeper understanding of China, its people and its culture.

Across Britain there are many Spring Festival celebrations like this one here in Trafalgar Square.

Today, this is the 11th year that Spring Festival is coming to Trafalgar Square.

This year I am delighted we are joined by performers from the Chinese Culture Ensemble and the Happy Spring Festival Ensemble. They have come all the way from China.

Together with Chinese artists from Britain they will entertain us with a brilliant performance shortly.

2012 will be a memorable year in the history of China and Britain relations:

- Together, our two countries will celebrate the 40th anniversary of China-UK ambassadorial diplomatic relations.
- London will follow Beijing and host the Olympic Games.

This gathering in London today is a symbol of our shared will to deepen exchanges and understanding.

Our meeting today is made possible by the Greater London Authority. Also key to this event is the City of Westminster and the London Chinatown Chinese Association. I want to thank them all most warmly for their 11 years of commitment and support to this event and to relations between China and the UK.

2012 is the Year of the Dragon. In China, the dragon is a symbol of bumper harvest.

The word "dragon" in Chinese is pronounced "龙", which is similar to the English word "LONG." Coincidently, "dragon" also carries the positive meaning of longevity and harmony.

Therefore, may I wish all of you good health and every success in the Year of the

Dragon!

May China and Britain enjoy greater prosperity and our people a better life!

May China-UK relations enjoy dynamic growth and our people a long-lasting friendship!

Thank you!

趣品中国味，厚植中英情 *

尊敬的英国科学博物馆馆长布莱奇福德爵士，

尊敬的英国数字、文化、媒体、体育部政务次官埃利斯阁下，

尊敬的英国科学博物馆董事会主席阿切尔女爵士，

女士们、先生们：

大家晚上好！

很高兴出席英国科学博物馆举办的"中国之夜"活动，与各位新老朋友共度这个蕴含中国风、富有中国韵的美好夜晚。我谨借此机会，对英国科学博物馆长期以来支持中英科技交流合作表示赞赏和感谢！

再过五天就是中国农历新年。我们越来越能感受到浓浓的年味。"中国之夜"以传播科学知识的方式庆祝中国春节，既有新意，也别有趣味。中国人过年有吃年夜饭的传统，全家人围坐一桌，品尝美味佳肴，共享天伦之乐。我认为，今晚英国科学博物馆也为大家烹制了一顿特殊的年夜饭，让大家能够品尝三道美味的"中国菜"。

第一道菜是"新鲜劲道"的中国科技。今晚的"天工开物 AR（增强现实）展""中国航天项目讲座""中国中生代化石展"等，不仅展示了中国古代科技的辉煌成就，也呈现了中国当代科技的最新成果。中国古代科学技术曾长期居于世界领先地位，特别是在数学、天文、医药和农学等领域成绩斐然，为世界文明进步做出了重要贡献。如今，中国正大力实施创新驱动发展

---

* 在英国科学博物馆"中国之夜"活动上的讲话。2019年1月30日，英国科学博物馆。

战略。2017年，中国全社会研发投入达1.76万亿元，占GDP（国内生产总值）的2.13%，其中企业投入占比高达78%。中国在航空航天、量子通信、高铁、核电等领域取得喜人成绩，为人类科技创新和社会进步贡献了中国智慧。前不久，"嫦娥四号"成功实现人类首次在月球背面着陆，首次实现月背与地球的中继通信，开启了人类探测月球的新篇章。

第二道菜是"余味回甘"的中国文化。在中国古代学术体系中，文化和科技密不可分。中国最早的诗歌总集《诗经》、讲变化之道的《易经》、讲礼乐制度的《礼记》等典籍都包含了丰富的数学、天文、地理、农林知识。春节不仅是中国的传统节日，也是重要的文化符号。例如，今天是腊月二十五，中国家庭有用剪纸等装饰窗户迎接新年的传统。今晚的活动也充分体现了文化与科技融合的独特魅力，除了科技知识，我们还能欣赏到舞狮、书法、手工、故事会等丰富的中华文化元素，这些都是几千年来中国百姓欢庆春节的文化习俗。

第三道菜是"历久弥香"的中英友谊。中国有句古语，"以利相交，利尽则散；以势相交，势去则倾；惟以心相交，方成其久远"。人文交流就是"以心相交"最生动的体现，也是中英两国关系中最具活力、最富成果的领域。今天英国科学博物馆举办的"中国之夜"活动就是最好的例证。还有，2018年"秦始皇和兵马俑"展在利物浦世界博物馆成功举办，观展人数超过60万，创该馆举办特展纪录。再有，每年在特拉法加广场举办的盛大春节庆典吸引了超过70万人次英国民众和各国游客，成为亚洲以外规模最大的春节庆典，我诚挚欢迎大家2月10日出席2019年的庆典活动。我也衷心希望，像"中国之夜"这样的活动越办越多、越办越好，使英国民众特别是青少年更好地了解中国的历史、现状和未来，为中英关系长远发展奠定更加深厚的民意基础。

2019年是猪年，在中国传统文化里，猪是幸运、福气和财富的象征。按照中国古代五行说，今年的猪年属土。土在传统中国哲学中意味着生养孕育，犹如希腊神话中的大地之母。土猪年的寓意是勤奋耕耘、真诚合作，为未来奠定坚实的基础，我想这也正是中英关系的应有之义。

最后，我祝愿各位在猪年吉祥如意、幸福安康！

谢谢大家！

A Delightful Taste of China, a Closer China-UK Bond*

Sir Ian Blatchford,

Under-Secretary Ellis,

Dame Mary Archer,

Ladies and Gentlemen,

Good evening!

It is a real delight to join you for the China Lates at the Science Museum. I look forward to a charming and beautiful night of Chinese culture and science with friends old and new!

Let me begin by taking this opportunity to express my appreciation to the Science Museum for your continued support for China-UK science and technology exchange and cooperation!

Although we are still five days away from the Chinese New Year, we can already feel the festive atmosphere. According to tradition, Chinese families always gather together to have a big "New Year Eve reunion dinner".

Here tonight, the Science Museum is celebrating the Chinese New Year through popular science. China Lates is your innovative and delightful "reunion dinner" that offers three delicious "courses".

The first course is the original and authentic science and technology of China.

Tonight's exhibitions showcase China's splendid achievements in science and

---

* Speech at the China Lates of the Science Museum. The Science Museum, London, 30 January 2019.

technology in both ancient and modern times, including "An ancient Chinese scroll in AR", "China's space programme" and "Flyers of Mesozoic China".

China had been a world leader in science and technology in ancient times. The achievements were remarkable in the fields of mathematics, astronomy, medicine and agronomy. These had been China's important contribution to the progress of human civilisation.

Today, China is pursuing innovation-driven development.

- In 2017, overall public and private R&D spending totaled 1.76 trillion yuan, accounting for 2.13% of China's GDP. Of this, company spending accounted for 78%.
- In areas such as aerospace, quantum communication, high-speed rail and nuclear energy, China has made gratifying progress. They are China's contribution to the scientific and technological innovation and social progress of mankind.
- Early this month, China successfully landed Chang'e 4 on the far side of the moon. It was the first time in human history that a man-made vehicle landed on the far side of the moon and communicated with the earth via a relay satellite. This marked the beginning of a new chapter in mankind's exploration of the moon.

The second course is the luscious Chinese culture.

In China's traditional academic system, culture, science and technology are interconnected. Classic books of Chinese culture such as the *Book of Songs*, the *Book of Changes* and the *Book of Rites* all contain knowledge of mathematics, astronomy, geography, agriculture and forestry. Tonight, China Lates offers the public an opportunity to appreciate the unique charm of Chinese culture through displays of science and technology.

The Chinese New Year itself is not only a folk festival but also a cultural symbol. There are many cultural and artistic elements in the celebrations of this festival. Take today for example. It is the 25th day of the last month of Chinese lunar calendar. On this day, Chinese families decorate their windows with paper cutting, an exquisite form of folk art.

I am delighted that China Lates also presents colorful displays of Chinese culture, such as lion dance, calligraphy, crafts and legends. These will offer a glimpse into the arts and customs with which the Chinese people have celebrated the Chinese New Year for thousands of years.

The third course is China-UK friendship with an enduring fragrance.

A Chinese adage goes, "Interests wane and power withers; Relations endure for those who stay heart-to-heart."

Cultural exchanges between China and the UK have been keeping us heart-to-heart. It is the most vigorous and productive elements in China-UK relations. A good example is the exhibition China's First Emperor and the Terracotta Warriors hosted by the World Museum Liverpool last year. It was a great success, drawing more than 600,000 visitors and setting a record for special exhibitions at the Museum.

Another example is the annual Chinese New Year Celebration in Trafalgar Square. More than 700,000 British people and tourists from all over the world gather to mark the Chinese New Year, making it the largest celebration outside Asia. This year's celebration will take place on 10 February. I hope to see you all in the Trafalgar Square.

Tonight, at the Science Museum, China Lates is also a fine example of such cultural exchanges. It is my sincere hope that there will be more and more such high-standard events to help the British people, especially the young people, to gain a better understanding of China's past, present and future. This will cement public support for the sustained development of China-UK relations.

The new year will be the Year of the Pig. In the Chinese tradition, the pig symbolises happiness and good fortune. According to the ancient Chinese theory of the Five Elements, 2019 is the Year of the Earth Pig. Earth is a symbol of productiveness, as Gaia is in Greek mythology. Therefore, in the Year of the Earth Pig, we have every reason to work hard and work together to lay a solid foundation for a brighter future of China-UK relations.

In conclusion, I wish everyone present tonight a happy and healthy Year of the Pig!

Thank you!

品尝中西交融美味，迎接互利共赢未来 *

尊敬的英国外交部经济和全球事务总司长罗林斯女士，
尊敬的英国议会上院国际关系委员会主席豪威尔勋爵，
女士们、先生们、朋友们：
晚上好！

欢迎大家出席第二届"行走的年夜饭"活动。很高兴与大家一起通过味蕾感受中国的年味儿，共同迎接中国子鼠新年的到来。我谨代表中国驻英国大使馆，感谢海德公园文华东方酒店和成都厨师团队的精心筹备和倾情奉献！

"行走的年夜饭"是中国"欢乐春节"系列活动的亮点之一。"欢乐春节"有三个主题词：希望（Hope）、家庭（Home）、和谐（Harmony），代表着几千年来中国人民对新年的美好期许和对世界的真诚祝福。希望大家也能在今晚中西合璧的年夜饭中品出三个"H"的味道。

一是希望的味道，只有坚持交流互鉴，才能不断酝酿新的希望。中国人讲："和羹之美，在于合异。"我们今天要品尝的川菜，就是最好的例子。川菜最常用的三种调料是花椒、胡椒和辣椒。花椒原产于中国；胡椒原产于南印度，约1500年前通过丝绸之路传入中国；辣椒则原产于墨西哥，约400年前通过海上丝绸之路传入中国。这三种原产地不同的调料，通过交流结合

---

* 在第二届"行走的年夜饭"活动上的讲话。2020年1月15日，伦敦海德公园文华东方酒店。

在一起，形成了川菜独有的味道。习近平主席说，"文明因交流而多彩，文明因互鉴而丰富"。饮食仅是文明交流互鉴的美好产物之一，人类不断发展的历史，就是世界各种文明交流互鉴的过程。只有加强交流互鉴，以海纳百川的胸怀跨越文明之间的鸿沟，以兼收并蓄的态度汲取各种文明的养分，才能绘就人类文明的美好画卷，酝酿人类发展的无限希望。

二是家庭的味道，只有坚持互利共赢，才能实现天下一家亲。春节最大的年味儿，就是举家团圆、相聚言欢，就像我们今天这样。世界也是一个大家庭。随着经济全球化深入发展，世界已变成一个你中有我、我中有你的地球村，各国已结成同舟共济、休戚与共的命运共同体。在这样的背景下，中英合作全面拓展，形成了互利共赢的良好格局。2019 年 1—11 月，中英货物贸易额超过 783 亿美元，同比增长 6.9%，全年有望再创新高；在英中国留学生人数接近 20 万，居各国留英学生之首；2019 年中英人员往来超过 200 万人次，中国已成为访英游客的重要来源国。随着中国进一步扩大开放和英国完成脱欧，两国合作的巨大潜力将进一步释放。双方应抓住机遇，深化合作，携手打造开放型世界经济，为世界大家庭做出更大贡献。

三是和谐的味道，只有坚持求同存异，才能推进和谐共生。人类文明多样性是世界的基本特征，也是人类进步的重要源泉。世界上有 200 多个国家和地区，各国历史背景、文化传统、社会制度不尽相同，基本国情、经济水平、发展模式千差万别，共同构成了世界文明的多样性。中国人强调，"万物并育而不相害，道并行而不相悖""君子和而不同"，英国价值观也主张相互尊重和包容。历史昭示我们，只有相互尊重、彼此包容、求同存异，才能和谐共处、交融共生、相得益彰。

女士们、先生们、朋友们，

金猪辞旧话新年，玉鼠迎春添秀色。2020 年对中英两国而言，都是承前启后、继往开来的重要一年。希望大家在新的一年里，怀揣希望、携手前行，为推动中英关系提质升级、为构建人类命运共同体做出新的更大贡献！

现在，我提议，让我们共同举杯，

为世界的和平与发展，

为中英两国的互利合作,
为在座朋友们鼠年吉祥幸福,
干杯!

Fusion of Flavours for a Fruitful Future[*]

Director General Menna Rawlings,

Lord Howell,

Ladies and Gentlemen,

Dear Friends,

Good evening!

It is a real delight to have you all with us at the event of A Bite of China on the eve of the Chinese New Year, or Spring Festival as it is more commonly known in China.

This is the second year that A Bite of China has come to London. It allows us to "taste" the festive atmosphere of New Spring and celebrate the Year of the Rat.

On behalf of the Chinese Embassy, I would like to thank Mandarin Oriental Hyde Park and the chefs from Chengdu for their thoughtful preparation and the passion they have put into this fascinating feast, which is a definite highlight of the Happy Chinese New Year events.

The theme of the Happy Chinese New Year events comes down to three "Hs", namely, hope, home and harmony. These three words have, for thousands of years, encapsulated the best wishes of the Chinese people for the new year and their sincere greetings to the world.

I hope tonight's feast not only pleases the palates but also, with its delicious fusion of Eastern and Western food, offers tastes of hope, home and harmony.

First, there is taste of hope in exchanges and mutual learning.

---

[*] Speech at A Bite of China: A Dinner to Celebrate the Chinese New Year. Mandarin Oriental Hyde Park, London, 15 January 2020.

As we Chinese often say, "Delicious soup is made by combining different ingredients." The Sichuan cuisine served today is a best example. There are three most commonly used seasonings:

- Sichuan pepper is native to China;
- Black pepper was brought to China from South India about 1,500 years ago via the Silk Road;
- And chili pepper originated in Mexico, and reached China about 400 years ago via the Maritime Silk Road.

Historical exchanges between people of different continents have enabled these three seasonings, born in three different places, to find their way into the same pot and create the unique flavor of Sichuan cuisine.

Food is just one of the wonderful fruits of exchanges and mutual learning between civilisations. As President Xi Jinping said, "exchanges and mutual learning enrich civilisations." Learning from other civilisations with an inclusive spirit could create a better future for human civilisations and bring more hope to mankind.

Second, there is a taste of home in win-win cooperation.

The happiest part of the Chinese New Year comes when family members get together, like what we are doing tonight.

In the ever-deeper economic globalization, win-win cooperation has turned the world into a global village that is our common home. Countries belong to an interdependent community with a shared future.

Against this backdrop, China-UK cooperation in various areas has expanded and delivered win-win results.

- In the first 11 months of 2019, China-UK trade in goods exceeded 78.3 billion US dollars, increasing by 6.9% year-on-year. The trade volume for the whole year is expected to reach a new high.
- Nearly 200,000 Chinese students are studying in the UK and continue to be the largest overseas student community here in this country.
- In 2019, mutual visits between China and the UK topped 2 million. China has

become an important source of the UK's inbound tourists.

China will continue to open its market wider and the UK is about to complete Brexit. This will unleash enormous potential of China-UK cooperation. We should seize the opportunities, deepen collaboration and join hands to build an open world economy and make greater contribution to the "big global family".

Third, there is taste of harmony in our pursuit for common ground despite differences.

Cultural diversity is a basic feature of the world. It is also an important source for the progress of mankind. There are more than 200 countries and regions in the world. They are different not only in history, cultural heritage and social system, but also in basic national condition, economic development stage and growth model. From these differences, cultural diversity arises.

Ancient Chinese wisdom tells us, "All living creatures grow together without harming each other; all roads run parallel without interfering with one another. A true gentleman respects diversity while seeking harmony."

Here in the UK, people also value mutual respect and inclusiveness.

The lessons of history tell us that we should respect each other, be inclusive and seek common ground despite differences. By doing this, we will not only live in harmony but also enhance exchanges and bring out the best of each other.

Ladies and Gentlemen,

Dear Friends,

Tonight we gather to say goodbye to the Year of the Pig and to usher in the Year of the Rat. The year 2020 is an important year for both China and the UK. Our two countries will build on past achievements and pursue new success.

It is my hope that in the new year, we will join hands, strive forward, pursue our dreams, and take China-UK relationship to a new level. Together, let's make new, greater contribution to building a community with a shared future for mankind!

Now may I invite you to join me in a toast:

To peace and development in the world,

To the mutually-beneficial cooperation between China and the UK,

To a happy and prosperous Year of the Rat for everyone present tonight,

Cheers!

共同建设美好世界大家庭 *

尊敬的各位议员，

女士们、先生们、朋友们：

晚上好！

欢迎大家做客中国大使馆！今天是中国农历腊月二十三，俗称"小年"。按照中国传统，这是筹备过年的开始。很高兴在这个吉祥的日子，与英国各界朋友欢聚一堂，辞旧迎新，共度佳节。今年是鼠年，鼠为十二生肖之首。在中国文化中，鼠象征着顽强、精明、机灵、活力。我祝愿各位朋友鼠年吉祥如意、幸福安康！

刚刚过去的 2019 年，我们过得很充实。中国人民的获得感、幸福感、安全感不断增强。2000 多年前，中国的先哲就强调，天下之本在国，国之本在家，家和万事兴。带领万千中国家庭过上幸福生活，正是中国政府的不懈追求，也是过去一年的最大收获。

一是推进高质量发展，为万千家庭增强获得感。随着中国特色社会主义进入新时代，中国经济由高速增长阶段转入高质量发展阶段。我们坚定不移贯彻新发展理念，持续推进供给侧结构性改革，推进产业转型升级和创新发展，推动新型工业化、信息化、城镇化、农业现代化同步发展，加快建设创新型国家，发展更高层次的开放型经济，不断满足人民日益增长的美好生活需要。2019 年，中国 GDP 总量超过 14 万亿美元，人均 GDP 将迈上 1 万美

---

* 在新春招待会上的讲话。2020 年 1 月 17 日，中国驻英国大使馆。

元新台阶，新增就业超过1300万人，民众获得感不断增强。

二是增进民生福祉，为万千家庭增强幸福感。我们始终坚持在发展中保障和改善民生，全面推进幼有所育、学有所教、劳有所得、病有所医、老有所养、住有所居、弱有所扶。2019年，中国再减少贫困人口1000万人以上，为实现2020年全部脱贫目标奠定了良好基础；蓝天、碧水、净土保卫战取得积极进展，空气质量大幅改良；建成包括养老、医疗、低保、住房在内的世界最大的社会保障体系，社保卡持卡人数覆盖中国93%以上人口；教育事业全面发展，来英留学人数接近20万。总之，民生措施有力度，民生发展有温度，民生改革有深度，民众幸福感不断增强。

三是加强和创新社会治理，为万千家庭增强安全感。改善社会治理，是当前世界各国面临的共同挑战。近年来，我们不断创新社会治理方式方法，提高社会治理法治化、智能化、专业化水平，打造共建共治共享的社会治理格局，民众安全感不断增强。仅以新疆维吾尔自治区为例，3年前新疆饱受恐怖主义和极端思潮侵害，暴恐势力大肆制造恐怖事件，造成数千名无辜民众伤亡。为维护新疆安全，自治区政府借鉴国际反恐经验，依法采取各项反恐和去极端化措施，成功遏制暴恐活动，连续3年多未再发生一起暴恐事件，有力保障了新疆安全与稳定，受到2500万当地各族人民的广泛支持和衷心拥护。

女士们、先生们、朋友们，

随着2020年的钟声敲响，世界将进入21世纪第三个十年。我们在为万千个家庭谋幸福的同时，也需要思考如何建设世界这个大家庭。我们生活在同一片蓝天下，拥有同一个地球家园，彼此命运紧密相连、休戚与共。着眼未来，我们应携手推动构建人类命运共同体，共同打造美好的世界大家庭。

一是构建开放合作的发展命运共同体。当今世界处于百年未有之大变局中，经济全球化仍是时代潮流，谋发展、求合作仍是时代主题。一段时间以来，逆全球化暗流涌动，保护主义、单边主义、民粹主义、霸凌主义甚嚣尘上，但全球化大势不可逆转。保护主义损人害己，单边主义失道寡助，霸凌主义扰乱秩序、危害世界经济发展，是一条走不通的路。开放带来进步，合作才能发展。我们应本着开放合作的精神，共建开放型世界经济，通过协商合作解决矛盾和摩擦，坚决反对单边主义、贸易保护主义，推动全球产业链、供应链、价值链协同发展，共同做大全球市场的"蛋糕"，推动经济全球化朝着更加开放、包容、普惠、平衡、共赢的方向发展。

二是构建交流互鉴的文明新形态。世界上的不同文明没有高下优劣之分，每一种文明都有其优点和长处，都是人类的共同财富。历史一再证明，认为自己的文明高人一等、执意改造甚至取代其他文明的做法都会带来灾难性后果。文明因多样而交流，因交流而互鉴，因互鉴而发展。只有欣赏、接纳并不断借鉴其他文明，人类文明才能长盛不衰。我们应该秉持平等和尊重，摒弃傲慢和偏见，加深对自身文明和其他文明差异性的认知，推动不同文明交流对话、和谐共生，共同为推动人类文明的整体发展和进步做出不懈努力。

三是构建共商共建共享的全球治理体系。当今世界面临各种问题和严重挑战，发展鸿沟日益突出，地区冲突此起彼伏，恐怖主义、极端主义、气候变化等全球性挑战层出不穷。在新形势下，现行全球治理体系的不完善、不合理、不适应等问题日益突出，消除全球治理赤字、推进全球治理体制变革已是大势所趋。我们应坚持共商共建共享的全球治理观，坚持全球事务由各国人民商量着办，倡导国家不分大小、强弱、贫富一律平等，树立共同参与、合作共建的理念，凝聚共识、通力合作，推动国际秩序和全球治理体系朝着更加公正合理的方向发展。

女士们、先生们、朋友们，

我担任驻英大使10年来出席了近百场春节庆典活动，今天是我第一次在使馆举办面向英国各界朋友的春节招待会。我感到春节已日益成为中英两国人民共同的节日。现在再把春节称为"中国新年"已经不够准确了，应归其本义。春节顾名思义是春天的节日，它既预示新年的开始，也寓意春天的到来。"一花独放不是春，百花齐放春满园。"我衷心期待中英两国携手努力，共建各国共享的百花园，为构建人类命运共同体贡献力量，让我们的世界大家庭更加和平、更加和睦、更加美好！

谢谢！

Build a Big Global Family Together[*]

My Lords,

Ladies and Gentlemen,

Dear Friends,

Good evening, and welcome to the Chinese Embassy!

Today is the 23rd day of the last month of the Year of the Pig. According to tradition, today is known as "Xiao Nian", or "Minor Chinese New Year". This is the day to start all the Chinese New Year preparations.

It is a real delight to have you, my British friends from all walks of life, with us on this auspicious day to say goodbye to the Year of the Pig and celebrate the Year of the Rat.

As the first of the 12 zodiac animals, the rat symbolises tenacity, shrewdness, cleverness and vitality. With these auspicious promises, I wish all the friends present today a happy and prosperous Year of the Rat!

The year 2019 was a fruitful year and a year of greater sense of gains, happiness and security for the Chinese people. More than 2,000 years ago, a Chinese sage taught us, "The root of the world is in the state, and the root of the state is in the family. So a happy family brings prosperity." Better life for tens of thousands of Chinese families has been the persistent pursuit of the Chinese government. In 2019, great success has been achieved in this aspect.

---

[*] Remarks at a Reception to Celebrate the Chinese New Year. Chinese Embassy, 17 January 2020.

First, high-quality economic growth provided Chinese families with a greater sense of gains.

As socialism with Chinese characteristics enters a new era, China's economy is shifting from high-speed growth to high-quality growth. In the past year, China

- remained committed to the new development concept,
- deepened supply-side structural reform,
- promoted industrial transformation and upgrading,
- advanced industrialisation, IT application, urbanisation and agricultural modernisation,
- pursued innovation-driven development,
- and built an open economy at a higher level.

In 2019, China's GDP exceeded 14 trillion US dollars, and per capita GDP is expected to reach a new high of 10,000 US dollars. More than 13 million jobs were created. These have helped meet people's growing needs for a better life.

Second, higher living standard gave Chinese families a greater sense of happiness.

China has persistently pursued greater development in order to safeguard and improve the life of its people.

- Babies are given the best care.
- Children have good education.
- Hard work gets paid.
- Sickness gets treated.
- The elderly are looked after.
- Everyone has a roof over his head.
- And the vulnerable get the help they need.

In 2019,

- China lifted more than 10 million people out of poverty. This is a critical step towards achieving the goal of eliminating poverty in 2020.
- We have made positive progress in preserving the blue sky, clear water, clean

land and better air quality.
- We have established the world's largest social security system, providing old-age pension, health care, basic allowances and welfare housing, and covering more than 93% of the population.
- We also made remarkable progress in education. Here in the UK alone, there are close to 200,000 Chinese students.

In a word, in improving people's life, the measures are effective, the progress is remarkable, and the reform has been deepening. The Chinese people now have a higher sense of happiness.

Third, strengthened social governance provided Chinese families with a greater sense of security.

Improving social governance is a common challenge to all countries in the world.

In recent years, China has explored new ways of social governance. We have worked to ensure that social governance is under the rule of law, supported by smart technologies and managed by professionals. The general public can contribute to and share in social governance, and in this process, their sense of security increase.

Take Xinjiang for example. Three years ago, Xinjiang suffered severely from terrorism and extremism. Violent terrorist forces launched numerous terror attacks, victimizing thousands of innocent people.

To safeguard security in Xinjiang, the Government of the Autonomous Region drew lessons from international counter-terrorism efforts and took a series of counter-terrorism and de-radicalisation measures in accordance with law. These measures have effectively deterred violent terrorist activities. In the past more than three years, there has not been a single terrorist attack in Xinjiang. With security and stability safeguarded, the counter-terrorism measures have won extensive and heartfelt support from the 25 million people of all ethnic groups in Xinjiang.

Ladies and Gentlemen,

Dear Friends,

As the new year bell for 2020 rings, the world enters the third decade of the 21st century. While pursuing happiness for tens of thousands of Chinese families, China is also thinking about what we can contribute to our global family.

All countries in the world live under the same blue sky. Planet earth is our one and same home. Our destinies are inter-connected. We should stand by one another, through thick and thin.

Going forward, it is important that we join hands to build a community with a shared future for mankind, namely, a global family.

First, in the community with a shared future, countries should pursue development through open cooperation.

The world is undergoing profound changes unseen in a century. Economic globalisation continues to be the overall trend. Development and cooperation remain the theme of our times.

Despite the raging anti-globalisation, protectionism, unilateralism, populism and hegemonism, they lead to nowhere.

- The trend of globalisation is irreversible.
- Protectionism is counterproductive.
- Unilateralism finds scant support.
- And bullying others will disrupt order and harm the world economy.

By contrast, openness brings progress, and cooperation leads to development.

- Therefore, we should work together to embrace cooperation and build an open world economy.
- We should stand firm against unilateralism and protectionism, and address frictions and differences through consultation and collaboration.
- We should pursue coordinated development of the global industrial chain, supply chain and value chain.
- We should work together to make the pie of global market bigger and make economic globalization open, inclusive, balanced and win-win.

Second, in the community with a shared future, different civilisations should enhance exchanges and learn from each other.

No civilisation is superior to others. Every civilisation has its unique advantages and strengths. Every civilisation is the treasure of all mankind. History has proved once and again that regarding one's own civilisation as superior to others, and insisting on changing or even replacing other civilisations will have disastrous consequences.

Diversity leads to interaction among civilisations, which in turn promotes mutual learning and greater development. Appreciating, accepting and learning from other civilisations is the only road to enduring prosperity.

It is important that we act in the spirit of equality and mutual respect, and discard unwarranted pride and prejudice. We should have a deeper understanding of the differences between civilisations, and promote exchanges, dialogue and harmonious co-existence. Our concerted and persistent efforts will lead to the development and progress of mankind as a whole.

Third, in the community with a shared future, global governance should follow the principles of extensive consultation and joint contribution.

The world today is faced with various problems and grave challenges:

- Development gap is widening.
- Regional conflicts are surging.
- Global challenges, such as terrorism, extremism and climate change, keep cropping up.

The current global governance system needs improvement because it does not reflect the reality in the world and this has created a deficit in global governance. To address this, the global governance system needs to go through reforms.

China proposes a new global governance concept. This follows the principles of extensive consultation, joint contribution and shared benefits.

- Global affairs should be handled through consultation between all the parties involved.
- All countries, big or small, strong or weak, rich or poor, are equals, and should all take part in and contribute to global governance.
- China is ready to work with other countries to form consensus on building a just and reasonable international order and global governance system.

Ladies and Gentlemen,

Dear Friends,

In my ten years as Chinese Ambassador to the UK, I have attended nearly 100 Chinese New Year celebration events and I have come to realize that Chinese New Year has become a festival for both Chinese and British people. Tonight, I am hosting the first-ever Chinese New Year celebration at the Chinese Embassy for my British friends.

In fact, "Chinese New Year" is more commonly known in China as "Spring Festival", because it is a festival for the spring. It marks the beginning of a new year, and heralds the coming of spring.

As a Chinese saying goes, "A single flower does not make spring. Hundreds of flowers in full blossom bring spring to the garden."

I sincerely hope that China and the UK will join hands to create a garden of hundreds of flowers for all to enjoy and contribute to building a community with a shared future for mankind, thus making our big global family more peaceful, harmonious and beautiful!

Thank you!

第三章　教育交流
PART Ⅲ　Educational Exchanges

英国是世界教育大国，全国有 110 多所大学和高等教育学院。2022 年，QS（全球高等教育分析机构）世界大学排名前 10 中，英国大学占 4 所；排名前 100 中，有 17 所是英国大学。每年有约 55 万名海外学生在英国院校学习，英国高等教育年收入超过 400 亿英镑，支撑了全国近 2% 的国民收入和几十万人的就业。

中英教育交流源远流长，特别是近年来赴英留学的中国学生与日俱增。我在英国期间访问了几十所英国高校，几乎每所高校都有中国学生，少则几百人，多则数千人。截至 2020 年，也就是我在英国工作的最后一年，中国留学生的数量达到 20 多万人，英国已取代美国成为中国留学生第一大海外去向国。英国来华大学生的数量也在不断增加，2019 年英国在华学生总数近 7000 人。

我高度重视中英教育交流，积极为两国高校建立联系、开展合作牵线搭桥，推动中英合作办学取得积极成果。截至目前，中英共同创建了 232 个本科以上中英合作办学机构和项目，其中中英合作办学机构 29 个，涵盖金融学、通信工程、生物医药等专业。中国已成为英国开展跨境联合办学的首选目的地，约占英国跨境联合办学总量的 11%。

我十分关心中国留学生的学习和生活。每到一所英国高校访问，我都要看望中国留学生，与他们座谈，转达党和政府对他们的关心和慰问，为他们的学习和生活排忧解难；激励他们好好学习，将来学成报效祖国；同时鼓励他们讲好中国故事，向身边的老师和同学介绍家乡的变化。我对他们说，每一个中国留学生都是中国的形象代言人，都是讲好中国故事的传播人，都是中国大使。使英 11 年，我每年出席几十场与教育有关的活动，全英学联春晚是我必到场的活动。无论我多忙，我都十分珍惜这个与数千名学生和家长见面的机会，并通过他们向全英 20 多万名留学生和学者转达祖国的问候，介绍国内发展和中英关系，为他们鼓劲加油。英国大学校长把我称作"教育界的朋友"，使馆教育处同志称我是"教育大使"。

The UK is a global leader in education, with over 110 universities and higher education institutions. In the 2022 QS World University Rankings, 4 British universities made to the top 10 and 17 were in the top 100. Approximately 550,000 international students study in the UK annually, contributing over 40 billion pounds to the UK's higher education revenue, supporting nearly 2% of its national income and creating hundreds of thousands of jobs.

China-UK educational exchanges have a long history, with an increasing number of Chinese students studying in the UK in recent years. During my time in the UK, I visited dozens of universities where the number of Chinese students ranged from a few hundred to several thousand. By 2020, my last year in the UK, the number of Chinese students had reached over 200,000, making the UK the top overseas destination for Chinese students, surpassing the United States. The number of British students studying in China also increased to nearly 7,000 in 2019.

I attached great importance to China-UK educational exchanges, actively facilitating connections and cooperation between universities of both countries, resulting in positive outcomes. To date, there are 232 China-UK cooperative educational institutions and projects at the undergraduate level and above, including 29 joint institutions in the fields of finance, telecommunications engineering, and biomedicine. China has become the top destination for British cross-border educational cooperation, accounting for about 11% of the UK's total cross-border educational partnerships.

I cared deeply about the study and life of Chinese students in the UK. Each time I visited British universities, I met with Chinese students to convey the concern and greetings from the Party and the government, help them tackle the problems in their studies and daily life, and encourage them to study hard to serve their homeland in the future. I also encouraged them to tell China's stories and the changes in their hometowns to their teachers and classmates. I told them that each Chinese student is an ambassador for China. During my 11 years in the UK, I attended dozens of education-related events every year. The Chinese Students and Scholars Association UK Spring Festival Gala was an event I never missed. Regardless of how busy I was, I cherished this opportunity of meeting thousands of students and their parents, conveying greetings from the motherland, sharing my thought on domestic developments and China-UK relations, and giving them encouragement. University presidents in the UK call me "a friend of the education community", and my colleagues at the Embassy's education section call me "Ambassador for education".

记忆中国，难忘母校 *

各位来宾，

女士们、先生们：

欢迎大家出席中国驻英国大使馆教育处举办的"记忆中国，难忘母校"英国赴华留学生招待会。

我的同事曾建议我今天用中文讲话，因为今天的招待会与以往不同，是为英国曾经赴华的留学生举办的。可是，我了解到，出席今天招待会的嘉宾不仅于此，还有许多目前虽不会讲中文，但为推广在英汉语教学、资助英国学生赴华留学而热心出力的人士和企业机构代表，我要感谢你们长期以来对中英教育交流的关心和支持。而我现在还无法要求你们所有人都听懂中文，因为在英国的孔子学院起步时间不长，数量也不够多。中国古语曰："行远必自迩，登高必自卑。"（语出《礼记·中庸》，意为走远路要从近处开始，登高要从低点起步。）所以，我决定今天还是用英文讲。我希望有朝一日，我们之间能用中文自由交流。

60年前，首批外国留华人员来到百废待兴的新中国。51年前，首批英国留学生踏上了中国的土地。2009年，有来自190多个国家和地区的23万多名留学生在中国的610余所高校、科研院所学习。60年来，中国接受留学人员累计169万人次。中国接受外国留学生事业是逐步发展的过程，特别是

---

* 在"记忆中国，难忘母校"英国赴华留学生招待会上的讲话。2010年9月24日，中国驻英国大使馆教育处。

在改革开放后取得了长足进步。

在中国，在母校，你们留下了欢笑和汗水，留下了青春的足迹和美好的回忆。当然，许多英国赴华留学生可能当初都经历了一个思考和抉择的过程，毕竟"汉语热"只是最近几年才出现的；也可能都经受了许多困难和挑战，因为既要学习一门复杂的东方语言，又要适应迥异的生活环境，更要了解完全不同的文化，我本人年轻时就曾赴国外留学，对此深有体会；你们也可能曾怀疑自己学成归来的前途，担心自己一辈子会坐"冷板凳"。

正如亚里士多德所言，"教育的根是苦涩的，但其果实是甜美的"。付出总会有所回报，如今，从中国学成归国的英国留学生在许多领域或功成名就，或崭露头角。你们利用自己的所学所长，提升了英国社会对华了解和认知的水平，促进了两国经贸合作和文化交流，推动了中英关系的发展。我很高兴得知，你们中的几位杰出人士，包括欧盟驻华代表团前团长魏根深博士、大英图书馆中文部主任吴芳思博士和英国民间机构筷子俱乐部的主任童海珍女士，不久将代表所有英国赴华留学生，前往中国出席纪念外国学生来华留学60周年的庆祝活动。

我最近统计了一下到任以来的活动，意外地发现其中与中英教育交流合作相关的最多。仔细一想，这也不足为奇。因为目前有近10万名中国学生在英国留学，据说2010年申请学生签证的人数又增加了60%。我最近从国内述职休假回来，飞机上几乎一半是年轻学生。现在英国已设立了12所孔子学院和53间孔子课堂，2009年，全英孔子学院举办的活动吸引了近10万名英国民众参与。中英两国的大学间建立了上百对校际交流机制，合作非常密切。

中英教育合作是中英关系的重要组成部分。2010年，虽然英国政府发生了更迭，但两国关系保持了良好发展的势头。我们愿与英方共同努力，推动中英关系长期健康稳定发展，进一步造福于两国和世界人民。

中英合作前景广阔，到中国留学、学习汉语前程似锦，大有可为。事实已经证明并将继续证明，你们的选择完全是明智和正确的。希望你们做中英友好的纽带、两国合作的桥梁，为中英关系发展做出更大贡献。

我希望大家多到中国参观访问，重回母校，重拾记忆，同时了解中国几十年来以及近年来的发展变化，及时更新对中国的认识。我也期待英国每年赴华留学人数在目前3000人的基础上进一步增长，不断扩大两国友好合作的力量。

最后，在我结束讲话之前，我愿为我馆教育处打一则广告：明年秋季，中国驻英国大使馆教育处将协助国内相关部门在伦敦举办首次"留学中国教育展"，欢迎你们和你们的亲朋好友届时前来参观和交流！

谢谢大家！

Share Experiences of Studying in China[*]

Distinguished Guests,
Ladies and Gentlemen,

May I warmly welcome you to the Education Section of the Chinese Embassy to refresh and share your experiences of studying in China.

My colleagues at the Chinese Embassy suggested that I speak in Chinese for tonight's event. But I learnt that apart from British students in China, there will be many other friends and business leaders, who do not speak Chinese but are keen to promote mandarin teaching in the UK and offer funding for British young people studying in China. I am thankful to them for their commitment and support to China-UK educational exchanges. Naturally I cannot expect all of them to understand Mandarin. We still need many more Confucius Institutes to spread Mandarin wider in the UK. As an old Chinese saying goes, "Going on a long journey, one must start from a short step, and climbing high, one must start from low." So I decided to speak in English today to make things easier for you to start, but I do hope one day we will be able to communicate in Chinese.

60 years ago, the first group of foreign students came to the newborn People's Republic. 9 years after that, the first group of British students came to China. Fast forward to 2009, over 230 thousand students from more than 190 countries and regions were studying in 610 Chinese universities and research institutes. The past 60 years have seen 1.69 million foreign students studying in China. Many of them came during

---

[*] Speech at a Reception "to Refresh and Share Experiences of Studying in China". Education Section, Chinese Embassy, 24 September 2010.

the past 32 years of reform and opening-up.

I hope you have spent some very nice time of your youth living and studying in China and brought back lasting memories. And I assume that for many of you, going to China might not be an easy decision to make. After all, the "Mandarin fever" has only been a thing of recent years. You must have gone through a difficult time, trying to learn a foreign language and at the same time adapting to a totally different culture and environment. You may also have worried about your future, unsure about whether speaking Mandarin will land you in a decent job. I also studied abroad in my younger years, so I can imagine how you felt when you were in China.

As Aristotle said, "The roots of education are bitter, but the fruit is sweet." Many of the British young people studying in China have gone through this bitter-sweet experience. They have now become leaders of their fields. Their knowledge and experience of China has also helped the British society to know more about China, and contributed to stronger business and cultural ties.

I am glad to learn that Dr Endymion Wilkinson, former EU Ambassador to China, Dr Frances Wood, Head of the Chinese Department at the British Library and H-J Colston, Director of the Chopsticks Club, are going to China as representatives of British students for the 60th anniversary celebration of foreign students coming to China.

I was pleasantly surprised to find that of all the events I have attended since I came to London, educational events account for the largest share. This is quite understandable, given the fact that nearly 100 thousand Chinese students study here. And the number of student visa applications grew by as much as 60% this year.

On my way back to London after a home leave in summer, I found that almost half of the seats on the plane were taken by Chinese students coming to the UK. There are now 12 Confucius Institutes and 53 Confucius Classrooms in Britain, attracting nearly 100 thousand British people last year. More than 100 pairs of university partnerships have also been set up between our two countries.

Education exchanges and cooperation are an important part of China-UK relations. We are committed to working with our British colleagues for a sound and steady growth of our relations, which serves the interests of both peoples and the world at large.

A flourishing China-UK partnership means promising prospects for studying in China and learning Mandarin. You have proven yourselves to be far-sighted in your choice and decision. I do hope that you will serve as a bridge of friendship and cooperation between the two countries and contribute more to China-UK relations.

I also hope you will find time to go back to China and visit your alma mater to refresh the memories of your days in China and see the latest development in the country. I wish to see more and more British students go to study in China, bring the current 3,000 per year to an even higher level. This will further strengthen the foundation for China-UK friendship and cooperation.

Before I conclude, let me put in an advertisement for our Education Section: The first Study in China exhibition will be held in London in autumn next year. We look forward to seeing you again or your families and friends there.

Thank you!

从相识到相知，从相知到相通 *

同学们、老师们：

欢迎你们来到中国驻英国大使馆！

今天是中国农历兔年正月初八，正值新春佳节，我祝大家兔年快乐！兔年使我想起一句英文谚语："要像兔子一样，不畏困难，跳跃前进。"我祝同学们学习进步！祝老师们事业有成！

"百校组织"是由英格兰著名的 50 所私立学校和 50 所公立学校组成的联盟。你们每年一次的年会具有重要影响。2011 年，你们把国际问题确定为年会主题，并选择年会期间到中国大使馆做客，我对此感到很高兴，希望你们今天的访问既能增进你们对中国的了解，又有助于你们年会的讨论，使你们不虚此行。

现在你们所处的这座建筑是英国 18 世纪的流行建筑，由英国著名建筑师罗伯特·亚当和他的弟弟詹姆斯·亚当合作设计，现为二级保护文物。1877 年，这座建筑成为中国历史上第一个驻外代表机构所在地。130 多年来，它见证了中国近现代外交的沧海桑田，记载了中英两国关系的变迁发展。大使馆的负责人当然就是大使，自 1972 年中英建立大使级外交关系以来，我是中华人民共和国第 11 任驻英大使。大使馆的主要任务是促进中国与英国在政治、经贸、教育、文化、科技、军事等各领域的双边交流与合作。

中国和英国都是伟大的国家，都是当今世界有重要影响力的大国。中

---

* 在会见英国"百校组织"师生代表时的讲话。2011 年 2 月 10 日，中国驻英国大使馆。

英正致力于建设全面战略伙伴关系，也就是说两国的合作是全方位和长期的。2010年底卡梅伦首相访问了中国，2011年初中国国务院副总理李克强访问了英国，两国政治关系非常紧密；中英贸易额2010年已突破500亿美元，今后5年要争取达到1000亿美元；双方人员往来总量每年达100万人次，2010年仅中国大陆来英游客就超过20万人次；中国现在有近12万名留学生在英学习，可能有些还是你们的同学；中英在上海世博会上进行了良好合作，英国馆的表现非常精彩；伦敦还将继北京之后举办奥运会，我们期待着伦敦奥运会同样精彩。作为中英友谊的象征，两只可爱的大熊猫不久将在爱丁堡动物园安家落户，欢迎你们前去观看。

年青一代是国家的未来，也是中英关系的希望。中英关系发展需要世代接力，两国合作友好需要薪火传承。年轻人接手中英友好事业，我认为最重要的是要了解和理解对方国家。

对你们而言，首先要多了解中国的基本国情。中国的一个很大特点是地广人多。中国幅员辽阔，国土面积有960万平方千米，是英国的40倍。中国人口众多，人口总量超过13亿，是英国的20多倍。

中国具有5000年文明历史，曾对人类的进步与发展做出伟大贡献。可能你们有些人知道中国古代的"四大发明"——指南针、造纸术、活字印刷术和火药。如果人类历史上没有这四项发明，我想我们可能至今还生活在中世纪。

今天的中国朝气蓬勃，万象更新，各项事业全面发展。中国经济突飞猛进，改革开放32年来，保持了年均近10%的增长速度，经济总量已位居世界第二。中国人民的生活水平显著提升，过去30多年有2.5亿人摆脱贫困。中国社会更加开放和进步，我们先后成功举办了北京奥运会和上海世博会，展现了中国的新形象。中国现有4.5亿网民和2亿多博客，微博在中国也很时髦。

当然，中国现在还是一个发展中国家，人均GDP只相当于英国的1/10，排在世界100位之后，仍有1.5亿人的生活达不到每天1美元的联合国贫困线标准。中国的发展仍任重道远。

若要进一步了解中国，我认为需要学习中国的语言。汉语现在不仅是世界上使用人口最多的语言，而且正成为国际化程度发展最快的语言，世界各国对汉语学习的需求与日俱增。目前，国外学习汉语的人数超过 4000 万，据估算，在欧美学习汉语的人数每年以 40% 的速度递增。英国也有"汉语热"，超过 500 所中小学开设了汉语课程，部分学校将汉语列入了必修课，GCSE（中等教育普通证书考试）也将汉语列为正式科目。目前在英国有 13 所孔子学院和 54 间孔子课堂。我听说，"百校组织"当中已经有不少学校设立了孔子课堂或开展了汉语教学。例如，布莱顿中学和金斯福德社区学校的孔子课堂都办得十分成功，两所学校的学生在近年的英国中学生汉语比赛中都取得了出色的成绩。

当然，要更深入地了解中国，最好是到中国留学。目前越来越多的外国学生选择到中国留学，这样不仅可以了解中国的悠久文化，更可以亲身体验当代中国的活力。2009 年，来自 190 多个国家和地区的 23 万多名学生在中国留学。中国正采取一系列措施吸引国际学生，包括增加奖学金、完善服务等。中国驻英国大使馆教育处将于 2011 年秋季在伦敦举办"留学中国教育展"，欢迎你们前来参观，与中国的大学生进行面对面交流，争取给自己的学习生涯添加流行的中国元素和色彩。

我希望你们以今天走进中国大使馆为起点，开始你们了解中国、喜欢中国、热爱中国的进程。我也衷心地希望中英两国青年从相识到相知，成为致力于促进中英友谊的新一代。

再一次欢迎你们的到来！

From Acquaintance to Understanding, from Understanding to Connection*

Boys and Girls,

Ladies and Gentlemen,

Welcome to the Chinese Embassy. Today is the 8th day of the Chinese New Year, the Year of the Rabbit. This is a time for festivity and celebration. Let me first of all wish all of you a happy and prosperous Year of the Rabbit. The Year of the Rabbit reminds me of an English idiom: "Hop over obstacles like a rabbit." That is my wish to you. I wish you, the students, a lot of progress in your studies, and teachers every success in your career.

The 100 School Groups is a distinguished group of schools in England. The annual conference is an important event for the group. I am glad that this year's conference focuses on international issues, and that you have included in the agenda a visit to the Chinese Embassy. I hope this visit will be both interesting and informative. It will help increase your knowledge of China and enrich your discussions at the conference.

Let me say a few words about the history of the Chinese Embassy and what we do here. This building you are now in has an architectural style that became popular in the 18th century. It is now a protected cultural site. It was designed by the renowned architect Robert Adam and his brother James Adam. In 1877, it became the office building for the first ever Chinese diplomatic mission overseas, and has served as our embassy building ever since. For the past 130 years, it witnessed great changes in China's diplomacy and its relations with Britain. I am proud to be the 11th Ambassador

---

* Remarks at the Meeting with Representatives of the 100 School Groups. Chinese Embassy, 10 February 2011.

of the People's Republic of China to the UK following the establishment of full diplomatic relations between the two countries in 1972. The main mission of the Chinese Embassy is to promote China's exchanges and cooperation with Britain in political affairs, commerce, education, culture, science, technology and military fields.

Both China and Britain are great nations and major players on the world stage. We are both committed to our comprehensive strategic partnership. We have strong political ties. Prime Minister Cameron visited China last November and Chinese Vice Premier Li Keqiang visited the UK early this year. We have vibrant trade ties. Our trade last year hit a record 50 billion US dollars. We will aim to double it in the next 5 years. We have growing people-to-people links. Every year a million visits are made between our two countries. Tourists from the Chinese Mainland alone reached 200 thousand last year. Close to 120 thousand Chinese students are studying in the UK. Some of them may even be your classmates. The UK Pavilion at the Shanghai World Expo last year was a great success. We are confident that London as the host city for the 2012 Olympic Games will stage an equally spectacular Games as Beijing. I also want to tell you that two giant pandas will be coming from China to settle in their new home in the Edinburgh Zoo. They will be living symbols of China-UK friendship. I do hope you will have an opportunity to see them and you will like them.

Young people are the future of their nations. You also represent the future of China-UK relations. China-UK partnership needs to be nurtured from generation to generation. We count on you to take our friendship and cooperation forward. To fulfill this mission, it is very important to better understand each other's country.

Let me share with you a few facts about China. China is a vast country, covering an area of 9.6 million square kilometers, 40 times the size of Britain. It has a population of over 1.3 billion, more than 20 times that of Britain.

China has a history of 5 thousand years. It contributed enormously to human progress. Some of you may know the four great inventions of ancient China—the compass, papermaking, movable type printing and gunpowder. Without them, we may still live in the medieval age.

Today's China is making rapid progress on all fronts. Its economy has been growing at double-digit rates for the past 32 years. Its GDP now ranks the second in the world. The Chinese people enjoy a much better life today than ever before. 250 million people have been lifted out of poverty over the past 3 decades. The Chinese society is increasingly open and diverse. Both the Beijing Olympic Games and the Shanghai World Expo have been immensely successful. They showed the world a New China. There has been an explosive growth of Internet in China, with 450 million Internet users and over 200 million bloggers. Micro-blog, which is similar to Twitter, is attracting ever more users. Having said all that, it is important to understand that China is still a developing country. Its per capita GDP is only one tenth that of the UK, and ranks behind 100 countries. 150 million people in China still live under the UN poverty line of one dollar a day. For China, development remains an arduous task and the road is long.

A good way to understand China is to learn its language. Mandarin is spoken by the largest number of people in the world. It is also the fastest growing language. More than 40 million people around the world are learning Mandarin. The number of learners in Europe and North America is growing by 40% annually. "Mandarin fever" has also hit the UK. I am pleased to learn that Mandarin has been put on the curriculum of over 500 primary and secondary schools, in some cases as a compulsory course. Last September, the British government made Mandarin GCSE subject. There are now 13 Confucius Institutes and 54 Confucius Classrooms in the UK. Some schools of the 100 Group, such as Brighton College and Kingsford Community School, have Confucius Classrooms. Some of the students there have done very well in Mandarin proficiency competitions in recent years.

An even better way to know China is to study in China. China is now becoming a popular destination for overseas students to experience its ancient culture and modern vitality. In 2009, over 230 thousand students from more than 190 countries and regions studied in China. China is offering more scholarships and better services for these students. The Education Section of Chinese Embassy will host a Study in China exhibition this autumn. You are all welcome to this event. It will be a good opportunity to get to know Chinese universities and make them a part of your student life.

I hope today's visit will foster your interest in China, and help you understand and like China. I also hope young people of our two countries will become friends and join hands in building a bond of friendship between our two countries.

Once again a warm welcome to the Chinese Embassy!

中英教育合作未来更美好 *

尊敬的埃里克·托马斯校长，

女士们、先生们：

非常高兴来到久负盛名的布里斯托大学。首先我要祝贺贵校在 QS 世界大学综合排名中高居第 28 位。

说起大学，经常有人拿英美做比较。比如，美国有"常春藤联盟"，英国有"罗素大学集团"；美国有哈佛、耶鲁，英国有牛津、剑桥。我们不要忘了，美国还有麻省理工学院，人们告诉我，布里斯托大学就是英国的麻省理工学院。刚才和校长托马斯教授交谈时，我详细了解了贵校的情况，也更加印证了这一点，这里曾产生 11 位诺贝尔奖获得者，其中 8 位是诺贝尔自然科学奖获得者。就贵校的历史和取得的成就而论，或许这样说更准确一些——麻省理工学院是美国的布里斯托大学。

我已经访问了英国的 20 多所大学，谈了许多关于中国、中国外交和中英关系的话题，今天是第一次谈"中英教育交流"这个主题。我不妨从中国的教育说起。

中国是五千年文明古国，其文化传统之一便是尊师重教。最有名的中国古代教育家就是大家熟知的孔子，相传弟子三千。孔子招收学生不像今天要收取高昂的大学学费，学生只需向老师赠拜师礼以示尊敬。礼物是什么呢？书上记载是"十条腊肉"（束脩），今天看起来这非常有趣。

---

* 在英国布里斯托大学的演讲。2013 年 2 月 7 日，英国布里斯托大学。

孔子有很多教育理念，如因材施教、循循善诱、温故知新、举一反三等，不仅对中国，也对世界的教育事业产生了深远影响。我记得两年前，我在威尔士兰德福瑞公学与威尔士亲王（即查尔斯王子）一起出席该校孔子课堂揭牌仪式时，他就引用了孔子关于教育的至理名言："知之为知之，不知为不知，是知也。"

重视教育、提倡阅读、研究技术是中华文明的传统。正因为如此，中国为人类贡献了火药、造纸术、活字印刷术和指南针四大发明。

但是，中国古代教育在发展和演变过程中也走了一些弯路，即过分注重仁义道德而忽视科学知识和技能培养。这在中国的明、清两朝尤为甚之，教育沦为了应试教育，"学而优则仕"则成了读书人的唯一目的，导致"所学非所用，所用非所学""士大夫囿于章句之学，而昧于数千年来一大变局"。当中国的教育与封建社会一起没落时，正是西方科学兴起、大学兴盛之时，于是随着近代中国被迫打开国门，"西学东渐"成为潮流。20世纪初，中国出现了新文化运动，高举"德先生"和"赛先生"两大旗帜。特别是1949年新中国成立之后，中国的教育体制发生了重大变革，在内容与形式上开始逐渐与世界接轨。

30多年来，中国实行改革开放，经济社会发展取得了巨大的成就，教育事业也蓬勃发展。中国"两基"人口（基本普及九年义务教育、基本扫除青壮年文盲）覆盖率达到了100%。中国高校规模居世界首位，在校生数量超过了3000万人，高等教育发展实现了从精英教育到大众化的转型。中国不断加大教育投入。2012年，中国首次实现了教育投入占GDP比重达4%的目标。中国形成了多层次、宽领域、全方位的教育对外开放新格局，大力引进海外智力和优质教育资源，积极借鉴国际上先进教育理念和教育经验，不断提高教育国际交流与合作水平。

中英两国的教育交流已有160多年历史。早在1850年，作为中国第一批出国留学生之一，医学家、教育家黄宽就来到英国爱丁堡大学学习医学并获得博士学位。中国最早的海军人才也产生于英国。曾获中国国家最高科学技术奖的物理学家、中国半导体技术奠基人黄昆曾于20世纪40年代在布里斯托大学学习并获得博士学位。中国著名的地质学家李四光曾留学于另一所著名大学——伯明翰大学。

中华人民共和国成立后，英国也是较早同新中国开展教育交流的西方国家之一。1957年，英国接受首批中国公派留学人员来英学习。1959年，中国开始向英国学生赴华留学提供奖学金。英国的"志奋领奖学金"项目在中国已开展30年，迄今为中国培养了3000多名人才。

当前，在中英双方的共同努力下，中英教育交流合作成果显著，形成了合作领域宽广、内容丰富、政府主导、民间活跃的交流格局。双边教育交流与合作内容覆盖了高等教育、基础教育、职业教育和语言文化等多个领域，合作主体包括各级政府教育部门、各级各类教育机构以及科研机构，合作形式更是涵盖了人员交往、项目合作与机制平台建设等多个方面。目前在英国学习深造的中国学生、学者有12万人。中国留学生是英国最大的国际学生群体，英国高校每6名国际学生中就有1名来自中国。我很高兴了解到贵校就有近2000名中国留学生。近年来，英国赴华留学人数也呈持续增长趋势。2012年有4250人在华学习，比2011年增长超20%。英国朋友经常对我说，虽说两者从绝对数量上尚有较大悬殊，但从人口比例上来看差距就没有这么大了。

2012年，在"罗素大学集团"举行的年度晚宴上，我是唯一受邀的外国驻英使节，这说明了英国高校对开展中英交流与合作的重视。正是在那次活动上，我与托马斯校长首次见面。中英教育交流与合作已经成为中英双边关系中最活跃的组成部分。

百年大计，教育为本。2010年，中国政府制定了《国家中长期教育改革和发展规划纲要（2010—2020年）》，提出了"优先发展、育人为本、改革创新、促进公平、提高质量"的工作方针，目标是到2020年基本实现教育现代化。2012年底举行的中国共产党第十八次全国代表大会明确提出，教育是民族振兴和社会进步的基石，要努力办好人民满意的教育。中国的教育事业正面临着前所未有的机遇。

当今是全球化时代，也是大交流、大合作的时代，国家无论大小，民族无论强弱，都需要增进彼此间的沟通、理解与合作。教育交流对于促进知识传播、消除认识差异、增进互信友谊、推动人类文明进步具有不可替代的作用。中英两国均为世界教育大国，具有重视教育的优良传统和优质丰富的教育资源，双方可以进一步发挥互补优势，实现合作共赢。

我认为，中英未来在教育领域应当着重加强在以下五个方面的交流与合作。

一是不断加强两国教育实质性合作。支持中英大学间的教师互派、学分互认和学位互授联授。加强双方高水平大学建立教学科研合作平台，联合推进高水平基础研究和高新技术研发。鼓励并支持双方高等职业教育机构建立可持续伙伴关系，共同开展课程开发，联合开展职业教育和技能培训。鼓励两国中小学结对，开展师生双向交流，一方面提高中国学生的动手能力、独立与创新思维；另一方面强化英国学生的数学、科学等基础知识，实现取长补短。

二是继续鼓励支持双向留学。我们将一如既往地支持中国学生出国留学，特别是到国外一流大学、一流专业学习，并号召他们学成后归国效力。希望像布里斯托大学这样的英国著名高校能招收更多、更好的中国学生，我也衷心希望他们之中将来产生中国的大师级人物。同时，中国也欢迎更多的英国学生到中国留学、深造。我们制订了"留学中国"计划及相应的一系列鼓励措施，如开展学分互认、提供短期赴华留学奖学金、增加高等院校外语授课的学科专业等，希望为英国学生留华创造更好的条件。

三是大力支持中英合作办学。支持两国知名大学和教育机构到对方国家合作设立教学、研究机构。中国愿意更多地引进包括英国在内的国外优质教育资源，不断提高合作办学层次和质量，同时也将不断探索来英办学的形式和途径。

四是进一步推动语言教学。中国有3亿人懂英语，这一数字超过了美国讲英语的人口总和，英语是中国大中小学的必修课。中国学生英语考试的成绩很好，但是实际使用英语的能力有限，特别是听、说、写的能力不足。我们欢迎英国的语言教学机构来"对症下药"，提供良方。目前，"汉语热"在英国不断升温，中英双方已建有23所孔子学院和66间孔子课堂，汉语已被列为英国中小学外语必修课七种供选语种之一。今后双方应继续大力支持孔子学院和孔子课堂建设，提升办学质量，同时应合作加强英国本土汉语师资队伍的培养、培训。

五是加强两国相互研究。中国在现代化进程中，将进一步学习与借鉴英国等发达国家的发展经验。我们也希望英国社会能更加客观、理性地看待当代中国的进步与发展，特别是希望英国的大学能发挥引领作用。目前，英国的数十所大学都已设有中国研究中心或中国学院，我衷心希望布里斯托大学也能整合资源，加大对当代中国的研究力度，在促进英国与中国的相互了解和理解方面发挥更大的作用。

贵校前名誉校长、诺贝尔文学奖获得者，当然也是贵国的前首相丘吉尔曾说，"不懈的努力是打开我们潜能的钥匙，而并非力量或智慧"。就中英教育交流与合作而言，我们既有力量也有智慧，我相信再加上我们不断共同努力，一定能发掘合作的无限潜能，实现更多互利与共赢，从而创造中英教育合作更美好的未来。

谢谢！

A Brighter Future for China-UK Educational Cooperation*

Vice-Chancellor Eric Thomas,

Ladies and Gentlemen,

It is a great pleasure to be back to campus, especially to be invited to one of the best universities in Britain!

I want to congratulate Bristol in its recent QS global ranking of 28th place as a leading university of the world.

When talking about higher education, people tend to compare British universities with their American cousins. For example, America has the Ivy League while Britain has the Russell Group. America has Harvard and Yale while Britain has Oxford and Cambridge. Yet we should not forget that America also has MIT.

I was told that Bristol was regarded as the "British MIT". For me this was proved true in my talk with Vice-Chancellor Thomas today. I have learned that Bristol produced 11 Nobel Prize winners. Eight of them won this honour for their exceptional scientific research. Given your long history and outstanding achievements perhaps I should say that MIT is "American Bristol"!

So far I have visited more than 20 British universities and talked a lot about China, Chinese diplomacy and China-UK relations. Yet this is the first time I have spoken on China-UK educational exchanges. I will start from education in China.

China is a five-thousand-year old civilisation. One of our cultural traditions is to stress education and respect teachers. The most famous ancient Chinese educator is

---

* Speech at University of Bristol. University of Bristol, 7 February 2013.

Confucius. Legend records that Confucius had three thousand disciples and students. Unlike universities today, Confucius did not charge expensive tuitions. Students only needed to present him with a gift as a token of respect. You might be interested to know what was the gift. According to ancient books this gift was "ten pieces of cured meat". This would be unimaginable in our time!

But we can still learn from Confucius today. Confucius developed a wealth of teaching philosophies and learning methods. For example:

- Teaching methods to match the aptitude of each individual student.
- Teaching by using approaches involving patience.
- The technique of learning new knowledge by going over what has been learned.
- And learning by analogy and through inferences.

These ideas have exerted a far-reaching influence on education in China and around the world.

Two years ago His Royal Highness the Prince of Wales and I jointly unveiled the Confucius Classroom in Llandovery College. In his speech His Royal Highness quoted a saying of Confucius:

"True knowledge is knowing the limitations of one's own knowledge."

For a long time, China has been a rich-in-books, literate and technological civilisation. The evidence is how China gave humanity many key inventions such as gunpowder, papermaking, movable type printing and the compass.

Despite the proud traditions, China's education also went through some twists and turns. The main problem was it focused so much on morals and credos that it neglected science and training of practical skills.

This narrow focus was especially the case during the Ming and Qing dynasties. In those times, education was reduced to a tool for passing exams to recruit government officials. The status of officials meant there was immense competition to pass the exams. However, the curriculum for the exams was useless in practical daily life. Literati and officialdom were indulged in playing with words and formats.

The approach turned a blind eye to what was happening in the real world. The result was an utter failure to move on with social and technological changes.

As China's education declined along with feudalism, Europe was vigorously pursuing the enlightenment of science. Countries like Britain became keen to educate the wider population through opening more universities.

Then came the sad chapter of Chinese history when the door of China was forced open by the gunboats of Western powers.

Consequently Western civilization was gradually introduced to China. In China the rise of the New Culture Movement in the early 20th century spread the ideas of science and democracy. Chinese people were greatly stimulated by these influences and this resulted in China's educational system being dramatically reformed, especially after the founding of the People's Republic in 1949. Step by step, China's education became compatible with the rest of the world in terms of what to teach and how to teach.

This education transformation has been integral to one of the greatest changes ever seen in human history. The past three decades has seen China emerge as the world's biggest exporter and rank as the second largest global economy. These changes were driven by the reform and opening-up policies. The result is that China has made remarkable achievements on economic and social fronts.

Education in China has also come a long way:

- Adult literacy rates in China are now at 100%.
- Chinese people now have nine-year compulsory education.
- Enrolment at universities has passed 30 million places and this figure is the highest for any country in the world.
- Higher education is open to the mass of people and far beyond a small elite group.

China has boosted investment in education:

- In 2012 China for the first time reached the target of investing 4% of GDP in education.
- China has also engaged in multi-tiered, wide-ranging and all-dimensional educational exchanges with foreign countries.

This means:

- We have introduced to China overseas intellectual and educational resources.
- We have learned advanced international educational philosophies and experience.
- We have improved the quality of educational exchanges and cooperation with other countries.

Educational exchanges between China and the UK started over 160 years ago. Many Chinese scientists received education in Britain:

- In 1850 one of the first Chinese students studying abroad was Huang Kuan. He came to study in Edinburgh University and won a doctor's degree in medicine. He later became a medical specialist and educator.
- The seminal figures in the development of the modern Chinese navy also studied in Britain.
- The founder of China's semi-conductor technology, Huang Kun, studied here in University of Bristol. He received a PhD degree from the H H Wills Physics Laboratory. He later won the most prestigious Chinese award in science.
- The highly accomplished Chinese geologist, Li Siguang, studied at the University of Birmingham.

Britain was also one of the early Western countries to have educational exchanges with China following the founding of the People's Republic of China in 1949:

- In 1957 Britain received the first group of government-funded Chinese students.
- Since 1959 China has been offering scholarships for British students.
- Britain's Chevening Scholarship program has run in China for 30 years. More than 3,000 people have benefited from this program.

In recent years, with the concerted efforts of both sides, China-UK educational exchanges and cooperation have been dynamic and productive.

It is wide in reach and rich in content. The areas include higher education, primary education, vocational education and teaching of language and culture.

There is strong support of both Chinese and the UK governments, but there is also active participation of educational and research agencies of various types and on various levels. The collaboration takes a variety of forms from personnel exchanges, joint programs to institutional building.

Currently, 120,000 Chinese students and scholars are studying in Britain. This makes Chinese students Britain's largest community of international students. This means in British universities one in every six international students is from China. I am glad to learn that University of Bristol is home to 2,000 Chinese students.

China and Britain are sharing a mutual trend in exchanging students. In recent years more and more British students are going to study in China. In 2012, 4,250 British students were studying in China. This was an increase of over 20% compared to the previous year. British friends often tell me that despite the big gap between the numbers of our students in each other's country, the shares are more or less balanced when compared with our respective populations.

At the annual dinner of the Russell Group last year, I was the only foreign ambassador invited. This testifies to the importance British universities place on exchanges and cooperation with China. It was at that event that I had the pleasure of meeting Vice-Chancellor Thomas. Now I am delighted to be his guest here in Bristol. These exchanges are symbolic of how we can proudly say that educational links have become a most dynamic part of China-UK relations.

Education is essential for the future. In 2010 the Chinese government formulated the Mid-and Long-term Plan for Educational Development and Reform. This covers the ten years until 2020. It established the following principles:

- Give top priority to education.
- Take cultivation of character as a primary task.
- Encourage reform and innovation.
- Promote educational fairness.
- Raise educational quality.

This Plan also set the target of realizing modernisation of education by 2020.

The 18th National Congress of the Communist Party of China held late last year also stressed the importance of education. The Congress emphasised that education is the cornerstone for national revitalisation and social progress. The government is determined to meet the people's demand for quality education.

All these developments will open up opportunities never seen before for China's education. These are the key trends:

- We live in a time of globalisation. That calls for greater exchanges and cooperation.
- All countries big or small and all nations strong or week need to increase communication, understanding and cooperation.
- Educational exchanges play an irreplaceable role in disseminating knowledge, dispelling misunderstanding, enhancing mutual trust and developing friendship.
- Both China and the UK have large educational programmes. Education has a long and important tradition in both countries.
- We both have rich and quality educational resources.
- For all these reasons we are well positioned to draw on each other's strengths and achieve win-win cooperation.

In my view China-UK educational exchanges and cooperation should focus on the following areas.

First, substantially upgrade cooperation.

- We should support our universities to exchange teachers. There is a need to recognise each other's academic credits and award joint degrees.
- Our leading universities should conduct joint teaching and research both in basic science and in high and new technologies.
- We should encourage our vocational schools to enter into sustainable partnership, jointly develop courses and provide vocational training.
- We should pair our middle and primary schools for two reasons.
    * It will strengthen hands-on ability of Chinese students and cultivate their independent and creative thinking.

* It can also help improve the study of maths and science for British students.

Second, continue to encourage our students to study in each other's country.

- We will as always support Chinese students to study overseas, especially in leading universities.
- Of course we encourage students to return to China after completing studies abroad. We want them to help advance China towards developed country standards.
- I hope British universities like Bristol will attract more and better Chinese students. I also hope they will become "masters in their fields".
- At the same time China welcomes more British students to study in China.
- To help British students we have formulated the Study in China program and worked out a series of supporting measures. These measures include mutual recognition of academic credits, short-term scholarships and teaching more classes in foreign languages.
- I hope these measures will make it easier for British students to study in China.

Third, support jointly running facilities.

- We should support our best universities and educational institutions to set up educational and research facilities in each other's country.
- China wants to import more fine educational resources from Britain and other foreign countries.
- We will also explore suitable forms and ways to open schools in Britain.

Fourth, further promote language teaching.

- 300 million people in China studied English. This is more than total English speaking population in the US.
- English is a compulsory course in Chinese primary schools, middle schools and universities. Chinese students usually do well in exams. But their English

listening comprehension, speaking and writing are poor due to limited practice.
- So, we welcome British language schools to recommend bespoke teaching methods in China.
- In Britain the enthusiasm for learning Chinese is also growing. As evidence, 23 Confucius Institutes and 66 Confucius Classrooms have been opened in Britain.
- Chinese language has become one of the seven foreign languages for British students to choose in their compulsory language course.
- In the future China and the UK should continue to support the development of Confucius Institutes and Confucius Classrooms and improve their quality.
- Meanwhile we should work together to strengthen the training of local Chinese language teachers in Britain.

Fifth, strengthen study of each other's country.

- In its process of modernization, China will draw upon experience of Britain and other developed countries.
- We hope Britain will view modern China's progress and development in an objective and reasonable light.
- In particular we hope British universities will lead this effort. Dozens of British universities have founded China Research Centres or China Institutes.
- I do hope University of Bristol will integrate resources, intensify studies of contemporary China and play a bigger role in promoting better mutual understating between China and the UK.

University of Bristol had a most eminent former Chancellor. This was the Nobel Prize laureate in literature and former British Prime Minister, Sir Winston Churchill. He once wisely said:

"Continuous efforts, not strength or intelligence, is the key to unlocking our potential."

In the case of China-UK educational exchanges, we already have both strength and intelligence.

So I am convinced so long as we make continuous efforts together, we will unlock our potential.

In this way we will bring benefits to both countries and create a brighter future for China-UK educational cooperation.

Thank you!

春华秋实结硕果，交流互鉴促发展 *

尊敬的英国文化教育协会首席执行官戴维信爵士，
尊敬的中英两国大学各位校长，
女士们、先生们：
很高兴出席"中英留学交流四十年论坛"活动。

这是我一周内第二次参加有关中英留学的活动。上周，我出席了在皇家海军学院旧址举行的严复主题展览。那既是一次纪念缅怀活动，更是一次对历史的反思。19世纪70年代，在中国积贫积弱、被瓜分豆剖之际，以严复为代表的中国第一批留英学子心怀救亡图存、民族复兴之梦负笈求学，学成归国后推动了西方近代先进思想和技术在中国的传播，影响了中国近代历史的发展进程。这是中英最早的留学交流。

今天也是纪念活动，但时代背景完全不同。这次是纪念新中国成立后，特别是20世纪70年代中英正式建立大使级外交关系之后，中英之间恢复留学交流，开启两国留学教育新篇章。40年来，一批又一批中国学生、学者来到英国学习，英国年轻人也纷纷赴华留学。40年春华秋实，40载桃李芬芳，40年中英留学交流给我们带来许多启迪和收获。

第一，蓬勃发展的中英关系是两国留学交流持续升温的保障和助推力量。自中英建立大使级外交关系42年来，两国关系实现了跨越式发展。我

---

* 在"中英留学交流四十年论坛"开幕式上的讲话。2014年11月21日，英国机械工程师学会。

们解决了重大历史遗留问题，香港回归祖国成为中国的特别行政区。我们确立了全面战略伙伴关系，建立了中英总理年度会晤、经济财金对话、战略对话和高级别人文交流机制等高层对话机制。双边贸易额从1972年的3亿多美元增长到2013年的700多亿美元。蒸蒸日上的中英关系为中英教育交流的蓬勃发展提供了适宜的环境。40年前，新中国首批留英学子只有16人，赴华留学的英国学生也只有11人，而今在英有超过13万名公费和自费中国留学生，英国成为世界第二、欧洲第一中国留学生目的国，中国留学生也成为英国最大海外留学生团体；同时，有5465名英国学生在华留学，按人口比例来说，与中国赴英留学规模相当。40年间，中国共有超45万人来英留学，英国共有约3.5万人赴华留学。中英留学交流伴随着中英关系的发展已从涓涓细流汇聚成滔滔江河。

第二，广大留英学子已成为今天推动中国经济社会发展的杰出人才和中坚力量。中英留学交流40年来，广大留英归国人员积极投身改革开放和社会主义现代化建设，学以致用，学有所为，锐意进取，开拓创新，在中国的政治、经济、外交、教育和科技等不同领域发挥了重要作用。据统计，在有留英学习或工作经历的回国人员中，27人担任中国科学院、中国工程院院士。在中国"985"高校现任校长和党委书记中，有13位是留英回国人员。这说明留学英国是成才的必要知识储备和人生历练过程，更说明留英归国后有着广阔的发展空间，可以把个人梦想与国家发展梦想融为一体。

第三，中英留学是两国人文交流的重要形式，是中英关系发展的桥梁和纽带。中英都是拥有悠久历史和灿烂文化的国家，双方通过平等交流，能实现互学互鉴，共谋发展，共创未来。40年来，中国留学人员作为对外开放的先锋，既学习了英国的先进科学技术和管理经验，也促进了中国文化的传播，增进了两国人民之间的了解和友谊。同时，两国留学人员充分发挥自身优势，牵线搭桥，促进中英在经贸、教育、科技等各领域广泛交流与合作，为两国关系发展起到了推动作用。若没有40年中英留学的大交流，就没有今天中英关系的大发展。

孔子曰："四十而不惑。"中英留学交流经过40年发展，其规模盛况空前，其成效有目共睹。今后，中国政府将继续推进中外青年交流和学习互鉴，继续扩大派出留学生规模，继续鼓励和资助更多各国学生来华留学。我希望并相信，在中英双方的共同努力下，中英留学交流在下一个40年，一定会结出更加丰硕的果实，谱写更加辉煌的篇章！

最后，预祝本次论坛取得圆满成功！

谢谢！

Develop Together through Exchanges and Mutual Learning[*]

Martin Davidson,

Principals of Chinese and British Universities,

Ladies and Gentlemen,

It is a real pleasure to attend this Forum on Forty Years of China-UK Student Exchange.

This is my second event on student exchange in one week.

The first was held at the Old Royal Naval College in Greenwich. That was for the opening of an exhibition about Yan Fu. It was both a commemoration and a reflection on history.

In the 1870s, when China was weak and being dismembered, Yan Fu came to Britain with the first group of Chinese students. These young students came with a dream of national salvation and revitalisation. The impact of their studies in the UK was historic. Yan Fu and his fellow students returned to China a few years later to spread the advanced modern Western ideas and technology in China. They had a profound influence on the modern history of China.

Yan Fu and his colleagues were the earliest exchange students between China and the UK.

Today's commemoration is against a completely different historical backdrop. We are gathered to commemorate China-UK student exchange after the founding of the

---

[*] Speech at the Forum on Forty Years of China-UK Student Exchange. The Institution of Mechanical Engineers, 21 November 2014.

People's Republic of China, especially after the establishment of diplomatic relations at the ambassadorial level between China and the UK in the 1970's. Bilateral educational cooperation since then has evolved on an unprecedented scale.

For the past four decades hundreds of thousands of Chinese students and scholars have studied in the UK. In turn, many young British students have gone to China. These 40 years of flourishing and fruitful China-UK student exchange is both hugely rewarding and inspirational for both nations. There have been many mutual benefits.

First of all, Sino-UK student exchange is built on a foundation of positive relations between our two countries. This sustains the student exchange and drives its momentum.

After 40 years, China and the UK have achieved a quantum leap in our bilateral relations:

- We have resolved the question left over from history. Hong Kong has returned and become a special administrative region of China.
- China and the UK have established comprehensive strategic partnership, and set up a number of high level dialogue mechanisms. These include the Prime Ministers' Annual Meeting, the Economic and Financial Dialogue, the Strategic Dialogue and the High-Level People-to-People Dialogue Mechanism.
- Two-way trade has grown from 300 million US dollars in 1972 to over 70 billion US dollars in 2013.

The ever-growing China-UK relationship is providing an enabling environment for educational exchange to prosper:

- 40 years ago, the first group of students sent by New China numbered only 16 and there were only 11 British students in China.
- Today, there are over 130,000 Chinese students in the UK. They are either government or privately funded.
- Britain ranks second in the world and first in Europe in receiving Chinese students.
- Chinese students have become the largest overseas student community in the UK.

- Meanwhile, almost five and a half thousand British students are now studying in China. This is on the same scale as the number of Chinese students in the UK—given the different size of the population of our two countries.
- In total, the number of students exchanged over the past four decades amounts to 450,000 Chinese and 35,000 British.

As a result of the development of overall China-UK relations, the student exchange has turned from a small stream to a rushing river.

Let me turn to the second mutual benefit from China-UK student exchange.

The vast number of Chinese students who have studied in the UK have become the backbone in China's social and economic development.

Throughout the four decades, most Chinese students returned to China upon finishing their studies in the UK. They have become active participants in China's reform, opening-up and economic development. Armed with what they have learned in Britain, these enterprising and innovative young people have gone on to excel and play important roles in a wide variety of fields:

- Politics.
- Business.
- Diplomacy.
- Education.
- Science and technology.

Statistics show the scale of influence of these returnees:

- 27 are now fellows of Chinese Academy of Sciences or Chinese Academy of Engineering.
- In addition, among the principals and leading officials of the 39 universities in the government "985 Project", 13 had studied in the UK.

These statistics show that studying in the UK prepares young Chinese students with knowledge and life experience that is vital for career advance.

These figures also show that back at home, China offers a broad platform for their career development.

The returning scholars can certainly expect to realise their personal dreams back at home and at the same time profoundly influence the realization of the Chinese Dream.

This leads me to the third gain from student exchange.

For our two nations the student exchange greatly advances our people-to-people interaction and builds a great bridge and bond between the people of China and Britain.

Both China and the UK have a long history and rich cultures. Exchanges on the basis of mutual respect for each other deliver huge benefits for our peoples. In this spirit of sharing and understanding, we are able to learn from each other, develop hand in hand and build our future together.

For forty years, Chinese students have been pioneers in China's opening-up endeavour. They have learned advanced science and technology and management expertise from Britain. They have also brought Chinese culture to British people and helped build mutual understanding and friendship between our two peoples.

Chinese and British exchange students are in the prime position to connect our two countries together. They have played special role and worked hard to push for extensive exchanges and cooperation in various fields:

- They are pioneers in economic cooperation.
- They have pushed forward collaboration in education.
- They have involved in deep exchange in science and technology.
- And they have always been strong promoters of China-UK relations.

It is without question that the exponential increase in student exchange has delivered enormous progress in China-UK relations.

Confucius observed wisely and said:

"At forty, one has no doubt."

Forty years on, there is no doubt about the immense value of China-UK student exchange. Today, we can join together to applaud the unprecedented growth and great achievement of student exchange, and its contribution to China-UK relationship.

Looking forward, the Chinese government will continue to send more students overseas, encourage and finance more foreign students to study in China.

We will continue to promote youth exchange and mutual learning with foreign countries.

It is my very sincere hope that the UK will continue to be a primary partner with China for student exchange.

I am confident that with joint efforts, we will harvest even richer fruit and write a more splendid chapter for China-UK student exchange in the next forty years.

In conclusion, I wish this Forum a complete success.

Thank you!

共谋中英关系百年大计 *

尊敬的英国商业、创新与技能部常务次官马丁·唐纳利先生,
尊敬的英国文化教育协会首席执行官邓克然爵士,
尊敬的各位大学校长,
各位留学中国同学会会员,
女士们、先生们:

今天我们欢聚一堂,庆祝英国留学中国同学会的成立。首先,我谨代表中国驻英国大使馆向同学会及全体留华学生表示热烈的祝贺!

2014年11月,我出席了"中英留学交流四十年论坛"。在那次论坛上,我们共同回顾了40年来中英留学交流走过的不平凡之路,总结了40年来取得的成就与经验。我认为,今天英国留学中国同学会的成立是中英留学交流中水到渠成的崭新成果,必将发挥其恰逢其时的积极作用。

第一,同学会的成立体现了当前中英留学规模持续增长、交流形式日益多元的局面。过去40年,共有超45万名中国学生到英国留学,约有3.5万名英国学生赴华学习。目前,约15万名中国留学生在英学习,英国成为世界第二、欧洲第一中国留学生目的地国。而中国成为继美国、英国之后世界第三大留学生输入国,超过37.7万名国际留学生在华学习。其中,7800多名英国学生通过"英国未来计划""中国政府奖学金""孔子学院奖学金",以及各

---

* 在"英国未来计划——留学中国同学会"启动仪式上的讲话。2016年2月26日,英国医学会。

地方政府奖学金、校际交流、校企合作等途径赴华学习或实习。

特别值得注意的是，在留学形式上，双方在保持传统的学历教育外，积极开拓教育交流新模式，内容丰富的定制式短期留学成为英国学生赴华学习的新趋势。两国政府继续通过国家级奖学金发挥关键作用，中英企业、高校等也纷纷参与和支持双边学生的留学或实习项目。2015年3月，萨塞克斯大学宣布投入75万英镑，为300名英国学生提供到中国工作和实习的机会；华为英国公司自2011年开展"未来种子"项目以来，至今已累计将英国高校的百余名学生送往中国，学习语言文化，了解中国企业发展。

第二，同学会的成立将有力促进中英两国政府鼓励双向留学政策的实施。2015年9月，国务院副总理刘延东与英国卫生大臣杰里米·亨特在伦敦共同主持中英高级别人文交流机制第三次会议期间，代表两国签署了《中英教育伙伴关系框架协议》，促进了中英教育领域各方面的合作。作为该框架的一部分，双方的旗舰项目"留学中国计划"及"英国未来计划"成为英国学生赴华的重要平台。其中"英国未来计划"作为英国高等教育国际发展战略的重要组成部分，将在2020年前累计输送超过8万名英国年轻人赴华交流或参与实习。

2015年10月，习近平主席对英国进行了成功的"超级国事访问"，在访问联合声明中，中英双方承诺促进文化教育联系，支持两国人员特别是青年往来，并将进一步为双边留学人员的往来提供便利。我相信，英国留学中国同学会的成员规模会如同滚雪球般越来越大，同时你们也将带动更多英国年轻学生以你们为榜样，争相赴华学习交流。

第三，同学会的成立必将为推进中英关系发展发挥积极作用。当前，中国即将开启"十三五"规划征程，我们正处在一个充满巨大机遇和美好前景的时代。中英双方将在政治、经贸、金融、人文和全球方面开展"五位一体"的全方位合作，围绕中方倡导的"一带一路"、中国"长江经济带"与英方基础设施建设升级改造计划、"英格兰北方经济中心"等开展战略规划对接。双方将加大在新兴产业，特别是在新能源、智慧城市、生物制药、科技创新、电子商务等领域的合作力度。这也为未来中英教育交流与合作构筑了广阔空间。今天，我们成立这个同学会，就是要汇聚中英两国青年学子的智慧和力量，同心协力为中英关系增光添彩！

最后，为祝贺英国留学中国同学会的成立，也为进一步鼓励英国学生赴华留学，我为你们准备了一份特殊的礼物。从2016年起，除现有的"中国政府奖学金"及"孔子学院奖学金"外，中方首次在英设立中国政府短期奖学金项目。2016—2017年该项目奖学金名额为150个，重点支持英方高校学生赴华参加为期2个月的留学、实习活动，同时鼓励中英高校间开展灵活多样的校际学生交流项目。我相信这必将进一步促进中英教育合作，增进两国青年学生的交流与友谊。

2016年春节大年初一，卡梅伦首相在唐宁街10号首相府举行的新春招待会上，引用了中国成语。他说，"一年树谷，十年树木，百年树人，千年树院"，并进而提出，"千年之计，莫如民心相通"，以此强调中英应发展长久持续的千年友好关系。

我们今天做的事情，就是中英关系的百年大计、千年大计。让我们携手，共同为中英关系的百年和千年大计添砖加瓦！

谢谢！

Plan for One Hundred Years of China-UK Relations *

Secretary Donnelly,

Sir Ciaran Devane,

Vice-Chancellors,

Members of the China Network,

Ladies and Gentlemen,

It is a great pleasure to join you this afternoon at this important event co-hosted by the Chinese Embassy and the British Council.

We are gathered to celebrate the founding of the China Network. On behalf of the Chinese Embassy, I would like to extend my warmest congratulations to the China Network and all those who have studied in China.

I remember attending the Forum on Forty Years of China-UK Student Exchange in November 2014. Back then, we reviewed the China-UK student exchange in the past 40 years. Together, we summarised the achievements and experience we have gained. Today, the founding of the China Network marks our latest progress. This is the natural outcome of decades of student exchange between China and the UK. There could not be a better time to form such an organisation.

Let me share with you my thoughts about the importance of the launch of the China Network.

First, it reflects the trend of ever-growing and increasingly diversified student

---

* Remarks at the Inauguration of Generation UK: China Network. British Medical Association (BMA), 26 February 2016.

exchange between China and the UK:

- In the past 40 years, more than 450,000 Chinese students studied in the UK.
- Over the same period about 35,000 British students have studied in China.
- At present, there are around 150,000 Chinese students in this country. As a destination for Chinese students, the UK is No.2 in the world and No.1 in Europe.
- China is also a major destination for foreign students, ranking third after the US and the UK.
- Now more than 377,000 students from around the world study in China.
- Among them, 7,800 are from the UK.

These British students came to China for study or internship through a series of channels that include:

- The Generation UK.
- The Chinese Government Scholarship.
- The Confucius Institute Scholarship.
- Local government scholarships.
- School-to-school exchanges.
- And university-business partnerships.

Notably, many new forms of student exchange have been adopted. In addition to the traditional degree programmes, the tailor-made short-term study programmes have become a prevailing trend among the British students going to China.

Of course, the governments of our two countries continue to play key roles through national scholarships. At the same time, Chinese and British enterprises, universities and colleges are getting more and more involved and starting to support student exchange and internship.

In March 2015, the University of Sussex announced a 750,000 pounds China Internship Scheme. This aimed at financing 300 British students for work and internship in China. The Huawei UK launched the "Seeds for the Future" Programme in 2011. More than a hundred British university students have benefitted from this programme by attending Chinese language and culture courses, and learning about doing business in China.

Let me turn to my second thought about the importance of the China Network. I believe it plays a vital role in helping facilitate the implementation of Chinese and British government policies with regard to student exchange. Last September, Vice Premier Liu Yandong and Health Secretary Jeremy Hunt co-chaired the Third Meeting of the China-UK High-Level People-to-People Exchange. During the meeting, the Framework for Strengthening China-UK Partnership in Education was signed to enhance our cooperation in this field. Under this framework, our respective flagship projects, the Study-in-China Scholarship and the Generation UK, are now major platforms for British students planning to study in China. The Generation UK is an important part of the UK's international strategy in higher education. Through this programme more than 80,000 young British will have studied or worked as interns in China by 2020.

Last October, President Xi Jinping paid a "super state visit" to the UK. In the Joint Statement issued during the visit, both China and the UK are committed to stronger cultural and educational connections. This means more people-to-people exchanges especially for young people, and greater facilitation for students. I expect the China Network to grow in scale. In turn, I am sure that more and more young British students will follow your footprints and take advantage of the opportunities to study in China.

Let me give you my third point about the China Network. It will have an active role to play in promoting China-UK relations.

China will soon begin a new journey, with the adoption of the 13th Five Year Plan for economic and social development in the coming five years. We have before us a promising future and huge opportunities. Much can be achieved when China and the UK work together.

- We can engage each other in all-round cooperation in the political field, in business and finance, in cultural exchanges and on global issues.
- We can dovetail our respective development strategies. For China this includes Belt and Road Initiative and the Yangtze River Economic Belt. For Britain there are the National Infrastructure Plan and the Northern Powerhouse.

- We can step up our cooperation in emerging industries, especially in new energy, smart city, bio-pharmacy, sci-tech innovation and e-commerce.

All these areas will open up wider space for our educational exchanges and cooperation. With the China Network set up today, I hope that young Chinese and British students will pool their wisdom and strength, and work together to create more splendid China-UK relations.

I want to congratulate you once again on the founding of the China Network. I also hope to encourage more British students to study in China.

To follow up my congratulations and encouragement, I have brought you a special gift today. This is the Short-term Chinese Government Scholarship Scheme. The scheme is the first of its kind for the UK students. It will run in parallel to the long-term Chinese Government Scholarship and the Confucius Institute Scholarship. In the academic year 2016—2017, this short-term scheme will fund 150 British university students for two-month study or internship in China. Meanwhile, Chinese and British universities are encouraged to take advantage of this scheme through flexible and diverse forms of exchange programs. I am sure such an initiative will definitely boost China-UK educational cooperation and help increase the communication and friendship between the young people of our two countries.

Ladies and Gentlemen,

On the very first day of this Year of the Monkey, Prime Minister Cameron hosted a Chinese New Year reception at No.10 Downing Street. In his remarks, the Prime Minister quoted a Chinese idiom and carried it further to develop his own version. He said:

"If you want one year of prosperity, you grow grain.

If you want ten years of prosperity, you grow trees.

If you want one hundred years of prosperity, you grow people.

If you want a thousand years of prosperity, you grow relationships between peoples."

He said this to highlight the importance of China and the UK working together for one thousand years of lasting friendship.

This is actually what we are doing today. We are planning for a hundred years—

even a thousand years of China-UK relations!

So, let us join hands together to build this great China-UK edifice by growing people and by growing the relationships between our two peoples.

Thank you!

凝聚智慧，共建世界和平与繁荣 *

尊敬的格林纳韦校长，

老师们、同学们，

女士们、先生们：

很高兴在金秋时节再次来到诺丁汉大学（以下简称诺大）。我曾多次访问诺大，每次都有新感悟、新收获。这次访问收获最大，我很荣幸地接受了诺大授予的荣誉法学博士学位。在此，我谨向诺大和格林纳韦校长表示衷心的感谢。

我认为，这不仅是给予我个人的荣誉，也是对中国驻英国大使馆工作的认可，更体现了诺大对中英教育合作的高度重视和做出的积极贡献。当然，这也进一步加深了我与诺大的缘分。

诺大是我担任中国驻英国大使后访问最早、访问次数最多的大学之一，但我与诺大的缘分可以追溯到16年前。

2001年，我出任中国驻埃及大使。同我一批向穆巴拉克总统递交国书的大使共有15位，除我之外，还有两位来自联合国安理会常任理事国。其中一位是我的弗莱彻校友美国大使大卫·韦尔奇，另一位就是诺大的杰出校友约翰·索尔斯。我们3位都是第一次当大使，而且都是40来岁。开罗外交界把我们称为"3个新兵"。索尔斯后来回忆称，他原以为自己是"最年轻的

---

* 在英国诺丁汉大学荣誉法学博士学位授予仪式上的演讲。2017年9月6日，英国诺丁汉大学。

驻埃及大使",没想到中国大使比他还年轻一岁。

在共同出使埃及的岁月里,我和索尔斯成了好朋友,我们经常就中东局势和国际形势交换意见。后来我们一直保持联系。我出任驻英大使之后,他在英国政府担任要职,我们共同为增进中英政治互信、深化战略合作贡献各自力量。从他的身上我了解了诺大,理解了诺大,读懂了诺大校训——"城市建于智慧之上"。因为智慧不仅是人成长、成功的基础,也是增进人与人之间、国家与国家之间友谊必不可少的能力。

弹指一挥间,16年过去了,当年"最年轻的驻埃及大使"成为"在任时间最长的中国驻英国大使"。7年多来,我有幸见证、亲历、推动了中英关系的蓬勃发展,特别是2015年习近平主席成功对英国进行国事访问后,两国建立面向21世纪全球全面战略伙伴关系,中英关系进入历史最好时期。

7年多来,中英各领域合作不断增量提质。双边贸易额从508亿美元增长至744亿美元。中国对英直接投资从13亿美元增长至180亿美元,增长了近13倍,高居欧洲各国之首。两国金融合作不断深化,中国各大银行相继在伦敦开设分行或子行,中英两国政府分别在伦敦发行首批人民币主权债券,伦敦成为中国境外最大人民币离岸中心。两国"一带一路"合作不断深入,英国在西方大国中第一个申请加入亚投行,继中国之后第二个向亚投行基础设施项目注资。在国际事务中,中英协作日益加强,从联合国到二十国集团,从网络安全到抗生素耐药性,从气候变化到野生动物保护,中英关系的内涵和外延持续拓展。

7年多来,中英人文交流亮点纷呈。两国成功互办"中英文化交流年",每年人员往来超过150万人次,"中国热"在英持续升温,汉语成为不少英国学校的首选外语,伦敦和英国各地的春节庆典活动跻身年度盛事,我连续7年出席的特拉法加广场春节庆典成为亚洲之外规模最大的中国春节庆典活动。"英伦风"在华风头更盛,《哈利·波特》《唐顿庄园》《神探夏洛克》等电影或英剧在中国拥有海量粉丝,来英旅游观光的中国公民数量逐年攀升。

7年多来,教育成为两国人文交流的最大亮点,并且创造了至少3个欧洲第一。一是英国吸引的中国留学生数量居欧洲第一,中国在英留学生从7

年前的 12 万人增长到近 17 万人。二是开办孔子学院和孔子课堂数量居欧洲第一，在英孔子学院和孔子课堂数量分别从 7 年前的 13 所和 57 间猛增至今天的 29 所和 140 多间。三是开展校际合作的名牌大学数量居欧洲第一，包括北京大学与剑桥大学、爱丁堡大学分别建立研究中心，清华大学与剑桥大学等大学联合设立低碳研究中心，以及成立"牛津大学－苏州先进研究中心""剑桥大学南京科技创新中心"等。

我高兴地看到，诺大在格林纳韦校长的领导下，在两国教育交流中一直发挥着引领和示范作用。诺大是第一所与中方合办高校、第一所任命中国人为校监的英国大学；诺大孔子学院被评为全球"示范孔子学院"；在诺大本校求学的中国学生超过 2000 人；诺大已成为研究当代中国的学术标杆。

中英人文交流的大发展不仅体现在数量上，而且体现在质量上。2012 年，中英建立了高级别人文交流机制，这是中国同欧洲国家建立的第一个人文交流机制。目前，这一机制已成为中英高层机制性对话的三大支柱之一。它的建立进一步加强了中英人文交流的顶层设计、政策支持和制度支撑。2017 年恰逢中英高级别人文交流机制成立 5 周年，新一轮对话将于 2017 年 12 月初在英国举行，我衷心期待此次对话取得更多实质成果。

展望未来，中英人文交流的发展将不仅惠及两国人民，为中英关系深入发展打下坚实的民意基础，而且会越来越具有世界意义和全球影响。中英人文交流的成果向世界展示，只要在相互尊重、平等相待的基础上加强对话、增进交流、深化合作，国与国之间的关系就能发展得更顺畅，就能为人类多元文明和谐共处做出积极贡献。

女士们、先生们，

7 年多来，中英关系也曾经历曲折，今天的局面来之不易，其难度也不亚于"建造一座城市"。中英历史背景、文化传统、社会制度不同，导致双方对一些问题的看法不可能完全一致，有时也会出现分歧和矛盾。每当处理这些难题时，我会从"城市建于智慧之上"的诺大精神中汲取营养，致力于运用"智慧"求同存异、求同化异，将中英关系"这座城市"建造得更加坚固。

此时此刻令我想起40多年前在母校大连外国语大学毕业时的情景。那时我也像在座的同学们这般年轻，眼中充满对未来的憧憬。我青年时代的梦想就是为中国外交、为世界和平与发展事业做点事。

幸运的是，我的梦想成真，成了一名中国外交官。在40多年的外交生涯中，我曾在非洲、美洲、亚洲、欧洲四大洲六次常驻。但无论走多远，我的心始终和祖国连在一起。我深知，只有祖国繁荣和强大，个人才能成功。因为外交不是个人行为，而是国家行为。担任驻英大使7年多的工作经历，使我对此有了更深刻的体会。最近中国国内正在热播六集大型政论专题片《大国外交》，其讲的是近5年来，在习近平主席的领导下，中国特色大国外交的发展历程。我在此隆重向诺大师生们推荐。我相信，随着中国的发展、随着中国特色大国外交的推进，中国必将为促进人类和平与发展事业贡献更多中国智慧，提供更多中国方案。

最后，我想对在座的诺大青年校友们说几句话：中英关系的未来依靠你们，世界的发展进步依靠你们。诺大的一位知名校友，英国文学家大卫·赫伯特·劳伦斯曾说，"不要被动地适应世界，而要积极地改造世界"。我衷心希望诺大的青年朋友们，能把眼界放得更宽、更广，秉持并发扬诺大精神，在充满变化和挑战的世界中挥斥方遒，奋发有为，为增进中英两国人民的友谊、为构建世界和平与繁荣贡献智慧和力量！

谢谢！

Build World Peace and Prosperity on Wisdom[*]

Professor Sir David Greenaway,

Teachers and Students,

Ladies and Gentlemen,

It is such a great delight to be back to the University of Nottingham on this beautiful autumn day. For me:

- Every journey to Nottingham brings new thoughts.
- Every visit to your University is highly stimulating.
- And every trip is rewarding.

Undoubtedly the biggest reward of this visit is receiving the Nottingham's honorary doctorate of law. I am deeply moved by this degree being conferred on me. Therefore, I would like to first of all extend my heartfelt thanks to University of Nottingham and to Professor Sir David.

I take this degree as not only an honour for myself but also the recognition of the work of the Chinese Embassy. More significantly, it represents Nottingham's strong commitment and remarkable contribution to the educational cooperation between our two countries. Furthermore, it strengthens my personal ties with University of Nottingham.

---

[*] Speech at the Awarding of the Degree of Doctor of Laws, Honoris Causa. University of Nottingham, 6 September 2017.

I have been Chinese Ambassador to the UK for over 7 years. Nottingham was among the very first universities that I visited. But, more than that, Nottingham is one of the British universities that I have paid the most visits to. However, my links with your university began much earlier. It reaches back to 16 years ago.

In 2001, I was appointed Chinese Ambassador to Egypt. At the ceremony of presenting credentials to Egyptian President Mubarak, there were 15 ambassadors. These included three representing the US, the UK, and of course China, all permanent members of the UN Security Council. The US Ambassador David Welch is my fellow alumnus from the Fletcher School of Law and Diplomacy. The British Ambassador is an eminent Nottingham alumnus, Sir John Sawers. We were all in mid-forties and serve as Ambassador for the very first time. So, we were known as the "three rookies" in the diplomatic community in Cairo. Sir John later told me that he thought at that time he was "the youngest Ambassador in Egypt" and later found out that the Chinese Ambassador was one year younger than him.

In the years we spent together in Cairo, Sir John and I became very good friends. We often exchanged views on the Middle East and international situation. After leaving Egypt, Sir John and I continued to stay in touch. When I came to Britain as Chinese Ambassador, Sir John was holding an important British government office. Both of us worked hard in our respective posts to increase the political mutual trust and deepen the strategic cooperation between China and Britain. It was through Sir John that I got to know about the great strengths of the University of Nottingham. Through Sir John I learned to appreciate your motto which is:

"A city is built on wisdom."

I believe that wisdom comes with maturity and lays the groundwork for success. Wisdom is indispensable for building friendship between people. And wisdom is the path to deliver mutual respect and understanding between nations.

Time flies and 16 years are like a "split second". The once youngest Ambassador in Egypt has now become the longest serving Chinese Ambassador to Britain. For seven years and more in Britain, I have had the honour to witness and personally contribute to a thriving China-UK relationship. This was most notable in 2015, when Chinese President Xi Jinping paid a successful state visit to the UK. China and the UK began a global comprehensive strategic partnership for the 21st century. Never before has

China-UK relationship been so strong and so close as it is now.

For seven years and more, China-UK cooperation across the board has been expanding both in quality and quantity:

- Bilateral trade grew from 50.8 billion US dollars to 74.4 billion US dollars.
- And investment from China to Britain expanded about 13 times from 1.3 billion US dollars to 18 billion US dollars. This is much more than Chinese investment in any other European country.

Progress is also being made in China-UK financial cooperation:

- All major Chinese banks have come to London one after another, setting up branches or subsidiaries.
- The Chinese and British governments respectively issued their first RMB sovereign bond in London.
- And London is now the largest RMB offshore market outside China.

China-UK cooperation on the Belt and Road is also deepening. Britain was the first major Western country to apply to join the Asian Infrastructure Investment Bank (AIIB) and the second only after China to contribute capital to the AIIB infrastructure project.

China and Britain are also enhancing collaboration on many international agendas:

- Strengthening the UN and G20.
- Advancing cyber security.
- Moving forward on antimicrobial resistance.
- Cooperating on climate change.
- And working together on protecting wild life.

For seven years and more, cultural and people-to-people exchanges have been a definite highlight in China-UK relations. There are many positive developments:

- Our two countries successfully co-hosted the Year of China-UK Cultural

Exchange.
- Every year, more than 1.5 million mutual visits are made between China and Britain.
- Enthusiasm for Chinese culture and language learning has been growing across Britain.
- More and more British schools offer Chinese as the first foreign language in their curriculum.
- The Chinese New Year has become a popular annual festival in London and across the UK. The celebration at the Trafalgar Square, in particular, is now the biggest Chinese New Year event outside Asia. For the past seven years, I have never missed one.
- In China, the rising interest in Britain can also be strongly felt. *Harry Porter, Downtown Abbey, Sherlock,* and many other British films and TV dramas have a huge number of fans in China. The number of Chinese tourists visiting Britain keeps growing every year.

For seven years and more, education has become the biggest highlight of China-UK cultural and people-to-people exchanges. In the field of educational ties with China, Britain has set at least three European records:

- Britain is the biggest European destination for Chinese students. This year, nearly 170,000 Chinese students came to the UK, compared to 120,000 seven years ago.
- Britain is home to the largest number of Confucius Institutes and Confucius Classrooms, increasing from 13 and 57 respectively seven years ago to 29 and 140 today.
- Britain is leading all European countries in joint research and studies with world-class Chinese universities. There are so many examples:
    * Peking University set up separately with University of Cambridge and University of Edinburgh cultural and area studies centres in each other's campus.
    * Cambridge, Tsinghua and others established joint low-carbon study centres.
    * There are also the Oxford Suzhou Centre for Advanced Research and the

centre for education on scientific innovation set up by Cambridge and Nanjing.

It is a great pleasure to witness the exceptional commitment of the University of Nottingham to China. Led by Professor Sir David, University of Nottingham has always played a leading and exemplary role in the educational exchanges between our two countries:

- University of Nottingham is the first British University to appoint a Chinese Chancellor and to set up a joint campus in China.
- The Nottingham Confucius Institute is named a Model Confucius Institute.
- University of Nottingham is home to more than 2,000 Chinese students.
- And University of Nottingham is a leader in the study of contemporary China.

The progress of China-UK educational exchanges is not only evidenced by numbers. More significantly, it is reflected in the growing quality of cooperation:

- In 2012, China and Britain co-established the High-Level People-to-People Exchange Mechanism.
- At present, this mechanism has become one of the three major pillars underpinning the development of China-UK relations.
- It helps strengthen the top-level design of our bilateral exchanges on cultural and people-to-people ties. It ensures stronger policy and institutional support.
- This year marks the fifth anniversary of the High-Level People-to-People Exchange Mechanism.
- The new round of dialogue is going to take place in Britain in early December this year, which, I am sure, will produce more concrete outcomes.

Looking ahead, the closer cultural and people-to-people exchanges between China and Britain will bring more benefits to the people of our two countries. In turn, this will further consolidate the public support for China-UK relations. Moreover, it will have a global significance and extensive influence. It will show that closer dialogue, deeper exchanges and stronger cooperation on the basis of equality and mutual respect delivers great benefits. It will smooth state-to-state ties and contribute to the harmonious co-existence between diverse civilizations.

Ladies and Gentlemen,

Over the past seven years and more, China-UK relationship is not free from problems. Like building a city, building sound China-UK relations as we enjoy today is no easy task. China and Britain are two nations differing in history, heritage and social system. So, it is only natural that we do not see eye to eye on every issue. It is only inevitable that sometimes we have different views and ideas. In dealing with these differences, I think Nottingham's motto offers food for thought:

- We should seek common ground while handling differences with wisdom.
- And we should always work to build China-UK relations on foundations of wisdom.

On today's occasion, I cannot help thinking about my graduation from my alma mater, Dalian University of Foreign Languages, more than 40 years ago. Back then, I was like each and every one of you sitting in this hall, young and eager to explore. At that time, my dream was to do something for China's diplomacy and for world peace and development.

Luckily, my dream came true. I became a Chinese diplomat. In my more than four-decade long diplomatic career, I have had six overseas postings in four continents: Africa, America, Asia and Europe. But wherever I go, my heart is always with my homeland, China. As I understand, without a strong and prosperous homeland, any individual success would be meaningless. For a diplomat, no individual behavior is really individual. Whatever you do, you represent your country. Indeed, my time here in Britain, over the past seven years, made me feel even more deeply about this.

Recently, a documentary being shown in China has become a big hit. It is called *China's Diplomacy*. This film series is an overview of China's diplomacy under the leadership of President Xi Jinping over the past five years. I highly recommend this documentary to Nottingham teachers and students. As China develops and as China's diplomatic endeavors unfold, I have every confidence that we will be able to contribute more of China's wisdom and China's solutions to the cause of world peace and development.

Before I conclude, I have these thoughts for my young Nottingham alumni:

- Young people like you will be the ones to shape the future of China-UK relations.
- And, you will be the ones to make sure the world continues to develop and make progress.

Just as another Nottingham alumnus, D. H. Lawrence said:

"Instead of chopping yourself down to fit the world, chop the world down to fit yourself."

It is my sincere hope that you will keep these words in mind, take a global vision and live up to the spirit of University of Nottingham.

I hope you will meet the changing and challenging world head on and prove your wisdom and capabilities:

- In developing China-UK friendship.
- And in building world peace and prosperity.

Thank you!

携手谱写中英教育交流与合作的"华彩乐章" *

尊敬的各位大学校长，

各位教授、学者，

女士们、先生们：

欢迎大家出席今晚的新春招待会。我很高兴第一次为中英教育界朋友举办专场中国春节招待会，也很高兴在接待梅首相成功访华返英后就与大家欢聚一堂。再过9天就是中国农历狗年春节，我谨向各位教育界新老朋友拜个早年，祝愿大家新春快乐，狗年吉祥！

刚刚过去的2017年是中英关系深入发展的一年，也是中英教育交流与合作蓬勃开展的一年。

一是奏响了政府间教育合作的"壮丽鲜明主旋律"。中英高级别人文交流机制第五次会议取得圆满成功，双方发表联合声明，为两国教育合作提质增速指明方向。第十次中英教育部长峰会成功举办，双方签署了多项谅解备忘录，规划了两国教育合作的新愿景。

二是奏响了全方位交流的"优美和弦"。从教学到科研、从大学到中小学、从数学到体育，中英教育各领域交流更加频繁、更加深入。中国医学科学院牛津研究所在牛津大学成立，成为牛津建校800多年历史上首个也是唯一的牛津与外国高校在该校园内设立的研究机构。北京大学汇丰商学院创办英国校区，成为中国高校在发达国家办学的新探索。牛津大学－苏州先进研

---

* 在中英教育界中国春节招待会上的讲话。2018年2月7日，伦敦O2剧场。

究中心、剑桥大学南京科技创新中心、萨里大学5G（第五代移动通信技术）创新中心等有效推动中英高等院校科研合作。英国哈珀·柯林斯出版集团首次翻译出版中国数学教材，推动中国数学走进英国中小学，目前已有超500名中英数学教师通过"上海数学教师交流项目"实现互访。曼彻斯特大学、拉夫堡大学、伯恩茅斯大学等为中英校园足球、橄榄球教练员培训等项目做出积极贡献。

三是奏响了语言和文化互鉴的"丰富和声"。中国在英国留学人员数量保持欧洲国家首位，英国赴华留学人员数量不断增多。如今，超过17万名中国学生和学者负笈英伦；约9000名英国学生赴华学习，2017年获得中国政府奖学金支持的英国学生近300名，较2016年大幅攀升。全英共建29所孔子学院和148间孔子课堂，注册学员超过16万，谢菲尔德大学、诺丁汉大学、伦敦南岸大学、思克莱德大学等7所孔子学院荣获全球"示范孔子学院"称号。600多所英国学校开设了中文课程，每年有近500名中国汉语教师和汉语志愿在英国大中小学任教。

2017年也是我本人对中英教育交流合作倾力投入、收获丰富的一年。我遍访英国各地，从英格兰到苏格兰，从皇家属地到海外领地，从牛津郡到诺丁汉郡，我总共出席了20多场教育活动，使馆教育处的同事们称我为"教育大使"。通过这些活动，我也深深感受到英国教育界朋友对中国的友好情谊和推进中英教育合作的热情意愿。2017年我还有幸获得诺丁汉大学荣誉法学博士学位，这进一步加深了我与英国教育界的不解之缘。

这次我陪同梅首相访华，又一次见证了中英教育交流与合作的丰硕成果。梅首相第一站就访问了历史悠久的武汉大学，启动了"英语很棒"培训项目，双方还决定将"中英数学教师交流项目"续期两年，加强学前教育和职业培训合作并深化就业教育信息共享。双方签署的教育协议总价值超过5.5亿英镑，将在英国创造800个职位。梅首相此次访问开启了两国教育交流与合作的升级版。

千淘万漉虽辛苦，吹尽狂沙始到金。中英教育交流与合作之所以能取得这么多成果，离不开在座各位朋友的辛勤耕耘和不懈努力，我谨借此机会向你们表示衷心的感谢！展望新的一年，我衷心希望中英教育界人士抓住中英关系的新机遇，通力协作，勤奋耕耘，携手谱写中英教育交流与合作新的"华彩乐章"！

谢谢！

A Symphony of China-UK Educational Exchanges and Cooperation*

Vice-Chancellors,

Professors and Scholars,

Ladies and Gentlemen,

A few days ago I had the honor of accompanying Prime Minister May on her successful visit to China. Now, it is a real delight to be back and join you at this special Chinese New Year reception for friends from the educational sector of both countries.

This is the first time that I host such an event. Let me first of all express my warmest welcome to all of you.

In nine days time, we will celebrate the Chinese New Year and embrace the Year of the Dog. Please allow me to take this opportunity to send New Year greetings to friends from the educational sector, both old and new.

I wish you a happy and prosperous Year of the Dog!

The year 2017 witnessed the consolidation of China-UK relations. It is also a year of thriving exchanges and cooperation in education between our two countries.

Firstly, if we compare China-UK educational exchange and cooperation to a "symphony", its "main theme" is loud and clear: Such cooperation enjoys full government backing from both countries.

The fifth China-UK High-Level People-to-People Dialogue was a huge success. A joint statement was issued, which serves as a guide for accelerating and improving

---

* Remarks at the Chinese New Year Reception for the UK Education Partners. O2 London, 7 February 2018.

China-UK cooperation in education.

Our two countries also held the tenth China-UK Education Summit. The MOUs signed at the summit outlined the blueprint for future cooperation.

Secondly, with flourishing exchanges on all fronts, this "symphony" offers delightful "chords".

From research to teaching, from universities to primary and secondary schools, and from maths to PE classes, China and the UK have increased and deepened exchanges across the field of education.

- The Oxford Institute of the Chinese Academy of Medical Sciences was established in the University of Oxford. This is the first time in its 800-year history that Oxford has a foreign university to set up a research unit on its campus. And it is the only one of its kind.
- The Peking University HSBC Business School opened a new campus in the UK. This is a pioneering effort by a Chinese university to run a school in a developed country.
- The cooperation on scientific research between universities of the two countries has been greatly advanced by the establishment of joint research centres. These include Oxford Suzhou Centre for Advanced Research, the centre for education on scientific innovation set up by Cambridge and Nanjing, and the 5G Innovation Centre at the University of Surrey.
- For the first time, the HarperCollins Publishers translated and published Chinese maths textbooks for use in primary and secondary schools in the UK. Up till now, over 500 maths teachers from the two countries have been on exchange visits through the China-UK maths teacher exchange programme.
- The University of Manchester, the Loughborough University and the Bournemouth University have been active participant in the China-UK Campus Football and Rugby Coach Training Programmes.

Thirdly, the "symphony" of educational exchange and cooperation presents a "rich harmony" of mutual learning of language and culture.

The UK has the largest Chinese student community in Europe. The number of

British students in China is also increasing. Now there are over 170 thousand Chinese students and scholars studying in the UK, and about 9,000 British students went to China for study. About 300 of them are on Chinese Government Scholarship. This number has increased by a large margin over the previous year.

Confucius Institutes is another highlight. Across the UK, there are 29 Confucius Institutes and 148 Confucius Classrooms, with a total of over 160 thousand registered students.

Seven Confucius Institutes were awarded "Model Confucius Institute", including the Confucius Institutes in the University of Sheffield, the University of Nottingham, the London South Bank University and the University of Strathclyde.

Moreover, over 600 British schools are offering Chinese language courses, hiring nearly 500 teachers and volunteer teaching assistants from China every year.

In 2017, I personally committed much more efforts to China-UK education exchange and cooperation. This has been an exceptionally bountiful year for me.

From England to Scotland, from Crown Dependencies to the British Overseas Territories, and from Oxfordshire to Nottinghamshire, I attended over 20 education-related events. My colleagues at the Education Section of the Embassy called me "Education Ambassador".

In all these events, I was deeply touched by the friendship of the British education community towards China. I could feel their readiness and enthusiasm to advance China-UK cooperation in education.

Last year, I had the honor of receiving an honorary doctorate of law from the University of Nottingham. I can now feel an even closer bond with the British education community.

During Prime Minister May's visit, I had the opportunity of witnessing once again the fruitful exchange and cooperation between the two countries in education.

- At her first stop in China, the Prime Minister visited the time-honoured Wuhan University and launched the 2018 "English is GREAT" campaign.
- The two countries agreed to extend the China-UK Mathematics Teacher Exchange Programme for another two years, to facilitate joint training of pre-school and vocational school staff, and to improve information-sharing on

vocational education.
- The education agreements signed during the Prime Minister's visit exceed 550 million pounds in value. They are expected to create 800 jobs in the UK.

The Prime Minister May's visit effectively upgraded the educational exchange and cooperation between the two countries.

Panning for gold from grains of sand is strenuous work, just as it is arduous to harvest the fruits of China-UK education cooperation that we have achieved.

I want to take this opportunity to express my heartfelt thanks to all of you present tonight whose relentless efforts are absolutely indispensable in what we have accomplished so far.

As we celebrate the New Year, I hope you will seize the new opportunities in China-UK relations. I hope the education sector of our two countries will join hands and work even harder to compose a new cadenza for the symphony of China-UK educational exchange and cooperation!

Thank you!

激扬青春梦想，共促中英合作 *

尊敬的鲍伯·克莱恩校长，
尊敬的蒂姆·桑顿常务副校长，
各位老师、各位同学，
女士们、先生们、朋友们：
上午好！

很高兴出席哈德斯菲尔德大学2018年毕业典礼。首先，我谨向所有毕业生表示衷心的祝贺，祝贺你们圆满完成学业，开启人生新航程，扬帆筑梦新旅程！我也要向辛勤耕耘的老师们致以崇高的敬意！

我来英工作8年多，到访过不少英国大学，但今天是第一次参加毕业典礼。此时此刻，看到这么多青春洋溢、朝气蓬勃的面庞，不禁感触良多。

这是盘点收获的时刻。哈德斯菲尔德大学被HEA（英国高等教育质量保证委员会）列为"教育质量最佳的大学"之一。据我了解，贵校在教学质量、学生满意度、学生实习就业、教师培训、科研共建等方面成就显著，尤其重视培育办学理念和人文精神。贵校不仅在2017年HEA首届全球教学优秀奖评比活动中获得总冠军的殊荣，还在2018年ISB（国际学生晴雨表）评选中荣获全英国际学生满意度第一名。这些优异成绩的取得离不开约克公爵安德鲁王子殿下的关心和支持，也离不开贵校全体教职员工及同学们的共同努力和辛勤付出。我谨对此表示衷心的祝贺！

---

* 在英国哈德斯菲尔德大学毕业典礼上的演讲。2018年7月9日，英国哈德斯菲尔德大学。

第三章　教育交流　　　229

这是分享友谊的时刻。近年来，中英教育交流合作成果丰硕，成为两国关系的一大亮点。贵校在对华交往合作方面不断迈上新台阶，为促进中英教育交流与合作做出积极贡献。现在，1000多名中国学生在贵校就读。贵校已与中国100多所大学建立校际合作关系，与数十家教育、文化、媒体等机构开展多种形式合作，2018年计划在华再开设一所分校。尤其令人感动的是，贵校还是在中国大陆第一所捐助希望小学的外国大学。

这是憧憬未来的时刻。变革创新是推动人类社会不断向前发展的不竭动力。当今世界，变革创新大潮涌动，中英创新合作潜力巨大。中国正在实施"大众创业、万众创新"的创新驱动发展战略，为扩大国际创新合作提供了广阔的市场、充沛的资本和人才机遇。约克公爵安德鲁王子殿下2014年创办的"龙门创将"项目顺应世界变革创新的潮流，推动全球创新创业产业快速发展。前不久，王子殿下赴华参加第二届"龙门创将"全球创新创业大赛中国区总决赛，进一步提升了该项目在华知名度和影响力。我衷心希望在双方共同努力下，中英创新合作不断取得新成果，为两国发展开创更加美好的未来。

同学们，

今天既是你们的毕业典礼，也是你们迈进社会大学的开学典礼，具有重要意义。在这个时刻，我给大家提三点希望。

第一，要以开放包容的态度拥抱世界。当今世界正处于百年未有之大变局，国际形势深刻演变。和平与发展仍是时代的主题，但是全球单边主义、保护主义、排外主义思潮上升，贸易战阴云笼罩。人类面临是开放还是封闭、是前进还是倒退、是唯我独尊还是互利共赢的重大抉择。历史发展规律和经验一再证明，开放带来进步，封闭必然落后，合作才能共赢。世界已成为你中有我、我中有你的命运共同体，只有推进互联互通、加快融合发展，才能促进共同繁荣，增进人类福祉；只有坚持兼容并蓄、和而不同，才能促进文明交流互鉴，增进各国人民友谊。与此相反，若一味妄自尊大、以邻为壑，则只会四处碰壁、害人害己。希望大家能把握历史前进大势，积极为全球开放合作、交流互鉴贡献"正能量"。

第二，要以与时俱进的眼光看待中国。2018 年是中国改革开放 40 周年。40 年来，中国人民成功走出一条中国特色社会主义道路，不仅自身面貌发生了翻天覆地的变化，还为世界经济增长和人类发展事业做出了重要贡献。过去 6 年，中国对世界经济增长平均贡献率超过 30%。展望下一个 40 年，中国将坚持以维护世界和平、促进共同发展为宗旨推动构建人类命运共同体，坚持以相互尊重、合作共赢为基础走和平发展道路，坚持以共商共建共享为原则推动"一带一路"建设，坚持以公平正义为理念引领全球治理体系改革。

第三，要以奋发有为的精神促进合作。今天在座的毕业生中有不少中国学生，你们是 17 万多名在英负笈求学中国学生和学者的代表。当前，两国各领域务实合作稳步推进，中英关系的战略性、务实性、全球性和包容性不断彰显。我衷心希望大家能珍惜时代，脚踏实地，勇当创新创业的弄潮儿，积极投身深化中英友谊与合作的事业，为促进中国与世界各国的交流合作添砖加瓦。

老师们、同学们，

"自古英雄出少年，敢为强者天下先。"青年是中英两国发展的未来，也是中英关系的未来。希望同学们抓住机遇，争做强者，在释放青春激情、追逐青春梦想的过程中书写人生华章，用青春和智慧创造无愧于时代的新业绩，谱写人类命运共同体更加灿烂辉煌的新篇章！

最后，祝愿哈德斯菲尔德大学不断取得新的更大成就！

谢谢！

Devote Your Youthful Vigour to China-UK Cooperation[*]

Vice-Chancellor Bob Cryan,

Deputy Vice-Chancellor Tim Thornton,

Teachers and Students,

Ladies and Gentlemen,

Dear Friends,

Good morning!

It is a real delight to join you at the Graduation Ceremony 2018 of the University of Huddersfield. Let me begin by extending my congratulations to all the graduates on completing your studies and embarking on a new journey to pursue your dream! I would also like to take this opportunity to pay tribute to all the faculty members for your hard work!

Since I became Chinese Ambassador to the UK eight years ago, I have visited many British universities. But this is the first graduation ceremony that I have attended.

Here, looking at so many youthful and eager faces, I know this is a significant moment.

First of all, this is a moment to review what you have achieved.

Huddersfield is one of the universities recognized by the Higher Education Academy (HEA) for excellence in teaching. I have learnt about your remarkable record in education, student satisfaction, internship and career opportunities, faculty training

---

[*] Speech at the Graduation Ceremony of the University of Huddersfield. University of Huddersfield, 9 July 2018.

and joint scientific research, and I admire your educational concepts and humane spirit. It therefore came as no surprise when you were given the HEA's 2017 Global Teaching Excellence Award and ranked highest in student satisfaction by the International Student Barometer this year.

These achievements could not have been possible without the personal care of His Royal Highness the Duke of York, and the hard work of all the faculty members and students. I congratulate you on these achievements!

Second, this is a moment to appreciate the friendship that you have built over the years.

For China and the UK, we have seen fruitful outcomes in educational exchanges in recent years. These are highlights in our overall bilateral relations. The contribution to these highlights by Huddersfield is particularly noteworthy. You are constantly scaling new heights in your cooperation with China.

As of today, Huddersfield is home to over 1,000 Chinese students.

- You have established partnership with over 100 Chinese universities.
- You have carried out various forms of cooperation with dozens of Chinese educational, cultural and media institutions.
- You are about to open another joint campus in China this year.
- What touched me most is that you are the first foreign university to donate to a Hope Primary School on the Chinese Mainland.

Third, this is a moment to embrace changes in your life and welcome a bright future.

Changes provide inexhaustible power for progress. Changes create opportunities. In today's world, the waves of reform and innovation are surging, and this promises great potential for China-UK cooperation.

China has adopted an innovation-driven strategy known as "mass entrepreneurship and innovation". This promises a huge market, abundant capital and capable minds for international cooperation on innovation.

Pitch@Palace founded by His Royal Highness the Duke of York in 2014 has moved along with this global trend of reform and innovation. It is designed to provide innovative industries and start-up businesses with opportunities to succeed. Not long ago, His Royal Highness visited China for the finals of the second Pitch@Palace China. That visit further increased the popularity and influence of this programme in China.

I sincerely hope that with our joint efforts, China-UK cooperation on innovation will bear new fruits and open up a more beautiful future for the development of our two countries.

Dear Students,

Today, while marking your graduation from Huddersfield, we are also celebrating the beginning of your education in another university, the "university of real life". At this significant moment, may I share with you my three hopes.

First, I hope you will embrace the world with an open mind and inclusive attitude.

The world is now undergoing profound changes unseen in a century. The international landscape is changing drastically. Peace and development are still the main theme of our times. But unilateralism, protectionism and xenophobia sentiments are surging, and the dark cloud of trade war is hanging low. The world faces a critical choice between openness and isolation, between progress and retrogression, between dominance and win-win cooperation.

History has showed us time and again that openness brings progress, isolation leads to backwardness and cooperation delivers win-win results. Our world is a community with a shared future, where the interests of all countries are intertwined.

Only with better connectivity and integrated development can we achieve common prosperity and improve the wellbeing of everyone. Only with inclusiveness and harmonious coexistence can we promote mutual learning between civilizations and enhance friendship between the people of all countries. Seeking dominance or adopting a "beggar-thy-neighbor" approach is counterproductive and will only lead to a dead end.

I hope that young graduates like you will seize the trend of the times and become champions of openness, cooperation and mutual learning between countries of the world.

Second, I hope you will open your eyes to a changing China.

This year marks the 40th anniversary of China's reform and opening-up policy. In the past 40 years, the Chinese people have successfully blazed a path of socialism with Chinese characteristics. This has not only brought profound changes to China itself, but also made important contribution to growth and progress in the world. China contributed over 30% to world economic growth every year in the past 6 years.

In the next 40 years,

- China will work with other countries to safeguard world peace and promote common development with a goal of building a community with a shared future for mankind.
- China will keep to the path of peaceful development based on mutual respect and win-win cooperation.
- China will build the Belt and Road Initiative under the principles of extensive consultation, joint contribution and shared benefits.
- And China will take part in the reform of the global governance system guided by the principle of fairness and justice.

Third, I hope you will promote cooperation with an enterprising spirit.

I can see many Chinese faces in the audience. You represent over 170,000 Chinese students and scholars here in Britain and while you are here, you have seen how China-UK relations have grown in the past years.

The overall cooperation between our two countries is making steady progress. We are building an increasingly strategic, practical, global and inclusive relationship.

I sincerely hope that my young Chinese friends will cherish the times, take a down-to-earth approach and dare to be innovative and enterprising. I hope you will devote what you have learned to China-UK friendship and cooperation. I hope I can count on your contribution to the exchanges between China and all the countries in the world.

Dear Teachers and Students,

Every nation looks to its young and daring to lead the way forward. In deed, our young people have in their hands the future of our countries and the future of China-UK relations.

So I hope you will seize the opportunities and aim for excellence. I hope you will give full play to your youthful vigour and intelligence to go after your dreams and achieve great feats that is worthy of our times. I hope you will join hands to write a new and more splendid chapter for a community with a shared future for mankind.

In conclusion, I wish the University of Huddersfield continued progress and greater success.

Thank you!

为中英教育交流合作增光添彩 *

尊敬的英国教育部国务大臣吉布阁下,
尊敬的各位校长、各位老师,
女士们、先生们、朋友们:
大家晚上好!

欢迎大家做客中国大使馆!很高兴在中国传统佳节来临之际,与中英教育界朋友们欢聚一堂,共叙友情,共迎新春。我谨对长期支持两国教育交流合作的各界人士,特别是参与"中英数学教师交流项目"的各位校长、各位老师表示衷心的感谢!

教育是立国之本、兴国之基。教育交流与合作是中英关系的重要组成部分,也奠定了两国关系的民意根基。我对此高度重视,倾注了大量时间和精力,使馆同事们称我为"教育大使",我对这一头衔感到骄傲。对于"中英数学教师交流项目",我认为有三方面的重要意义。

第一,这是促交流、拓合作的品牌项目。近年来,中英教育合作内涵日益丰富,涵盖了从学龄前教育、基础教育到职业教育、高等教育、语言文化交流等广泛领域。"中英数学教师交流项目"应运而生。在短短 4 年里,该项目一路走来,从无到有,从小到大,现在已经成为两国教育合作的一大亮点。双方迄今已互派 5 批中小学教师共 720 多人次,有力地推动两国教育交

---

* 在"中英数学教师交流项目"新年招待会上的讲话。2019 年 1 月 25 日,中国驻英国大使馆。

流合作走深走实。

第二，这是打基础、利长远的互惠平台。数学是十分重要的基础学科，有"学科之母"的美誉。在本次"中英数学教师交流项目"中，有86位上海中小学数学教师来英，90多位英国数学老师前往上海交流。项目紧扣提高教师教学能力的主题，设计了形式灵活、内容丰富的学习研修模式。两国中小学数学老师深入交流、相互学习、切磋技能，直接惠及中英数百所学校及数万名学生，产生了广泛积极影响，为提升两国基础教育水平注入了新动力。

第三，这是增互鉴、促了解的有益实践。文明交流互鉴是不可阻挡的历史潮流，是推动人类文明进步和世界和平发展的重要动力。中国和英国是东西方文明的代表性国家。"中英数学教师交流项目"是中国与西方发达国家开展的首个大规模教师交流项目，对促进东西方文明交流互鉴具有重要意义。我相信，参与该项目的师生在教学和学习的过程中，都能亲身体验彼此的文化，促进互学互鉴，增进了解与友谊。

女士们、先生们，

中国人常说，"百年大计，教育为本；教育大计，教师为本"。这对教育及教师来说，既是一种重视与肯定，也是一份责任与使命。借此机会，我想就"中英数学教师交流项目"未来发展提两点希望。

一是相互学习，共同提高。中英数学教学的理念和方法各有所长。英国作为世界上最早建立现代教育体系的国家，诞生了牛顿、图灵等伟大的数学家。中国古代也产生了刘徽、祖冲之等伟大的数学家，他们对人类科学的贡献，至今仍为我们享用。中英两国教师可以通过数学项目合作相互学习，互通有无，取长补短，共同提高。

二是教书育人，传承友谊。国之交在于民相亲，民相亲在于心相知。中英历史文化、社会制度不同，发展阶段各异，加强交流与沟通尤显重要。2019年是中英建立代办级外交关系65周年，中英关系历经沧桑，不断发展，在很大程度上得益于两国人民之间的密切交往和深厚友谊。青年是国家的未来，也是中英关系的未来。我希望各位老师在传授数学知识的同时，也将友好的种子播种在青年学生的心田，使中英友谊世代相传。

女士们、先生们，

再过 9 天就是中国农历新年猪年。猪在中国文化中象征着财富和吉祥。我希望并相信，新的一年，在双方共同努力下，"中英数学教师交流项目"一定会不断开拓创新、开花结果，为中英教育交流合作增光添彩！

最后，我提议，

为中英关系行稳致远，

为中英教育交流合作不断发展，

为在座的各位朋友猪年吉祥、万事如意，

干杯！

Make Greater Contribution to China-UK Educational Exchanges and Cooperation*

Minister Nick Gibb,

Headmasters,

Teachers,

Ladies and Gentlemen,

Dear Friends,

Good evening, and welcome to the Chinese Embassy!

It is a real delight to invite you all to celebrate the Chinese New Year with us. I would like to begin by extending my heartfelt thanks to all of you. I want to thank you for your support for China-UK educational exchange and cooperation. And I wish to pay particular tribute to the headmasters and teachers who have taken part in the China-UK Mathematics Teacher Exchange Programme.

Education makes a country strong and prosperous. I have personally committed much of my time and efforts to China-UK educational exchange and cooperation. My colleagues at the Embassy call me "Education Ambassador". I am proud of this title because the educational partnership between our two countries is an important part of our bilateral relations. It is also crucial for cementing public support for our bilateral ties.

As far as the China-UK Mathematics Teacher Exchange Programme is concerned, I believe this Programme is significant in the following three aspects.

---

* Speech at the China-UK Mathematics Teacher Exchange Programme Reception. Chinese Embassy, 25 January 2019.

First, it is a signature programme for China-UK educational exchange and cooperation.

In recent years, China-UK educational cooperation has been greatly enriched. It now covers pre-school education, basic education, vocational education, higher education and language training and cultural exchanges.

To meet the increasing need for further cooperation, the China-UK Mathematics Teacher Exchange Programme was launched. In just four years, this Programme has grown from strength to strength. It has now become a highlight in China-UK educational cooperation.

As of today, five visits have been made between the two sides, involving more than 720 primary-school and middle-school teachers. This helps deepen and enrich the educational partnership between our two countries.

Second, this Programme is a mutually-beneficial platform that helps students strengthen the foundation for long-term academic achievements.

Mathematics, known as the "mother of all sciences", is an important and basic academic discipline.

In recent exchanges under this Programme, 86 math teachers from Shanghai came to Britain and more than 90 British math teachers went to Shanghai. Focusing on improving their teaching ability, these teachers took part in various forms of learning and training. They had in-depth discussions, learned a great deal from each other and improved teaching skills.

This has been hugely influential. It has brought direct benefits to hundreds of schools and tens of thousands of students in both our countries. It has given a fresh boost to our basic education.

Third, this Programme is a useful experiment that enhances mutual learning and mutual understanding.

Exchange and mutual learning between different civilizations are the irreversible trend of history. These are the sources for human progress as well as world peace and development.

China and the UK are both great civilizations. As the first large-scale teacher exchange programme between China and a Western developed country, this Programme is of great significance to enhancing exchanges and mutual learning between China and the West.

I am sure that, by teaching and learning together, the teachers and students participating in this Programme could have a better understanding of each other's culture and forge a deeper friendship.

Ladies and Gentlemen,

The Chinese people often say, "If you plan for one hundred years, educate the children." "If you make a plan for education, begin with the teachers." These words underline the importance we attach to education and teachers. These words also highlight the great responsibility and glorious mission.

Now, as we anticipate greater progress in the China-UK Mathematics Teacher Exchange Programme, I would like to share with you my two hopes.

First, learn from each other and improve teaching skill.

China and the UK have respective strengths in math teaching ideas and practice. The UK is the world's first country to establish a modern education system. It is home to great mathematicians such as Isaac Newton and Alan Turing. China has its great mathematicians such as Liu Hui and Zu Chongzhi. Their contribution to the world of science has enduring influence today.

I hope that through this Programme, our teachers could learn from each other to complement the strengths of our two countries and achieve common progress.

Second, educate our young people and build closer friendship between our two countries.

State-to-state relations hinge upon close people-to-people exchanges and heart-to-heart communication. China and the UK differ in history, culture and social system. We are at different stages of development. This makes it all the more important for us to enhance exchanges and communication.

This year marks the 65th anniversary of China-UK diplomatic relationship at the chargé d'affaires level. Over the years, China-UK relations have continued to grow despite twists and turns. And the reason for this lies, to a large extent, in the close exchanges and deep friendship between our two peoples.

Young people are the future of our two countries. They are also the future of China-UK relations. Therefore, I hope that when you teach math, you will at the same time sow the seeds of friendship in the hearts of our young students. This will help pass our friendship from generation to generation.

Ladies and Gentlemen,

In just nine days, we will be celebrating the Chinese New Year of the Pig. In the Chinese culture, pig symbolizes good fortune and happiness.

I hope and believe that, in this auspicious new year, with concerted efforts from both sides, the China-UK Mathematics Teacher Exchange Programme will explore new fronts, bear new fruits and make new contribution to China-UK educational exchange and cooperation!

Now may I invite you to join me in a toast:

To the steady and sustained development of China-UK relations,

To continued progress in China-UK educational cooperation,

To a happy and prosperous Year of the Pig for all of you present today.

Cheers!

第四章　孔子学院
PART Ⅳ　Confucius Institutes

语言教学与合作是中英教育交流的重要内容，孔子学院在其中发挥了重要作用，它不仅促进了中英教育文化交流，而且在传播中国语言文化、增进英国民众对中国的了解、深化两国人民友谊方面起到了独特作用。

英国是拥有孔子学院和孔子课堂最多的欧洲国家，目前共有30所孔子学院，164间孔子课堂。在英国，孔子学院均建在大学，向大学生和社会各界人士教授汉语和介绍中国文化，而孔子课堂大都建在中小学。全英每年约有20万人在孔子学院和孔子课堂学习，约有170万人次参加孔子学院和孔子课堂开展的各类文化活动。

在担任中国驻英大使期间，我多次出席孔子学院和孔子课堂的揭牌仪式，其中有两次给我留下了深刻印象：一次是"规格最高"的，另一次是"学校最小"的。

"规格最高"的一次是我陪同英国王储查尔斯为威尔士兰德福瑞公学的孔子课堂揭牌。英国王储又叫威尔士亲王，这个封号起源于1301年英王爱德华一世征服威尔士后，爱德华一世将他的长子、王位继承人封为威尔士亲王。从此，历任英国王储都与威尔士结下了不解之缘。此次查尔斯王储亲自为威尔士兰德福瑞公学的孔子课堂揭牌，体现了他的高度重视，因为这是威尔士第一所孔子课堂。这也是迄今为止英国孔子学院和孔子课堂最高规格的揭牌仪式，这在其他西方国家也是不多见的。

"学校最小"的揭牌仪式是在苏格兰中耶尔中学，它位于英国领土最北端的设得兰群岛，该群岛也是地球最偏远的群岛之一，散落在苏格兰以北210千米的海洋上，由15个有人居住的岛屿和100多个无人居住的荒岛组成。我经过两次转机、一次渡轮，登上设得兰群岛的第二大岛耶尔岛（人口仅1000人左右），为该岛中耶尔中学的孔子课堂揭牌（全校只有100名学生）。这是我访问过的最小的学校，我不仅成为第一位登岛的中国大使，也是第一位登岛的外国驻英使节。许多人问，为什么中国大使千里迢迢为一个偏僻的中学孔子课堂揭牌？我告诉他们，中耶尔中学校长劳森给我写了一封非常感人的信。他曾随旅游团访华，中国之行给他留下了深刻的印象。他看到了一个充满活力的国家，他认为中国代表了21世纪，只要学会了汉语，就等于掌握了打开21世纪大门的钥匙。因此他希望他的学生学习汉语，也希望能得到我的帮助，为他们开办一间孔子课堂。我很受感动。虽然学校小，距离远，交通不便，但它代表了中英关系的未来，因此我决定前往。此行我把中国文化传播到英国最遥远、最偏僻的地方，把中英友谊的种子播撒到了孩子们的心田。

Language teaching and cooperation are key aspects of China-UK educational exchanges, with Confucius Institutes playing a vital role. These institutes not only promote educational and cultural exchanges between China and the UK, but also enhance the understanding of Chinese language and culture among the British public and deepen the friendship between the peoples of our two countries.

The UK has the most Confucius Institutes and Confucius Classrooms in Europe, with 30 Confucius Institutes and 164 Confucius Classrooms. Confucius Institutes in the UK are established in universities, teaching Chinese and introducing Chinese culture to university students and the general public, while Confucius Classrooms are mostly set up in primary and secondary schools. Each year, approximately 200,000 people study at Confucius Institutes and Confucius Classrooms in the UK, with around 1.7 million people participating in various cultural activities organized by these institutes.

During my tenure as the Chinese Ambassador to the UK, I attended many unveiling ceremonies for Confucius Institutes and Confucius Classrooms. Two events left me the deepest impression: The "highest-profile" and the "smallest school".

The "highest-profile" event was when I accompanied Prince Charles, The Prince of Wales to unveil the Confucius Classroom at Llandovery College in Wales. The title "Prince of Wales" dates back to 1301 when Edward I of England invested his eldest son, the heir to the throne, after conquering Wales. Since then, successive holders of this title have had an indelible connection with Wales. Charles's unveiling of the first Confucius Classroom in Wales in person underscored his high regard for it. This remains the highest-profile unveiling ceremony for Confucius Institutes and Confucius Classrooms in the UK, and such high-level participation is rare in other Western countries.

The "smallest school" event was at Mid Yell Junior High School in Scotland, located in the Shetland Islands, the northernmost part of British territory and one of the most remote archipelagos on the earth. I had to take two flights and a ferry to reach Yell Island, the second-largest island in the Shetlands with a population of about 1,000, to unveil the Confucius Classroom at the school, which has only 100 students. This was the smallest school I had visited, and I was the first Chinese Ambassador and the first foreign envoy to the UK to visit the island. Many people asked why the Chinese Ambassador would travel so far to unveil a Confucius Classroom at a remote school. I told them that Mid Yell Junior High School's principal, Lawson, had written me a very moving letter. He had visited China with a tour group, and the trip left a profound impression on him. He saw a vibrant country which represented the 21st century and believed that learning Chinese was commanding the key to the 21st century. He hoped his students could learn Chinese and sought my help in establishing a Confucius Classroom. I was deeply touched. Despite the school's small size, remote location, and inconvenient travel, it represented the future of China-UK relations. So I decided to go. This trip brought Chinese culture to the most remote and far-flung part of the UK, and planted the seeds of China-UK friendship in the hearts of the children.

学习语言，传承友谊[*]

尊敬的英国王储查尔斯殿下，
尊敬的威尔士三一圣大卫大学校长休斯先生，
尊敬的兰德福瑞公学董事会主席盖洛普先生，
尊敬的兰德福瑞公学校长亨特先生，
各位来宾，
老师们、同学们：

很高兴有机会访问兰德福瑞公学，感谢同学们刚才精彩的演出。

今天是一个大喜的日子。首先，今天是威尔士最重要的节日——圣大卫节。其次，就在163年前的今天，兰德福瑞公学正式成立。最后，今天也是一个新的纪念日，因为兰德福瑞公学孔子课堂在今天正式揭牌，并且由威尔士亲王殿下亲自揭牌。我对亲王殿下热心支持汉语教学和中英文化交流表示衷心的感谢。

同学们可能会问，为什么叫作孔子课堂？我想告诉大家，因为孔子是中国古代伟大的思想家和教育家，是中华文化最具代表性的人物之一。孔子主张的和谐、仁爱、德治等政治社会思想至今仍富有现实意义，他提倡的"三人行必有我师""温故知新""学而不思则罔，思而不学则殆"等教育思想对同学们的学习也具有启发性。

---

[*] 在威尔士兰德福瑞公学孔子课堂揭牌仪式上的讲话。2011年3月1日，威尔士兰德福瑞公学。

孔子课堂的作用是什么？大家可能首先想到的是教学中文。没错，目前在英国，"汉语热"持续升温，已经有13所孔子学院和54间孔子课堂。孔子课堂配备专业的中文老师、适宜的教材，大家可以学到标准的中文。

学习一门外语，不仅是学习语言本身，也是在了解一个国家。威尔士有一句名言："没有语言的民族是没有思想的民族。"由此，我们也可推出另一个结论：只有学习一国的语言，才能真正了解这个国家，了解这个国家的人民，了解这个国家的思想。中国是一个值得你们了解的国家，因为它既古老，具有五千年的文明历史和深厚的文化底蕴；又现代，它的经济和社会正在飞速发展，中华民族正在实现伟大复兴。

对于同学们来说，学习中文还有另外一层意义：你们是国家的未来，也是中英友谊的未来，你们今天学习好中文，明天就可以成为中英友谊的传承人和中英合作的促进者，为我们两个伟大国家的共同发展与繁荣做出贡献。

最后，祝同学们在兔年"兔"（突）飞猛进，取得新的更大进步！

谢谢！

Study Language, Promote Friendship[*]

Your Royal Highness,
Professor Medwin Hughes,
Mr Ian Gallop,
Mr Ian Hunt,
Distinguished Guests,
Teachers and Students,

It is a great pleasure for me to visit Llandovery College. Thank you, boys and girls, for your wonderful performance.

Today is a most memorable day for many reasons. It is first and foremost St David's Day, the most important festival of Wales. Today is the 163rd anniversary of the founding of Llandovery College. Today we also have the honour of attending the official unveiling of the Confucius Classroom by His Royal Highness. I would like to sincerely thank His Royal Highness once again for his personal support for Mandarin teaching in Britain and for China-Britain cultural exchanges.

Many of you may wonder how Confucius Classrooms got their name. They were named after Confucius, a great thinker and educator in ancient China. He was an enormous influence on the Chinese civilization. Many of his political and social values, such as harmony, benevolence and rule by virtue, are still relevant today. He also left behind many popular sayings that have guided the Chinese people for thousands of years. The following quotes are just a few examples: "In any group of three people,

---

[*] Remarks at the Official Unveiling of the Confucius Classroom in Llandovery College. Llandovery, Wales, 1 March 2011.

there must be someone to learn from"; "Review what you have learnt, and you shall gain new knowledge"; "Learn without thinking, one will be lost. Think without learning, one will not get far."

Then what can we expect from the Confucius Classroom? Learning Mandarin is one obvious answer. Thanks to the emerging "Mandarin fever" in Britain, 13 Confucius Institutes and 54 Confucius Classrooms have come into being. These classrooms are equipped with professional teachers and easy to use teaching materials. They are the places for learning good Mandarin courses.

On the other hand, learning a language is not just about the language itself. It is also about understanding a country. As a Welsh proverb goes, "Cenedl heb iaith, cenedl heb galon."(A nation without a language is a nation without a heart.) To really understand a country, its people and its way of thinking, one must learn the language. There is a lot to learn about China. China is an ancient country, with a 5,000-year civilisation and rich culture. China is also a modern country with fast economic and social progress. It has embarked on the road of rejuvenation.

For you, boys and girls, learning Mandarin is also important because you represent the future of your country and the future of China-UK friendship. With a good command of Mandarin, you will be better equipped for taking China-UK friendship and cooperation forward. We count on you to contribute to the development and prosperity of our two great countries.

In closing, boys and girls, I wish all of you ever greater progress in the Year of the Rabbit!

Thank you!

为"汉语热"助阵 *

尊敬的英国议会下院副议长林赛·霍伊尔先生，
尊敬的英国议会跨党派中国小组主席马克·亨德里克先生，
尊敬的伦敦南岸大学校长马丁·艾尔维克教授，
女士们、先生们：

很高兴出席全英孔子学院大会，与全英国从事汉语教学和支持汉语教学的院长和校长们齐聚一堂。首先，我要感谢此次会议的主办方——英国议会跨党派中国小组和伦敦南岸大学，使此次会议能在英国议会保得利大厦这样一个特殊的地点举行。同时，我也要感谢中国国家汉办多年来对在英推广汉语的重视和支持。

我出任中国驻英国大使已一年半有余，出席过中英之间举办的各种文化活动，其中有关汉语推广、孔子学院和孔子课堂的活动，我不仅有请必到，而且优先参加。

2010年3月我刚到任时，参加的第一场公众活动是第九届"汉语桥"世界大学生中文比赛英国区预选赛，随后我参加了第二届欧洲孔子学院联席会议，不久后为伦敦圣玛丽小学孔子课堂揭牌。2011年1月，我陪同到访的李克强副总理会见了英国汉语学习爱好者；3月，我同查尔斯王储一同出席了威尔士兰德福瑞公学孔子课堂的揭牌仪式；当月，我出席了第十届"汉语桥"世界大学生中文比赛英国区预选赛。今天，我出席全英孔子学院大会；

---

* 在全英孔子学院大会上的讲话。2011年9月14日，英国议会保得利大厦。

后天，我还要在中国驻英国大使馆为历届参加"汉语桥"比赛的英国选手及老师、亲友举行招待会，祝贺他们在比赛中接连取得优异成绩。

为什么我这么重视汉语在英国的推广？我想，原因有三个。

第一，汉语是中国最精美、最畅销的文化产品。许多来英国访问的中国代表团曾问我，英国目前最大宗出口产品是什么？我告诉他们：英语。全球正在学习英语的人口数量约为10亿，另有15亿～20亿人口每天使用、接触英语。而汉语是全世界母语人口最多的语言，使用人数超过10亿，汉语代表着5000年来一直延绵不断的文明——中华文明。令人高兴的是，随着中国的全面发展及影响力扩大，现在全球有4000多万人学习汉语，孔子学院经过近6年从无到有的跨越式发展，全球数量超过300所，注册学员达到36万人。汉语正在成为中国增长最快、影响最大的对外文化产品和交流工具。

第二，汉语是了解当代中国的最直接、最有效的钥匙。当代中国，发展日新月异，进步包罗万象，如果仅从英国当地媒体的视角认识中国，难免管中窥豹，甚至被一些偏见误导。但是，如果借由汉语这一门径，就能透过语言，认识当代中国社会的方方面面，由表及里，从外至内。所以，了解中国，自汉语始。孔子学院和孔子课堂应时应需，在全球建立了合作开展汉语教学的专业场所，提供了非营利性的、获得广泛认可和赞誉的优质平台。

第三，汉语学习和交流是当前中英关系中最热门、最活跃的领域。我很高兴看到英国"汉语热"不断升温，无论是工商精英，还是年青一代，甚至是冲龄幼童，都在积极学习汉语，总人数超过10万，正合孔子的一句名言："有教无类。"

在我7月底回国述职前，英国有13所孔子学院和54间孔子课堂；而当我上周回到伦敦时，这组数字增长到17所孔子学院和57间孔子课堂，继续在欧洲名列第一。现在，全英各地包括英格兰、苏格兰、威尔士和北爱尔兰都已设有孔子学院，布局全面、合理。英国的孔子学院和孔子课堂培养出一大批精通汉语、了解中国文化、热爱中国的优秀人才，他们在"汉语桥"比赛中表现出色，在增进两国交流和理解方面作用突出。

近年来，中国领导人在访英期间，经常参观孔子学院或会见英国青年汉语学习爱好者，活动成为访问中的突出亮点。两国政府教育部门也全力推动，2010年签署了在英开展汉语教学的框架合作协议，决心促进提升在英汉语教学水平和提供更多资源便利。我赞赏英国议会跨党派中国小组同样热心支持在英汉语教学，特意参与主办此次会议。作为中国大使，我乐见"汉语热"持续升温，也愿继续为它添火助阵。

本次会议的一大主题是"在英孔子学院的可持续发展"。我认为，这一讨论在当前阶段尤为必要和重要。当前孔子学院建设速度很快，取得很大成绩，树立了良好的品牌。在此大好形势下，我们应保持头脑冷静，调整发展思路，转变工作重点，重视提升教学质量，注重资源共享，加强经验交流，强化当地师资培养，借重教学新科技和新方式，不断固本强基，开拓创新，使在英汉语教学走上一条可持续发展道路。

最后，祝本次会议圆满成功，祝在英孔子学院和孔子课堂的发展更上一层楼！

谢谢！

Add to the Momentum of Rising Demand for Mandarin[*]

Mr Lindsay Hoyle,

Mr Mark Hendrick,

Professor Martin Earwicker,

Ladies and Gentlemen,

It's a real delight for me to be with you again today.

Let me first express my warm thanks to the organisers of the UK Confucius Institute National Conference. These are the All Party Parliamentary China Group and London South Bank University. It is your support that has brought the conference to such a distinguished and unique location, the British Parliament.

My thanks also go to Hanban for leading the effort for Mandarin promotion in Britain.

In my first 18 months in the UK, I have attended many cultural activities. Among them, events related to Mandarin promotion, Confucius Institutes and Confucius Classrooms have always been a priority for me. Whenever my schedule allows, I will always turn up and take part.

In fact, the first event I attended as Chinese Ambassador to the UK was the UK Regional Preliminary for the 9th "Chinese Bridge" Competition. As you may know, this is a highly successful global contest organised by Hanban.

Then last September, I spoke at the Second Joint Conference of European Confucius

---

[*] Speech at the UK Confucius Institute National Conference. Portcullis House, London, 14 September 2011.

Institutes.

Shortly afterwards, I unveiled the Confucius Classroom at the St Mary's Primary School.

When Vice Premier Li Keqiang was here on an official visit this past January, I was with him at an exchange with British students learning Mandarin.

Two months later, I joined His Royal Highness the Prince of Wales at the official unveiling of the Confucius Classroom at Llandovery College in Wales.

The same month, I attended the UK Regional Preliminary for the 10th "Chinese Bridge" Competition.

In two days time I will be giving a reception at our Embassy for the UK contestants in the "Chinese Bridge" Competitions. They will be joined by their teachers and families.

That will be another occasion for us to celebrate the outstanding performances of these young British contestants. It is a proud symbol of the success in Mandarin teaching in this country.

You may now be asking: Why is the Chinese Ambassador devoting so much time on Mandarin promotion in the UK?

There are three reasons. Let me take each in turn.

First, Mandarin is at the very core of Chinese culture and civilization. It is one of the most popular cultural products of China.

So if China is to be truly understood and integrated with the world, we must promote the learning of Mandarin.

One question put to me by many visiting Chinese delegations is this: "What does Britain sell most to the rest of the world?"

I respond: "That must be English."

Let me give you some compelling statistics. Today, roughly 1 billion people are learning English worldwide. An additional 1.5 to 2 billion are speaking or exposed to English every day.

In contrast, Mandarin is spoken by over 1 billion users. This means Mandarin has more native speakers than any other language.

More importantly, Mandarin is part of the very "DNA" of Chinese civilisation, the core building block of Chinese culture. China is the longest continuous civilisation in the world. Mandarin has been an integral part of the development of China for the past five millennia.

Coming back to the language statistics, Mandarin now has more than 40 million learners across the globe. This is a key trend for the people of the world outside China to truly grasp the depth and breadth of Chinese culture and civilization.

One powerful example of Mandarin's growing popularity is the Confucius Institutes initiative.

Confucius Institutes started from scratch six years ago. No one then could have imagined how far this initiative could come in so short a time. Today, global numbers are over 300. There are 360,000 registered students benefiting from its language teaching programmes.

Mandarin is now well on its way to become China's fastest-growing cultural export and means of communication.

The second reason I devote so much time to this vital effort is this: Mandarin is the most effective key to understanding today's China.

As you may be aware, the development of China is moving very quickly. In China today many aspects, such as cities, can change beyond recognition in a short period of time.

If one relies on British media coverage and journalists perspectives alone, he will fail to understand the larger picture of my country, or even be influenced by biased and misguided reports.

This lack of reporting and analysis means it is vital to equip young British people with Mandarin skills. By being able to speak Mandarin, the youth of Britain can go and explore China themselves. They can then learn first hand the reality of my country today. Mandarin offers a path to grasp all facets of the Chinese society, from outside to inside. So understanding China truly starts from Mandarin.

The Confucius Institutes and Confucius Classrooms couldn't come at a better time. They have offered high-quality venues around the world for Mandarin teaching and learning. In turn they have created non-profit and excellent platforms that have earned wide recognition and respect.

My third reason for devoting time to Mandarin learning is its role in China-UK relations. From my visits to many Confucius Institutes and Classrooms I have seen the evidence that here is the most dynamic and vibrant core of Sino-UK cultural exchanges.

Such eagerness to learn Mandarin is shown by so many people. Business leaders, young people and even children: Overall more than 100,000 Britons are learning Mandarin. What is happening now can be best described by a well-known observation of Confucius. That is: "Education is for all."

At the end of July when I left Britain for consultations back home, I had noted that there were 13 Confucius Institutes and 54 Confucius Classrooms in Britain. When I returned to London last week, I was told their numbers had jumped to 17 and 57 respectively. I am delighted to note that these figures mean Britain will remain in the pole position across Europe in developing Mandarin education.

Today, Confucius Institutes and Confucius Classrooms now reach out across all parts of Britain. They have spread around England, Scotland, Wales and Northern Ireland.

This movement is already having results. Confucius Institutes and Confucius Classrooms have educated and trained a large number of students. These pupils now speak Mandarin and as a result better understand Chinese culture and appreciate my country.

Some of these students have done extraordinarily well in the global "Chinese Bridge" Competition. In turn these contestants have now become active in boosting cultural exchanges and building understanding between our two nations.

In recent years, Chinese leaders coming to Britain have made frequent visits to Confucius Institutes and met with young Mandarin learners. These visits reflect strong high-level support for the further advance of Mandarin teaching.

As a result the government education departments of both our countries are giving a big push to Mandarin teaching. One recent development was last year's signing of a Sino-UK government framework cooperation agreement. The objective is to provide higher quality Mandarin education and more resources in support of such programmes.

I highly appreciate the All Party Parliamentary China Group warmly supporting such teaching programs and co-hosting today's conference. As Chinese Ambassador, I hope this rising demand for Mandarin will become an even stronger force. I will do everything I can to add to its momentum.

Your theme for this conference is "The Sustainable Development of Confucius

Institutes in Britain". I fully support the choice of this theme. It is a vital and necessary task to ensure there are solid foundations that will last for all time.

Of course, we have every reason to be proud of the achievements to date. New Confucius Institutes are being created quickly. All around the world they have made a big difference to Mandarin teaching outside of China. And the plan to create a global network has been largely successful.

As you explore the theme of this conference, I would encourage deep thinking and analysis. We should never stop searching for better approaches to promote the development of Confucius Institutes.

More needs to be done to raise teaching standards, and promote sharing of resources and the spread of best practices.

In addition, we need to put more efforts in training local teachers. Then there is the use of new techniques and methodologies to make Mandarin teaching more productive.

So I encourage you in this conference to build on the success and bring forward a new vision for the future. I believe that this is the only way we can set Mandarin education in Britain on a sustainable course.

In closing, I wish this conference a great success!

Thank you!

中英、中欧合作结硕果 *

尊敬的苏格兰首席部长萨蒙德先生，
尊敬的爱丁堡大学校长蒂莫西·奥谢爵士，
各位中欧大学校长、孔子学院院长：

非常高兴出席在爱丁堡大学苏格兰孔子学院召开的 2012 年欧洲地区部分孔子学院联席会议。

这是我第二次出席欧洲孔子学院联席会议。中国有一句俗语："一回生，二回熟。"可以说我与今天大多数与会者已经是熟人了。同时，我也看到一些新面孔，这说明在短短不到两年的时间里，欧洲的孔子学院、孔子课堂又增加了许多新成员。以英国为例，我上次出席会议的时候，英国建立了 12 所孔子学院和 53 间孔子课堂；而今天，这组数字已经增长到 20 所孔子学院和 63 间孔子课堂。我相信下次再出席这个会议的时候，数字还会增长，因为据我所知，英国还有 20 多所大学在"排队"，它们已经提出申请并正在积极筹备，希望能早日开设孔子学院。

当前孔子学院的建设，得到了来自欧洲的各个大学，以及政府层面的大力支持。2012 年 4 月，中欧和中英都建立了高级别人文交流机制，其目的就是促进两国在教育、文化、科技和青年等领域的交流与合作。在首次交流对话中，中欧、中英双方明确将语言合作作为增进人文交流的一个重要手段，

---

* 在 2012 年欧洲地区部分孔子学院联席会议开幕式上的讲话。2012 年 6 月 6 日，爱丁堡大学苏格兰孔子学院，苏格兰。

支持加强汉语教学合作。

苏格兰地方政府对孔子学院也是鼎力支持，特别是萨蒙德首席部长本人。2011年，他曾亲自参加格拉斯哥大学孔子学院的揭牌仪式。2012年，他亲临此次欧洲孔子学院联席会议的会场，刚才发表了热情洋溢的讲话。

孔子学院和孔子课堂发展形势很好，但我们必须保持"两个清醒"。

我们必须清醒地认识到孔子学院的发展不是一朝一夕的事，而是一个长期任务。当前，孔子学院的发展正从数量向质量转变，由快速成长向可持续发展演进。这就更加需要提升管理水平，强化本土教师培养，注重资源共享，加强经验交流，从而不断提升教学质量，培养更多、更优秀的学生。我很高兴地看到，本次会议主题侧重于欧洲孔子学院的发展、评估和评价以及新汉学国际研究计划。这样的横向交流非常有必要，因为只有交流才会促进共同进步。

同时，我们也必须清醒地认识到，孔子学院的发展并非没有挑战。一些人因孔子学院的快速发展感到不安。他们抓着陈旧的冷战思维不放，指责孔子学院是中国的"国家宣传工具"，教学汉语是在搞"意识形态渗透"。因此，他们不时在西方报纸上发表一些不负责任的言论。这就需要孔子学院和孔子课堂的院长们、校长们站出来讲话，因为你们最有发言权。

我希望你们告诉欧洲的公众，孔子学院是中英、中欧共同办学、合作办学，适应当前欧洲对汉语学习的巨大需求，有助于中英、中欧在文化、教育、经贸等各领域开展合作，有利于增进中英、中欧之间民众特别是年青一代的相互了解，能为中英、中欧关系的长远发展奠定良好的基础。我相信，任何了解孔子学院和孔子课堂办学模式、教学内容和教学成果的人，都会支持孔子学院，都会支持这一中英、中欧合作的成果。

最后，我衷心祝愿欧洲孔子学院和孔子课堂健康发展，为增进中英、中欧人民之间的了解和友谊，为促进中英、中欧关系的全面发展做出更大贡献。

预祝会议取得圆满成功！

谢谢！

Fruits of China-UK and China-Europe Cooperation[*]

First Minister Salmond,

Professor Sir Timothy O'Shea,

Principals and Chancellors,

Directors of Confucius Institutes,

It is a delight for me to attend the Joint Conference of European Confucius Institutes.

I congratulate the Confucius Institute for Scotland in the University of Edinburgh for hosting this important event.

This is the second time I have attended a joint conference of European Confucius Institutes. I can say most of you present here are my "old friends", because there is a Chinese saying: "first time, strangers; second time, old friends."

I also see some new faces. This shows in less than two years, the family of Confucius Institutes and Confucius Classrooms in Europe has gained many new members.

Take Britain as an example. When I attended the 2010 conference, there were 12 Confucius Institutes and 53 Confucius Classrooms. Today, the figures have respectively increased to 20 and 63. I have no doubt that when I meet you again at the next conference, the number will be even more impressive!

As far as I know, more than 20 other British Universities are already waiting to set up Confucius Institutes. They have made their applications and are making relevant

---

[*] Speech at the Opening Session of the Joint Conference of European Confucius Institutes. Confucius Institute for Scotland, Scotland, 6 June 2012.

preparations. They all hope Confucius Institutes will be open in their universities at an early date.

Apart from immense interest from universities in the UK and other European countries, Confucius Institutes have been given great support at government level.

In April, High-Level People-to-People Dialogue Mechanism were launched between China and the UK and between China and the EU. They were designed to promote exchanges and cooperation in education, culture, science and technology and youth affairs.

In the first dialogues, all sides agreed language cooperation was an important means to strengthen people-to-people links. All parties pledged more support for cooperation in Mandarin teaching.

The government of Scotland is also a strong supporter of Confucius Institutes, especially First Minister Salmond. Last year he attended the launch of Confucius Institute in the University of Glasgow. This year, he joins us again at this Joint Conference of European Confucius Institutes. Just a few minutes ago, he delivered a very warm speech.

These are all very positive trends. Yet we must have awareness on two issues.

First, we must be aware that the development of Confucius Institutes is not a one-off easy effort. It is a long task. Now the development of Confucius Institutes is shifting from growth in numbers to improvement in quality. The current trend is turning from rapid growth to sustainable development. This requires us to do the following:

- Improve management.
- Strengthen training of local teachers.
- Share resources and experience.
- Raise teaching quality.
- And produce more and better students.

I am glad that this conference has a focus on two areas:

- "Assessment and future development" of European Confucius Institutes.
- And the Neo-Sinology International Research Plan.

Dialogue on these topics is an essential step on the road to winning higher quality and sustainability. Only exchanges will lead to progress.

Turning to my second awareness point. We must also be aware that development of Confucius Institutes is not without challenges.

Some people are not comfortable to see the rapid growth of Confucius Institutes.

- They cling to the outdated Cold War mentality.
- They criticize Confucius Institutes for being a tool of China's "national propaganda".
- They label teaching Mandarin "ideological infiltration".
- So they have from time to time made irresponsible remarks in Western media against Confucius Institutes.

All these require you, Heads of Confucius Institutes and Confucius Classrooms, to make your case and tell your stories. You are in the best position to speak.

I hope you will tell the general public in Britain and around Europe the following messages:

- Confucius Institutes are jointly run by China and Britain, and by China and Europe.
- Confucius Institutes are there to meet the huge demand for learning Chinese language in Britain and Europe.
- Confucius Institutes facilitate China-UK and China-EU cooperation in culture, education, economy and many other fields.
- Confucius Institutes help promote mutual understanding between peoples of China, Britain and Europe, especially young people.
- Confucius Institutes aim to lay a good foundation for future development of China-UK and China-EU relations.

I believe anyone who knows the operation model, curriculum and teaching achievements of Confucius Institutes and Confucius Classrooms will support this collaboration of China and Britain and China and Europe.

I wish Confucius Institutes and Confucius Classrooms in Europe sound and sustainable growth.

I hope they will make a greater contribution to deeper understanding and friendship between Chinese, British and European peoples.

I also believe Confucius Institutes and Confucius Classrooms have a key role to play in building comprehensive development of China-UK and China-EU relations.

In conclusion, I wish this conference a great success!

Thank you!

拿起手中"魔法棒",谱写中英关系新篇章*

尊敬的苏格兰中耶尔中学校长劳森先生,
尊敬的苏格兰设得兰群岛议会主席贝尔先生,
尊敬的苏格兰国家语言中心主任马珍娜女士,
老师们、同学们,
女士们、先生们、朋友们:
大家上午好!

很高兴在春暖花开的季节来到风景秀美的耶尔岛,为中耶尔中学孔子课堂揭牌。我谨代表中国驻英国大使馆向中耶尔中学表示热烈祝贺!对苏格兰中小学孔子学院和中耶尔中学老师们的辛勤付出表示衷心的感谢!

中国古人说,"志之所趋,无远弗届。穷山距海,不能限也",意思是求学之路虽然充满艰辛,但只要秉持坚韧不拔、锲而不舍的精神,就能超越山海所限,达到成功的彼岸。

7年前,我曾与英国王储查尔斯王子共同为位于英国西南部的威尔士兰德福瑞公学孔子课堂揭牌。今天,我又来到苏格兰北部设得兰群岛的耶尔岛,为全英最北端的孔子课堂揭牌。无论在哪里,我都能深深体会到英国学生学习中文的热情和求学致知的渴望,感受到"中文热"正跨越时空、超越山海,火遍英伦。

---

* 在苏格兰中耶尔中学孔子课堂揭牌仪式上的讲话。2018年5月1日,设得兰群岛中耶尔中学,苏格兰。

春天是万物生长的季节。英国的中文教育正处在这样一个季节，英国的孔子学院和孔子课堂正迎来一个美好的春天。

8年前，在我刚刚出任中国驻英国大使时，英国只有11所孔子学院和47间孔子课堂。如今，全英共开设29所孔子学院和156间孔子课堂。仅2017年，全英就有16万人在孔子学院和孔子课堂学习，各孔子学院共开展了4074场文化活动，参与人数达到102万人。放眼全球，截至2017年底，已经有146个国家和地区建立了525所孔子学院和1113间孔子课堂，各类学员累计达916万人，相当于欧洲一个中等国家的人口规模。孔子学院和孔子课堂的蓬勃发展是中英汉语教学合作的一个经典缩影。

很多同学也许会问：为什么这么多人愿意学习中文？为什么孔子学院和孔子课堂在英国这么受欢迎？我的答案是：中文是一种神奇的力量，就像哈利·波特手中的"魔法棒"。

拿起这个"魔法棒"，你将能弥补浅尝辄止的遗憾，深度感受中华文化的无限魅力。语言是一个国家和民族文化的基本要素。若不会中文，虽然你仍然可以去爱丁堡动物园看大熊猫"甜甜"和"阳光"，可以坐飞机去中国登长城、尝美食，但你不会知道中文中"大熊猫"是两种动物的组合，也不会深刻理解长城在中国悠久历史文化中的独特地位。只有掌握了中文，你才能了解中华文明的丰富内涵，才能读懂精妙绝伦的唐诗宋词，才能知晓儒家、道家、法家哲学的深邃思想。我听说，中耶尔中学的毕业生杰克·路易斯·埃尔文获得了到中国学习的奖学金，将前往天津师范大学学习一年。我注意到，杰克今天也来参加我们的活动，他就坐在台下。杰克，我衷心地祝贺你！祝你学有所获，学有所成。

拿起这个"魔法棒"，你将能搭上中国经济发展的快车，拥有更多人生机遇。中国已是世界第二大经济体、第一大工业国、第一大货物贸易国、第一大外汇储备国。近14亿人口和快速增长的中产阶层，还使中国成为全球最大、最具潜力的市场。改革开放40年来，中国国内生产总值年均增长约9.5%，对外贸易额年均增长14.5%，近年来中国对世界经济增长贡献率保持在30%左右。英国是中国在欧盟内第二大贸易伙伴，中国是英国第三大贸易伙伴。现在已经有500多家中国企业落户英国，它们需要大量双语人才。目前最大的3家中国公司共雇用2000多名当地员工，占比均超过它们在英雇员总数的80%。随着中国对英投资迅速增长，可以预见，"懂中文"今后将大有用武之地，一定会为你们的履历加分，为你们的事业助力。

拿起这个"魔法棒"，你将能看到更全面、更真实的中国，做增进中英友谊的使者。了解是信任的前提，信任是合作的基石。汉语是了解中国、走近中国的一把钥匙。如果只从西方媒体的报道观察和认识中国，难免管中窥豹，甚至会被一些偏见误导。如果你懂汉语，就能更多地与中国民众直接交流，就能更多地去中国各地走一走，亲眼看一看中国的变化，亲耳听一听中国人自己讲述的中国故事，你就能看到、听到一个真实的中国。我相信，学好中文不仅有利于你们更好地认识中国，而且有助于你们为增进中英友谊与合作做出更多贡献。

我知道，坐落在苏格兰的"魔法学校"不止霍格沃茨一所，还有众多孔子学院和孔子课堂，包括你们中耶尔中学孔子课堂。孔子是中国古代伟大的思想家和教育家，他的经典著作《论语》开篇第一句就是："学而时习之，不亦说乎？"今天我给大家带来了100本讲解汉语、介绍中国的书籍，希望能助大家一臂之力，更好地掌握了解中国的"魔法棒"，找到走近中国的"金钥匙"，搭建中英友好的"友谊之桥"！

最后，我祝你们好好学习，天天向上，为中英友好事业不断积累知识才干，将来为谱写中英关系新篇章做出你们的贡献！

谢谢大家！

Wave Your Magic Wand to Contribute a New Chapter to China-UK Relations[*]

Mr Mark Lawson,

Mr Malcolm Bell,

Ms Fhiona Mackay,

Teachers and Students,

Ladies and Gentlemen,

Dear Friends,

Good morning!

It is a real delight to come to the beautiful island of Yell in this blossoming season of Spring for the launch of the Confucius Classroom at Mid Yell Junior High School. On behalf of the Chinese Embassy, let me begin by extending my warmest congratulations!

I also wish to thank the teachers from the Confucius Institute for Scotland's Schools and Mid Yell Junior High School for your hard work and vigorous contribution!

An ancient Chinese sage said, "For he who is unstoppably determined, there is no place too far to reach, no mountain too high to climb and no sea too vast to cross." This line explains how perseverance is the only path to success.

Seven years ago, I had the honour to join His Royal Highness the Prince of Wales, to unveil the Confucius Classroom in Llandovery College in the southwest of Britain. Today, I have come to Yell to unveil the Confucius Classroom in the farthest and northernmost part of Scotland and Britain.

---

[*] Remarks at the Launch of the Confucius Classroom at Mid Yell Junior High School, Shetland Islands. Mid Yell Junior High School, Scotland, 1 May 2018.

From the south to the north, I can see the strong and growing enthusiasm in the British students for learning the Chinese language. That is why the distance between China and the UK, the barriers of mountains and seas, can not stop the Chinese language from reaching every corner of Britain, including Yell!

And I think I have come at a good time. This is the season for flowers to bloom and for trees to grow. It is also a good time for Chinese language education in Britain, for the Confucius Institutes and Confucius Classrooms, to grow.

Eight years ago when I took the office of Chinese Ambassador to the UK, there were only 11 Confucius Institutes across Britain. Today, there are 29.

Eight years ago there were 47 Confucius Classrooms. Today, there are 156.

In 2017 alone, these Confucius Institutes and Confucius Classrooms enrolled 160,000 students, hosted 4,074 cultural events and drew over one million visitors and participants.

Across the world, the numbers are also encouraging. As of the end of last year, there were 525 Confucius Institutes and 1,113 Confucius Classrooms in 146 countries and regions. The total number of students was 9.16 million. That was the size of the population of an average country in Europe.

You may wonder:

- Why are so many people falling in love with the Chinese language?
- Why are the Confucius Institutes and Confucius Classrooms so popular in Britain?

My answer is this: The Chinese language has the power of Harry Potter's magic wand.

Wave this magic wand, and you will have the power to appreciate the charm of Chinese culture.

Language is the basic element of culture. If you do not speak Chinese, you can still visit the giant pandas Tian Tian and Yang Guang at the Edinburgh Zoo; you can also fly to China, visit the Great Wall and enjoy Chinese food.

But you will not know that "Da Xiong Mao", the Chinese word for giant panda, consists of two different animals; neither will you fully understand why the Great Wall has a unique place in China's time-honored history and culture.

The Chinese language gives you the key to unlock the rich heritage of the Chinese civilization, to savour the fascinating poems of the Tang and Song dynasties, and to decipher the profound philosophies of Confucianism, Taoism and Legalism.

I learnt that Jack Louis Irvine, a graduate from Mid Yell Junior High School, has won a scholarship to study in Tianjin Normal University for a year. I saw him sitting among you. Jack, May I take this opportunity to express my heartfelt congratulations to you. I wish you a fruitful year in China.

The magic wand of the Chinese language will also unveil before your eyes the opportunities that China has to offer.

China is the world's second largest economy, largest industrial producer, largest trader in goods, and largest holder of foreign exchange reserves. Moreover, with its large population of nearly 1.4 billion and a rapidly growing middle class, China is the world's largest and most promising market.

Over the past four decades, China has undergone reform and opening-up. These policies have enabled China's economy to grow at around 9.5% every year, and its foreign trade to grow at 14.5%. In recent years, China's contribution to global growth has been around 30%.

China's strong growth is benefiting the UK, because the UK is the second largest trading partner of China in the EU, and China is the third largest trading partner of the UK.

Moreover, more than 500 Chinese companies have set up businesses here in Britain. They need a large number of bilingual employees. The top three Chinese companies in the UK have employed more than 2,000 people locally. That is over 80% of their total employees here in Britain.

As more and more Chinese investments come into the UK, I have no doubt the language capability you will acquire will become a bonus in your resume and boost your future career opportunities.

I also hope you will use the magic wand of the Chinese language to see the complete picture of a real China and become an envoy for China-UK friendship.

Understanding is the precondition for trust, which in turn lays the foundation for cooperation. The Chinese language is a key to understanding China.

Western media alone will not show you the complete picture of China. Worse still, some of their biases can be misleading. But if you can read and speak Chinese, you will be able to hear directly from the Chinese people and learn directly about the China's story. You will be more than just a tourist when you visit China and you will be able to see the country's development with your own eyes.

In a word, mastering the Chinese language will open your ears and eyes to the real China. And you will be better equipped to make greater contribution to closer friendship and cooperation between our two countries.

Hogwarts is not the only "school for witchcraft and wizardry" in Scotland. There are also the Confucius Institutes and Confucius Classrooms, including yours in Mid Yell Junior High School. Here you will learn how to wave the magic wand of the Chinese language.

Confucius, the eponym of the classroom we are opening today, was a great philosopher and teacher of ancient China. His great work, *The Analects of Confucius*, begins with this line, "Isn't it a pleasure to study and practice what you have learned?"

To add to the pleasure of learning the Chinese language, I have brought with me 100 books about China and the Chinese language. They are your text books on how to wave the magic wand, how to find the golden key to understanding China, and how to build the bridge of friendship between China and the UK.

In conclusion, I wish you will study well and make progress everyday. I hope this will get you ready for building closer China-UK friendship and contributing your own new chapter to China-UK relations!

Thank you!

秉持交流初心，共建理解之桥 *

尊敬的伦敦董事协会主席拉马尔先生，

各位评委、各位选手，

老师们、同学们，

女士们、先生们、朋友们：

大家晚上好！

很高兴再次出席"汉语桥"活动。每次来"汉语桥"致辞，我都为一件事感到纠结，那就是不知道该讲中文还是英文。王永利公参建议我讲中文，因为这是一场中文演讲比赛，选手们都说中文。2018年我用中文致辞，但发现除参赛选手外，现场多数英国听众不懂中文，我们未能充分沟通。看来，学习语言并非一日之功，不能急于求成，所以今天我还是讲英文。为了保险起见，我们做个现场调查，请不懂中文的英国听众朋友举手。果真不少。看来我今天讲英文的决定是正确的。希望在不久的将来，我可以用中文在"汉语桥"致辞。

今天的"汉语桥"活动有特殊意义。这是第十八届"汉语桥"世界大学生中文比赛全英大区赛决赛。在中英两国，18岁都是法定成年的年纪，是人从青涩到成熟的里程碑。18年来，"汉语桥"从最初的鲜为人知，到如今已成长为中外人文交流的知名品牌。它的成长，离不开在座各位的热情支持与

---

* 在第十八届"汉语桥"世界大学生中文比赛全英大区赛决赛开幕式上的讲话。2019年4月6日，伊丽莎白二世女王会议中心。

积极参与。在此，我谨为所有致力学习中文的同学们点赞，向长期在英从事汉语教学、传播中华文化的老师们表示敬意，向所有关心和支持"汉语桥"的中英各界人士表示感谢！

2019年是中英建立代办级外交关系65周年。65年来，教育始终是推动中英关系发展的重要动力，始终是滋养中英友谊的厚沃土壤，也是中英合作最具活力、最有潜力的领域之一。中国古代典籍《庄子》谈道，"其作始也简，其将毕也必巨"。"汉语桥"不仅是汉语教学的"质检中心"和"成品展示会"，更是中英教育合作的瑰宝。它起步于语言，而超越语言；它发源于中国，而走向世界；它产生于课堂，而走进心灵。不忘初心，方得始终。在"汉语桥"的"成年礼"上，有必要再问一个问题：为什么要学习汉语？对于这个问题，我愿与大家分享三点体会。

第一，语言是探索中华文化深厚魅力之桥。语言是一个国家和民族文化的基本要素。只有学好汉语，才能真正走进五千年未曾间断的中华文明；才能读懂"不独亲其亲，不独子其子，使老有所终，壮有所用，幼有所长，矜、寡、孤、独、废疾者皆有所养"的和睦观念为何深植中国人民的心底；才能读懂"各美其美，美人之美，美美与共，天下大同"的和谐理念为何已深入中国人民的基因。中华民族5000年文明史，中国人民近代以来170多年斗争史，中国共产党90多年奋斗史，中华人民共和国70年发展史，改革开放40多年探索史，事实上是一脉相承、不可割裂的历史，只有学习好汉语，读懂历史，才能真正掌握和了解中国过去、今天和未来的钥匙。

第二，语言是促进中英两国合作共赢之桥。近年来，英国的"汉语热"持续升温。2017年，英格兰在中小学启动"中文培优"项目，截至目前已有64所学校的1300多名学生参与其中。2018年，汉语首次超越德语，成为英国A-Level（普通中等教育证书考试高级水平课程）考试中最受学生欢迎的第三大流行语言。中英教育机构迄今共建29所孔子学院和161间孔子课堂，成为英国朋友学习汉语、了解中国文化的热门平台。同时，中国的"留英热"也不断升温。2010年我刚出使英国时，约有13万中国学生在英求学。9年过去了，这一数字增长到了19万。"汉语热"和"留英热"反映出中英两国人民对彼此的友好情谊，也折射出中英人文交流的蓬勃生机。

第三，语言是推动东西方文明交流互鉴之桥。在世界多极化、经济全球化、文化多样化深入发展的今天，人与人之间的沟通尤为重要，文明与文明之间的交流互鉴愈显必要。语言就是我们沟通交流的工具，就是帮助我们理解差异性、坚守共同性、相互尊重、平等相待的基石。中英两国社会制度、历史文化、发展阶段不同，但都拥有深厚的历史文化积淀，两国代表的东西方文明也有许多共通之处。比如英国人注重优雅、诚实、独立等品质，中国人则坚守仁、义、礼、智、信等道德准则。只要我们不断跨越语言的障碍，就能达到增进了解、凝聚共识的新境界。

各位来宾、朋友们，

英籍著名哲学家维特根斯坦曾说，"我的语言之局限就是我的世界之局限"。希望"汉语桥"世界大学生中文比赛能够帮助我们不断突破能力和认知的局限，培养大批会汉语、懂中国的人才，为推进中英关系发展、为构建人类命运共同体贡献力量！

我祝愿今天的各位选手取得优异成绩，期待你们成为"汉语桥"上耀眼的明珠！

现在，我宣布：第十八届"汉语桥"世界大学生中文比赛全英大区赛决赛正式开始！

谢谢大家！

Build a Bridge of Exchanges and Understanding*

Chairman David Stringer-Lamarre,

Judges and Contestants,

Teachers and Students,

Ladies and Gentlemen,

Dear Friends,

Good evening!

It is a real delight to join you again at the "Chinese Bridge" Competition.

Every time I speak at the "Chinese Bridge", I struggle over whether I should speak Chinese or English. Last year Minister Counsellor Wang Yongli suggested I speak Chinese, because this is a Chinese proficiency competition. I accepted his suggestion and spoke Chinese, but I found that most British friends in the audience could not understand, and it was not a communication success.

Language is not learned in a day. So I have decided to speak English tonight.

Before doing it I would like to double-check if my decision is right. Let's do a survey. Those who don't understand Chinese, please raise your hand.

It seems I am right in choosing to speak English. Nevertheless I hope that in the near future, I could speak Chinese at the "Chinese Bridge".

Ladies and Gentlemen,

Tonight's "Chinese Bridge" is special. It is the 18th "Chinese Bridge" Chinese

---

* Speech at the 18th "Chinese Bridge" Chinese Proficiency Competition for Foreign College Students the UK Regional Final. Queen Elizabeth II Centre, 6 April 2019.

Proficiency Competition the UK Regional Final.

In China as well as the UK, the age of 18 is a milestone in life. It marks the end of adolescence and the beginning of adulthood.

In the past 18 years, the "Chinese Bridge" has grown from obscurity to international fame. It is now a brand name for cultural exchanges between China and the world. This could not have been possible without the ardent support and active participation of all of you present today.

I would like to give the thumbs up to all the students who have been devoted to learning Chinese!

I would also like to pay tribute to all the teachers. Thank you for your hard work over the years to impart knowledge about the Chinese language and culture to the British people!

My thanks also go to those from both our two countries who have given their care and support for the "Chinese Bridge"!

This year marks the 65th anniversary of the establishment of China-UK diplomatic relationship at the chargé d'affaires level.

In the past 65 years,

- Education has been an important driving force for China-UK relations.
- It has provided nourishment for China-UK friendship.
- And it has been one of the most dynamic and promising areas of China-UK cooperation.

Ancient Chinese philosopher Zhuangzi said, "A simple endeavour could have significant influence."

The "Chinese Bridge" is such a simple endeavour of great significance. For Chinese language proficiency, "Chinese Bridge" is a "centre of quality inspection" and a "display of excellent results". It is also a crown jewel of China-UK cooperation.

- It begins with language learning but is more than language learning.
- It originates in China and gains popularity all over the world.
- It starts in the classrooms and ends in people's heart.

To know where we are going next, we should never forget why we started in the first place.

At this coming-of-age moment for the "Chinese Bridge", it is necessary to ask yourself this question: Why do you want to learn Chinese?

This is what I think:

First, the Chinese language is a bridge leading to the world of profound Chinese cultural charm.

Language is the basic element of the culture of a country and a nation. The Chinese language holds the key to the five-thousand-year uninterrupted Chinese civilisation.

A good command of the Chinese language would enable a thorough understanding of ancient Chinese literature which constitutes the foundation of the Chinese value, such as this one:

"Treat other's kin and children as your own; let all the elderly be supported, the young be employed and the children be educated; ensure all the widowers, the widows, the orphans, the childless elders, the disabled and the sick are properly taken care of."

Or this one:

"Harmony arises from the ability to appreciate different cultures for their unique beauty."

These adages are the very root of the ideals of good-neighbourliness and harmony, which the Chinese people hold dear.

With a good command of the Chinese language, one would find it easier to see how:

- the more than 170 years struggle of the Chinese people in modern history,
- the more than 90 years of strenuous efforts of the Communist Party of China,
- the 70 years of progress of the People's Republic of China,
- and the more than 40 years of the exploration of reform and opening-up, are all parts of a continuous, uninterrupted 5,000-year history of the Chinese nation.

This is the key to understanding China's past, present and future.

Second, language is a bridge for win-win cooperation between China and the UK.

Over the past years, learning the Chinese language has become increasingly popular in Britain.

- In 2017, the Mandarin Excellence Programme was introduced to primary and secondary schools in England. As of today, the programme has covered more than 1,300 students from 64 schools.
- In 2018, the Chinese language overtook German for the first time and became the third most popular foreign language in A-Level exams.
- Chinese and British education institutions have jointly built 29 Confucius Institutes and 161 Confucius Classrooms, which have become popular platforms to learn the Chinese language and culture.

At the same time, more and more Chinese students choose to study in Britain. In 2010, my first year as Chinese Ambassador to the UK, there were about 130,000 Chinese students here. Today, after nine years, this figure has increased to 190,000.

All these figures reflect the close bond between the Chinese and British people. They also demonstrate the vigour of China-UK cultural and people-to-people exchange.

Third, language is a bridge for exchange and mutual learning between Eastern and Western civilizations.

In an age of deepening multi-polarization, economic globalization and cultural diversity, the communication between people and the exchange and mutual learning between civilizations are becoming increasingly important.

Learning a foreign language gives us a tool for such communication and exchange. This helps us understand differences and seek common grounds. This also builds the foundation for equality and mutual respect.

China and the UK differ in social system, history, culture and development stage. But both have created profound civilizations, and many of our values are similar.

For example, the British people prize the qualities of elegance, honesty and independence, while the Chinese people value benevolence, integrity, courtesy, wisdom and good faith.

As long as we overcome the barrier of language, we could reach a new stage of better understanding and stronger consensus.

Distinguished Guests,

Dear Friends,

Ludwig Wittgenstein said, "The limits of my language are the limits of my world."

I hope the "Chinese Bridge" Competition will help us break the limits of ability and knowledge, and encourage more people to learn the Chinese language and understand China. This will be an important contribution to advancing China-UK relations and building a community with a shared future for mankind!

In conclusion, I wish all the contestants success in this competition. I hope you will become super stars of the "Chinese Bridge"!

Now I have the honour to announce:

The 18th "Chinese Bridge" Chinese Proficiency Competition for Foreign College Students the UK Regional Final now begins!

Thank you!

●**2017年1月24日**
在英国皇家莎士比亚剧团为庆贺中国合作项目成功举办招待会上发表讲话：《海纳百川，有容乃大》

●**2017年1月29日**
在伦敦特拉法加广场春节庆典活动上发表讲话：《民相亲与心相通》

●**2017年5月9日**
在英国第三届年度体育商业大会上发表主旨演讲：《深化中英体育合作，共创世界美好未来》

●**2017年9月11日**
在中国驻英国大使馆举办"编织梦想——中国手工艺文化时装秀"活动并致辞

2017 年 10 月 3 日
在中国人民解放军海军第二十六批护航编队访英新闻发布会上发表讲话：《把握时刻，开启新程》

2018 年 2 月 7 日
在中英教育界中国春节招待会上发表讲话：《携手谱写中英教育交流与合作的"华彩乐章"》

2018 年 2 月 25 日
为全英华裔教授学者举行新春招待会并发表讲话：《秉持"石头精神"，推进中英合作》

2018 年 5 月 1 日
在苏格兰中耶尔中学孔子课堂揭牌仪式上发表讲话：《拿起手中"魔法棒"，谱写中英关系新篇章》

2018 年 7 月 9 日
在英国哈德斯菲尔德大学毕业典礼上发表演讲：《激扬青春梦想，共促中英合作》

2019 年 1 月 14 日
为斯蒂芬·佩里荣获"中国改革友谊奖章"举行招待会并与其全家合影

2019 年 1 月 25 日
在"中英数学教师交流项目"新年招待会上发表讲话:《为中英教育交流合作增光添彩》

2019 年 1 月 30 日
出席英国科学博物馆"中国之夜"活动并发表讲话:《趣品中国味,厚植中英情》

2019 年 1 月 31 日
出席英国首相特雷莎·梅在首相府举办的春节庆典活动

2019 年 4 月 6 日
在第十八届"汉语桥"世界大学生中文比赛全英大区赛决赛开幕式上发表讲话：《秉持交流初心，共建理解之桥》

2020 年 1 月 17 日
在 2020 年中国驻英国大使馆新春招待会上发表讲话：《共同建设美好世界大家庭》

2020 年 1 月 24 日
出席英国首相约翰逊在首相府举办的春节庆典活动

第五章 军事往来
PART V　Military Exchanges

中英两军关系是两国关系的重要组成部分。自 2002 年两军建立防务磋商机制以来，双方已举行六次磋商，并保持交流合作。在我任期内，中国海军第十八批和第二十六批护航编队分别于 2015 年和 2017 年访问英国，特别是第二十六批护航编队舰艇首次停靠在英国首都伦敦，引发国际舆论关注和热议。2016 年，英国皇家空军"红箭"特技飞行表演队首次亮相珠海航展。两军还开展联合撤侨室内推演，并在联合国维和行动以及反恐、反海盗、人员培训等领域开展了卓有成效的合作。

　　本章收录了我在接待中国海军两批护航编队访问英国时的演讲和在庆祝中国人民解放军建军 91 周年招待会上的演讲。

China-UK military relations are an important component of the bilateral relationship. Since the establishment of the Defence Consultation Mechanism between the two militaries in 2002, six consultations have been held, and exchanges and cooperation have continued. During my tenure, the 18th and 26th Chinese Naval Escort Task Forces visited the UK in 2015 and 2017 respectively, with the first docking in London by Chinese naval ships in 2017 attracting significant international attention. In 2016, the Royal Air Force Red Arrows made their debut at the Zhuhai Airshow in China. The two militaries have also conducted joint evacuation tabletop exercises and cooperated effectively in the UN peacekeeping operations, counter-terrorism, anti-piracy, and personnel training.

This chapter includes my speeches during the visits of the two Chinese naval escort task forces to the UK and at the reception celebrating the 91st anniversary of the founding of the People's Liberation Army of China.

威武之师，和平之师，友谊之师 *

尊敬的英国皇家海军舰队司令菲利普·琼斯中将，

尊敬的中国海军第十八批护航编队指挥员张传书少将，

尊敬的朴茨茅斯市副市长戴维德先生，

各位来宾，

女士们、先生们：

非常高兴在这"军港之夜"，出席在中国海军护航编队战舰上举行的甲板招待会。

首先，我代表中国驻英国大使馆，对中国海军第十八批护航编队的来访表示热烈欢迎！向为此来访做出精心和周到安排的英国皇家海军和朴茨茅斯市表示衷心的感谢！

这次中国海军舰艇编队访英，是在圆满完成亚丁湾、索马里海域护航任务后顺访5国的第一站，也是中国军舰时隔7年再次访英。

我们迎来的是一支威武之师。这次编队的三艘中国军舰：两栖登陆舰长白山舰、导弹护卫舰运城舰以及综合补给舰巢湖舰，都是近年来服役的中国新一代主力舰艇，代表着中国海军装备的前沿水平，代表着中国海军建设的历史性跨越。编队官兵800多人，特战队员近百名，他们在浩瀚的印度洋经受了考验，圆满完成了任务，全方位锻炼和检验了执行远海军事行动的能力

---

* 在中国海军第十八批护航编队访问英国招待会上的讲话。2015年1月12日，英国朴茨茅斯军港。

水平，充分展现了中国海军官兵的过硬素质。

我们迎来的是一支和平之师。自 2008 年 12 月以来，中国已先后派出 19 批护航编队赴亚丁湾、索马里海域，出色完成了近 6000 艘船舶的护航任务。今天来访的第十八批护航编队于 2014 年 8 月 1 日启航，共完成 48 批 135 艘中外船舶护航任务，保持了被护船舶和船员零伤亡的纪录，有效遏制了相关海域的海盗活动，为维护国际海上安全做出了重要贡献。事实证明，中国军队不仅是中国和平发展的基本保障，也是维护世界和平与地区稳定的坚强力量。

我们迎来的是一支友谊之师。护航编队在执行护航任务期间，与包括英国皇家海军在内的各国海军开展了广泛交流，加深了彼此的了解和互信。从第二批护航编队开始，每批编队完成任务后，都对一些国家进行友好访问，迄今已到访近 50 个国家。这些访问加强了军事交流，促进了双边关系。这次护航编队到访英国，满载着中国人民和中国军队对英国人民和军队的友好情谊。我相信，中国海军护航编队与具有悠久历史的英国皇家海军开展深入交流和相互学习，必将进一步增进两国海军的了解和友谊，有力促进中英两军关系不断向前发展。

新年伊始，中国海军护航编队访问英国，拉开了新一年里中英关系的序幕，为 2015 年两军交往开了个好头，为两国关系带来了新气象。

再过一个月，我们将迎来中国农历羊年。羊在中国文化中象征着祥和、圆满。

让我们共同举杯，

祝愿中国海军护航编队访英取得圆满成功！

祝愿中英两国、两军关系迈向更加美好的明天！

祝愿各位来宾三阳开泰、羊年吉祥！

谢谢！

A Valiant Force for Peace and Friendship*

Vice Admiral Philip Jones,

Rear Admiral Zhang Chuanshu,

Deputy Lord Mayor David Horne,

Ladies and Gentlemen,

It is such a great pleasure to join you all at the deck reception for the Chinese Navy fleet.

On behalf of the Chinese Embassy, may I first of all extend my very warm welcome to the 18th Escort Task Force of the Chinese Navy.

May I also express my heartfelt appreciation to the Royal Navy and the City of Portsmouth for their thoughtful and gracious arrangement.

The Chinese Navy ships calling at Portsmouth this time have just fulfilled an escort mission in the Gulf of Aden and off the coast of Somalia. The UK is the first stop in their five-country tour and their visit to the UK is the first by Chinese Navy ships in seven years.

The 18th Escort Task Force of the Chinese Navy gathered here can take great pride that they are a valiant force.

The Naval Escort Task Force consists of amphibious transport dock Changbai Shan, missile frigate Yuncheng and replenishment ship Chaohu. They are all part of China's new generation of active main naval ships. They represent the best of China's naval equipment. They mark a historic leap of advance for the Chinese Navy.

---

* Remarks at a Reception for the 18th Chinese Naval Escort Task Force. Portsmouth, 12 January 2015.

This Naval Escort Task Force consists of over 800 officers and sailors on board, including some one hundred members of the special task force. They have stood the test of the vast Indian Ocean and accomplished their mission. They have trained and tested their "blue sea" capability. They can take great pride in their performance as they have shown the true colors of the Chinese Navy.

It is important to understand that the Chinese Navy is a force for peace.

Since December 2008, the Chinese Navy has sent 19 Escort Task Force successively to the Gulf of Aden and the waters near Somalia. They have all accomplished their missions with distinction and offered protection to nearly 6,000 ships.

The 18th Escort Task Force we are greeting here today set off from China on 1st August 2014. It has since offered protection to 135 Chinese and foreign ships in 48 groups. In all those operations, there was not a single accident or casualty.

Thanks in part to the efforts of the Chinese Navy ships, piracy in those waters is being effectively curbed and maritime security along that route is being safeguarded.

All these facts speak volumes about the role of the Chinese military. In addition to being the basic guarantor for China's peaceful development, the Chinese military is also a staunch force in safeguarding world peace and regional stability.

The Chinese Navy is also a force for friendship.

While carrying out escort missions, successive Chinese Naval Escort Task Force always engaged in extensive exchanges with the naval forces of other countries, including the Royal Navy. This has helped deepen mutual understanding and trust among navies.

The escort missions were always followed up with good-will port calls in a number of countries. This has become the tradition since the second Escort Task Force. To date, Chinese Escort Task Forces have altogether visited nearly 50 countries. Their visits have enhanced military-to-military exchange as well as bilateral relations between China and the relevant countries.

With its arrival at Portsmouth today, the 18th Chinese Naval Escort Task Force is bringing with it the friendship of the Chinese people to the British people. It will also enhance the military-to-military links between our two countries.

I welcome the exchange and mutual learning between the Chinese Navy and the Royal Navy which has centuries of heritage. I am confident it will surely lead to greater understanding and mutual trust between our navies. It will also give a strong push to the relations between our military forces.

The new year has just begun. Today's port call launches China-UK relations into action in 2015. It signifies a good beginning for exchanges between our military forces. It heralds a great start for our bilateral relations as a whole in the coming year.

In a month's time, Chinese around the world will be celebrating the Lunar New Year and ringing in the Year of the Ram. The Ram in Chinese culture symbolizes fulfillment and satisfaction.

In this spirit of the Ram, I now invite you to raise your glasses and drink a toast:

To the fulfillment and success of the visit of the 18th Escort Task Force of the Chinese Navy!

To a better tomorrow for the relationship between our two countries and our two military forces!

And to a happy and prosperous Year of the Ram for each and everyone present!

Thank you!

忠诚、使命、奉献 *

尊敬的中国海军第十八批护航编队指挥员张传书少将，
尊敬的中国海军第十八批护航编队政委周名贵大校，
同志们：
晚上好！

首先，我谨代表驻英使馆全体人员，对中国海军第十八批护航编队的全体指战员表示热烈欢迎！

你们自2014年8月1日从湛江军港启航，在外执行任务已经整整166天。远行的人总是盼望早点回家。今晚，你们就回家了。

中国大使馆就是你们在英国的家。如果说，军舰是一国在海上的"流动领土"，那么，大使馆就常被称作一国在海外的陆上"固定领土"。我们在这片"固定领土"上的使命，就是积极促进中国与英国在政治、经济、文化、教育和军事等各领域合作，就是忠实履行保护中国公民、侨民的职责，使我们的国民不论走到哪里，都能感到祖国的关怀，都会感到家就在身边。

关于我们在伦敦的这个家，我想多谈几句，因为它在中国外交史上有特殊的地位。中国驻英国大使馆是中国第一个驻外使馆，其历史可上溯至1877年晚清政府设立的中国驻英公使馆。第一任中国驻英公使是郭嵩焘先生，他

---

* 在中国海军第十八批护航编队与驻英使馆联谊活动上的讲话。2015年1月13日，中国驻英国大使馆。

是湖南湘阴人，也是我们护航编队周名贵政委的同乡。他是一位杰出的外交家，可惜生不逢时。当时他被派到英国的首要使命不是与英国发展友好关系，而是作为清朝皇帝的钦差大臣履行不平等的《中英烟台条约》，赴英向维多利亚女王当面"道歉"。他作为中国首位常驻使节向外国元首递交的第一份文件不是国书，而是一封道歉信。这就是中国近代的一段屈辱历史。

100多年过去了，中国人民在中国共产党的领导下实现了国家独立和民族解放，结束了那段屈辱历史，现在正为实现中华民族伟大复兴的中国梦而奋斗。中英关系也发生了翻天覆地的变化，平等互利、合作共赢成为今天中英关系的主旋律。

这次，中国海军舰队在圆满完成亚丁湾、索马里海域护航任务后，雄赳赳、气昂昂地访问英国，展现威武之师、和平之师、文明之师和友谊之师的风采，展现中国综合国力的强盛、军事实力的强大和大国外交的气派。这是时代进步、国家发展和中英关系发生质变的充分体现。

说到回家，我还想说，我们的确是一家人。你们是穿军装的人民解放军，周恩来总理把外交人员称为"文装解放军"。我们的穿着不同，但我们的核心价值观是相同的，这就是"忠诚、使命、奉献"。

我们都高度忠诚。忠于党、忠于国家、忠于人民，这是人民军队和外交队伍的相同品质和灵魂。

我们都肩负光荣使命。维护国家的主权、安全和发展利益，维护和促进世界的和平与稳定，这是人民军队和外交队伍的共同使命和责任。

我们都具有奉献精神。在困难和挑战面前，我们从不畏惧、不怕牺牲、顽强拼搏。这是人民军队的精气神，也是外交队伍的精气神。

所以，作为一家人，我们热烈欢迎你们回家，希望与你们共同度过一个愉快的夜晚。

最后，我再次祝贺你们出色完成护航任务！

预祝你们访英和此后各站访问圆满成功！

衷心祝愿你们归程一帆风顺，早日回家，回到祖国母亲的怀抱！

谢谢！

把握时刻，开启新程 *

尊敬的英国皇家海军海上部队司令阿莱克斯·伯顿少将，
尊敬的中国海军第二十六批护航编队指挥员王仲才少将，
各位记者朋友，
女士们、先生们：
上午好！
欢迎大家出席今天的新闻发布会。

从今天起到 10 月 7 日，中国海军第二十六批护航编队将对英国进行友好访问。其间，舰队将举行开放日、甲板招待会、中英两军业务交流等一系列丰富多彩的活动。这些活动将不仅展示中国海军的风采，增进英国各界对中国海军的了解，而且将促进中英两国和两军关系的发展。

这是我时隔近三年，第二次迎接中国海军舰队来访。我为中国海军的快速发展感到骄傲，也为中英两军关系的深入推进感到高兴，同时对中国海军护航编队访英的重要意义也有了更深刻的体会。

第一，从两军关系层面看，这是书写历史的时刻。这次访问创造了多个"第一次"：这是中国海军舰队历史上第一次访问英国首都伦敦，第一次在不到三年的时间里再次访英，第一次有这么多英军将领出席中国海军舰队举行的活动，两军在此访问期间还将第一次举办人道主义救援交流会。所有这些

---

* 在中国海军第二十六批护航编队访英新闻发布会上的讲话。2017 年 10 月 3 日，英国伦敦西印度码头。

都充分表明中英两军关系日益密切，更显示出中英两国战略互信不断深化。在这次编队访问期间，两国海军将就反海盗、人道主义救援等广泛议题进行交流。这些交流将进一步加深两军之间的互信与合作。

第二，从双边关系层面看，这是谱写新篇的时刻。2015 年，习近平主席对英国进行了成功的国事访问。2017 年是中英建立大使级外交关系 45 周年，也是中国人民解放军建军 90 周年。值此承前启后、继往开来的重要年份，中国海军舰队到访英国，必将在中英两国和两军交往史上留下浓墨重彩的一笔。

第三，从全球层面看，这是彰显和平的时刻。当今世界并不太平，地区冲突、恐怖主义、海盗活动、跨国犯罪、难民危机此起彼伏。为了让和平薪火代代相传，中国倡导国际社会共同构建人类命运共同体，建立以合作共赢为核心的新型国际关系。中国军队积极参与联合国维和行动，与包括英军在内的各国军队一道应对全球性安全挑战，为维护世界安全与稳定做出了重要贡献。实践证明，中国军队是维护世界和平的中坚力量。

女士们、先生们，

中国 2000 多年前的古代思想家荀子曾说："锲而舍之，朽木不折；锲而不舍，金石可镂。"英国前首相丘吉尔也说："发挥潜能的关键是不懈努力，而不是力量或者智力。"我相信，中国海军第二十六批护航编队此次访英，必将为中英两军友好交往与合作开启新航程，为中英关系行稳致远注入新动力，为建设一个持久和平、共同繁荣的世界做出新贡献！

谢谢！

Seize the Moment and Start a New Journey[*]

Rear Admiral Alex Burton,
Rear Admiral Wang Zhongcai,
Friends from the Press,
Ladies and Gentlemen,
Good morning!

It is a pleasure to have you all with us today for the press conference.

The 26th Chinese Naval Escort Task Force is calling at London from today to 7 October. In the coming days, there will be a series of events, including an open day, a deck reception and professional meetings between Chinese and British navies.

- These events will showcase the best of the Chinese Navy.
- They will be an opportunity for British people to get to know the Chinese Navy better.
- And they will strengthen China-UK bilateral ties and military-to-military relations.

This is my second time greeting Chinese Navy fleet in Britain. Last time was nearly three years ago.

- I feel proud of the rapid development of the Chinese Navy.

---

* Remarks at a Press Conference of the 26th Chinese Naval Escort Task Force. West India Quay, London, 3 October 2017.

- I feel happy about the ever deeper links between the Chinese and British militaries.
- And I feel excited about what this visit truly means to our military ties, to our bilateral relations and to our global partnership.

First, this visit is making history for China-UK military-to-military ties.
This visit has set many records.

- It is the first time ever for Chinese navy ships to call at Britain's capital city, London.
- It is also the first time for the Chinese navy fleet to be back in the UK after just two old years.
- It is the first time that so many British admirals and generals will come to the events to be held by the Chinese Navy fleet.
- And during this visit, our two navies will hold the first humanitarian rescue symposium.
- All these reflect the ever closer military ties and strategic mutual trust between our two countries.

During this visit, our two navies will exchange views on a broad range of issues from anti-piracy to humanitarian rescues. I believe such extensive engagement will help deepen the mutual trust and cooperation between our two militaries.

Second, this visit is writing a new chapter for the overall China-UK relations.

President Xi Jinping paid a successful visit to the UK in 2015.

This year marks 45 years of ambassadorial diplomatic ties between China and Britain. It is also the 90th anniversary of the founding of the People's Liberation Army. It is a year of great significance that calls on both countries to strive for further progress based on past achievement.

This visit by the Chinese Navy fleet will leave its mark in the history of our military-to-military exchanges and state-to-state relations.

Third, this visit is reaffirming the commitment of China and Britain to world peace.

Today's world is far from being peaceful. Regional conflicts, terrorism, piracy, cross border crimes and refugee crisis are on the rise.

To meet the challenges and uphold peace, China proposes to build a community of shared future for mankind and calls for a new type of international relations featuring win-win cooperation.

The Chinese military have been an active contributor to the UN peacekeeping missions.

- Chinese peacekeepers have worked together with the British military and armed forces of other countries to deal with global security challenges.
- They have made significant contribution to world peace and stability.
- They have proven to the world with concrete actions that the Chinese military is a staunch force for world peace.

Ladies and Gentlemen,

The great Chinese thinker Xun Zi said this 2,000 years ago:

"Giving up halfway, one cannot even cut into rotten wood; but with unremitting efforts, one can shape metals and stones."

Winston Churchill had this to say with similar sentiments:

"Continuous effort—not strength or intelligence—is the key to unlocking our potential."

I believe the visit to Britain by the 26th Chinese Naval Escort Task Force will mark a new beginning of closer, friendly exchange and cooperation between Chinese and British militaries.

It will create new impetus to sustain China-UK relations.

And it will contribute to a world of lasting peace and common prosperity.

Thank you!

为中英关系增彩，为世界和平担当 *

尊敬的英国皇家海军舰队司令本·基中将，
尊敬的中国海军第二十六批护航编队指挥员王仲才少将，
各位将军，
女士们、先生们：
大家晚上好！
很高兴出席中国海军护航编队甲板招待会。

首先，我谨代表中国驻英国大使馆，对中国海军第二十六批护航编队来访表示热烈欢迎！对英国皇家海军为此访所做的精心筹备和周到安排表示衷心的感谢！

在中英两国、两军交往史上，这是中国海军舰队第四次访问英国，也是第一次停靠英国首都伦敦。作为中国驻英大使，这是我第二次欢迎中国海军护航编队到访，我对此深感荣幸。

今天，我们在这里只能看到两艘军舰，但编队总共有三艘军舰：导弹护卫舰黄冈号、导弹护卫舰扬州号和停靠在伦敦皇家港口国王乔治五世码头的综合补给舰高邮湖号。三艘军舰都是中国自行设计制造的新一代主力舰艇，代表了中国海军装备前沿水平。此次，中国海军护航编队圆满完成亚丁湾、索马里海域护航任务，不远万里来到英国，带来了"三大信息"。

---

* 在中国海军第二十六批护航编队访问英国甲板招待会上的讲话。2017 年 10 月 3 日，英国伦敦西印度码头。

第一，这是一次维护和平之旅。第二十六批护航编队于 2017 年 4 月 1 日启航，在 4 个多月里，共对 42 批 64 艘中外船舶进行护航，移交 3 名疑似海盗，并多次完成特殊护航和延伸护航。自从 2008 年以来，中国海军已累计派出编队 27 批、舰艇 86 艘次、官兵 2.2 万余人次奔赴亚丁湾、索马里海域执行护航任务，有效遏制海盗的猖狂活动，圆满完成 1074 批中外商船的护航任务。就在 6 天前，第二十七批护航编队成功处置一起疑似海盗小艇袭击外国商船事件，被保护的商船包括一艘英国籍集装箱船。正因为如此，中国海军护航编队被各国商船誉为"值得信赖的保护伞"，并被国际海事组织授予"航运和人类特别服务奖"。

第二，这是一次深化友谊之旅。第二十六批护航编队在执行任务期间，与欧盟 465 编队及各国海军开展广泛交流，加深了彼此间的了解与信任，也结下了深厚的友谊。第二十六批护航编队这次先后访问比利时、丹麦、英国和法国。在伦敦，编队将举办开放日等一系列活动，与英军官兵和英国民众进行互动。事实上，从第二批中国海军护航编队开始，每批编队完成任务后都对一些国家进行友好访问，这些访问将中国海军的友好情谊传递到近百个国家。

第三，这是一次拓展合作之旅。当前，中英两军交流与合作已成为中英关系的重要组成部分。近年来，两军各层级交往频繁，务实合作稳步推进，在反恐、反海盗、救灾等领域开展卓有成效的合作，在专业技术领域和人员培训等方面展开深入的交流。2017 年是中英建立大使级外交关系 45 周年。中国海军护航编队此时来访，必将进一步丰富两军合作内涵，为中英关系增光添彩。

英国海军名将纳尔逊有句名言，"英格兰期盼人人恪尽职责"。当前，国际形势复杂多变，传统和非传统安全威胁相互交织，世界并不太平。在这样的形势下，中英两国军队恪尽职守，携手合作，共同为维护世界和平与稳定勇敢担当，这不仅符合中英两国利益，也必将造福整个世界！

明天就是中国传统节日中秋佳节，是阖家团圆的日子。在此，我谨向大家致以诚挚的节日问候！

最后，让我们共同举杯，

祝愿中国海军护航编队访英取得圆满成功！

祝愿中英两国、两军关系迈向更加美好的明天！

祝愿各位来宾身体健康、诸事顺遂！

干杯！

For World Peace and More Splendid China-UK Relations *

Vice Admiral Ben Key,

Rear Admiral Wang Zhongcai,

Admirals, Generals,

Ladies and Gentlemen,

Good evening!

It is such a great pleasure to join you at the deck reception for the Chinese Navy fleet.

On behalf of the Chinese Embassy, may I first of all extend my very warm welcome to the 26th Escort Task Force of the Chinese Navy.

May I also express my heartfelt appreciation to the Royal Navy for all the thoughtful arrangements for the visit!

This is the fourth Chinese Naval fleet to visit Britain, but definitely the first to call at London. As Chinese Ambassador, I feel hugely honoured to greet the Chinese Navy fleet in Britain for the second time.

The 26th Escort Task Force consists of three ships:

- FFG Huanggang and FFG Yangzhou, the two missile frigates we see here.
- And the AOR Gaoyouhu, berthed at King George V Dock in the London Docklands.

---

* Remarks at a Reception for the 26th Chinese Naval Escort Task Force. West India Quay, London, 3 October 2017.

- They are all part of China's new generation of principle ships. They represent the best of China's naval prowess.

These Chinese Navy ships have just fulfilled an escort mission in the Gulf of Aden and off the coast of Somalia. Traveling thousands of miles, they are here to deliver three messages:

First, their mission is to uphold peace.

- The 26th Escort Task Force set off from China on April 1st.
- In over four months' time, they provided security escort to 64 Chinese and foreign vessels in 42 groups.
- They handed over three suspected pirates.
- They fulfilled a number of special tasks and extended their escort mission.

Since 2008, more than 22 thousand officers and sailors, and 86 navy ships have taken part in 27 escort missions to the Gulf of Aden and the waters near Somalia. They have effectively cracked down on piracy and offered protection to 1,074 groups of Chinese and foreign merchant vessels.

Just six days ago, the 27th Escort Task Force successfully dealt with a suspected pirate attack. The merchant vessels under their protection included a British container.

This is a latest example of the efforts of the Chinese Navy fleet. They are widely regarded as providing "a trustworthy protective umbrella" for merchant ships worldwide. And for this, they have been conferred with the "Special Award for Shipping and Human Services" by IMO.

Second, their mission is to deepen friendship.

During the mission, the 26th Escort Task Force had extensive contacts and exchanges with other naval forces, including the EU Combined Task Force 465. Such exchanges have helped increase understanding and build deeper trust and friendship.

After completing the escort mission, the 26th Escort Task Force began its four-country tour to Belgium, Denmark, Britain and France.

Here in London, the Chinese navy will hold a number of events, including an open day and meetings with their British counterparts and with the wider British public.

Paying friendly visits upon completion of the escort mission has been a tradition since the 2nd Escort Task Force. Over the years, these visits have taken the Chinese Navy ships to nearly one hundred countries and helped spread friendship all around.

Third, their mission is to expand cooperation.

Military exchange and cooperation have become an indispensable part of China-UK relations. Recent years have seen frequent military exchanges at all levels and ever growing cooperation between our two militaries.

Our two militaries worked together effectively in such fields as counter-terrorism, anti-piracy, disaster relief and so on. We had close exchanges in professional skills and personnel training.

This year marks the 45th anniversary of China-UK ambassadorial diplomatic relationship.

This visit of the Chinese Naval Escort Task Force will surely enrich our military-to-military ties and contribute to advancing China-UK relations.

Horatio Nelson has a famous saying:

"England expects that every man will do his duty."

We live in a complex and changing world, a world far from being a safe place due to conventional and non-conventional security threats.

In such a world, Chinese and British military forces must work closely together. It is our shared responsibility to safeguard world peace and stability. This will not only serve the interests of our two countries but also benefit the whole world.

Tomorrow will be the Mid-Autumn Festival, a traditional Chinese festival for family reunion. Here I would like to wish everyone a very happy Mid-Autumn Festival.

Now may I invite you to join me in a toast:

To the successful visit of the Chinese Navy fleet,

To a splendid future for China-UK relations and the relations between our two militaries,

To the health and success of everyone present tonight!

Cheers!

捍卫和平，促进发展 *

尊敬的英国皇家空军詹姆斯少将，

各位使节、各位武官、各位来宾，

女士们、先生们、朋友们：

大家晚上好！

欢迎大家出席今晚的招待会，与我们共同庆祝中国人民解放军建军91周年。

近一个世纪之前，中国人民解放军诞生。这一个世纪，风云激荡，战事不断，有热战，有冷战；有局部战争，有世界大战。人类经历了正义与邪恶的搏斗、光明与黑暗的决战。历史告诉我们：和平来之不易，和平需要珍惜，和平需要捍卫。

这一个世纪里，中国人民解放军始终秉持全心全意为人民服务的宗旨，不懈奋斗，砥砺前行，从无到有，由弱变强，为中国人民赢取民族独立、为维护世界和平与安全做出了重要贡献。历史证明：

第一，中国人民解放军是中国人民的守护者。91年来，人民解放军始终在中国共产党领导下为中国人民求解放、求幸福，为中华民族谋独立、谋复兴，历经硝烟战火，一路披荆斩棘，付出了巨大牺牲，从胜利走向胜利，成就了彪炳史册的伟大功勋。当前，中国军队正着眼新时代新目标，坚持走中国特色强军之路，为实现中华民族伟大复兴的中国梦提供坚强保障。

---

* 在中国人民解放军建军91周年招待会上的讲话。2018年7月26日，中国驻英国大使馆。

第二，中国人民解放军是世界和平的捍卫者。在联合国维和行动中，中国是联合国安理会"五常"国家中派遣维和人员最多的国家，累计派出维和军事人员 3.7 万余人次。现在仍有 2507 名中国军人在世界多地执行维和任务。中国也是联合国第二大维和摊款贡献国，2017 年度缴纳维和摊款 6.97 亿美元，占摊款总额的 10.25%。中国军队迄今已派出 29 批 92 艘次舰艇、62 架直升机赴亚丁湾、索马里海域执行护航任务，累计安全护送中外船舶 6500 余艘，其中一半为外国船舶。中国军队还积极组织和参与国际人道主义救援行动，迄今已执行 30 多次国际紧急人道主义物资援助任务。中国人民解放军以实际行动向世界宣告，他们是世界和平与安全的坚定捍卫者。

第三，中国人民解放军是新安全观的践行者。当今世界正处于大发展大变革大调整时期，和平与发展仍是时代的主题。但与此同时，保护主义、单边主义沉渣泛起，强权政治、霸权主义阴魂不散，地区冲突、局部战争持续不断，恐怖主义、跨国犯罪、传染性疾病、气候变化、难民危机等非传统安全威胁日益上升，世界和平稳定面临严峻挑战。中国主张打破冷战思维、不搞集团对抗，反对以牺牲别国安全换取自身绝对安全的做法，倡导共同、综合、合作、可持续的安全观，为应对各类全球性挑战做出重要贡献。

女士们、先生们，

2015 年，习近平主席对英国的国事访问开启了中英全面战略伙伴关系。2018 年初，梅首相成功访华，两国领导人一致同意增强中英关系的战略性、务实性、全球性和包容性。中英两军关系是两国关系的重要组成部分，近年来，中英两军交流与合作空前活跃。仅近 1 个月，中国空军上将于忠福率团成功访英并出席英国空军成立 100 周年活动；英国第一海务大臣菲利普·琼斯上将顺利访华；第六次中英防务战略磋商成功举行。2017 年，中国海军护航编队首访伦敦。英国皇家空军"红箭"特技飞行表演队首次亮相珠海航展，两军还成功开展联合撤侨室内推演，并在联合国维和行动以及反恐、反海盗、人员培训等领域开展了卓有成效的合作。

女士们、先生们，

习近平主席说，要"树立正确的历史观"。他告诫我们应端起历史的望远镜回顾过去，总结历史规律，把握历史大势。20世纪，世界经历了血与火的考验、战争与和平的洗礼。进入21世纪，我们应以史为鉴，更好地维护世界和平，促进世界发展。为此，我衷心希望，中英两国、两军能把握世界和平大势，着眼世界发展大局，一起走好"三条路"。

一是走好增进互信之路。互信是合作的基础。中英历史文化、社会制度不同，但两国都倡导多边主义，反对单边主义；都支持自由贸易，反对保护主义；都主张维护联合国权威，维护以规则为基础的国际秩序。双方应在相互尊重与平等相待的基础上，加强对话，增进互信，深化合作。

二是走好扩大合作之路。双方应抓住机遇，进一步拓展交流与合作的广度、深度、高度和频度，共同应对各类全球性安全与发展挑战，提升中英关系的战略性和全球性，使两国和两军关系在合作中成长，在合作中成熟，在合作中共赢。

三是走好维护和平之路。中英同为联合国安理会常任理事国，都是世界上有重要影响的国家，都肩负着维护人类和平的时代重任。中英两国、两军应携手努力，积极履行国际责任和义务，珍惜和平、捍卫和平，为构建人类命运共同体，为建设持久和平、普遍安全的美好世界贡献力量！

最后，我提议：

为庆祝中国人民解放军建军91周年，

为中英两国和两军关系更上一层楼，

为世界的持久和平与普遍安全，

干杯！

Safeguard Peace and Promote Development[*]

Air Vice Marshal Warren James,

Your Excellencies,

Military Attachés,

Distinguished Guests,

Ladies and Gentlemen,

Dear Friends,

Good evening!

First of all, a very warm welcome to the Chinese Embassy!

It is a great delight to have you all with us tonight to celebrate the 91st anniversary of the People's Liberation Army of China (PLA).

It has been nearly a century since the founding of the PLA.

In this century, the world saw much turbulence and incessant wars. There were hot wars and cold wars, regional wars and world wars. In these arduous times, mankind fought decisive battles between justice and evil, and between light and darkness.

The lesson of history is clear:

- Peace is hard won.
- Peace needs to be valued.
- Peace must be safeguarded.

---

[*] Remarks at the Reception Marking the 91st Anniversary of the People's Liberation Army of China. Chinese Embassy, 26 July 2018.

And the PLA has lived up to its mission in the past century.

- It has been devoted wholeheartedly to serving the people.
- It has forged ahead relentlessly.
- It has grown from strength to strength.
- It has made important contribution to the independence of the Chinese nation.
- It has done its very best for world peace and security.

In the past 91 years, the PLA has been the protector of the Chinese people. Under the leadership of the Communist Party of China,

- The PLA has always fought for the liberation and happiness of the Chinese people.
- It has always pursued independence and rejuvenation of the Chinese nation.
- In this lofty cause, the PLA has braved the flames of war, overcome immense hardships and made tremendous sacrifice.
- Its tenacity has led it to win one victory after another and make glorious marks in history.

In the new era, the PLA strives to achieve new goals, that is,

- To build a strong military with Chinese characteristics.
- And to provide effective safeguard for pursuing the Chinese Dream of national rejuvenation.

Looking back, we see that the PLA has been a defender of world peace.

- In the UN peacekeeping missions, China is the largest contributor of peacekeepers among the five permanent members of the UN Security Council. The PLA has sent more than 37,000 military personnel to various peacekeeping missions. As we speak, 2,507 Chinese servicemen are on active the UN duty around the world.
- China is the second largest contributor to the UN peacekeeping budget. With 697

million US dollars paid in 2017, China accounts for 10.25% of the total budget.
- At sea, the PLA has to date sent 29 fleets, including 92 naval vessels and 62 helicopters, on escort missions in the Gulf of Aden and off the coast of Somalia. They have altogether escorted the safe passage of over 6,500 ships from around the world, half of which are foreign ships.
- In international humanitarian operations, the PLA is also taking an active part. It has so far carried out over 30 emergency humanitarian missions.

All these speak loud and clear about the PLA's concrete actions of defending world peace and security.

Looking back, we also see that the PLA has been an implementer of the new security concept.

The world is undergoing profound changes and transformations. Peace and development remain the theme of our times.

But at the same time, world peace and stability face severe challenges from

- surging protectionism and unilateralism,
- lingering hegemonism and power politics,
- chronic regional wars and conflicts,
- and rising non-traditional threats such as terrorism, transnational crime, epidemics, climate change and refugee crisis.

To address these challenges, countries must renounce the Cold War mentality, reject confrontation between blocs of countries and work together. We must come to the conclusion that in this new era, there is no place for absolute security of oneself at the expense of others' security.

China champions common, comprehensive, coordinated and sustainable security. In line with this new security concept, China is determined to make important contribution to addressing global challenges.

Ladies and Gentlemen,

President Xi Jinping's state visit to the UK in 2015 ushered in China-UK comprehensive strategic partnership. At the beginning of this year, Prime Minister May paid a successful visit to China, during which the leaders of our two countries agreed to build a more strategic, practical, global and inclusive bilateral relationship.

Military-to-military relationship is an important part of China-UK relationship. In recent years, our two militaries have seen more active exchanges and cooperation than ever.

In the recent month alone,

- General Yu Zhongfu of the PLA Air Force led a delegation to the UK and attended the events marking the 100th anniversary of the Royal Air Force.
- The First Sea Lord Admiral Sir Philip Jones paid a successful visit to China.
- And the sixth China-UK Defence Strategic Consultation was successfully held.

Last year,

- The Chinese Navy Escort Taskforce paid its first visit to London.
- The Red Arrows performed at the Airshow China in Zhuhai for the first time.
- The two militaries held a successful joint evacuation tabletop exercise.
- And they have engaged in effective cooperation on the UN peacekeeping, counter-terrorism, anti-piracy and personnel training.

Ladies and Gentlemen,

President Xi Jinping said that we should have the right historical perspective. What he means is that we should review the past, draw lessons from history and grasp the historical trend.

In the last century, the world went through tests of fire and blood, endured wars and enjoyed peace. In the 21st century, it is important that we draw lessons from history and do our utmost to safeguard world peace and promote development.

I sincerely hope that China and the UK, and the militaries of our two countries will keep in mind the big picture of world peace and development.

First, we should enhance mutual trust.

Mutual trust is the basis of cooperation. China and the UK differ in history, culture and social system.

- But both our countries champion multilateralism and oppose unilateralism.
- Both support free trade and stand against protectionism.
- And both uphold the authority of the UN and the rule-based international order.

Our two countries have every reason to enhance dialogue, build mutual trust and deepen cooperation on the basis of equality and mutual respect.

Second, we should expand cooperation.

China-UK strategic partnership offers opportunities for our two sides to expand, deepen, upgrade and increase our exchanges and cooperation. This will enable us to pool our strengths in addressing the challenges to global security and development, and enhance the strategic and global significance of China-UK relations.

Through cooperation, the relationship between our two countries and our two militaries will grow strong and prosperous.

Third, we should safeguard peace.

China and the UK are permanent members of the UN Security Council. Both are countries of global influence. Both shoulder the important mission of safeguarding peace for mankind. It is our international responsibilities and obligations to join hands, cherish peace and safeguard peace.

The world is a community with a shared future for mankind. The people of the world deserve a better future—a future of lasting peace and universal security.

Together, we can make this happen.

Now, may I invite you to join me in a toast:

To the 91st anniversary of the People's Liberation Army of China,

To ever-growing China-UK relationship and military-to-military cooperation,

To lasting peace and universal security in the world!

Cheers!

第六章　华侨华人
PART VI　Chinese Community

华人移民英国已有200多年历史，利物浦是华人最早移民欧洲的城市，据史料记载，利物浦还建有欧洲最早的唐人街。目前在英国的华侨华人总数超过70万人，老侨、新侨和华裔新生代约各占1/3，华人大多集中在伦敦等主要城市，其中大伦敦地区的华侨华人约占总数的1/3。目前在英国高校工作的华侨华人超过6200人，其中正教授近600人。英国现有侨社经办的中文学校200余所。

旅英华侨华人有着光荣传统，他们始终情系家乡，心系祖国。19世纪末，孙中山先生在英国从事革命活动时，得到了旅英华侨华人的支持和帮助。抗日战争爆发后，旅英华侨华人成立了"抗日救国会"，声援国内抗战。新中国成立后，特别是改革开放以来，侨胞们更加爱祖国、爱家乡，支持国内经济建设，支持北京奥运会，倾情为汶川地震灾区捐款捐物，热心资助各项公益事业，为国家的发展做出了重要贡献。新冠疫情暴发以后，侨胞们团结互助、齐心抗疫，设立守望互助组、咨询群、救助站、应急队等，向在英中国公民和英国社会各界提供援助，为英国的医院和各类慈善机构抗疫捐资捐物，展现了中国人民兼善天下、关怀社会的仁爱情怀。

使英11年，我出席了近百场华侨华人活动，在整理这些演讲时，我与侨胞们的一幕幕往事历历在目。2015年，习近平主席对英国进行国事访问时，白金汉宫前林荫大道两边集聚了长达1000多米的华侨华人欢迎队伍，锣鼓喧天、红旗招展；2017年，中国海军护航编队访问伦敦时，码头上侨胞们齐整站立、摇旗欢呼；2019年，第十五届世界华商大会在伦敦隆重举办时，侨胞们共商合作，共谋发展，成果丰硕；每年特拉法加广场春节庆典人山人海，舞龙舞狮热烈奔放，花车巡游鲜艳夺目；还有全英华侨华人为庆祝中国国庆而举办晚宴、晚会；等等。这些活动都凝聚着侨胞们对祖国的深深热爱和血浓于水的同胞感情，每一场活动都是对中英友好合作的悉心呵护和有力推动。

本章收录了我的6篇演讲，从侨界欢迎招待会到第11次华侨华人新春招待会，这场新春招待会也是我离任前在英国出席的最后一场大型公共活动，活动上我发表了最后一篇演讲，这为我出使英国11年画上了一个圆满句号。

Chinese immigration to the UK has a history of over 200 years, with Liverpool being the first European city where Chinese migrants settled. Historical records show that Liverpool also had the first Chinatown in Europe. Currently, there are over 700,000 Chinese nationals and people of Chinese descent in the UK, with the communities of old immigrants, new immigrants, and new-generation Chinese each making up about one-third of the population. Most of the Chinese community live in major cities like London, with about one-third residing in Greater London. Over 6,200 Chinese nationals and people of Chinese descent work in British universities, including nearly 600 full professors. There are over 200 Chinese schools run by Chinese communities in the UK.

The Chinese community in the UK has a proud tradition of always being connected to their homeland. During the late 19th century, when Sun Yat-sen was engaged in revolutionary activities in the UK, the Chinese community in the UK supported and helped him. After the outbreak of the Anti-Japanese War, the Chinese community in the UK formed the "Anti-Japanese National Salvation Association" to support the war effort back home. Since the founding of the People's Republic of China, especially since the reform and opening-up, there has been an outpouring of passion among the Chinese community to support the economic development of their ancestral home and the Beijing Olympics, and donate generously to the Wenchuan earthquake disaster area as well as various public welfare causes. They have made significant contribution to the country's development. After the outbreak of the COVID-19 pandemic, the Chinese community in the UK united and helped each other, setting up mutual aid groups, consultation groups, rescue stations and emergency teams to provide assistance to Chinese citizens in the UK and various sectors of British society, and donate funds and materials to British hospitals and charities. They have demonstrated the benevolent spirit of the Chinese people.

During my 11 years in the UK, I attended nearly a hundred events hosted by the Chinese community. Reviewing my speeches in these events brings back many memories: In 2015, during President Xi Jinping's state visit to the UK, Chinese community members lined the Mall in front of Buckingham Palace, welcoming with red flags and drum beats; in 2017, during the visit of the Chinese naval escort task force to London, Chinese community members stood in neat rows at the dock, waving flags and cheering; in 2019, at the 15th World Chinese Entrepreneurs Convention in London, the Chinese community discussed cooperation and development, achieving fruitful results; every year, the Spring Festival celebrations at Trafalgar Square, with vibrant dragon and lion dances and colourful parade floats, are packed with people; and there are also the gala dinners and performances celebrating China's National Day organized by the Chinese community across the UK. These activities reflect the deep love of the Chinese community for their motherland and the strong bond between compatriots. Each event also served to nurture and promote China-UK friendship and cooperation.

This chapter includes 6 of my speeches, from remarks at the welcome reception of the Chinese community to words of farewell at the 11th Spring Festival reception, which was the last large public event I attended before leaving the UK. This event and my final speech marked a successful conclusion to my 11-year mission in the UK.

众人拾柴火焰高 *

各位侨领、各位侨胞：

非常感谢各位侨胞为我和我的夫人举行如此热烈的欢迎仪式，这不仅是大家对我们来英履新的热烈欢迎，更体现出大家对祖国和家乡的拳拳之心。

来英国之前，我就听说不少关于英国侨界的佳话。令我印象深刻的是英国华侨华人享有的之"最"。从历史来说，英国的利物浦是华人最早移民欧洲的地方，据英国1782年史料记载，利物浦建有欧洲最早的唐人街；成立于1901年的"英国致公总堂"是欧洲最早的华人社团；1894年在伦敦创刊的《中英商工机器时报》是欧洲最早的华文报纸。就现状而言，英国华侨华人人数已超过60万，在欧洲国家中数一数二；每年在伦敦特拉法加广场举办的中国春节活动是亚洲之外规模最大的春节庆典活动。还有一个之"最"，那就是大家公认的英国中餐在欧洲做得最地道。

当然，最令我感动的还是旅英侨胞始终情系家乡，心系祖国。1896年孙中山先生在英国从事革命活动时，得到了旅英华侨的支持和帮助。抗日战争爆发后，旅英华侨成立了"抗日救国会"，声援国内抗战。新中国成立后，特别是改革开放以来，侨胞们更加爱祖国、爱家乡，支持国内经济建设，支持北京奥运会，倾情为汶川地震灾区捐款捐物，热心资助各项公益事业，为国家的发展做出了重要贡献。你们的爱国爱乡行动，感人至深。在此，我向你们致以崇高的敬意和诚挚的谢意！

---

* 在英国侨界欢迎招待会上的讲话。2010年3月30日，伦敦唐人街。

我刚从国内来，古诗曰："君自故乡来，应知故乡事。"我愿向侨胞们介绍一下国内的情况。2009 年，受全球金融危机影响，国内经济较困难，但我们坚定信心，迎难而上，超额实现"保八"目标。2010 年国家经济面临的形势依然复杂严峻，这既有国内外因素，也有短期问题和长期矛盾。我们将化挑战为机遇，着力加快经济发展方式转变和经济结构调整，努力保持经济平稳较快发展。祖国的发展，离不开广大海外华侨华人的支持，希望你们一如既往，继续参与，共建祖国，同铸中华。

还有一个月，上海世博会即将开幕，听说你们将组织一个"百人团"赴上海观看。我们有信心像举办北京奥运会一样，将上海世博会办成一届有特色的、成功的、精彩的、难忘的盛会，既让中国了解世界，也让世界了解中国。希望大家大力支持上海世博会，踊跃前往参观，共襄盛举。

各位侨胞一直支持祖国和平统一大业，坚决反对"台独"。我们高兴地看到，近年来两岸关系呈现和平发展的良好势头，交流合作不断深入，全面直接双向"三通"得以实现，经济关系正常化迈出重要步伐。今后，我们将进一步密切两岸经贸金融交往，深化产业合作，加强民众和社会各界交流，使两岸关系持续改善和发展。在新的形势下，我们希望各位侨胞继续与我们齐心协力，推动两岸关系百尺竿头，更进一步。

各位侨胞也一直关心中英关系的发展，积极参与和推动中英友好交流与合作。中英关系是当今世界上最重要的大国关系之一，具有全球性和战略性。前一阶段，中英关系虽然出现了一些波折，但在双方的共同努力下，目前中英关系正朝好的方向发展。不久前，米利班德外交大臣访问了中国，双方决定提升中英战略对话级别，深化两国全面战略伙伴关系，为两国关系掀开了新的一页。事实证明，只要中英坚持相互尊重、平等相待的原则，坚持从战略高度把握和维护两国的共同利益，坚持加强对话和沟通，妥善处理分歧，中英关系就一定会保持长期健康稳定的发展。众人拾柴火焰高，希望侨胞们充分利用你们的独特地位，继续发挥两国间的桥梁作用，为中英全面战略伙伴关系的发展做出新的更大贡献。

我高兴地听说，在英华侨华人近年来与当地社会的沟通和交流得到不断加强，侨胞们大力传播中华文化，努力提升华人形象，积极参与公共事务，取得了很大的成绩。英国首相布朗每年都向英国华侨华人祝贺新春，2010年还在首相府专门为华侨华人举行招待会，高度评价华侨华人对英国社会的贡献和作用。伦敦及英国各地的新春庆典活动成为品牌，得到了英国各级政府的支持，受到了当地民众的喜爱。华人参政议政的意识也日益提高，2010年将有7位华裔候选人报名竞选议会下院议员。希望你们加强团结互助，积极融入当地社会，为自身发展争取更大的话语权。

作为新任驻英国大使，我本人和中国大使馆将继续全力支持你们。我们将继续支持侨胞们在英国的发展，努力维护你们的合法权益，推动解决大家关心的问题；我们将积极为你们与国内开展各方面合作牵线搭桥，提供更多的资讯和往来的便利；我们将进一步支持华文教育，在经费和师资方面提供帮助；我们将大力支持华侨华人社团举办各种有意义的活动。

我也衷心希望各侨团之间、新老侨之间加强团结，群策群力，更深入地参与当地的政治和社会生活，继续关心祖国的发展，支持祖国的统一大业，支持中英关系的发展，支持我和中国大使馆的工作。

一些华人朋友告诉我，伦敦唐人街将再建新的牌楼。我预祝牌楼早日建成，为唐人街增光添彩。到时，我一定来出席剪彩仪式。

最后，我祝愿侨胞们事业发达、身体健康、家庭幸福！

谢谢大家！

虽有智慧，不如乘势 *

各位教授、各位学者、各位专家：

首先，我热烈欢迎大家来中国大使馆出席今天的座谈会。

见到各位旅英专家学者，我不由得想起了20世纪70年代末的一部电影，想起了一位杰出的科学家。可能在座的很多人都看过电影《李四光》，也知道李四光先生的事迹，但大家可能不完全知道，李四光先生曾三度来英。第一次是1913—1918年，他在伯明翰大学攻读采矿和地质学。第二次是1934—1936年在英讲学。第三次是1948年来英参加第18届国际地质学大会，并在英国养病一年多。获悉新中国成立后他毅然回到祖国，投身国家的建设，为我国地质科学的发展做出了不可磨灭的贡献。

海外华人专家学者是我们国家的宝贵财富，是联系中国与世界的重要纽带。你们长期奋战在教育、科研的第一线，深谙国外教育、科技的体制和机制，学有所长、术有专攻，并建有全球化的人际网络，这些都是无可比拟的优势条件。国家始终关心你们，重视你们，一直支持你们在国外的发展，也期待你们为国家的建设发挥更大的作用，为促进中国与世界的合作与交流做出更大的贡献。

今天，我想通过座谈，了解大家在英国治学研究的体会，同时也愿听取你们对国内教育、科技发展的宝贵建议，对中英教育和科技合作的宝贵建议，对中国大使馆工作的宝贵建议。

---

* 在与旅英专家学者座谈会上的讲话。2010年4月25日，中国驻英国大使馆。

刚才大家结合自己多年来在英国学习和工作的切身体会，发表了各自的观点，其中充满真知灼见，我深受启发。

大家都是旅英专家学者中的高端人才，在各自的领域取得了突出成绩，也一直心系祖国，支持祖国的建设和发展，推动中英两国的教育和科研合作。在此，我向大家表示敬意和感谢！

在经济全球化的今天，各国实力的竞争越来越表现为高科技的竞争，高科技的竞争又体现在人才的竞争，人才的竞争归根于教育的竞争，所以教育与科技在当今世界经济社会发展中占有重要的地位。

中国政府高度重视实施科教兴国战略和人才强国战略，把科技进步和自主创新作为经济社会发展的重要推动力，把发展教育和培养高素质人才摆在更加突出的位置，努力建设创新型国家和人力资源强国。

2006年，国家颁布了《国家中长期科学和技术发展规划纲要（2006—2020年）》，提出到2020年全社会研究开发投入占国内生产总值的比重提高到2.5%以上，科技进步贡献率达到60%以上，对外技术依存度降低到30%以下等目标。国家目前正就《国家中长期教育改革和发展规划纲要（2010—2020年）》公开征求意见，其中提出，到2020年中国要基本实现教育现代化，基本形成学习型社会，进入人力资源强国行列。同时，国家还正在制定《国家中长期人才发展规划纲要（2010—2020年）》，提出人才资源是经济社会发展第一资源的思想，把人才的地位和作用提到了一个新的高度。

中国教育科技事业的兴盛，需要拔尖创新人才的引领。2008年，国家制定了《中央人才工作协调小组关于实施海外高层次人才引进计划的意见》，主要目标是围绕国家发展战略，用5~10年，引进并有重点地支持一批能够突破关键技术、发展高新产业、带动新兴学科的战略科学家和领军人才回国或来华创新创业。目前承担国家"863""973"等重大国家科技项目的首席科学家中，有一半以上是海外归国人员；在2006年度国家自然科学奖、国家技术发明奖和国家科技进步奖获奖项目第一完成人中，海外归国人员分别占67%、40%和30%以上。孟子曰："虽有智慧，不如乘势；虽有镃基，不如待时。"国家需要你们，建功立业正当其时！

当然，我们的政策是"支持留学，鼓励回国，来去自由"。出于事业和家庭等各种原因，大家可能选择继续在英发展，对此我们十分理解，也同样充满期望。

"水尝无华，相荡乃成涟漪；石本无火，相击乃发灵光。"我希望大家利用经常与国内高校、研究机构交流的机会，多向国内介绍英国的先进教育、科研理念，推动国内教学和科研水平的提高；希望大家积极促进中英高校、科研机构的沟通与合作，取长补短；也希望大家多招收一些来自国内的优秀年轻人到自己的研究机构学习和工作，多为我们国家培养高层次人才。

你们直接面向英国高端社会，面向英国知识精英和青年学子。希望大家在工作和生活中，多向你们身边的英国朋友、同事和学生介绍中国，以你们的故事、经历讲述一个现代的、真实的、充满活力的中国；也希望你们多通过自身的科研精神、科研成果展示中华民族的聪明才智，让英国民众更加了解中国、认识中国。

在座的各位教授、专家、学者都来自祖国大陆，无论在哪里，血浓于水的祖国感情都不会被隔断。祖国人民始终关注着你们，祖国始终是你们温暖的家，中国大使馆就是你们在英国的家。我们将一如既往地关心和帮助大家，为大家提供好服务。我也衷心地希望我及中国大使馆的工作今后继续得到大家的支持和协助。

再次感谢大家来使馆座谈！

越是民族的就越是世界的 *

尊敬的约克公爵安德鲁王子殿下,
尊敬的伦敦华埠商会邓柱廷主席,
尊敬的西敏寺市沙莫斯市长,
各位来宾,
女士们、先生们:
大家上午好!

今天,我很高兴与约克公爵殿下及各位来宾一起,出席伦敦华埠新牌楼的落成仪式。

首先,我代表中国驻英国大使馆对牌楼的落成表示热烈祝贺!对为筹建牌楼付出巨大辛劳和贡献的伦敦华埠商会及中国太平保险集团有限责任公司等赞助商表示衷心的感谢!

俗话说,越是民族的就越是世界的。

牌楼是中国特有的建筑艺术和文化载体,往往坐落于宫廷、寺院、园林门口或繁华大街路口,以其独特建筑风格和恢宏气势,尽显属地之高贵荣耀。

现在屹立在我们面前的新牌楼无疑是伦敦华埠的新地标,它不仅是一座具有中国特色的建筑,而且是一座丰碑,象征着广大英国华侨华人顶天立地、团结协作的精神,与人为善、敞开胸怀广迎天下客的情怀。"天行健,君子以自强不息;地势坤,君子以厚德载物。"祝愿牌楼为伦敦华埠商会乃

---

* 在伦敦华埠新牌楼落成仪式上的致辞。2016 年 7 月 25 日,伦敦中国城华都街牌楼。

至整个英国华社带来和谐繁荣、太平盛景。

这座牌楼也是中英友好的象征。牌楼的建设得到中国国务院侨办等中方机构和部门的帮助，也得到伦敦市及西敏寺市政府的大力支持，今天约克公爵殿下又亲临落成仪式，这说明中英双方都很重视发展中英友好关系。

2015年10月，习近平主席对英国的"超级国事访问"开创了中英面向21世纪的全球全面战略伙伴关系，目前两国间政治、经济、人文等各领域的交流与合作蓬勃发展。

我希望并相信，中英关系发展的良好势头不会因英国公投脱欧而改变，也不会因英国政府变动而变化，就像我们面前这座牌楼一样，"任尔东西南北风，我自岿然不动"。

最后，祝今天走过华埠新牌楼的各界人士身体健康、家庭幸福、事业发达！

What Is Unique to a Nation Is Precious for the World[*]

Your Royal Highness,

Chairman Tang,

Lord Mayor,

Distinguished Guests,

Ladies and Gentlemen,

Good Morning!

It is a great delight for me to join Your Royal Highness and all of you today in celebrating the completion of the new Chinese Gate in London Chinatown.

On behalf of the Chinese Embassy, let me begin by extending warm congratulations and sincere appreciation to the London Chinatown Chinese Association, China Taiping, and other sponsors. You have made tremendous efforts and contributions to create this new gate.

This gate is typical of many found across China. It reflects highly distinctive Chinese architecture that goes back many millennia. There are all rich details and cultural symbols. They are mostly found in front of palaces, temples and gardens or at the entrance to major streets. Everywhere, these magnificent gates honour the place where they stand.

There is a popular saying in China:

"What is unique to a nation is precious for the world."

---

[*] Remarks Marking the Completion of the New Chinese Gate in London Chinatown. Wardour Street, 25 July 2016.

Now this brand new magnificent Chinese gate, providing a most fitting focal point and entrance into London's Chinatown, is undoubtedly a new landmark:

- It is more than an architecture with Chinese features.
- It is a monument to the unity and indomitable spirit of the Chinese community in the UK.
- It is a symbol of their hospitality and kindness.
- It is a reflection of their perseverance, hard work and social commitment.
- It stands for their aspiration for harmony, peace and prosperity—not only in London Chinatown—but also for all the Chinese communities across Britain.

At the same time, this gate is also a symbol of China-UK friendship:

- The construction of the gate is symbolic of the collaboration of our two nations. It had the assistance and support of relevant Chinese and British authorities. They are, respectively, China's Overseas Chinese Affairs Office of the State Council, Greater London Authority and Westminster City Council.
- Today, His Royal Highness is joining us to witness this event. This is yet another example of the great support from the British Royal family to China-UK relations.
- The Gate is symbolic of how China and the UK reach out to each other and greatly value the importance of building friendship.

Last year, President Xi Jinping paid a "super state visit" to Britain. During the visit, our two countries agreed to build a global comprehensive strategic partnership for the 21st century.

At present, exchanges and cooperation between China and the UK are flourishing in the political, economic, cultural and many other fields.

It is my sincere hope and firm belief that the momentum in China-UK relations will remain strong and unaffected by the Brexit referendum or the change of the British government.

It is my sincere wish that China-UK relations will grow even stronger. Just as this gate will always stand tall and firm, whatever the elements, through sun, rain and wind.

In conclusion, I wish everyone who walks through this gate good health, happiness and success!

秉持"石头精神",推进中英合作[*]

尊敬的各位大学校长,

各位皇家工程院院士,

各位教授,

各位学者:

大家过年好!

今天是大年初十,按照中国传统习俗,"十"谐音"石",所以今天是"石头生日",也称"石头节"。国内有些地方还会专门举办仪式,祭石谢地,以表达感恩之情。

石头与留英中国学者也有不解之缘。著名地质学家李四光在年轻时,因为一块大石头而萌生对地质学的兴趣。他后来专门赴英学习地质学,并通过考察大石头,研究出长江流域第四纪冰川活动的重要成果,震惊世界。

李四光的"石头精神"激励着一代代负笈英伦的中国学生和学者,地球物理学家黄大年就是其中一位优秀代表。他是听着李四光的故事长大的,他在李四光创办的长春地质学院求学,也曾在英国多所大学深造,并像李四光一样放弃了在英国的优越条件,学成回国,走上了科技报国之路,为祖国发展贡献了一系列重大科技成果。

黄大年的先进事迹感动了千千万万中国人,习近平主席号召大家向他学

---

[*] 在为全英华裔教授学者举行的新春招待会上的讲话。2018年2月25日,中国驻英国大使馆。

习。我认为，黄大年身上这种至诚报国的爱国情怀、敢为人先的开拓精神、甘于奉献的高尚情操，既是李四光"石头精神"的传承，也是当前 6000 多名在英华人教授学者的缩影。

20 世纪 80 年代初我也曾在海外留学，深知在欧美国家高校当上教授很不容易，中国人在英国的名校当上教授则更不容易，而当上校长、当上皇家工程院院士就更是难上加难。大家排除万难，迎难而上，通过奋斗不仅获得自身成功，也为中国人赢得了尊敬和荣誉。我作为中国驻英国大使，为你们感到骄傲和自豪。

最近，习近平主席在会见英国梅首相时，又一次引用莎士比亚的名句："凡是过去，皆为序章。"中英关系如此，我们每个人的事业、学业恐怕也是如此。因此，我希望大家在新的一年里继续秉持李四光的"石头精神"，不断取得新的成就。为此，我向大家提"三点希望"。

第一，在参与国内建设上，要"坚如磐石"。中共十九大胜利召开，标志着中国特色社会主义进入新时代。新时代更加需要我们海内外全体中华儿女团结一心、坚定信念、发愤图强，把爱国之情、报国之志融入祖国改革发展的伟大事业之中，融入人民创造历史的伟大奋斗之中，为实现"两个一百年"奋斗目标、实现中华民族伟大复兴的中国梦贡献智慧和力量。大家身在英国，可以充分发挥各自在学科、学校及社会上的影响，通过指导和培养优秀青年人才、推动设立创新科技园区、建设联合实验室等多种形式为祖国发展做出贡献，使国家发展"坚如磐石"。

第二，在促进中英合作上，要"点石成金"。春节前夕，梅首相成功访华，两国领导人就增强两国关系的战略性、务实性、全球性和包容性达成重要共识。双方签署了一系列合作协议，其中教育合作协议总价值超过 5.5 亿英镑，包括"中英数学教师交流项目"延期、加强英语教师赴华教学等项目。教育合作已日益成为中英人文交流的一大亮点。我本人也非常重视促进中英教育合作，仅 2017 年就参加了 20 多场与教育有关的活动，被使馆同事们称为"教育大使"。中英务实合作还有很多潜力可以挖掘，大家在教育、科研等领域可以发挥重要作用。比如英国在科技创新、创意等领域世界领先，而中国在市场、资金等方面有优势，如果能找到对接点，有效整合双方优势，则必能"点石成金"。

第三，在讲好中国故事上，要"踏石留印"。英国不少民众对中国缺乏了解，英国媒体对中国还存有不少偏见。从我开展公共外交的经验看，讲好中国故事要掌握三个要点：一要有自信，关于中国的发展道路，要理直气壮地讲，要旗帜鲜明地讲，要坚持道路自信、理论自信、制度自信、文化自信；二要接地气，要用英国民众熟悉的语言和方式讲中国故事，要让英国民众听得进、听得懂、听而信；三要坚持不懈，久久为功。我担任驻英大使8年来，遍访各地，每到一地都演讲发声，并在英国各大报刊上投书撰文，接受各大电视台、电台采访，可以说实现全覆盖，目的就是让英国民众了解一个真实的中国。讲好中国故事不仅是外交官的事，也是每个在英中国人的责任。各位教授、院士、学者德高望重，是中国的形象大使，希望大家多向英国朋友讲中国的故事、讲中国人民的故事，努力做到"踏石留印"。

金鸡振翅去，瑞犬迎春来。狗年寓意着忠诚和勤奋，象征着兴旺与发展。大家在报效祖国、努力工作的同时，也要保重身体，维护自身权益，团结一致，更好地形成合力。

中国驻英国大使馆始终是大家在英国的家，是大家的坚强后盾。今天既然是"石头节"，我向大家承诺，使馆也要当好"三块石头"：一是"铺路石"，为大家参与国内建设开山铺路、牵线搭桥；二是"压舱石"，确保中英关系行稳致远，为大家在英发展保驾护航；三是"上马石"，为大家讲好中国故事提供助力和便利。

最后，恭祝大家狗年大吉、身体健康、工作顺利！

牢记共同的血脉，开创共赢的未来 *

尊敬的各位中英企业家，

女士们、先生们：

大家下午好！

很高兴出席第十五届世界华商大会闭幕式，我谨代表中国驻英国大使馆对大会的成功举办表示热烈祝贺！

过去3天，全球华商首次云集英国，乡音萦绕、忆祖溯根，放眼世界、擘画未来，不仅开创了世界华商大会历史上参会国家数量之最，更向英国、向欧洲、向全球展示了世界华商大会的"三大品牌"。

一是互联互通的枢纽。全球华商同源、同文又同行，可以说是当今世界最大也最富有潜力的资本网络、人脉网络、资讯网络之一。正如中国全国政协主席汪洋在贺信中所说，世界华商大会是凝聚全球华商力量、展示各国华商形象、促进各方交流合作、具有全球影响力的重要平台。这样一个平台，是互联互通的天然枢纽。我们期待这个枢纽在"一带一路"高质量发展的伟大征程中，在推动构建人类命运共同体的伟大事业中，发挥独特的联通作用。希望大家继续深挖潜力、整合资源、拓宽渠道，积极践行共商共建共享共赢理念，联通世界华商与欧洲及各地工商界，联通中国与世界，为世界经济增长开辟新空间、提供新机遇。

二是华人精神的引擎。自强不息、重情重义、兼容并蓄是华人精神的内

---

* 在第十五届世界华商大会闭幕式上的致辞。2019年10月23日，伦敦展览会议中心。

核,也是全球华商的品牌形象。这股精神成就了各位华商的光辉事业,也为新中国发展的伟大奇迹做出了重要贡献。习近平主席指出,"中国改革开放事业取得伟大成就,广大华侨华人功不可没","实现中国梦,是海内外中华儿女的共同愿景,也将为世界各国人民带来更多利益和机遇"。希望世界华商大会继续弘扬华人精神,鼓励全球华商抓住新一轮产业革命带来的新机遇,把握新时代中国特色社会主义建设带来的新机遇,抢占先机,接续奋斗,成为中华民族伟大复兴征程上的一支生力军。

三是文明交融的样板。正如自然界需要物种多样性,人类社会同样需要文明多样性。爱好和平、相互尊重,是全世界华夏儿女的传统美德;学贯中西、融通中外,是全世界华商的独特优势。世界华商大会已经发展成为增进和平与友好的民间论坛,来自世界各地的华商通过论坛开展丰富多彩的交流活动,团结更多爱好和平、谋求发展的各国人民,影响更多决策者和行业精英,倡导文明对话,促进包容互鉴,使爱好和平的薪火代代相传,使文明交融的光芒熠熠生辉。

女士们、先生们、朋友们,

第十五届世界华商大会即将落幕,但它已在全球华商发展史以及中英经贸合作史上留下浓墨重彩的一笔,激励着我们牢记共同的血脉、开创共赢的未来!

最后,祝愿世界华商大会不断谱写新篇章,不断铸就新辉煌!

谢谢大家!

Our Common Roots, Our Shared Future[*]

Chinese and British Entrepreneurs,

Ladies and Gentlemen,

Good afternoon!

It is a pleasure to join you at the closing ceremony of the 15th World Chinese Entrepreneurs Convention(WCEC). On behalf of the Chinese Embassy, I wish to extend my warmest congratulations on the success of the Convention.

The three-day Convention brought Chinese entrepreneurs from all over the world to the UK. It is a great reunion of the Chinese entrepreneurs' family. It is a moment to reconnect with our ancestry roots. More importantly, it is a platform that enables the entrepreneurs to adopt a global vision and make plans for future development. It will not only go down in history as a WCEC that attracted participants from the greatest number of countries. It has also displayed the three major features of the WCEC to the UK, to Europe and to the world.

First, WCEC is a hub of connectivity. Sharing a common ancestor, speaking the same language and involved in the same trade, Chinese entrepreneurs form the most extensive network with the greatest potential in capital, connections and information in the whole world.

Just as CPPCC Chairman Wang Yang said in his message of congratulations, the WCEC can pool the strength of the Chinese entrepreneurs in the world, highlight their image, and promote exchange and cooperation. It is an important platform of global

---

[*] Remarks at the Closing Ceremony of the 15th World Chinese Entrepreneurs Convention. ExCel London, 23 October 2019.

influence.

This platform is a natural hub of connectivity. It could play a unique role in the high-quality development of the Belt and Road Initiative and the great cause of building a community with a shared future for mankind.

I hope the Chinese entrepreneurs will continue to tap your potential, integrate your resources and explore new business channels. I hope you will put the concepts of extensive consultation, joint contribution and shared benefits into practice. I hope you will be the bridge linking the Chinese entrepreneurs in the world with your counterparts in Europe and other places, and linking China and the world. In doing so, you could open up new space and create new opportunities for world economic growth.

Second, WCEC is an engine of Chinese spirit. At the core of the Chinese national spirit is the continuous desire to reach for the best, the firm belief in friendship and brotherhood, and the open mind that tolerates differences. This is a summary of the image of the Chinese entrepreneurs all over the world. This spirit enabled the Chinese entrepreneurs to achieve success in their own business and make important contribution to the great miracle in the development of New China.

President Xi Jinping said, the vast majority of the overseas Chinese and Chinese descendents have made an indelible contribution to the great achievements of China's reform and opening-up; realizing the Chinese Dream is the common aspiration of the Chinese sons and daughters home and abroad, and will deliver more benefits and create more opportunities for the people all over the world.

I hope the WCEC will carry forward the Chinese spirit and encourage Chinese enterprises to seize the new opportunities of the new round of industrial revolution and the opportunities of socialism with Chinese characteristics in the new era. I will count on you to make relentless efforts and become a strong and reliable force on the journey towards the great renewal of the Chinese nation.

Third, WCEC is a perfect example of coexistence between different civilizations. Nature depends on biodiversity. Likewise, the human society thrives because of diverse civilizations. The Chinese people are known for their traditional ethics, such as the love for peace and the respect for each other. The Chinese entrepreneurs are uniquely positioned to understand both Chinese and Western thinking.

This is why the WCEC has grown into a people-to-people forum devoted to peace and friendship. Chinese entrepreneurs from all over the world come together for this Convention, where they engage one another in lively discussions, bring together peace-loving and development-oriented people from other countries and influence decision-makers and industry leaders.

This is a forum for dialogue between different civilisations. This is a platform for inclusive exchanges and mutual learning. This is the way forward to carry the torch of peace and shine the light of mutual learning.

Ladies and Gentlemen,

The curtain is about to fall on a successful convention, but the 15th WCEC will leave its indelible mark on the history of global Chinese business development and the economic cooperation between China and the UK. It will remind us of our common roots and encourage us to build a win-win future.

In conclusion, I wish the WCEC continued success and greater achievements in the future.

Thank you!

共庆新春佳节，共筑复兴伟业 *

侨胞们、同学们、同志们：

大家好！

值此新春佳节即将到来之际，很高兴在线上与大家欢聚一堂，共度佳节，共贺新春。在此，我给大家拜个早年！祝大家牛年大吉！

刚刚过去的2020年在新中国历史上是极不平凡的一年。

这是攻坚克难、成果丰硕的一年。面对突如其来的新冠疫情，中国采取了科学的防控措施，坚持人民至上、生命至上，用全民一心、众志成城，书写了抗疫斗争取得重大战略成果的壮丽史诗。我们在疫情防控的同时，经济社会发展也取得重大成就。"十三五"圆满收官，"十四五"全面擘画。新发展格局加快构建，高质量发展深入推进。我国在世界主要经济体中率先实现正增长，2020年国内生产总值迈上百万亿元新台阶。"天问一号""嫦娥五号""奋斗者"号等科学探测实现重大突破。全面建成小康社会取得历史性成就，决战脱贫攻坚取得决定性胜利。

这是和衷共济、守望相助的一年。面对疫情全球肆虐危机，中国从一开始就积极倡导国际抗疫合作，同各国携手抗击疫情，以实际行动践行人类命运共同体的理念。我们已向150多个国家和10个国际组织提供抗疫援助，我们还最早承诺将疫苗作为全球公共产品，致力于让发展中国家用得上、用得起疫苗，积极推进国际抗疫合作。英国疫情暴发以来，大家团结互助、齐心

---

* 在2021年华侨华人新春招待会上的讲话。2021年1月27日，中国驻英国大使馆。

抗疫，设立守望互助组、咨询群、救助站、应急队等，向在英中国公民和英国社会各界提供援助，中医界发挥中医独特优势提供咨询和用药服务，大家还为英国的医院和各类慈善机构抗疫捐资捐物，展现了中国人民兼善天下、关怀社会的仁爱情怀，难能可贵，值得点赞！我们坚信，在各国人民共同努力下，疫情一定会被战胜，危机一定会被克服，人类必将取得最终的胜利！

这是脚踏实地、孕育希望的一年。我们释放对外开放"新红利"，签署《区域全面经济伙伴关系协定》，完成中欧投资协定谈判，积极推进高质量共建"一带一路"，为全球经济复苏注入关键动力。我们担当多边合作"领头羊"，高举多边主义旗帜，积极参与应对气候变化国际合作，宣布碳达峰、碳中和国家自主贡献新目标，提出《全球数据安全倡议》，主动引领全球治理体系的变革。我们坚信，一个走向复兴、充满机遇、开放合作的中国，必将为世界注入更多"正能量"和稳定性，必将为世界和平、稳定和繁荣做出更大贡献。

侨胞们、同学们、同志们，

2021年是中国共产党百年华诞，也是"十四五"规划开局之年。站在"两个一百年"的历史交汇点上，我们要接续奋斗、砥砺前行，在全面建设社会主义现代化国家新征程上勇往直前，在实现中华民族伟大复兴的壮阔道路上再创辉煌。

今年的招待会，对我和我的夫人胡平华而言，具有格外特殊的意义。这是我们第十一次举行华侨华人新春招待会，也是我离任前在英国出席的最后一场大型公共活动。回首出使英伦这11年，我与同胞们的一幕幕往事历历在目。记得2015年习近平主席访英时，白金汉宫前林荫大道两边集聚了长达1000多米的华侨华人欢迎队伍，锣鼓喧天、红旗招展；2017年中国海军护航编队访问伦敦时，码头上同胞们齐整站立、摇旗欢呼；2019年第十五届世界华商大会在伦敦隆重举行、成果丰硕；每年特拉法加广场春节庆典人山人海，舞龙舞狮热烈奔放，花车巡游鲜艳夺目，"四海同春""欢乐春节"演出精彩纷呈；还有全英华侨华人为庆祝中国国庆而举办晚宴、晚会；等等。这些激动人心的场面不胜枚举、令人难以忘怀。每一场活动都有侨领侨胞、留学生和中资机构人员的忙碌身影和倾情奉献，每一场活动都凝聚着大家对祖国的深深热爱和血浓于水的同胞感情，每一场活动都是对中英友好合作的悉心呵护和有力推动，也都是对中国驻英国大使馆和我本人工作的巨大鼓舞和支持。

  临别之际，我们想要对大家说的话很多，千言万语化为一句衷心的感谢！我们将带着无限美好的回忆返回祖国，我们将永远不忘同胞们的深情厚谊。我们将继续关心中英关系，继续关注同胞们在英国的生活、工作、事业、学业。希望大家继续做好防疫、保重身体。最后，祝大家牛年吉祥、平安健康、阖家幸福！我们后会有期。

  谢谢大家！

第七章　英国友人
PART Ⅶ　British Friends

中英关系的发展离不开英国各界友好人士的支持，他们在不同的时期、不同的领域，为中英关系的发展做出了重要的贡献。本章收录了我的 5 篇关于英国友人的演讲，他们都是英国友人中的杰出代表。

其中有政治家希思，在他任英国首相期间，中英建立了大使级外交关系。他在卸任后访华 26 次，为推动中英关系发展不辞辛劳，获得中国民间外交最高荣誉"人民友好使者"称号，他也是最后一位见过毛泽东、周恩来和邓小平三位中国领导人的外国领导人。也有为中英达成香港问题解决方案、实现香港顺利回归中国做出历史性贡献的英国前副首相兼外交大臣杰弗里·豪。还有终其一生投入中国科技史研究的著名汉学家和科学家李约瑟，他的巨著《中国科技史》卷帙浩繁，蔚为大观，改变了世界对中国的认知，对中西文化交流产生了深远影响。更有为中英教育交流和合作做出重要贡献的英国诺丁汉大学前校长大卫·格林纳韦，他领导的诺丁汉大学在中英教育交流中创造了多个第一。最后还有获得"中国改革友谊奖章"的英国四十八家集团俱乐部主席斯蒂芬·佩里。20 世纪 50 年代，佩里的父亲杰克·佩里与数十位英国工商界人士冲破重重阻力，开启了"破冰之旅"，打开同新中国贸易往来的大门。多年来，佩里继承父志，积极推进中英经贸合作和人文交流，支持中国改革开放事业，使破冰精神薪火相传。当今世界多重挑战交织叠加，我们更需要"破冰者"。正如习近平主席所说，希望中英各界有识之士传承富有远见、开放合作、敢为人先的破冰精神，奋力开拓合作共赢新局面。

The development of China-UK relations has always benefited from the support of friends across various sectors in the UK, who have made significant contributions at different times and in different fields. This chapter includes 5 of my speeches about a few outstanding representatives of my British friends.

They include political leader Edward Heath, under whose premiership the UK established ambassadorial diplomatic relations with China. After stepping down, he visited China 26 times, worked tirelessly to promote China-UK relations, and was awarded the highest honour in Chinese people's diplomacy, the "Friendship Ambassador". He was also the last foreign leader to meet Mao Zedong, Zhou Enlai, and Deng Xiaoping. Also included is Geoffrey Howe, the former Deputy Prime Minister and Foreign Secretary of the UK, who made a historic contribution to the resolution of the Hong Kong question and the smooth return of Hong Kong to China. Another notable figure is Joseph Needham, a renowned sinologist and scientist whose monumental work *Science and Civilization in China* profoundly changed the world's perception of China and had a far-reaching impact on China-Western cultural exchanges. There is also David Greenaway, former Vice-Chancellor of the University of Nottingham, who made significant contributions to China-UK educational exchanges and cooperation, leading the University of Nottingham to achieve several firsts in China-UK education cooperation. Lastly, there is Stephen Perry, Chairman of the 48 Group Club, who received the "China Reform Friendship Medal". In the 1950s, Stephen's father, Jack Perry, and several British business people broke through numerous obstacles to open the door to trade with the newly established People's Republic of China. This was known as the "Icebreaking Mission". Over the years, Stephen Perry has carried forward his father's legacy, actively promoting China-UK economic and cultural exchanges and supporting China's reform and opening-up. He has made sure that the spirit of the "Icebreakers" lives on. In today's world, facing multiple challenges, we need more "Icebreakers". As President Xi Jinping said, we hope that visionary individuals from all sectors in China and the UK will carry forward the visionary, open, cooperative and pioneering spirit of the "Icebreakers" to open up new prospects for win-win cooperation.

研究历史,关注当代 *

尊敬的李约瑟研究所董事会主席约翰·博伊德爵士,
尊敬的李约瑟研究所所长克里斯托弗·库伦教授,
女士们、先生们:
很高兴再次来到李约瑟研究所并参加今天的赠书仪式。

中国有句古语:"触景生情,睹物思人。"在李约瑟先生亲手创办的研究所举办这样有意义的活动,我想我们首先应该共同缅怀李约瑟先生的非凡一生,追忆他与中国的不解之缘。

李约瑟先生是一位杰出的生物化学家,但是更让人们记住的是,他是一位伟大的汉学家和科技史专家。他于20世纪30年代末与中国结缘,在此后的50多年里,他始终以满腔的热情投入中国科技史的研究中。他的皇皇巨著《中国科技史》卷帙浩繁,蔚为大观,系统地改变了世界对中国的认知,对中西方文化交流产生了深远影响,确立了他在中国乃至世界科技史研究领域的崇高学术地位。1995年李约瑟先生逝世时,英国《独立报》在其讣告中写道:"李约瑟的去世是学术界的重大损失,他的学术成就寰宇之内无人与其比肩,古往今来无人望其项背。"

李约瑟先生不仅是一位震古烁今的学者,还是一位矢志不渝的友好使者。1942—1946年,李约瑟先生在中国最困难的时期,在华担任中英科学合作馆

---

* 在向英国剑桥大学李约瑟研究所赠书仪式上的讲话。2013年10月18日,英国剑桥大学李约瑟研究所。

馆长，与中国的科学界结下了深厚的情谊。1950年，他亲自创办了英中友好协会，在中英尚未建立外交关系的年代，为促进中英民间友好发挥了巨大作用。1965年，他担任英中了解协会的首任会长，积极推动该组织全面介绍中国，为英国民众了解中国打开了一扇窗户。2009年，李约瑟当之无愧地被评为"百年来为中国做出杰出贡献的十大国际友人"之一。

李约瑟先生不仅自己著作等身，而且带动了英国乃至西方的东方科技史研究，其最重要成果便是李约瑟研究所的创立。今天，李约瑟研究所已经成为中国和东方科技史研究领域首屈一指的国际性研究中心，吸引了大批世界各地的科研人员来此从事研究。不仅如此，李约瑟研究所东亚科技史图书馆的丰富馆藏和珍贵的中文古籍善本在西方国家中独一无二，成为东亚研究学者们向往的圣地。

今天，我代表中国文化部、中国国家图书馆和中国驻英国大使馆向李约瑟研究所赠送关于中国文化和历史等方面的书籍约200册，并赠送中国国家图书馆网上阅览贵宾卡。这既是为李约瑟研究所图书馆增加馆藏，也是与时俱进，为李约瑟研究所"电子扩容"贡献一份力量。我衷心希望这些书籍和网上阅览贵宾卡有助于李约瑟研究所继续加强中国科技研究，在学术上百尺竿头，更上一层楼。

李约瑟先生是研究中国古代科技史的学者。古代的中国，科技成就斐然，文化灿烂辉煌；今天的中国，经济飞速发展，社会全面进步。中国人民正在为实现国家富强、民族振兴、人民幸福的"中国梦"而努力奋斗。如何客观认识并深入研究当代中国，对英国乃至世界来说，既是一个现实问题，也是一项艰巨挑战。我希望，英国和西方的学术界，不仅知古，也要出古厚今；既要研究古代中国，更要关注当代中国；既要继承李约瑟先生从事的事业，更要开拓李约瑟先生在学术上未及涉足的领域。这是对李约瑟先生事业最好的继承和发展。

我们对前人总是充满尊重和景仰，但作为后人，面对时代赋予的使命，我们也必须进行突破与超越。只有这样，我们才能增进中英人民之间的了解和友谊，深化两国之间的交流与合作；才能不断攀登科学高峰，为人类文明与进步事业做出新的更大贡献。

谢谢！

Study History and Focus on the Present[*]

Chairman Sir John Boyd,

Professor Cullen,

Ladies and Gentlemen,

It is a real pleasure for me to revisit the Needham Research Institute and join you at this book donation ceremony.

As an old Chinese saying goes:

"Memories revive at hearing of familiar names, and a particular sight stirs up feelings."

We are today gathered in the Institute founded by Dr Needham and named after him. So, it is timely and fitting to recollect the exceptional life of Dr Needham and in particular his extraordinary relationship with China.

Dr Needham was an outstanding biochemist, but he is best remembered as a great Sinologist and historian of science.

His passion for China started in late 1930s. In the more than half a century that followed, he was devoted heart and soul to the research of history of science in China.

His voluminous magnum opus, *Science and Civilization in China* radically changed Western perception of China. In addition, Dr Needham's scholarship made a far and deep influence on cultural exchanges between China and the West.

His study of China is recognized as a masterpiece. It also established his elevated academic status in the research of Chinese and world history of science.

---

[*] Speech at the Book Donation Ceremony at the Needham Research Institute. Cambridge University, 18 October 2013.

In 1995 Dr Needham passed away. In an obituary *The Independent* newspaper wrote:

"With the death of Joseph Needham, the world of learning has lost one of the greatest scholars in this or any country, of this or any century."

Dr Needham was not only an extraordinary scholar, but also a committed envoy of China-Britain friendship.

From 1942 to 1946 in the war-torn China, Dr Needham supervised the Sino-British Science Cooperation Office in Chongqing. Through this work he developed deep friendship with Chinese scientific communities.

In 1950 he personally founded the British-China Friendship Association. In the absence of diplomatic relations between China and Britain, the association played a huge role in promoting China-Britain people-to-people exchanges.

In 1965 Dr Needham became the first president of the Society for Anglo-China Understanding. Through the Society, he worked tirelessly to present the British public a full and comprehensive view of China.

In 2009 in China, Dr Needham was rightly honored "one of the top ten international friends for making exceptional contributions to the country in the past 100 years".

Apart from his own academic attainments, Dr Needham generated a wide interest in the history of oriental science in Britain and in the West at large. A landmark development was the founding of the Needham Research Institute.

Today this Institute has become a world-class centre for the research of oriental and Chinese history of science. The Institute attracts a multitude of researchers from across the world and offers a unique asset for understanding China.

Moreover, the library of the Needham Research Institute is of global importance, with a vast number of manuscripts, periodicals, and microfilms about China and a large quantity of traditional Chinese thread-bound books.

No other collection of this kind exists outside of China. This means the library is a magnet for researchers of East Asian studies.

Today, I represent the Chinese Ministry of Culture, the National Library of China and the Chinese Embassy.

On their behalf, it is my great pleasure to donate to the Needham Research Institute about 200 books on Chinese culture and history, and a VIP permit for on-line access at the National Library of China.

This donation has two aims. First, to enlarge the physical collection of the Institute's library. Second, to contribute to the digital development of the Needham Research Institute.

Looking forward, I do hope these books and the on-line reading card will help the Institute make greater academic achievements.

Dr Needham's research focused on science in ancient China.

We all agree that China in the past indisputably led the world in science and civilization.

But, we should also realize that China today enjoys extraordinarily rapid economic growth and comprehensive social progress. The Chinese people are now striving to achieve the Chinese Dream, a dream of bringing about prosperity of the country, renewal of the nation and happiness of the people.

How to get a true and full picture, as well as a deep understanding of modern China? This is a pressing task and a daunting challenge for Britain, as well as for the rest of Western world.

I hope that British and Western academic communities will not only study ancient China, but more importantly, focus on what is happening in today's China. I hope your Institute will open new frontiers as well as build on the foundations created by Dr Needham. I believe this would be the best way to make his legacy last and show our respect for him.

We can always benefit through reflection about great figures in history. But, we are a new generation in a new era. We should strive to make our own breakthroughs and set new records.

This is the only way to deepen understanding and friendship between Chinese and British people.

This is the only path to strengthen exchange and cooperation between China and Britain.

This is the only route to scale new heights in science and make greater contributions to human civilization and advancement.

Thank you!

友谊的记忆永不褪色 *

尊敬的亨特议员，

各位受托人，

女士们、先生们：

我和我的同事今天怀着崇敬的心情，前来拜访希思先生故居。我想首先感谢亨特议员的热情邀请和周到安排，感谢各位故居受托人出席今天的活动，也感谢各位本地和远道而来的记者朋友。

虽然我是第一次来，但很早就听说这里是"英国最佳风景地"。据说一位来访者曾对希思先生赞叹这所房子完全可以列入"英国十佳风景之一"，主人反问道，"为什么？另外九处在哪里？"

希思先生是一位颇具传奇色彩的人物。在英国人的记忆里，他是首相，是保守党领袖，是议会下院之父（曾是连续任期最长的下院议员），是把英国带入欧共体的领路人，是反绥靖的斗士，是参加反法西斯战争的军人，是音乐家，也是顶级的帆船手。对大多数人来说，能做到其中之一已是莫大成就，但希思先生却囊括了全部。

在中国人的记忆里，他是"中国人民的老朋友"。正是在希思首相任期内，中英两国于1972年建立了大使级外交关系，开启了两国关系正常化的时代。从1974年起，他27年里访华26次，是继李约瑟博士后第二位获得

---

* 在英国前首相希思故居的讲话。2014年7月11日，希思故居，英国索尔兹伯里镇。

中国民间外交最高荣誉"人民友好使者"称号的英国友人，也是最后一位见过毛泽东、周恩来和邓小平三位中国领导人的外国领导人。

经过40多年的发展，希思先生与中国老一辈政治家开创的中英关系已经今非昔比。中英双边贸易额从1972年的3亿多美元增长到2013年的700多亿美元，有望到2015年突破千亿美元。相互投资从无到有，规模从小到大，到2013年底，中英双向投资存量已超过500亿美元，其中中国对英投资存量323亿美元，英国也成为中资在欧洲首要投资目的地。中英人文交流蓬勃发展，人员往来从1972年的200人次增长到2013年的100万人次以上，中国在英留学生从首批16人增长到目前的13万人，仅次于美国，居世界第二。

前不久，李克强总理访问英国并举行两国总理年度会晤。双方领导人就打造共同发展、包容增长的伙伴关系达成共识，为进一步深化中英全面战略伙伴关系绘制了蓝图。

中国有句古话："吃水不忘掘井人。"中英关系能够达到今天的高度、深度和广度，离不开60多年前英国工商界人士的"经贸破冰"，离不开希思先生等英国有识之士的"政治破冰"，也离不开在场的佩里先生和彼得先生等人士数十年如一日推动中英友好合作的不懈努力。

今天，中国与世界的交往空前密切，我们在各国、各界结交了不少新朋友，但是我们没有也不会忘记为中国发展建设、为中国与世界各国友好合作做出过历史性贡献的老朋友。

培根说过，"友谊不但能使人摆脱暴风骤雨的感情而走向阳光明媚的晴空，而且能使人摆脱黑暗混乱的胡思乱想而走入光明与理智的思考"。中英关系发展到今天，中英合作未来持续健康稳定发展，都离不开友谊的滋养，离不开我们共同的呵护。

这次我来此访问，就是要以中英友好之根深，促中英合作之叶茂。我们带来了20多幅图片，既包括希思先生生前与中国交往的珍贵记录，也包括中英关系几十年发展历程的一些重要时刻。展出结束后，这些图片将全部赠送给希思故居收藏。

我衷心希望通过这次访问，能带动更多中英两国年轻人来此追寻中英友好永不褪色的历史记忆，激励他们加入促进中英友好与合作的事业中，共同书写新的更加美好的篇章。

谢谢！

The Memory of Friendship Never Fades[*]

Lord Hunt,

Trustees,

Ladies and Gentlemen,

We are grateful to Lord Hunt for his invitation to visit Arundells House, the former home of Sir Edward.

We have come to Arundells House with feelings of reverence for Sir Edward Heath made great efforts during his life to build deeper understanding and friendship between China and the UK.

We wish to thank Lord Hunt for his very warm welcome. We are grateful for his fellow trustees for joining us today. We also thank the journalists from local and faraway places.

This is my first time here. But, I heard a long time ago about Arundells being a most beautiful house in Britain.

I read a story that one visitor once marveled at the beauty of Arundells and said to Sir Edward:

"This must be one of the ten most beautiful views in Britain."

Sir Edward retorted:

"Why, what are the other nine?"

Sir Edward Heath was by any measure a legend. To British people, he was a Prime Minister, a Tory leader and Father of the House. Possibly most significantly, he led Britain into the European Economic Community.

---

[*] Speech at Arundells House. Salisbury, England, 11 July 2014.

Sir Edward was also a fighter against appeasement and in the military during the Normandy Landings. Outside politics, he was a musician of near professional standard and a world-class yachtsman.

For most people it would be a severe challenge to accomplish any one of these achievements. Yet Sir Edward was worthy of all the titles.

To all of us in China who cherish his memory, Sir Edward is highly regarded as "an old friend of the Chinese people".

Sir Edward's premiership oversaw the establishment of ambassadorial diplomatic relations between China and the UK in 1972.This launched a new era of relations between our two countries.

Since 1974 Sir Edward visited China 26 times during the following 27 years. After the famous British scholar Dr Joseph Needham, he was the second British person to be awarded "People's Friendship Envoy". This is the highest honour of people-to-people diplomacy that China ever gives to a foreigner.

Sir Edward was also the last foreign leader who had met the three Chinese leaders: Mao Zedong, Zhou Enlai and Deng Xiaoping.

Forty years on, China-UK relationship, launched by Sir Edward together with Chinese leaders, has gone through a sea change.

Figures tell the remarkable story:

- In 1972 China-UK trade was merely 300 million US dollars.
- Last year the figure was more than 70 billion US dollars.
- It is expected to pass 100 billion US dollars by 2015.

Our two-way investment has increased exponentially:

- By the end of last year, mutual investment had exceeded 50 billion US dollars.
- Chinese investments were more than 32 billion US dollars, making up over 60% of the total.

Across Europe, Britain has become the first choice for Chinese investors. But the progress is far wider than just economics and trade:

- China-UK people-to-people exchange is flourishing.
- The number of people visiting each other's country has surged from 200 in 1972 to more than one million last year.
- The number of Chinese students in the UK has leaped from 16 in 1972 to the current 130,000 only second to the USA.

In June this year Chinese Premier Li Keqiang paid a successful visit to the UK and held the annual summit with Prime Minister David Cameron. The two leaders agreed to build a partnership of common growth and inclusive development. They drew up a blueprint to further deepening the China-UK comprehensive strategic partnership.

As an old Chinese saying goes:

"When drinking the water, you should not forget those who dug the well."

In that spirit China never forgets the contribution of old friends.

We owe the height, depth and breadth of today's China-UK relationship to many old friends. These include:

- British business leaders 60 years ago who broke the economic ice.
- British political leaders represented by Sir Edward who broke the political ice.
- Of course such true supporters include Mr Stephen Perry and Mr Peter Batey who, over the past decades, have never ceased their efforts for a single day to promote China-UK friendship and cooperation.

In the era of globalization, China's links with the rest of the world are becoming ever closer.

China has made many new friends in different countries and different sectors. But we have not, and will never forget these old British friends. They made a historic contribution to China's development, to China-UK relations and to connecting China with the rest of the world.

Francis Bacon once wrote of friendship like this:

"For friendship maketh indeed a fair day in the affections, from storm and tempests; but it maketh daylight in the understanding, out of darkness, and confusion of thoughts."

Friendship has escorted China-UK relationship and partnership a long way to where it is today. Friendship will remain essential to the healthy and stable development of China-UK relations in the future.

Lord Hunt, fellow Trustees and Friends of Arundells,

The purpose of my visit today is to build on this friendship and promote greater China-UK cooperation.

For that reason we have brought a number of photos recording both Sir Edward's contacts with China and some historic moments in China-UK relations. We will donate these photos to you and hope they will enrich the collection of Arundells House.

I also hope that my visit today will go further to generate interest among Chinese and British young people. I want them to visit this beautiful part of England and be inspired by the memories that never fade and the feelings that never change. That will encourage them to join the cause of China-UK friendship and cooperation.

With their participation, we will write a new and even more glorious chapter of China-UK relations.

Thank you!

老骥伏枥，志在千里 *

尊敬的杰弗里·豪勋爵，
尊敬的卫奕信勋爵，
尊敬的外交国务大臣斯瓦尔先生，
尊敬的英中协会主席戴维信爵士，
女士们、先生们：

很高兴出席今天的招待会，与大家一起向杰弗里·豪勋爵表达敬意和感谢。在来英工作的五年多里，我曾经在许多场合与豪勋爵见面交谈，我受益匪浅。在我心目中，豪勋爵代表着资深、智慧和友谊。

就资深而言，他已年届90高龄，在威斯敏斯特宫从政长达51年，先后担任过英国政府的副总检察长、贸易国务大臣、财政大臣、外交大臣、议会下院领袖和副首相，又任上院议员达23年，可谓英国政坛的"长青树"和"不老松"。当今英国政坛还有谁可与豪勋爵比肩？

就智慧而言，豪勋爵是中英解决香港问题的参与者和贡献者。香港问题曾是中英关系中最棘手的难题，豪勋爵在1983年出任英国外交大臣后，直接参与中英两国关于香港问题的谈判，以其勇气和睿智，与中国领导人共同创造性地达成了解决方案，扫清了影响两国关系发展的最大障碍。中英《联合声明》为香港在1997年顺利回归中国奠定了基础，为国与国之间解决历

---

* 在英中协会名誉主席杰弗里·豪勋爵卸任招待会上的讲话。2015年7月8日，英国议会上院。

史遗留问题创造了一个范例。"一国两制"原则在今天依然是保持香港稳定和繁荣的基石。可以说，豪勋爵为中英关系发展做出了历史性贡献。

就友谊而言，豪勋爵是中国人民的老朋友。自从豪勋爵1978年首次访华，他与中国的交往已有近40年。他亲身经历了两国关系的许多重大事件，与几代中国领导人相识共事，是中方一直十分尊敬的英国政治家。他在担任英中协会名誉主席的23年间，一直致力于促进中英在政党、司法、青年等领域的交流，增进两国政治互信和民众友谊。同时也正是由于他的直接领导，英中协会成为中英交流与合作的桥梁，在促进中英关系发展中发挥着越来越重要的作用。

中国古人说："老骥伏枥，志在千里；烈士暮年，壮心不已。"用这句话来形容豪勋爵，真是再贴切不过了。他虽年已九旬，但依旧精神矍铄、老当益壮。我希望您从上院退休和卸任英中协会名誉主席之后，继续关心和支持中英关系的发展，继续培养和鼓励青年一代献身中英友好事业。

女士们、先生们，

当前中英关系正面临着重要发展机遇。中国国家主席习近平将应女王陛下邀请于2015年10月对英进行国事访问。我们愿与英王室、政府、议会及社会各界共同努力，使这次访问成为中英关系新的里程碑。我相信，这是豪勋爵最期望的前景，也是我们向豪勋爵表达敬意的最好方式。

谢谢！

A Steed Aspires to Gallop a Thousand Miles [*]

Lord Howe,

Lord Wilson,

Minister Hugo Swire,

Sir Martin Davison,

Ladies and Gentlemen,

It is my truly great delight to attend today's reception.

I feel honored to have this opportunity to show my respect and regard for Lord Howe.

Since I came to work in London five years ago, I have met Lord Howe many times on different occasions. I have benefited a great deal from his insight and vision.

Whenever I think of Lord Howe,

- I think of a statesman of global standing.
- I think of a man of profound wisdom.
- And I think of a symbol of friendship between China and Britain.

Lord Howe is a revered senior statesman.

At 90, Lord Howe has given exceptional public service to the people of Britain:

---

[*] Remarks at the Retirement Party in Honour of Lord Geoffrey Howe. House of Lords, 8 July 2015.

- He has served in the Palace of Westminster for 51 years and has held many important public offices.
- He has been, successively, the Minister of State for Trade and Consumer Affairs, Chancellor of the Exchequer, Secretary of Foreign and Commonwealth Affairs, Leader of the House of Commons and Deputy Prime Minister.
- Following his retirement as an MP, Lord Howe has served in the House of Lords for 23 years.

I cannot think of any other public figure in contemporary British politics who has given such dedicated and distinguished public service as long as Lord Howe.

In China, we would describe someone who has given such a long and great commitment as "an evergreen and never-aging pine tree".

Lord Howe is also a man of immense wisdom.

He has participated in and contributed to the solution of the most complex question between China and the UK—the return of Hong Kong.

After assuming the office of Foreign Secretary in 1983, Lord Howe became directly involved in the negotiations between China and the UK over Hong Kong.

Lord Howe showed great courage and wisdom in those negotiations, and worked creatively with Chinese leaders. Together, they reached the *Sino-British Joint Declaration* and cleared away the biggest obstacle to the development of China-UK relations.

Sino-British Joint Declaration laid a solid foundation for the smooth return of Hong Kong in 1997. Not only that, Sino-British Joint Declaration has also set an example for solving historical questions between states.

Today, the principle of One Country, Two Systems remains the bedrock of stability and prosperity in Hong Kong.

All of these speak volumes about Lord Howe's historic contribution to China-UK relations.

But above all, Lord Howe is a great friend of the Chinese people.

Since his first visit to China in 1978, Lord Howe has been committed to a better relationship between China and the UK for nearly four decades:

- Lord Howe has lived through many significant events in China-UK relations.

- He has made friends and worked closely with generations of Chinese leaders.
- To his Chinese friends, Lord Howe has always been a highly respected British statesman.

For 23 years Lord Howe has served as Honorary President of the Great Britain-China Centre(GBCC). In this role, Lord Howe has been working relentlessly to promote exchanges between political parties, the judiciaries and the young people of our two countries.

Through his wisdom and leadership, Lord Howe has contributed tremendously to advance political mutual trust and friendship between the peoples of China and the UK.

Under his guidance, the GBCC has served as a bridge of communication and cooperation between our nations. It will play an even greater and more important role in promoting China-UK relations.

Ladies and Gentlemen,

Let me quote an ancient Chinese poem:

"A mature steed in the stable still aspires to gallop a thousand miles! And a mature hero still cherishes high aspirations!"

There can't be a more apt description than this! At 90, and retiring from the House of Lords and GBCC, Lord Howe remains hale and hearty, and as vigorous as ever!

Lord Howe, I hope you will continue to care for and support China-UK relations.

In that spirit I know you will continue to inspire and encourage the younger generations.

Your great wisdom can rouse the youth of today to follow your lead with so many years of dedication.

Ladies and Gentlemen,

China-UK relationship today is faced with significant opportunities.

President Xi Jinping will pay a state visit to the UK in October at the invitation of Her Majesty The Queen. We are ready to work with the Palace, the UK government, the Parliament and various communities for the success of the visit. We should make this visit a new milestone for China-UK relations.

I am sure that is what Lord Howe wants most for China-UK relations. That is also our best way of paying respect to Lord Howe.

Thank you!

踏遍青山人未老，前路更加美好 *

尊敬的诺丁汉大学校监安德鲁·威特爵士，
尊敬的诺丁汉大学前校长大卫·格林纳韦爵士，
女士们、先生们：
晚上好！

前不久我回国出席了中国共产党第十九次全国代表大会，上周五刚返回英国。尽管回来后公务繁忙，我仍来参加诺丁汉大学为格林纳韦爵士退休举办的晚宴，这不仅是因为格林纳韦爵士是"我的校长"，更因为他是我十分敬重的教育家，是中国人民的好朋友，是中英教育合作的先行者。格林纳韦爵士为促进中英教育交流合作、深化两国人民友谊做出了重要贡献，我谨向他表示崇高的敬意和衷心的感谢。

时隔两个月再次来到诺大，我感到景色已大不相同，上次还是霜林初染、秋水长天，此时已是落叶满地、秋意深浓。看着行人在成堆的落叶中走出一条条路来，我想说说关于"路"的三句话。

第一句话："地上本没有路，走的人多了，也便成了路。"正是在格林纳韦爵士的带领下，诺大在中英教育交流中走出了一条"合作共赢"之路。在所有英国大学中，诺大率先与中方合办高校、任命中国人为校监；诺大与清华大学、浙江大学等中国数十所大学建立了校际联系；诺大成立的当代中国

---

* 在英国诺丁汉大学前校长格林纳韦爵士退休晚宴上的讲话。2017年11月9日，英国诺丁汉大学。

学学院、中国政策研究所和孔子学院，成为英国与其他西方国家研究和了解中国的重要窗口，诺大孔子学院成为全球首批"示范孔子学院"之一。

宁波诺丁汉大学尤其值得称道，已成为中外合作办学的成功典范，并得到习近平主席的肯定。习主席说，"宁波诺丁汉大学的创建和成立，开中国高等教育与国外优质高等教育资源相结合的先河，为中国教育走向世界创造了一种全新的模式"。13年来，宁波诺丁汉大学从最初的254名学生，发展到今天拥有来自70多个国家和地区的7300多名学生，已为世界培养出1.2万余名优秀的毕业生。

第二句话："地上有了路，走路的人就会越来越多。"中英教育"合作共赢"之路深受双方欢迎，走这条路的人越来越多。我担任中国驻英国大使7年多来对此深有体会，教育已成为中英人文交流的最大亮点。英国吸引的中国留学生数量、开办的孔子学院和孔子课堂数量、开展校际合作的名牌大学数量都是欧洲第一。中国还与英国建立了欧洲第一个高级别人文交流机制。教育也是我发表演讲涉及最多的话题之一，是我大力推动互利合作的重要领域之一。我的使馆同事们称我为"教育大使"，这都要归功于中英教育合作走上了正确的道路。

正确的道路必将通向光明的未来。刚刚闭幕的中国共产党第十九次全国代表大会具有重大意义，标志着中国在中国共产党的领导下，成功地走出一条中国特色社会主义道路。这是一条中国人民致富路，也是一条世界人民共赢路。中国走出的这条道路，不仅为深入探索人类更好的社会制度贡献了智慧，而且为发展中国家走向现代化提供了更多选择，也将为中英关系的深入发展带来新机遇，为推动构建人类命运共同体注入新动力。

第三句话："走路的人一起走，路就会越走越宽。"格林纳韦爵士对中国怀有深厚感情，工作不仅限于教育领域，还积极推动宁波市与诺丁汉市缔结为友好城市，促进双方在商贸、教育、文化、体育等多个领域的交流与合作，吸引了中英两国的同道之人，让合作共赢的路越走越宽。

一个人的职业生涯是有限的，而大家共同奋斗的中英友好事业是无限的。格林纳韦爵士在有限的职业生涯中积极践行"互尊互鉴、合作共赢"的精神，找到了促进中英民心相通的金钥匙，为推进中英关系深入发展做出了积极贡献。

踏遍青山人未老，前路更加美好。中英关系发展仍需要格林纳韦爵士的丰富经验、知识和智慧，仍需要诺大这支积极发展对华关系与合作的模范团队。我希望并相信，诺大将继承和发扬格林纳韦爵士留下的宝贵财富，继续为促进中英教育交流合作、增进两国人民友谊做出更多新的贡献。我也愿与在座诸位一道，共同为建设中英合作大厦添砖加瓦。

谢谢！

A Better View Further down the Road[*]

Sir Andrew Witty,

Professor Sir David Greenaway,

Ladies and Gentlemen,

Good evening!

I was back in London only last Friday, after attending the 19th National Congress of the Communist Party of China in Beijing. My in-tray is full, and so is my diary. But I told myself, I have to come to this dinner, because:

- You, Professor Sir David, are my Vice-Chancellor.
- You are an educationist whom I deeply respect.
- You are a good friend of the Chinese people.
- And you are a pioneer in advancing China-UK educational cooperation.

I would like to pay my highest tribute and extend my sincerest thanks to you, for the significant contribution you have made to closer educational cooperation and deeper friendship between China and Britain.

This is my second visit to Nottingham in two months. In a matter of two months, the early autumn chill has turned the University into spectacular shades of gold. Looking at the paths formed on the thick carpet of autumn leaves as people walked by, I thought a lot and had three observations about paths that I would like to share with you.

---

[*] Remarks at the Retirement Dinner of Professor Sir David Greenaway. University of Nottingham, 9 November 2017.

The first is:

"There is no path until people take the first step and create one."

The University of Nottingham, led by Professor Sir David, was the one who took the very first step in the field of educational exchanges between China and Britain. You have created the path of win-win cooperation.

- Of all the British universities, Nottingham is the first to set up a joint campus in China, the first to appoint a Chinese Chancellor and the first to set up a Confucius Institute in China.
- Your ties with China are so close that you have twined with Tsinghua University, Zhejiang University and dozens of other Chinese universities.
- Here in Nottingham, you have established the School of Contemporary Chinese Studies, China Policy Institute and Confucius Institute. You have become an important window through which Britain and other Western countries can study and understand China.
- Moreover, the Nottingham Confucius Institute was among the first to be awarded as a Model Confucius Institute.

Of all your achievements, the most notable is the establishment of the University of Nottingham Ningbo China(UNNC). This is a successful example of international cooperation. It was commended by President Xi Jinping, who said, "The founding of the University of Nottingham Ningbo China is the very first joint effort between Chinese and foreign higher learning institutions to pool their respective educational strengths. It creates a new model for a world-class and international education system in China."

Thirteen years ago, there were only 254 students at the UNNC. Today, the UNNC is home to more than 7,300 students from over 70 countries and regions and has 12,000 alumni all over the world.

Let me turn to my second observation.

"Where there is a path, there are more people who will follow."

The path of win-win cooperation is gaining popularity among educational institutions in both China and Britain. It is attracting more and more people.

Education is undoubtedly the biggest highlight of the cultural and people-to-people exchanges between China and Britain. That's what I have learnt after seven years as Chinese Ambassador to the UK.

In the field of educational cooperation with China, Britain has set at least three European records:

- First, Britain has the largest number of Chinese students in Europe.
- Second, Britain is home to more Confucius Institutes and Confucius Classrooms than any other European country.
- Third, British universities have more cooperation with China than their counterparts in Europe.

It is especially worth noting that Britain was the first European country to set up High-Level People-to-People Dialogue with China.

Education is also one of the most frequent topics for my speeches. It is a most important field that I have been working on to promote mutually beneficial cooperation.

At the Embassy, I am known as a "Education Ambassador". I would attribute that to the right path that we are taking in advancing China-UK educational cooperation.

Right path leads to promising future. This is true for China-UK educational cooperation. This is also true for China's cause as a nation.

The 19th National Congress of the Communist Party of China, which concluded not long ago, was most significant for China because it points to the right path forward.

- This is a path of socialism with Chinese characteristics.
- It is a path led by the Communist Party of China.
- It is a path towards prosperity and happiness for the Chinese people.

It is also a path towards win-win cooperation for the people of the world.

- This path is a contribution to man's exploration for a better social system.
- It offers a new option for other developing nations who are striving to achieve

modernization.
- It brings new opportunities to China and the UK as our two countries promote in-depth development of China-UK relations.
- It adds momentum to building a community of shared future for mankind.

Now let me share with you my third observation about paths.

"A path will become broader when more people walk on it."

Sir David, with the deep love you cherish for China, you have broadened the path you helped to create. Thanks to your contribution, the win-win cooperation between China and Britain has been expanded into more fields than just education.

- Ningbo and Nottingham have established twin city relationship.
- The two cities have increased exchanges and cooperation in the fields of education, business, culture and sports.
- More and more people have come to share the same ideal and work together.
- This path of win-win cooperation has become a broad thoroughfare to success.

While there is always an end to one's career, there is no end to what we can do and achieve for China-UK friendship.

- Sir David has dedicated a successful career to living up to the spirit of mutual respect, mutual learning, and win-win cooperation.
- You have found the key to heart-to-heart communications between the Chinese and British people.
- You have contributed to strengthening China-UK relations.

Retirement is a new beginning. There is always a better view further down the road.

Sir David, we still need you in building a better future for China-UK relations. We still need your rich experience, extensive knowledge and great inspiration in order to get there. We still count on the wonderful team here at the University of Nottingham to actively engage in growing ties with China.

It is my hope and belief that University of Nottingham will carry forward what Sir David has started and continue to contribute to the educational exchanges and cooperation and the close friendship between China and Britain.

I look forward to working with everyone present to contribute our part to China-UK relations.

Thank you!

改革促发展，合作促友谊 *

尊敬的四十八家集团俱乐部主席斯蒂芬·佩里先生，

尊敬的佩里夫人萨拉·佩里女士，

佩里夫妇的孩子们——乔迪、萨姆、罗西，

尊敬的各位议员，

尊敬的各位勋爵，

女士们、先生们、朋友们：

大家晚上好！

欢迎大家出席今天这场有特别意义的招待会。2018年12月18日，中国改革开放40周年庆祝大会在北京隆重举行。在庆祝大会上，习近平主席等中国领导人向10名国际友人颁发"中国改革友谊奖章"。佩里先生是唯一获此殊荣的英国友人。让我们用热烈的掌声对佩里先生和他的家人表示衷心祝贺！

回首过去40年，改革开放是中国与世界携手同行、共同发展的伟大历程，中国人民始终敞开胸怀、拥抱世界。在这一历史进程中，许多国际友人深度参与中国改革开放，积极促进中外交流合作，为此做出了突出贡献。

20世纪50年代，佩里先生的父亲杰克·佩里与数十位英国工商界人士冲破重重阻力，开启"破冰之旅"，打开同新中国贸易往来的大门。多年来，佩里先生继承父志，积极推进中英经贸合作和人文交流，倡导成立"青年破

---

* 在庆祝斯蒂芬·佩里先生荣获"中国改革友谊奖章"招待会上的讲话。2019年1月14日，中国驻英国大使馆。

冰者"和"女性破冰者"组织，使"破冰"精神薪火相传。佩里先生不愧为中国改革开放的见证者、支持者、贡献者，不愧为中国人民的老朋友、好朋友。佩里先生获得"中国改革友谊奖章"当之无愧。

这是一项至高无上的荣誉，意义重大、影响深远。它不仅凝聚着对佩里先生一家三代支持中国改革开放事业的诚挚谢意，蕴含着对中英关系发展成就的充分肯定，更充溢着对英国各界人士参与中国改革开放新征程的美好期许。

回首过去40年，中英关系历经风雨，迎来全面战略伙伴关系。这是两国各界人士不懈努力的结果，来之不易，值得加倍珍惜。我们庆祝佩里先生获得"中国改革友谊奖章"，就是要从中获得启迪，不忘初心，继往开来，共同推动中英关系行稳致远。我认为，佩里先生获奖对中英关系长远发展有三点启示。

一是打破意识形态樊篱，坚持通过接触交流促进理解包容。新中国成立之初，西方国家对中国实行经济封锁。杰克·佩里先生打破"坚冰"，开了中英合作的先河，用实际行动彰显了平等、开放、包容的合作精神。

60多年过去了，中国与世界的关系发生了历史性变化，中英关系的广度和深度今非昔比。但冷战思维并未绝迹，仍有人将中国发展视为挑战甚至威胁。这种背离时代潮流的观念，需要我们继续弘扬"破冰"精神，打破意识形态窠臼，消除偏见和误解，增进中英互信，深化中英合作。

二是聚焦利益汇合点，坚持通过友好合作实现互利共赢。多年来，佩里先生等有识之士始终着眼于中英利益汇合点，不断推动和扩大两国互利合作，为两国人民带来实实在在的利益。1978—2018年，中英双边贸易额由不足每年10亿美元增长至约800亿美元，增长了近80倍；相互投资从无到有，今天英国对华直接投资达260多亿美元，中国对英直接投资超过210亿美元。

当前，中英均处于各自发展关键阶段。双方应当积极探寻利益汇合点，不断加强政策对接，推进务实合作，实现互利共赢。我衷心希望英方排除各种干扰，继续为中资企业在英投资兴业提供公平、透明的营商环境，使双方合作更好惠及两国人民。

三是顺应历史发展大势，坚持通过互学互鉴实现共同进步。交流孕育融合，融合产生进步。人类历史就是一个不同文明相互交流、彼此借鉴、和合融通的进程。佩里先生等中英友好交往的先行者，积极参与中国改革开放进程，大力推动中英人文交流与合作，不断增进双方相互了解和友谊。

在当前形势下，双方更应顺应世界发展大势，秉持相互尊重、和而不同的精神，坚持互学互鉴、兼收并蓄，为中英合作奠定良好的民意基础，共同为构建人类命运共同体做出贡献。

女士们、先生们，

同舟共济扬帆起，乘风破浪万里航。2019年中国将迎来建国70周年，英国将进入"后脱欧时代"。我期待着中英各界人士秉持"破冰"精神，不断开拓创新、锐意进取，共同为两国关系更加美好的明天不懈努力！

谢谢！

Reform Promotes Development and Cooperation Enhances Friendship[*]

Chairman Stephen Perry,

Saraph,

Jodie, Sam and Rosie,

My Lords and MPs,

Ladies and Gentlemen,

Dear Friends,

Good evening!

Welcome to the Chinese Embassy!

Tonight's reception is very special. On 18 December 2018, a grand gathering was held in Beijing to celebrate the 40th anniversary of China's reform and opening-up. At the gathering, President Xi Jinping and other Chinese leaders presented the China Reform and Friendship Medal to ten foreign friends. Among them, Chairman Perry is the only one from the UK. Let's give him and his family a big hand. Congratulations!

The 40 years of reform and opening-up was a great journey. China embraced the world with open arms and joined hands with global partners to achieve common development. In this historical process, friends from all over the world have participated deeply in China's reform and opening-up, and played an active role in promoting the exchanges and cooperation between China and the rest of the world. They have all made outstanding contribution to this great cause.

---

[*] Speech at a Reception Celebrating Mr Stephen Perry Being Awarded the China Reform and Friendship Medal. Chinese Embassy, 14 January 2019.

As we celebrate Mr Perry being awarded the China Reform and Friendship Medal, we need to take a moment to recall the first generation of "Icebreakers" led by Mr Perry's late father Mr Jack Perry. In 1950s, Mr Jack Perry overcame various obstacles and "broke the ice" to trade with New China.

Over the years, Mr Stephen Perry has carried on the "Icebreakers" spirit. He has made active efforts to enhance China-UK cooperation on economy, trade, culture and people-to-people exchanges. He has also initiated the "Young Icebreakers" and the "Women Icebreakers". He has witnessed, supported and contributed to China's reform and opening-up. He has been an old friend and good friend of the Chinese people. He well deserves the China Reform and Friendship Medal.

This award is the highest honour. The conferment of this award on Mr Perry has profound significance.

- It represents the sincere thanks of the Chinese people to three generations of the Perry family for their support for China's reform and opening-up.
- It is in recognition of the progress of China-UK relations.
- It embodies our expectation that the people from all walks of life in Britain will take part in China's new round of reform and opening-up.

Over the past 40 years, China-UK relations have gone through twists and turns. The Chinese and British people have made relentless efforts and come a long way to build a comprehensive strategic partnership. This has not been easy and it deserves our greatest care and attention.

As we celebrate Mr Perry's award, we also need to take a moment to renew our commitment to China-UK relations. We need to think about how to build on our past achievements and forge ahead to make steady and sustained progress in China-UK relations. I believe from Mr Perry's award we can learn three important things.

First, we should break though ideological barriers, engage each other and exchange ideas in order to enhance mutual understanding and promote inclusiveness.

In the early years of the People's Republic, Western countries imposed economic blockade on China. Jack Perry "broke the ice" and spearheaded China-UK cooperation. His brave action lived up to the spirit of equality, openness and inclusiveness.

Now, more than 60 years have passed. The relations between China and the world have experienced historic changes. China-UK relations have reached unprecedented breadth and depth.

However, the Cold War mentalities die hard. Some in the world still regard China's development as a challenge or even threat. Yet, such views go against the trend of the times. The ideological mind-set, prejudice and misunderstanding are the "new ice" that we must break. We must carry on the "Icebreakers" spirit to promote deeper trust and closer cooperation between China and the UK.

Second, we should focus on common interests and achieve win-win results through friendly cooperation.

Over the years, a large number of visionary people like Mr Perry have acted in the common interests of China and the UK. They have worked to enhance mutually-beneficial cooperation and delivered tangible benefits to the people of our two countries.

From 1978 to 2018, our bilateral trade increased by nearly 80 times, from less than 1 billion US dollars to about 80 billion US dollars a year. Two-way investment was zero 40 years ago. Today, UK's direct investment in China exceeds 26 billion US dollars, and China has invested more than 21 billion US dollars in the UK.

Now China and the UK have both come to a crucial stage in our respective development. Our two countries should actively explore new areas of cooperation for the benefit of both sides. By matching our development policies and promoting business cooperation, we could achieve win-win results.

I sincerely hope that the UK will resist all kinds of interruption and continue to provide a fair and transparent business environment for Chinese enterprises in the UK, so that China-UK cooperation could deliver more benefits to the people of both countries.

Third, we should follow the trend of history and achieve common progress through mutual learning.

Exchanges lead to integration. Integration in turn promotes progress. The history of mankind is a process of exchanges, mutual learning and integration between different civilisations.

This is exactly what Mr Perry and other pioneers of China-UK exchanges have been working on. They have actively engaged in China's reform and opening-up. They have promoted China-UK cultural and people-to-people exchanges. Their efforts have resulted in better mutual understanding and stronger friendship between our two countries.

Today, as we speak, it is all the more important that our two countries go along with the trend of the times. When we learn from each other in the spirit of mutual respect and "harmony without uniformity", we can build solid public support for China-UK cooperation. This will enable us to contribute to the building of a community with a shared future for mankind.

Ladies and Gentlemen,

In the ocean of globalisation, China and the UK could ride the waves and sail far if we sail together.

2019 is an important year for both China and the UK. China will celebrate the 70th anniversary of the founding of the People's Republic, and the UK will enter a post-Brexit era.

I hope that the "Icebreakers" spirit will continue to inspire people across all sectors from both China and the UK to stay at the forefront of the times and to break new grounds. Together we can create an ever-brighter future for China-UK relations!

Thank you!

第八章　中英认知
PART Ⅷ　Understanding between China and the UK

英国著名作家鲁德亚德·吉卜林曾说，东方与西方永远无法完全理解对方。有一次我在接受英国广播公司采访时，主持人问我对这句话如何评价。我表示不同意这种说法。我认为东方和西方是可以相互理解的，现在的问题是西方没能很好地了解东方，特别是一谈到中国，西方一些人总是摆脱不掉冷战思维。他们往往以观察苏联的视角来看中国，从而无法了解一个全面的中国，更无法理解一个真实的中国。我认为西方要理解东方，就要端正态度，摒弃"西方中心论"；应少一些傲慢与偏见，多一些理智与情感。在我结束使英任期时，一些朋友问我，11年里最令我遗憾的是什么。我说，中英之间仍存在很大的"了解赤字"和"认知赤字"。

本章收录了我的6篇演讲，从中可以看到我在努力减少这些赤字，但要消除赤字仍任重道远。

The famous British writer Rudyard Kipling once said that the East and the West would never fully understand each other. During an interview with the BBC, the host asked about my thoughts on this statement. I expressed my disagreement. I believe that the East and the West can understand each other. The problem now is that the West fails to try to understand the East. Especially when it comes to China, some people in the West couldn't help hanging onto the Cold War mentality. They often view China the same way they viewed the Soviet Union, thus failing to understand a comprehensive and real China. I believe that for the West to understand the East, it must adopt the right attitude, abandon "Western-centrism", cut the pride and prejudice, and get more sense and sensibility. At the end of my tenure as the Chinese Ambassador to the UK, some friends asked me what my biggest regret was over the 11 years. I would say there is still a significant "understanding deficit" and "perception deficit" between China and the UK.

This chapter includes 6 of my speeches, reflecting my efforts to reduce these deficits, though much work remains to be done.

筷子与刀叉，中西方文明共存互鉴 *

尊敬的童海珍主席，

女士们、先生们、朋友们：

我和我的夫人胡平华很高兴首次参加筷子俱乐部的活动。童海珍主席，您刚赴北京参加了"记忆中国，难忘母校"活动，欢迎您满载美好的记忆归来。

2010年初我刚来到英国不久，就听说有筷子俱乐部这么别具一格的民间组织在推崇中华美食，宣传中国文化，促进中英了解，因此我一直期待着有时间与大家见面交流。我也特别喜欢"筷子俱乐部"这个可谓形神兼备的名字：一是俱乐部活动形式上多借用聚餐安排演讲和交流；二是筷子作为餐具，尽管平常简单，但许多学者认为这是东方智慧的体现。

我今天的演讲就想从筷子谈起。第一点，我认为筷子是具有中国特色的一种餐具，是历史的选择和文化的反映。

关于筷子的起源，史无明确记载，只有各种传说或推测。文献中最早提到筷子的使用者是三千多年前的商纣王，当时他使用"象牙箸"。我个人比较倾向这么一种说法：中国的先民最初以树枝或细竹从陶锅中夹取热食，慢慢地筷子就产生了。这情形就仿佛我们今天吃四川火锅，徒手不能，刀叉也不便，只能借助筷子帮忙。

三千多年来，中国人为什么保留了使用筷子的习惯，我认为这与中国长

---

* 在英国筷子俱乐部的演讲。2010年10月19日，英国皇家学会。

期的农耕文明和饮食结构有关。中国人的饮食一直以谷物等种植物为主，即使食肉，也一直如孔子所说："食不厌精，脍不厌细。"因此，餐桌上一双细细的筷子足矣。可见，使用筷子是由中国的经济、历史和文化等多种因素决定的。

我由此想起这么一句听来富有哲理的话：这个世界上没有什么是最好的，只有适合自己的才是最好的。筷子是这样，社会制度、经济发展模式也是这样。中国的社会制度是中国近代历史发展的必然结果，是中国人民的历史选择，也是中国对人类文明多样性所做的贡献。中国的经济发展模式，则是中国人民根据人口多、底子薄的国情，"摸着石头过河"，不断探索开辟出来的一条新型发展道路。大家可能听说过邓小平先生的名言："实践是检验真理的唯一标准。"改革开放32年来，中国政治稳定、经济发展、文化繁荣、社会进步，这就从实践上充分证明了中国的社会制度、经济发展模式是行之有效的，符合中国的国情，有利于中国的发展。

谈到中国的发展，我最近一直对英国朋友们说，要全面看待和了解中国。比如，在经济上，不能仅看到中国已成为世界第二大经济体，中国东部沿海地区一派繁荣景象，也要看到中国仍是一个发展中国家，人均GDP只有约3700美元，相当于英国的1/10，城乡区域发展还很不平衡。我曾经在处于中国大西北的甘肃省担任省长助理，所以我经常以甘肃为例，说明中国西部地区经济仍欠发达，不少地方人畜饮水都很困难。最近，甘肃的朋友碰到我开玩笑说："刘大使，你能不能不再拿我们当典型？"我对他们说："我这是给你们做广告啊！现在英国许多民众都知道了甘肃，知道你们那里自然条件恶劣，干旱少雨，但是你们发展经济、促进民生、保护文化的成绩非常显著，而且发展潜力很大，很多英国人现在都很想去甘肃看一看。"

我想说的第二点是，筷子与刀叉并非水火不容，只是代表着两种不同的文化。

为什么西方人使用刀叉吃饭呢？这个问题我并没有考证过。但是直觉告诉我，当你面对盘子里的一大块牛排时，筷子尽管不能说完全没用，但肯定比不上使用刀叉的那份优雅。这是由于中西方饮食结构、食物制作方法不同，所以在餐具上体现出了区别。但无论使用何种餐具，都不会妨碍我们享用本民族的美食。广而言之，只要东西方国家根据自身国情选择政治制度和经济模式，也就不会妨碍我们享用发展的盛宴。

中国的社会制度、经济发展模式与西方不同，这是不争的事实，但并不影响中西方的和平共存、共享繁荣。正如阳光因七色而斑斓，世界因多样而美丽。从人类历史上看，正是不同文明之间的相互接触和吸纳，才导致了新观念的萌芽，产生了新思想的火花，孕育了人类文明今天的成果。

第三点，既会用筷子，又会用刀叉，世界将会更加和谐。

我高兴地看到，今天到中餐馆就餐并使用筷子的外国人越来越多，同时许多中国人拿起刀叉吃顿西餐也轻松平常。中国古训说，"民以食为天"。人类学家、美籍华人张光直先生也曾直言："达到一个文化核心的最佳途径之一就是通过它的肚子。"如果在餐具和饮食方面中西方能够彼此接受和喜爱，我们有什么理由不处理好中西方关系呢？

处理好中西方关系，相互了解和尊重是关键。我一直认为，中国对西方的了解比西方对中国的了解要多得多。这主要是因为，近现代一百多年来中国一直在虚心地学习西方。今天，中国的孩子从小学一年级开始就学习英文。而西方有些人总丢不掉"文明优越论"，总认为自己的政治、经济、社会制度和文化高人一等，视自己的价值观为"普世价值观"，总想把别人的文化变成自己的"亚文化"。他们不愿也不想正视中国的变化，对中国的发展和进步感到不适应、不舒服，总想把这种情绪发泄出来，不断给中国制造困难和麻烦，唯恐中国不乱。我确信，这些人不代表西方社会的主流，他们阻止不了东西方相互学习、共谋发展的大趋势，更阻挡不了中国人民前进的步伐。

我认为，实现文明和平共存、共同进步，需要承认不同文明的平等地位，要以开放、包容的态度对待其他文明，要相互理解、相互尊重和相互学习。因此，中国主张"和而不同"，主张"求同存异"，主张"取长补短"，主张"和谐世界"。和谐世界，这是充满东方智慧的词，同时这也是最符合世界根本利益的思想。

朋友们，

我来英国后，曾对在英华侨华人说，英国的中餐在欧洲做得最地道。其实，我还有后面半句话没有说，那就是英国人用筷子在欧洲也最熟练。我发现在中餐馆里，很少有英国人用刀叉，都是"入乡随俗"，而且"驾轻就熟"。

中英关系是当今世界很重要的一组大国关系，我有时认为，中英关系就好比一双筷子。

第一，筷子是没有长短、不分左右的，中英关系也是平等的。中英是合作伙伴，既然是伙伴，两国关系就应当建立在互相尊重、平等对话的基础上，就应当加强战略互信，妥善处理分歧。

第二，筷子使用起来讲究协调与配合，中英关系也需要加强合作。今天的中英关系，早已超出了双边范畴，具有全球性和战略性。中英关系要想发展得好，双方一方面要加强在双边经济、教育、文化等各领域的务实合作，扩大利益基础，造福两国人民；另一方面应当在国际事务中携手合作，同舟共济，共同致力于促进世界的和平、稳定和繁荣。

第三，筷子不仅是用来夹食物的，关键是要把食物夹起来送到嘴里，中英关系也不能满足于现状，要不断提升发展。过去十多年来，中英关系取得了长足发展，两国建立了全面战略伙伴关系。2010年5月英国联合政府执政以后，致力于发展"更紧密的英中关系"。中方也高度重视发展中英关系，愿与英方共同努力，推动中英关系朝着友好合作、互利共赢的方向不断迈进。同年11月，卡梅伦首相即将对中国进行首次正式访问，这是中英关系发展的一个重要机遇，必将对双边关系起到进一步提升作用。

朋友们，

今天是星期二，在1993年的一个星期二，一个名叫中国星期二的团体在杜伦大学成立了，当时成员只有数十人。今天，中国星期二有了新的名字——筷子俱乐部，其注册会员也增加到500多人。借此机会，我要祝贺筷子俱乐部17岁生日快乐！我也衷心地希望筷子俱乐部不断成长，在促进中英了解和友谊方面发挥更大作用。

谢谢大家！

Chopsticks vs Knives and Forks[*]

Ms H-J Colston,

Ladies and Gentlemen,

Friends from the Chopsticks Club,

It is a great pleasure for me and my wife to attend our first event with the Chopsticks Club. I know Ms Colston has just been invited to Beijing as a representative of the British students who studied in China. I hope she had an enjoyable visit.

I got to know the Chopsticks Club soon after arriving in London. It is a unique non-governmental organization committed to promoting Chinese food and culture in Britain and increasing mutual understanding between the two countries. And I have been looking forward to this opportunity to meet you. I like the name of your club, as Chopsticks for us are much more than just something we use everyday for eating. I was glad to know that you have a good tradition of networking over delicious food, as chopsticks are also believed by many scholars to embody oriental wisdom.

Let me start my speech with the origin of chopsticks.

One story has it that King Zhou of the Shang Dynasty over 3,000 years ago was the first user of chopsticks, which were made of ivories. Personally, I tend to believe that chopsticks came about when ancient Chinese used tree branches or thin bamboo splits to pick up hot food from ceramic pots. Those of you who tried Sichuan hotpot would know that you could never take food from the hotpot with hand or a knife and fork; chopsticks seem to be the only practical choice.

The 3,000-year tradition of using chopsticks has a lot to do with our farming culture.

---

[*] Speech at the Chopsticks Club. Royal Society, London, 19 October 2010.

This meant that our diet has included grain as its mainstay, with meat being sliced or shredded. As Confucius said, "Eat no rice except when it is the finest and no meat except when finely minced." So it seems that economic, historical and cultural factors have all contributed to the continued use of chopsticks.

I remember a saying that makes sense to me: "Nothing is better than what suits one best." Apart from chopsticks, this may well apply to other things, such as a country's social system or model of economic growth.

The current social system in China, for example, came about as a natural outcome of the historical evolution in China and the choice of the Chinese people. It is also a contribution China has made to the diversity of human society.

China's economic model, on the other hand, has been developed through experience. As Deng Xiaoping put it, "crossing the river by feeling for the stones." For a country like China, with a large population and weak foundations, it has been a challenging task. You may have also heard another famous quote of Deng Xiaoping: "Practice is the only criterion for truth."

In the 32 years of reform and opening-up, China has achieved political stability, economic growth, cultural diversity and social progress. This has proved that the Chinese social system and economic model are well-suited to China's national conditions and effective in meeting the aspirations of the Chinese people.

I have been telling my British friends that to gain a balanced understanding of China's development, one needs to view China from different perspectives. Take China's economy as an example; many tend to see China as the second largest economy in the world, as they pay more attention to the richer coastal areas in the east and fail to recognise the slower development in the larger rural areas and regions. Our per capita GDP was merely 3,700 US dollars in 2009, one tenth that of the UK.

I used to work in China's north-western province of Gansu as Assistant Governor. So I often use Gansu's example to illustrate how much less developed western China is, with even access to drinking water being a problem for humans and animals sometimes. My friends in Gansu are now asking me not to use them as an example of poverty, but I've told them they should thank me for the free advertising.

A lot of people in Britain now know about Gansu's tough natural conditions and lack of rain. But they are also learning about what is being done to grow the economy, improve people's livelihood whilst preserving their culture, to the point that many people are now very keen to visit Gansu.

Chopsticks and knives and forks, rather than being incompatible, are just symbols of two different cultures.

Although I have not done any research on why Westerners use knives and forks, experience has taught me that if you have a large piece of steak in front of you, you had better use knives and forks, which would be much more elegant and effective than chopsticks. This is a reflection of our different ways of cooking and dietary structure. In a broader context, whatever political systems and economic models countries adopt, as long as the systems and models serve them well, they would be able to enjoy the feast of development.

China has a different social system and economic model from the West. But this does not mean that China and the West are not capable of living in peace with each other and sharing prosperity. Sunshine is made up of seven colours, and our world is beautiful for its diversity. Throughout history, dialogue and mutual learning between civilizations have always been a source of new ideas and progress.

I noticed with pleasure that more and more foreigners are eating in Chinese restaurants with chopsticks. And many Chinese now seem to be at ease using knives and forks. As an ancient Chinese saying goes, "Food is the paramount want of the people." Mr Zhang Guangzhi, a Chinese American anthropologist, pointed out that "one of the best channels to reach the heart of a culture is through its stomach". So when every Chinese is able to use a knife and fork, and every Westerner can use chopsticks, our world will be a better place.

Mutual understanding and mutual respect are the key to a better East-West relationship, and my impression is that China knows more about the West than the other way round. This is because China has been learning from the West for over a century. Today Chinese children start to learn English in the first year at primary school. Some people in the West, on the other hand, have been preoccupied by a sense of cultural superiority, believing that the West has the best political, economic, social and cultural system. They also tend to regard their own values as universal, expecting others to adapt their cultures according to Western culture. Some people are reluctant to see the changes in China and feel uneasy about the development and progress of China.

Some go so far as to attempt to create problems or even chaos for China. I'm sure they do not represent the mainstream in the West. They can in no way prevent China and the West from learning from each other and engaging each other in the general trend of common development. Nor can they obstruct the Chinese people's progress.

I believe that peaceful coexistence between cultures requires a sense of equality and an open and accommodating approach based on mutual understanding and respect. That is why China stands for the principles of "harmony but not uniformity", "seeking common ground and putting aside differences" and "drawing on the strong points of others to make up for one's weak points". This is also why China stands for building a harmonious world. We believe this term of harmony is full of oriental wisdom and best serves the fundamental interests of our world.

Dear Friends,

I told the Chinese community here that the UK has the best Chinese food in Europe. And I must add that the British are probably best at using chopsticks in Europe as well, as I have discovered that people here seldom use knives and forks when eating in a Chinese restaurant.

When it comes to describing China-UK relationship, I think we can also use the chopsticks analogy.

Firstly, the two chopsticks are of equal length, just as China and the UK are equals in our relationship. This means that we should hold dialogues on an equal footing and with mutual respect, enhance mutual trust on strategic issues and properly handle differences.

Secondly, just as it takes coordination of your fingers to use chopsticks properly; it takes cooperation for our relationship to grow stronger. Our relations have gone beyond being bilateral and become more global and strategic. A better relationship also calls for strengthened cooperation in areas such as the economy, education and culture, along with wider common interests in international affairs and a shared commitment to world peace, stability and prosperity.

Thirdly, the most important function of chopsticks is not only to pick up food, but to bring food to your mouth. Similarly, we should seek to upgrade our relations instead of resting on past progress. China-UK relations have come a long way in the past decade and a comprehensive strategic partnership has been established. Since the British coalition government took office in May, it has been committed to developing "closer engagement" with China. We in China also give the same priority to our relations with the UK to ensure we achieve friendly and mutually beneficial cooperation. Prime Minister David Cameron's first official visit to China next month will be an important opportunity for elevating China-UK relations to a new high. We will work closely with the British colleagues to make the visit a great success.

Dear Friends,

It is Tuesday today and it was on a Tuesday in 1993 that a group called China Tuesdays was founded with several dozens members. Today with a new name Chopsticks Club, the membership has increased to more than 500. So, may I take this opportunity to congratulate the Chopsticks Club on its 17th birthday. And I wish you continued growth in strength and hope you will contribute more to the mutual understanding and friendship between our two countries!

Thank you!

相互尊重，同舟共济 *

尊敬的休·戴维斯主席，

各位中国协会的朋友，

女士们、先生们：

很高兴在圣诞节前与大家相聚，首先祝大家圣诞快乐！新年快乐！

中国协会是英国历史最悠久的致力于促进中英经贸合作的组织，已历经123年的岁月变迁，可以说，中国协会是中英商业往来的先行者和两国关系发展的见证者。在此，我要对中国协会为发展中英经贸合作和推动中英关系做出的长期不懈努力表示赞赏和敬意。

这是我到伦敦后过的第一个冬天。据说2010年的冬天是英国近十几年来最冷的一个冬天，大雪纷飞，寒风凛冽。但当我走进这里，看到各位支持中英关系的朋友济济一堂，不由得感到浓浓暖意。刚才戴维斯主席说，今天出席午餐会的会员之多，创历史最高纪录。这表明了大家对中英关系的热情和关心。我认为，当前的中英关系也正如大家的热情一样，具有相当热度并且还在持续升温。

首先是高层交往热。2010年，尽管英国政府发生了更迭，但中英关系实现了平稳过渡和持续发展。就在11月，卡梅伦首相率英方有史以来规模最庞大的代表团成功访华，两国领导人就进一步增强政治互信、促进各领域合

---

* 在英国中国协会圣诞午餐会上的主旨演讲。2010年12月15日，伦敦海德公园文华东方酒店。

作达成了广泛共识。截至目前，英国联合政府外交、财政、商业、教育和气候变化五位内阁大臣相继访华。中英经济财金对话、战略对话、经贸联委会等重要交流机制运作良好，成效卓著。

其次是经贸合作热。2010年，两国经贸合作不仅走出国际金融危机的阴影，而且有新突破和新亮点。1—10月，中英货物贸易额达402亿美元，同比增长近30%，创历史同期最高纪录，其中英对华出口增幅达43%。双向投资掀起热潮。英国最大零售商乐购宣布今后5年斥资20亿英镑在华扩建购物广场和大型超市。中国投资项目数在英国投资来源国中居第6位，中国在伦敦投资的企业数量在各国中居第2位。

最后是人文交流热。2010年的上海世博会是两国合作的一大亮点，英国馆以其创意和创新吸引了800多万名中国观众，并获得世博会设计金奖。中国赴英留学生数量在欧洲仍然最多，并且保持大幅增长。中英双方签署协议，将合作加快培养英国本土汉语教师，以满足目前英国的"汉语热"需求。具有特殊意义的是，英国大学生蒋思哲获得了2010年"汉语桥"世界大学生中文比赛的特等奖。英国也正吸引越来越多的中国游客。据英国旅游局统计，2010年1—10月中国大陆赴英旅游人数激增80%，创下历年之最，全年有望超过20万人。

总之，当前中英关系正站在新的起点上，前景广阔。双方应抓住良好机遇，进一步从全球视角和战略高度规划好两国关系，深化各领域合作与交流，实实在在地造福两国和世界人民。

在我们为中英关系的发展感到欣慰的同时，也对一些杂音感到担忧。当我们每天翻开英国的报纸或打开电视时，总会看到有一些被炒作的所谓涉华"热点"，有些报道和评论充满了对中国的偏见。这些现象尽管不代表英国社会的主流，但不利于增进中英了解，也不利于两国关系的长期稳定健康发展。

孔子说，做人的道理是要"绝四"——"毋意，毋必，毋固，毋我"，即不臆测、不武断、不固执、不自我。我认为，这些道理今天同样适用于国与国之间，也就是说彼此之间要客观看待、增强信任、相互尊重和同舟共济。

第一，客观看待。西方要以发展的眼光和全面的视角看待中国，看到中国社会的最新全貌。比如，在政治领域，中国"开门立法"已经成为常态，公众参与程度越来越深；实行政务公开，制定实施了《中华人民共和国政府信息公开条例》；在重大决策中，听证会等征求民意、吸纳民智的形式普遍展开，目前中国举国上下正在热烈讨论"十二五"规划就是一个明证。在社会领域，中国更加多姿多彩，更加开放自信。中国现有4.2亿名网民，2.3亿个博客用户，7500多万个微博用户，上百万个论坛。超过66%的中国网民经常在网上发表言论，就各种话题进行讨论，充分表达思想观点和利益诉求。西方不能漠视中国各领域全面进步的现实，也不能只承认中国的经济成就和社会进步，而否定中国成功背后的制度性、体制性原因。

第二，增强信任。现在西方总有一些人对中国持怀疑态度，他们不确信中国的对外政策走向，担心中国强大了会称王称霸。持这种心态的人必然认为，中国的发展是一种威胁，中国越发展，威胁就越大。这种看法不仅反映了他们对中国缺少信任，更反映了他们对中国缺少了解。了解是信任的基础。我希望他们多了解中国的历史和现在。从历史传统上看，中华文化主张内敛和包容，没有扩张性。近现代史上，中国既没有侵略，也没有殖民，而是饱受欺凌。今天，中国尽管成了世界第二大经济体，但中国人均GDP仍排在世界百位之后，按照国际贫困线标准还有1.5亿人没有脱贫，中国仍然是一个不折不扣的发展中国家，发展的任务仍然相当艰巨，发展的道路仍然相当漫长。中国要实现发展，就需要和平安宁的外部环境，就需要与世界各国友好相处、互利合作，就需要成为国际体系中负责任的一员。即使中国将来发展起来了，中国也不会抛弃传统和忘记历史，去干扩张称霸之事。反对霸权主义不仅写进了中国的宪法，成了中国的基本国策和战略选择，而且永远刻在了中国人民的心中。中国将坚定不移地走和平发展的道路。

第三，相互尊重。世界上没有标准普适的发展模式，只有适合各国国情的发展道路。中华人民共和国成立以来，特别是改革开放30多年来走过的道路，就是中国人民根据国情，"摸着石头过河"探索出来的成功实践。民主是千百年来人类发展所追求的目标，但民主没有固定的模式，即使在西方也是如此。以某一种特定的民主模式为标准评判其他国家民主政治实践的优劣，既在理论上站不住脚，在实践中也十分有害。中国的民主随着新中国应运而生，是中国人民的历史选择。1949年，当中华人民共和国成立时，美国的一些政客大喊大叫："谁失去了中国？"事实上，美国从来没有拥有过中国，因而根本不存在失去的问题。美国政客受其价值观和世界观的限制，很难理解这样一个事实，即"中国人民赢得了中国"，中国人民把自己的杰出代表中国共产党人推上执政的舞台。今天，中国的民主就是在政体上坚持人民代表大会这一根本政治制度，在政党制度上坚持中国共产党领导的多党合作和政治协商制度，在基层民主上实行基层群众自治制度。这既符合现阶段国情，又有利于中国的发展和稳定，具有鲜明的中国特色。中国不会将自己的民主模式强加到别人头上，也不愿被别人强加。正如阳光因七彩而绚烂，世界也因多样而美丽。我们需要平等交流和对话，需要相互开放和包容。我们也希望西方的政治家不要重犯60多年前美国政客的错误，尊重中国的政治和社会制度，尊重中国人民的选择。

第四，同舟共济。今天的世界相互联系、相互依存、利益交融。每个国家作为国际大家庭的一员，只有与各国利益共享、责任共担，才是最符合自己和别国利益的。当风暴来临时，我们需要在同一条船上和衷共济；当风暴渐退，我们仍然需要守望相助。当前，世界经济仍然非常脆弱，甚至是一波未平，一波又起，我们需要加强各国宏观经济政策的协调，避免只顾刺激自己的经济，丝毫不考虑政策的溢出效应；我们需要理性探讨和合作解决世界经济失衡问题，不随意地将责任归咎于他人；我们需要继续维护开放的多边贸易体制，反对贸易保护主义；我们需要积极合作应对能源危机、粮食安全和共同发展等全球性问题，追求可持续发展。

各位中国协会的朋友，中英关系及中西方关系需要我们，也需要你们来共同努力。我衷心地希望各位能秉承协会的宗旨和使命，积极发挥自己的作用和影响，为中英经贸合作水平的不断提升、为中英关系的健康稳定发展、为中西方关系的美好明天做出最大贡献。

这寒冷的冬季不由得让我想起了贵国诗人雪莱的名句："冬天来了，春天还会远吗？"

谢谢！

Respect Each Other and Stand Together through Thick and Thin*

Chairman Hugh Davies,

Members of the China Association,

Ladies and Gentlemen,

It is a great pleasure for me to address the China Association before the holiday season. May I begin with warm festive greetings to all of you: Merry Christmas and Happy New Year!

The China Association, with a history of 123 years, is the oldest UK organisation in promoting business cooperation with China. It has been a forerunner and a witness to our growing business ties over the years. I take this opportunity to express my appreciation and respect to you for your long-standing commitment and hard work for China-UK business cooperation and our bilateral partnership as a whole.

This is my first winter in London, which I was told may be the coldest in the UK for more than a decade. But with so many of you here, I could feel the warmth of your enthusiasm for China-UK relations. And I am glad to say that our relationship has not only maintained its warmth, but is getting warmer and warmer.

First, we have had heated high-level exchanges. China-UK relations have made a smooth transition following the change of government in Britain. Prime Minister Cameron led the largest delegation ever to visit China last month and reached extensive agreement with Chinese leaders on strengthening political mutual trust and cooperation

---

* Speech at the China Association Christmas Lunch. Mandarin Oriental Hyde Park, London, 15 December 2010.

in all fields. Five cabinet secretaries have so far visited China. Important mechanisms such as the Economic and Financial Dialogue, the Strategic Dialogue and the Joint Economic and Trade Commission have run smoothly.

Second, we have enjoyed ever warmer business cooperation. We have put the worst impact of the financial crisis behind us and managed to make new progress. Our trade in goods for the first ten months of this year reached 40.2 billion US dollars, growing almost 30% year-on-year, a record increase. The UK exports to China jumped 43%. We have also seen robust investment both ways. TESCO, for example, has announced a plan to invest 2 billion pounds in China for the next 5 years. This year China also became the sixth largest investor in the UK in the number of projects. It ranks as the second largest investor in London in the number of companies.

Third, we have developed dynamic people-to-people and cultural exchanges. The Shanghai World Expo was a major highlight of China-UK cooperation this year. I must congratulate you on the huge success of the UK Pavilion—it attracted more than 8 million visitors and won the gold prize of the Expo in best design. The UK remains home to the largest number of Chinese students in Europe, with more coming each year. The two countries signed an agreement to train more Mandarin teachers to meet the demand of the emerging "Mandarin fever" in the UK. I am particularly pleased to see that a British college student Johnson Stewart won the top prize at this year's international Mandarin proficiency competition. The UK is also becoming a popular destination for Chinese tourists. According to VisitBritain, the number of tourists from the Chinese Mainland jumped a record high 80% from January to October. By the end of this year, over 200 thousand Chinese tourists will have visited the UK.

China-UK relations now stand at a new starting point and promise broad prospects. Now is the time to chart the course for our relationship from the global and strategic perspective and deepen cooperation in all areas, to the benefit of our countries and peoples.

While we are encouraged by the sound momentum of our relations, we should also be mindful of the potential challenges. One of the challenges is how to bridge the gap of understanding about China in this country. If you read the newspapers and watch TV, you would not miss China-related hot topics and some negative reporting and biased comments. They do not represent the mainstream here, but they could have a negative impact on our effort to promote friendship and understanding between the two countries.

Confucius told us, "There are four things one should beware of: arbitrary judgment, prejudice, obstinacy and egoism." This may well apply to how countries handle their relations with one another. In other words, it would serve bilateral relations well if countries could do the following:

First, view each other in an objective way. Only with a comprehensive and historical perspective, can one get a full picture of what's going on in China right now.

Today's China is a dynamic and ever more open and confident society combining tradition and modernity. There are now 420 million internet users, 230 million bloggers, 75 million microbloggers and 1 million online bulletin boards. Over two thirds of Chinese internet users, that is 280 million of them, regularly air their views online.

The legislative process has become much more open with increasing input from the people. A new regulation was put in place to make government disclosure of information mandatory. And extensive public consultations are held in the major decision-making process. The ongoing heated discussions on a national scale over the 12th Five-Year Plan are a case in point. While recognising the economic successes and social progress in China, the West should not ignore the political and institutional underpinnings of this progress.

Second, enhance mutual trust. Some people in the West have misgivings about China. They are unsure about where China is heading and fear for a "hegemonic China". They see China's development as a threat; the more developed China is, the greater the threat. Such a view shows a lack of trust in China, and even greater lack of understanding about China. Better understanding is key to building trust. I do hope those China-skeptics will try to understand the country in the context of both its history and its current development.

History has shown that China is a non-expansionary power. And culturally China believes in humility and tolerance. It has never invaded or colonized other countries in its modern history, but has fallen victim to aggression. It is true that China is now the world's second largest economy. But it is also a developing country, whose per capita GDP ranks behind 100 other countries. 150 million Chinese still live below the UN poverty line. Development remains a long and tortuous task for China. To fulfill this task, China needs a peaceful international environment. It needs to live in amity and develop win-win cooperation with other countries. It needs to be a responsible player in the international system. The last thing China will do is to seek hegemony or expansion in disregard of its tradition and history. Anti-hegemonism is not only a constitutional principle and strategic choice for China. It has become part of the consciousness of every Chinese. The only option for China is peaceful development.

Third, respect each other. There is no "one-size-fits-all" model for all countries. Models can only serve countries well when they are country-specific. The journey of China since the founding of the People's Republic, especially in the past 30 years of reform and opening-up, has been one of "crossing the river by feeling for the stones". Eventually China found its own road of development. Democracy is an ideal pursued by all people around the world. It does not take a single form, not even among the Western countries. It is neither reasonable nor useful to judge one country's democracy and political system by another country's standard.

The democratic system in China was born with the People's Republic in 1949 and was the choice of the Chinese people. At that time, some US politicians were loudly complaining "who lost China?" In fact, the US never owned China in the first place. There was no such a question for them to lose China. Constrained by their values and thinking, it was very hard for some US politicians to understand a simple fact. It was the Chinese people who won China. And it was the Chinese people who chose the Communist Party. Today, China's democratic system has evolved with reform and opening-up. It draws upon the best political experience of mankind. China's democracy is built on the fundamental political system of the National People's Congress. It follows a system of multi-party cooperation and political consultation under the leadership of the Communist Party and grassroots democracy. This uniquely Chinese system works best for the Chinese national conditions and serves development and stability of the country. China does not impose its model upon others, nor does it want to be imposed upon. Just as we admire the sunshine for its spectrum of colours, we should appreciate the world for its diversity. We need exchanges and dialogues with an open mind. We do hope Western political leaders would not repeat the mistake US politicians made 61 years ago. China's political and social systems should be respected, so should the choices of the Chinese people.

Fourth, work together for the common good. A defining feature of our world is its inter-connectedness and interdependence. Only by sharing interests and responsibilities can countries serve their own interest and the interest of others. When a storm rages, we are all fighting the waves in one boat; when it recedes, we offer each other help in repairing damages. Global economic recovery remains fragile and fraught with challenges. We need to step up macroeconomic policy coordination and prevent negative spill-over effect of stimulus measures. We need rational dialogue and cooperation to address global economic imbalances. We need to ensure that the multilateral trade regime upholds openness and rejects protectionism. And we need active global cooperation to tackle global issues such as energy crisis, food security and common development, and work for sustainable development.

Members of the China Association,

Building a partnership of trust and cooperation between China and the UK, between China and the West calls for efforts of all of us. I sincerely hope that the China Association will continue to play an active part in this respect. I look forward to even greater contributions by the China Association to a closer China-UK economic partnership, to a healthy and stable China-UK relationship and to a promising relationship between China and the West.

This cold winter reminds me of two lines from Shelley's poem, "If winter comes, can spring be far behind?"

Thank you!

兼听则明，偏信则暗[*]

尊敬的司法部国务大臣麦克奈利勋爵，
尊敬的克莱门托-琼斯勋爵，
女士们、先生们：

欢迎各位出席2011年的自民党秋季年会"中国论坛"。2010年，我首次参加了在利物浦举办的自民党秋季年会"中国论坛"，并与自民党的朋友们就如何发展中英关系进行了交流。今天，我想就如何认识中国与各位交流看法。

我不妨从英国媒体上对华报道的几个关注点谈起，因为许多朋友是通过媒体报道了解中国的，而英国媒体涉华报道往往不够全面、客观和公正。

英国媒体的第一个关注点是中国经济前景。

一些观点认为，中国经济以年均近10%的高速持续增长了30多年，现在中国劳动力成本上升、人民币升值、资源对外依赖度提高，中国作为"世界工厂"快没有优势了，快没有增长动力了，一个"中等收入陷阱"正在等着中国。也有人拿不久前中国动车追尾并脱轨事故说事，认为这预示着中国经济即将脱轨。

中国经济确实面临不少挑战和困难，例如，外部世界经济复苏不稳定，美欧形势不太乐观；中国内部存在着发展不平衡不充分的问题，如资源消耗

---

[*] 在英国自民党秋季年会"中国论坛"上的主旨演讲。2011年9月21日，英国伯明翰市会议中心。

过大、环境不堪重负、科技创新不足、内需消费欠缺。

但是，正如温家宝总理9月初在大连举行的夏季达沃斯论坛上讲到的那样，"对中国经济的未来，有看好的，也有唱衰的。对此，我们的头脑是清醒的，胸中是有数的，信心是坚定的"。

应当看到中国经济发展的有利因素仍然很多。中国经济内在动力很充沛。中国正处在工业化、城镇化和国际化中期，基础设施建设、地区和城乡差别的缩小、消费结构的升级都将继续带动经济的发展。中国与发达国家相比也还有很大差距，我们的人均GDP只有美国、英国的1/10左右，不到世界平均水平的一半。水力学上有一个原理：落差产生势能。经济学上也一样，中国与发达国家的差距，就是中国经济继续加紧追赶的动能。

除了内在条件，更鼓舞人心的是中国正在调整发展思路，进行"对症下药"，解决发展中存在的一些问题。2011年中国制定了"十二五"规划并开始实施，着力转变发展方式，调整经济结构，改善社会民生。我们还采取措施主动放缓经济增速，比如2011年上半年，中国经济增速为9.6%，低于2010年全年的10.4%，这样的适当降速有利于促进产业升级，实现经济可持续发展。我们对中国经济发展的前景充满信心。

英国媒体的第二个关注点是中国政治改革。

最常见的观点是认为中国经济改革很成功，但是不搞政治改革。中国到底有没有搞政治改革？应当说，一直在进行。取消领导干部终身制、完善人民代表大会制、发展党内民主、扩大基层民主，这些都是步骤和措施，改革是全方位的、逐步推进的。

那么为什么外界还是认为中国没有搞政治改革呢？关键问题是什么样的政治改革。如果以西方的标准衡量中国，自然会得出不同的结论。但西方的标准并不是普适标准，而且西方的政治制度本身也存在不少问题和弊端，在最近这轮金融危机中这些弊端更加暴露无遗，对此，西方的有识之士也在大声疾呼改革。

2011年中国庆祝了中国共产党成立90周年，当我们总结党90年来的风雨历程时，认为很重要的一条经验是"与时俱进"，就是勇于变革、勇于创新、永不僵化、永不停滞。中国的政治制度建设同样如此，始终是在不断变革和创新中向前发展。正是因为中国不断推行政治体制改革，完善上层建筑，才奠定和带动了30多年的经济发展、民生改善和社会稳定。任何政治制度优越与否，关键要看是否符合本国国情，是否使国家发展、人民幸福。我们认为中国的政治制度符合中国国情，它不仅使国家繁荣昌盛，而且使人民幸福安康。

英国媒体的第三个关注点是中国的自由和人权。

在这个问题上，你只要问中国的普通民众，他们就会将现在的自由与以前相比；他们就会告诉你，今天中国人比以前历史上任何时期都自由、都幸福。

中国的4.85亿名网民和约2亿个微博用户在这个问题上也很有发言权。他们通过网络、微博对国家和社会事务发表意见，往往一个社会事件会引来数百万网友"围观"、几万条评论。中国现在提出要加强和创新社会管理，其中心就是要让人民群众成为社会管理的主体，最大限度激发社会活力，而网络、微博就成为民众参与社会管理的一种有效方式，既是民众利益表达的顺畅平台，也是政府了解民意的"直通车"。

当然，无论是在现实生活中还是在网络上，自由都是相对的，都必须受法律和道德的约束。这种约束的界限在哪里，往往是中西方分歧所在。其中既有价值观因素，也有文化因素，更有社会因素。在东方文化中，集体总是高于个人，责任总是大于自由，这与西方崇尚个人的绝对自由主义有很大不同。在历史上，中国经历过太多的社会动荡，耽误了太多的发展时间，所以我们现在高度珍惜社会稳定，不愿发展大局受任何干扰和破坏。我们正在建设法治国家，依法治国，依法维护社会稳定。任何人在法律面前都是平等的，既受法律保护，又受法律约束。任何人，不管他是"异见分子"还是"同见分子"，只要违犯法律、破坏社会稳定，就都要受法律的惩处。稳定犹如空气，尽管身处其中有时可能感觉不到，但一旦没有，就会难以生存。在2011年8月伦敦发生骚乱后，英国的民众是否也有这种感觉？

英国媒体的第四个关注点是中国对外政策。

中国近来被西方媒体描述成一个在世界上咄咄逼人的国家：在南海示强；发展航空母舰；在非洲搞"新殖民主义"；等等。

中国与一些周边国家存在领土和海洋权益争端，这是客观事实，但中国始终高度克制，努力通过外交谈判来维护主权、化解争端，避免破坏地区和平与稳定。中国不会以大欺小、以强凌弱，但也绝不会允许一些国家以小欺大，蚕食中国的领土和海洋权益。

中国发展航母，是出于维护国家领土主权和海洋权益的需要。中国有1.8 万千米漫长的大陆海岸线，以及依据《联合国海洋法公约》合法管辖的约 300 万平方千米广阔海域。美国拥有现役航母 11 艘，并还在建造新一代航母；英国也计划建造两艘"伊丽莎白女王"级新一代航母。即使是印度、巴西、泰国等发展中国家也都拥有航母。所以，中国拥有航母，实在没有什么值得大惊小怪的。

中国与非洲的合作历史悠久，从 20 世纪 50 年代起，中国向非洲提供了大量的经济援助，派出了近 2 万人次援外医疗队员。中国在非洲援建铁路 2000 多千米、公路 3000 多千米，援建 100 多所学校和 60 所医院。近 10 年来，中国减免了非洲 200 多亿元债务。近年来除对非援助外，中国在非投资和生产合作越来越多，普遍采用政府主导、市场运作、企业参与的合作模式，实现了中非互利双赢。

不久前，中国政府发布了《中国的和平发展》白皮书，再次向世界宣示，中国始终不渝地走和平发展道路，在坚持自己和平发展的同时，致力于维护世界和平，积极促进各国共同发展繁荣。这是中国的真诚愿望，也是我们的实际行动。

以上就是我针对近期媒体涉华报道谈的一些看法和想法，希望借此为大家了解中国提供多一点角度，多一点思考。当然，我说的并非英国媒体的所有观点，因为英国不乏有识之士，涉华报道也并非千篇一律。最近，我就看到一些呼吁客观看待中国发展及其对世界影响的文章。我希望这样的声音越来越多，越来越引起英国社会的共鸣。

近几十年来，西方一直在争论如何对待中国、怎样和中国打交道。最近，我看到英国报纸上出现了一个词"拥抱"。或许，拥抱不是中国人的常用礼节，但中国人的礼节是：当你想拥抱我们时，我们也会张开双臂。

　　谢谢！

A Clear Head Comes from an Open Mind[*]

Lord McNally,

Lord Clement-Jones,

Ladies and Gentlemen,

Welcome to this year's China Forum.

I am delighted to be addressing China Forum at your Party Conference.

I have warm memories of meeting with many of you at the China Forum we held last year in Liverpool.

I see this as an important opportunity to share ideas and strengthen our friendship.

Last year we explored what should be done to take China-UK relations forward. This year I hope we can use the China Forum to deepen understanding between our countries.

On this issue of understanding, I think a useful starting point is to analyse those issues about my country that are the focus of attention for the British media.

I suggest this approach since British media coverage is the primary source for many of you to find out about what's going on in China.

However, I must say at the outset that British media coverage on China is nowhere near comprehensive, objective and fair.

British media generally places its attention on four areas:

- China's economic future.

---

[*] Keynote Speech at China Forum at the Lib Dems Party Conference. International Convention Centre, Birmingham, 21 September 2011.

- Political reform.
- Freedom and human rights.
- And foreign policy.

Let me take each in turn.

First, China's economic future.

Some observers suggest that China's economy is running out of steam. In early September, at the China Summer Davos in Dalian Chinese Premier Wen Jiabao reflected on the differing views about the Chinese economy.

Premier Wen said: "Some are optimistic about China's economic future, while some others say that China is in trouble. But we in China remain clear-headed and are firm in our confidence."

Let me analyse what some media describe as "trouble".

Some believe that China is under pressure from rising labor costs, more expensive Renminbi and higher dependence on imported resources.

Those commentators suggest that China's days as a "world factory" are numbered and its growth is losing momentum. In addition, they say that in China, a middle-income trap is looming.

Some take the recent tragic rail crash as a sign that the Chinese economy will "come off the rails entirely".

Yes, the Chinese economy is confronted with many challenges.

For example, the fragile global recovery and the bleak economic landscape in America and Europe.

At the same time, China must find a solution to many problems internally as well. Premier Wen Jiabao has publicly pointed to these facts in the Chinese economy:

- A lack of balance and coordination in development.
- Inefficient use of resources.
- Environmental strains.
- Poor innovation capacity.
- And flagging demand and consumption.

All these cry out for effective responses.

Despite all these challenges, I'd like to bring to your attention these points.

For 32 years China has had consistent annual average growth of over 10%. Despite the turmoil in global financial markets over the past three years, our economic fundamentals remain strong.

China is half way through industrialisation and urbanisation and we're moving faster to integrate into the global economy.

Other contributors to economic growth are:

- Our infrastructure building in roads, rail, air and seaports.
- Narrowing regional gaps and the urban-rural divide.
- And encouraging greater domestic consumption.

China is still far behind developed countries in terms of per capita GDP. Ours is only around 10% of that of America and Britain; it is merely half of the world average.

Since China adopted its reform and opening-up policies three decades ago, my country has industrialized at an unprecedented speed. This means China is on a journey from developing towards developed status. This has created a strong driving force for China to catch up with the developed countries.

In addition China is reorienting its development strategy and seeking solutions to its problems.

Early this year, China unveiled the 12th Five-Year Plan, and it's being implemented with rigour. According to the plan China is taking these major steps:

- Readjusting its growth model.
- Restructuring the economy.
- And improving public services.

China has also taken measures to slow down economic growth. The objective is to create a favourable macroeconomic environment to reach all the Plan goals.

As a result, in the first 6 months this year, the growth speed has stabilized at 9.6%. That's below the 10.4% full-year rate in 2010.

As Premier Wen Jiabao reflected at this year's Summer Davos held in China that we have many reasons to be confident about China's economic future.

Second, China's political reform.

A prevailing opinion in British media is that China only goes for economic reform, but not political reform.

As an ambassador I must be "diplomatic" and avoid comment on political reform in Britain!

So let me focus on political reform in China.

The answer is clear. There is a political reform in China and it has never stopped.

In this significant reform, we have:

- Put an end to lifelong tenure of leadership positions.
- Improved the system of people's congresses.
- Strengthened democratic institutions within the Party.
- And expanded democracy at the grass-roots level.

Our reform covers many aspects of the political life and its steady progress is there for all who choose to see.

Then why do many outside of China still take the view that China has no political reform?

To answer this question, we need to clarify what kind of political reform they are talking about.

If China was judged by the standards of Western countries, then people would come to the above conclusion. But the truth is that the Western standards are not universal, and the Western political system has its own flaws.

These problems have become more visible and better understood in the ongoing financial crisis. Some visionary people in the west have come out strongly in favour of a decisive reform.

This year China celebrated the 90th birthday of the Communist Party of China. It was a time to take stock of the extraordinary journey of the Party over 90 years. There was a consensus that the Party's success wouldn't have been possible without a commitment to move forward with time.

The Party is always ready to change. The Party has been bold enough to reinvent itself and it has never stood still.

The same is true of the political reform in China, which keeps going ahead amidst adjustment and innovation.

To sum up, it is China's relentless push to reform and strengthen its political institutions that has helped to deliver over 30 years of economic growth.

Most importantly, such reforms have also underpinned people's rising living standards and social stability.

There is a core yardstick with which to judge the legitimacy and effectiveness of a political system. The benchmark of the system is this:

- It matches well with the conditions on the ground.
- It contributes to the development of a country.
- And it promotes the well-being of all the people.

We believe China's political system is tailored to our national circumstances.

The evidence is that the system has contributed to national prosperity and a better life for the people.

Third, freedom and human rights in China. If you ask the average Chinese about their views, they may compare their freedom with the past. They may also point out that they are freer and happier than any time in history. China's 485 million internet users and 200 million micro-bloggers are also a key voice on this issue. They speak their minds on political and public affairs online and by micro-blog. In many cases, one single issue may attract the attention of millions in cyberspace and tens of thousands of comments may be posted online.

China is talking about exploring new approaches to better and innovative governance. At the heart is a desire by the government to encourage the public to be leading players in the society. The Internet and micro-blog have every potential to be an effective platform for the public to be heard, and for the government to hear their concerns.

Of course, either in our daily life or in cyberspace, freedom is a relative concept. Freedom must operate within the boundary of laws and ethics.

China and the developed countries like Britain are quite often at odds over where the boundary of freedom lies. Part of our differences is about values, and part of them is cultural and social.

In Asian cultures, collectivity is more important than individual rights. Responsibility always outweighs freedom. This is quite different from the pursuit of absolute individual freedom by the Western countries.

China in the past two centuries went through too much turmoil and instability. That is why we Chinese people highly treasure social stability. We will not allow our development efforts to be disrupted or damaged in any way.

China is strengthening its legal framework and promoting the rule of law. We are determined to maintain social stability according to law.

In China, people are all equal before the law. They have the protection of the law and at the same time must act within the law. Anyone, whether he or she is a "dissident" or not, must be held to account if he or she breaks the law or damages social stability.

Stability, like air, may not be felt if it is present. But its absence may threaten people's survival.

Maybe the importance of stability was more apparent to the British people after the August riots in London.

Fourth, China's foreign policy.

Recently, China has been labeled by the Western press as getting assertive. Headlines touched on territorial questions in the South China Sea. Then there was China unveiling an aircraft carrier. And how China pursues "neo-colonialism" in Africa.

It's true that China has disputes with some neighbours over territory and maritime rights and interests. But we always show restraint and seek diplomatic and negotiated solutions. This is the way to uphold sovereignty and regional peace and stability. China will not threaten or intimidate smaller, weaker countries. Yet at the same time we will not allow anyone to damage our interests or encroach upon our territory and maritime rights and interests.

China does have one aircraft carrier now, and it is not yet in service. China seeks to have an aircraft carrier as this is necessary for the protection of territorial sovereignty and maritime interests. China has a 18,000-kilometre coastline. In addition, China has under its jurisdiction 3 million square kilometers of waters according to the United Nations Convention on the Law of the Sea.

In contrast, America today has 11 aircraft carriers in service and the latest super carriers are already under construction. Britain plans to build two Queen Elizabeth class aircraft carriers. And even such developing countries as India, Brazil and Thailand have deployed aircraft carriers. Therefore, I don't see why people should take fright at China's refitted aircraft carrier.

Turning to China-Africa relations. Our cooperation with Africa has a long history. Starting from the 1950s, China has provided substantial economic assistance and sent nearly 20,000 medical workers to Africa.

We have built over 2,000 kilometres of rail line, more than 3,000 kilometres of highway, 100-plus schools and 60 hospitals in Africa.

Over the past decade, we have cancelled over 20 billion yuan, or roughly 2 billion pound of African debt. In recent years, apart from aid, we have made more investment and run more joint-production programs in Africa. These are government-led, commercial programmes where companies are major players. This is a win-win cooperation model for both China and Africa.

To highlight its commitment to peaceful development, the Chinese government recently published a White Paper on China's Peaceful Development. The White Paper reaffirms to the world China's commitment to a path of peaceful development and its dedication to world peace.

We seek common development and shared prosperity with the world. This is our sincere aspiration and it has been matched with firm actions.

These are the thoughts I'd like to leave you with about China. I hope they can offer you new perspectives when you read about China in the British media or deal with China.

Of course, I'm not speaking about all of British media. In the UK there's no shortage of far-sighted people and even-handed views about China.

What has encouraged me in particular is that I found a new word in British newspapers on relations with China.

That word is "embrace".

As you may be aware, "embrace" is not what we Chinese always do traditionally to show goodwill and respect.

But when you want to "embrace" us, we will surely open our arms warmly.

Thank you!

共促合作，共同发展 *

尊敬的大卫·谢拉德主席，

尊敬的马克·加文先生，

女士们、先生们：

很高兴出席美欧工商协会的午餐会，与大家就中国的发展及中国与美欧关系进行交流。

我知道美欧工商协会是一个致力于促进北美和欧洲之间理解与合作，同时推动全球发展的组织。那么，我首先想问大家一个问题：北美和欧洲之间地理上间隔的是什么？可能大多数人会不假思索地回答：大西洋。没错，但你是否想过，这不是唯一正确的答案，因为地球是圆的，所以答案也可以是太平洋和亚洲。

我之所以问这个问题，就是想说明两点。第一点，人的思维往往是有惯性的，而这种惯性往往会导致思维的局限，有时还会产生误解甚至偏见。在如何看待中国发展这个问题上，现在西方就存在一种思维惯性。

比如，对于中国经济发展，西方从"经济周期"理论或"中等收入陷阱"现象出发，认为中国经济已经高速增长了30多年，很难再持续，经常找各种可能导致中国经济"突然刹车"或"硬着陆"的理由，如劳动力成本上升、房地产泡沫及银行信贷和地方债务风险等。但是，如果不拘泥于局部和具体问题，从整体上看中国经济发展的基本面，看到中国经济发展水平与

---

* 在美欧工商协会午餐会上的演讲。2011年10月26日，摩根大通集团英国公司，伦敦。

发达国家仍有相当大的差距，中国城乡区域发展仍相当不平衡；看到中国经济发展的积极面，中国正在加速调整经济结构和转变发展方式，即增长主要由出口和投资拉动向内需和科技创新驱动转型，就不难得出乐观的结论，中国经济目前适当放缓并不足虑，中国未来仍有较大的增长空间，中国经济能够实现更长时期、更高水平、更好质量的发展。

又如，看待中国的政治改革问题，美欧舆论显得很消极，有一种"失望"情绪。但如果多一些包容性，不以自己的标准来衡量，多一些客观性，深入了解中国并进行纵向比较，就会看到中国政府越来越以人为本、执政为民；中国的人民代表大会制度日益完善，人大代表越来越发挥监督职能；中国的基层民主自治充满活力，人民群众当家做主的意识越来越强烈，实现形式也越来越丰富，包括网络、微博等现代方式。

再如，看待中国的外交政策，西方的逻辑是"国强必霸"，因而喜欢给中国贴一个"咄咄逼人"的标签。比如，有人认为中国在南海问题上显得很强硬。但是他们往往忽视了两个基本事实：一是南海诸岛自古以来就是中国的领土，中国的主权要求在国际法上有充分的依据，相关国家以前也是明确承认的；二是中国一直主张在南海问题上"搁置争议，共同开发"。现在有些国家加强对南海的所谓"占有"，加大与第三国搞所谓的"共同开发"，中国自然要对这种侵犯中国主权和领土、损害中国海洋权益的行动做出必要反应。即使这样，中国也继续主张相关各方通过双边协商和谈判，以建设性的态度处理出现的问题，特别是要保持冷静和克制，不采取使争端复杂化、扩大化的行动，共同维护南海和平与稳定。这充分表明中国谋和平、顾大局，不靠强权、不搞霸权，推动合作共赢。

与南海相关联的另一个话题是航母，外界目前对中国发展航母似乎颇有"担心"，认为这是中国在搞军力扩张。中国有1.8万千米漫长的大陆海岸线，以及依据《联合国海洋法公约》合法管辖的约300万平方千米广阔海域，中国发展航母完全是出于维护国家领土主权和海洋权益的需要。从全球层面看，据英国《卫报》的统计，现在世界上8个国家拥有航母，其中不仅有发达国家，如美国、法国、意大利和西班牙，而且印度、巴西和泰国等发展中国家也都拥有航母，航母并不是什么"霸权的标志"。英国虽然没有现役航母，但正计划建造"伊丽莎白女王"级新一代航母。所以，中国建造航母，只是中国作为一个负责任大国提高国防能力的正常行为，中国无意与某些国家去搞军备竞赛，更不会去争夺海洋霸权。

因此，要打破旧有思维惯性，全面看待和多角度认识中国的发展，这是我想说的第一点。回到最初美欧地理间隔的问题，我想说一下第二点。

大家可以看我手中的这一幅中国出版的世界地图，与你们以往在英国看到的地图不同，中国正好处于美欧的中间，中、美、欧将地球纵向做了三个等分，彼此之间距离差不多。

当然，这只是地理上的距离，更重要的是在经济上，中国与美欧现在均保持着密切的合作关系。中国和欧盟、美国互为最主要的贸易投资伙伴。中国是欧盟第二大出口市场和第一大进口来源地，是美国第三大出口市场和第一大进口来源地；欧盟、美国分别是中国第一和第二大出口市场，第二和第五大进口来源地。不仅如此，中欧、中美经贸合作现已从商品贸易向服务贸易、投资并购、技术转让、研发合作及品牌营销等宽领域、多层次格局拓展。例如，欧盟和美国现在分列中国第一和第三大投资目的地。2011年，中国的"十二五"规划出台，提出要扩大内需和促进消费，预计今后五年中国将进口超过8万亿美元的商品。联系到此前美国制定的"出口倍增计划"和欧洲启动的"欧洲2020战略"，我认为中国与美欧的利益契合点增多，经贸合作前景更加广阔。

这就是全球化时代的特点，各国经济利益相互依存，形成利益共同体。经济繁荣时，世界各国共同增长，共享合作"蛋糕"；经济危机时，没有一国能够独善其身。用一句西方俗语："大家同在一条船上。"

事实上，中国有一句类似的成语："同舟共济。"显然，"同舟共济"相比之下多了一层意思，即强调"共济"。在目前世界经济复苏乏力、危机跌宕起伏、下行风险增大的情况下，"共济"无疑是关键。

我认为，"共济"应立足于增强信心，加强合作，共同应对挑战，共同促进世界经济持续复苏。"共济"的基础是"自济"，各国政府要真正承担起责任，把自己的事情尽力做好，把自己的问题尽力解决好。"共济"不是转嫁危机，而是携手消解危机。"共济"的方式应是开放和合作，而不是保护和限制。越是在世界经济面临复杂困难形势时，越要坚持自由贸易和全球化进程，而不是限制高新技术出口，推行保护主义措施和实行"去全球化"。

中国积极参与"共济"，采取了一系列行动：中国始终表明对欧洲、对欧元具有信心，不会减持欧元债券，并支持欧盟和国际货币基金组织应对危机的努力；中国及时实施强有力的内需刺激政策，组织30多个大型采购团赴海外采购，努力加大进口；中国积极鼓励企业加大对外投资，投资数量年均增长40%以上，2010年已达688亿美元，居世界第五位，这有力地促进了投资地的就业和经济增长；中国2010年6月进一步推进人民币汇率形成机制改革，目前人民币兑美元汇率已升值7%。中国深知，世界的繁荣稳定离不开中国，中国的发展也离不开世界。

最后，让我再次回到最初的地理问题，当前我们的世界越来越小，已经成为"地球村"，但毋庸置疑，世界还未小到没有足够的空间来容纳中、美、欧的共同发展。只有中、美、欧共同发展，这个地球才会更加稳定、更加繁荣、更加和谐。

谢谢！

Collaborate and Grow Together[*]

Mr David Shellard,

Mr Mark Garvin,

Ladies and Gentlemen,

It's with great pleasure that I join you at this luncheon of the American European Business Association.

I have been invited to discuss China's development and its relations with America and Europe.

Through the past 30 years, the American European Business Association has built a strong reputation. It has progressed transatlantic understanding and cooperation and advanced opportunities in a globalized world.

That globalized world means that it is very appropriate to include China in any dialogue about Europe and America. So I am delighted you have hosted this discussion on the shared future of China, America and Europe.

I guess two issues are very much at the front of your minds. First, the future of the Eurozone, and second, the political debate in the US over economic decisions. Both these matters are having a profound impact on the world.

The media is brimming over with discussions on these issues, so today for a change I want to take you to a different view of the world.

Let me start off with this question. Geographically, what lies between North America and Europe?

---

[*] Speech at the Luncheon Hosted by the American European Business Association. JP Morgan, London, 26 October 2011.

The answer appears so simple — the Atlantic Ocean. You might say it is such an easy answer that it's a no-brainer question.

But the instant answer means you are thinking of the world in only one dimension.

The world is round and so there is another correct answer to the question of what lies between America and Europe. That answer is the Pacific Ocean and Asia.

That second correct answer is a vivid reminder of two important things.

First, people tend to perceive the world looking back into the past. Or, in other words, there's an inertia out there resisting new ways of thinking.

However, such inertia quite often leads to misjudgment and bias.

Sadly, this is the way the Western countries have been looking at China for decades. This deeply entrenched paradigm creates a fog of thinking that blinds seeing the real China.

In economics, there are those in Western countries who argue that China is unable to go beyond the "boom-and-bust cycles" and the "middle-income trap".

Other commentators say that they doubt China's economic sustainability after over 30 years of high growth. They point to selective evidence such as higher labour cost, property bubbles, lending squeeze and local government debt risks. Many make the case that the Chinese economy will have a hard landing.

However, if you choose to do a deep analysis, and from within China, you will come to a different conclusion.

Obviously, there are short term challenges in the Chinese economy. But it is clear that China's economic fundamentals are strong and its long-term growth trend is positive.

There has been a lot of focus in past months on two facts. First, China is the world's biggest exporter. Second, China ranks as the second largest economy. I believe that it is very important to view these strengths in the context of the comparative weakness of China.

It is really important to grasp these facts:

- China is far from a developed country.
- China's per capita income is way lower than the developed world.
- China faces a wide urban-rural divide and sharp regional disparities.

- China is moving faster to restructure its economy and recast its growth model.
- The heart of this strategy is to reorient from export and public investment to greater consumption and technology innovation.

All this means that China's slowdown right now is temporary. The growth potential of China over the next twenty years is enormous.

We have reason to believe that China's development is sustainable and its growth quality will be even higher.

Let me now turn to politics and China.

When it comes to China's political reform I always find that media coverage in America and Europe is negative and gloomy.

A sense of "disappointment" seems to be the prevailing mood. This stems from continuous comment suggesting China should adopt the political systems in Western countries.

I believe that if the foreign media coverage of politics in China were more inclusive and objective, then the conclusions can be vastly different.

An analysis of China in greater depth will show that China has come a long way in promoting democracy:

- The Chinese government has increasingly put public interests above other considerations.
- The People's Congress system has been continuously strengthening.
- Deputies elected to Congresses are playing ever more effective supervisory roles.
- The grass-roots democratic organisations are vibrant.
- Chinese people have a clearer sense of ownership of society.
- The voices of Chinese people in public affairs are louder through the Internet, micro-blog and other public channels.

Turning to foreign policy.

The developed countries' logic tends to be "power leads to hegemony". In some foreign media China has recently been labeled as "being assertive".

These media point to China playing tough on the South China Sea question. This is interpreted as a sign of China's new diplomatic posture.

However, two basic facts are often ignored.

First, those South China Sea islands have been part of the Chinese territory reaching deep into our history.

China's sovereign claims are supported by sufficient evidence in the international law, and such claims were explicitly recognized by other countries.

Second, China supports the principles of "shelving disputes and carrying out joint development" by relevant claimants as the best way toward a solution.

In contrast, some countries are strengthening the grip over their "illegitimate gains" and bringing in countries from the outside as development partners.

These counterproductive actions further complicate the situation and violate China's sovereignty, territory and maritime interests. In such a context, China's reiteration of its established position is a natural and necessary response.

Against this background there is still a clear will from China to talk and negotiate.

China wishes to deal with problems in a way that is constructive.

Right now, all sides must be cool-headed and show restraint. No action should be allowed to complicate and expand the disputes. The pressing priority is to keep the South China Sea peaceful and stable.

China's stance on the South China Sea is a clear example of our broader approach to the international relations.

The characterisitics of China as a nation are:

- Peaceful.
- Rational and conscious of the larger picture.
- China knows the days of power politics and hegemony are over.
- And win-win cooperation is the only choice in our time.

Another topic associated with the South China Sea is China's aircraft carrier.

There seem to be immense concerns about it as a symbol of China's military expansion.

The reality is China has an 18,000-kilometre coastline.

China has 3 million square kilometers of waters under its jurisdiction according to the UN Convention on the Law of the Sea.

So it is obvious that our aircraft carrier is important in protecting our sovereignty and maritime interests.

According to The Guardian newspaper eight countries own aircraft carriers today.

These countries include developed countries such as America, France, Italy and Spain, and developing countries like India, Brazil and Thailand.

So I don't see why a Chinese aircraft carrier is billed as the "mark of hegemony".

Britain has no aircraft carrier in service now, but is building a new generation of aircraft carrier called the Queen Elizabeth Class.

So, China's unveiling of an aircraft carrier shouldn't be regarded as a surprise move. It's merely what China should do to strengthen defense capabilities as a large, responsible country.

You can be certain that China is not intending to be locked into an arms race. Still less does China pursue any sort of hegemony over the sea.

So, the first thought I want to leave you with is the need to have a broader picture and develop a balanced view about China.

As I said this means having a fresh perspective of the world.

I now return to my earlier reference to the transatlantic geography.

I will draw your attention to a second point.

If you look at world maps published in China, they look very different from those in Europe and the USA.

What you find is that Chinese maps put China at the centre. On either side of the map you find America and Europe.

Chinese maps roughly divide the globe into three major parts, which are evenly spaced apart.

These three major parts have great symbolism in current global trade patterns. It is a most important fact that in economics and trade, the ties among China, America and Europe are closer than ever. We are each other's major trade and investment partners.

To be specific:

- China is the EU's second largest export destination and the largest source of imports.

- The EU is China's largest export market and the second largest source of imports.

Meanwhile:

- China is America's third largest export destination and number one source of imports.
- And America is China's number two export market and the fifth largest source of imports.

In addition, China's commercial ties with Europe and America are widening: from trade in goods to services, investments, merger and acquisition, technology transfer, and R&D cooperation and marketing.

The best examples of the deepening of our economic partnership include:

- The EU and America are respectively China's number one and number three investors today.
- This year, China published its 12th Five-Year Plan, announcing to boost internal demand and consumption and projecting an import of over eight trillion dollars worth of goods over the next five years.
- This plan followed America's National Export Initiative and the EU's 2020 Strategy.
- And all this means more opportunities for Chinese companies and their European and American peers to cooperate to create mutual economic benefits.

This is what our globalized era is all about.

Economies are more interdependent and their interests and destinies are inseparable.

In good times, all economies grow and gain from cooperation and prosperity. In tough times, no one is immune from the crisis. As one Western saying goes, "We are all together in the same boat."

In China we have a similar proverb, "cross the river together in the same boat."

It not only shows the fact of "all being in the same boat", but also stresses the need to "cross the river together".

As you are fully aware the world is in its third year of financial crisis. I feel sure you will agree that solutions will only come through collaborations. So, we badly need this spirit of "crossing the river together" to overcome the crisis.

To "cross the river together", we must build up confidence and strengthen cooperation to battle the crisis and promote a sustained recovery.

But the mutual help of the international community can only be effective when it's based on self-help of individual countries.

The number one priority for governments around the world is to take real responsibility to put their own house in order. This is the essential first step for any rescue plan to take hold.

As we combat the crisis together, we must make sure the homegrown crisis is not shifted to others. And "beggar-thy-neighbour" politics should have no place in our strategy.

What we need is openness and cooperation, instead of protectionism and restrictions.

It is vital for all countries that we all commit to free trade and globalization.

What is very clear is that protectionism and anti-globalization are false choices that will only suck the world deeper into the crisis.

China has taken decisive actions on many fronts to support globalization and so help pull the world economy back from the current financial crisis:

- China has shown strong confidence in Europe and Euro.
- China has pledged not to reduce its holdings of euro bonds.
- We support the counter-crisis measures by the EU and the IMF.
- And China has not only put together a strong package to stimulate demand at home, but also sent out over 30 large purchase missions abroad, mainly to America and Europe, to increase imports.

In addition, China is encouraging its businesses to ramp up outward investment.

Figures show that China's outbound investment keeps growing by over 40 percent each year. It had reached 68.8 billion US dollars by 2010, making China the world's fifth largest investor. This is a strong boost to job creation and economic growth in host countries.

And since June last year, when China announced further reforms to its exchange rate regime, our currency, the Renminbi, has strengthened by 7% against the US dollar.

The reason behind such moves is self-evident.

China is deeply aware that a prosperous world needs China's contribution and China's own development is inseparable with the world.

In closing, I return to the question of geography at the outset.

Our world is indeed getting smaller. Our globe is closer to becoming a global village than ever in human history.

I say this to skeptics who say the world is too small to provide enough space for China, America and Europe to grow together. My view is that history will prove the opposite to be true.

And here's what I believe in and what I think will happen.

A world in which China, America and Europe all prosper will be more stable, more prosperous and more harmonious.

Thank you!

构建新型中西方关系 *

尊敬的沈祖尧校长，

各位老师、各位同学：

首先感谢香港中文大学盛情邀请。

这是我任中国驻英国大使近两年来第 9 次到世界百强大学做演讲，不过前 8 次都是在英国大学，这还是第一次在中国的世界百强大学发表演讲，而且是第一次用中文。当我走上英国著名大学的讲台时，我感到很自豪，我为作为一名驻外使节代表自己的国家而感到自豪。今天，在中国香港的著名大学讲台上，我更加感到骄傲，我为中国香港能有这样的一流大学感到骄傲。

这也是我第一次到一个比我年龄小的大学。你们大多数人被称为"80后"或"90后"，按照这个说法，香港中文大学建于 1963 年，是"60后"。因此，我要祝贺香港中文大学在建校不到 50 年里进入世界大学 50 强。同时祝香港不仅保持国际经济金融中心地位，而且香港的大学不断提升其在世界级高等学府中的地位。

我从事外交工作近 40 年，大半时间在与美英等西方国家打交道，目睹了中西方关系几十年来的发展历程，也深感中西方关系仍处在一个信任与合作的十字路口。今天我来到香港这个中西方文化交汇之地，来到香港中文大学这座致力于"结合传统与现代，融会中国与西方"的学术殿堂，我愿就中西方关系谈一点体会和思考。

---

* 在香港中文大学的演讲。2011 年 11 月 23 日，香港中文大学。

中西方之间尽管交往历史很长，但真正的碰撞与交融只有从鸦片战争起到现在的 100 多年时间。正是在这 100 多年里，中西方关系可谓沧海桑田。

中西方关系的变化首先是中国地位的变化。过去中国受西方列强的任意宰割，国家被瓜分豆剖，"人为刀俎，我为鱼肉"。香港遭受英国殖民统治，"东方之珠"离开了祖国的怀抱长达 155 年；上海租界林立，"华人与狗不得入内"的牌子触目惊心。帝国主义列强把一个又一个不平等条约强加给了中国。

中国第一位驻外使节——清朝首任驻英公使郭嵩焘，也可算我的最早一位前任，但他出使的起因并不是因为中英建立了公使级外交关系，而是由于清廷与英国签订了丧权辱国的条约。1875 年初，英国驻华公使馆官员马嘉理在云南境内与当地居民发生冲突后被打死。英国政府一口咬定这是当地政府蓄谋所为，胁迫清政府签订《烟台条约》，规定中国赔偿白银 20 万两，开放宜昌等四个通商口岸，并要求清廷派钦差大臣赴英赔礼道歉。清政府不得不从，后来考虑既然派使臣赔礼道歉，不如干脆让其留下常驻，这样可保留一点面子。中国第一位驻外使节就这样成了一位赔罪使臣，他向英王递交的"国书"竟是一封丧失国格的道歉信。这就是一百多年前中国与西方的关系。

还有，过去的中国一直被西方称为"东亚病夫"，不仅是国家积贫积弱，人民的身体也是羸弱不堪。新中国成立前，中国人的平均寿命是 35 岁，中国也从来没有获得过一块奥运会奖牌。

今天，中西方之间的不平等历史已经被彻底改写，中国经济飞速发展，综合国力迅速提高。中国已经成为世界第二大经济体、世界第二大贸易体，外汇储备高居世界第一。中国作为联合国安理会五常之一和二十国集团的重要成员，在世界政治、安全、经济事务中都发挥着举足轻重的作用。

今天，香港与澳门都已经回归祖国。这是我第二次访问香港，第一次是 14 年前参加历史性的香港政权交接仪式，见证五星红旗和紫荆旗同时在香港会议展览中心冉冉升起。

今天，"东亚病夫"的帽子早已被扔进了历史的垃圾堆。中国人的人均寿命已经达到 73 岁，"十二五"规划更将这一目标提高到了 74.5 岁，接近西方国家 76 岁的水平；中国大陆的基本医疗保障制度已覆盖超过 12.5 亿人口，成为世界上覆盖人口最多的医疗保障制度。中国成为世界体育强国，在2008年北京奥运会中勇夺金牌总数第一。2012年，第30届夏季奥运会将在伦敦举行，我相信中国运动员能够再次取得优异成绩，我到时也将在现场为他们加油助威。

中西方关系的另一个巨大变化是中西方交往与合作的变化。过去，中国在西方国家对外贸易投资中的比例无足轻重。今天，中国和美欧互为最主要的贸易投资伙伴。中国是欧盟第二大出口市场和第一大进口来源地，是美国第三大出口市场和第一大进口来源地。中国对西方国家的投资近年加速增长，特别是英国，非常看重和欢迎中国企业投资。按年度计，中国对英投资在英国投资来源国中已经排到第7位，在伦敦投资的企业数量已经居各国第3。

中西方人员往来和人文交流的频繁和密切也是前所未有的。中英之间每天至少有13个直飞航班，中美之间每天有9000多人往返于太平洋两岸；中国在英国留学生数量有12万人，在美国约有13万人；孔子学院在英国有17所，在整个欧洲有120所，在美国也有70所。

在国际事务中，过去西方不认为中国有发言权，后来把中国看成一个地区性大国，今天西方越来越认识到，中国是一个全球性大国，许多全球性事务和国际热点问题的解决离不开中国的参与和支持，世界经济的繁荣和稳定也离不开中国的作用和贡献。因而，中西方在国际事务中的磋商与协调现在非常紧密。

一百多年来中西方关系发生了翻天覆地的变化。今天中国要发展，离不开与世界的良性互动，这也包括离不开与西方国家的交流与合作。我们高度重视发展与西方国家的关系，将其置于中国外交全局中的重要位置。因为一个良好的中西方关系不仅造福中国与西方国家人民，而且对于维护世界和平与繁荣至关重要。近年来，我们与欧盟等都建立了全面战略伙伴关系，我们也与美国共同致力于建设"相互尊重、互利共赢的合作伙伴关系"。

当然，中西方关系的发展并不稳定，分歧和矛盾时起时伏。青年同学们从媒体报道中可能都会感受到这一点。为什么会出现这种现象？我认为主要有两大原因。

一个主因是西方的心态问题。西方自与中国交往以来，长期面对的是一个弱势的中国，形成了居高临下的思维惯性，如今中国强大了，西方要重新摆正自己的位置，一时很难适应，担忧和焦虑感上升。它们的逻辑就是"国强必霸"，担心中国会与它们争夺在国际事务中的主导权，要与它们在世界范围内争夺资源和能源。

近几年，大家可以看到西方先后推出各种版本的"中国威胁论"，比如中国"军事威胁论""经济威胁论""能源威胁论""环境威胁论""文化威胁论"等，2011年的一个突出论调是中国"网络威胁论"，无端指责中国发动网络攻击、搞网络间谍。西方也对中国与非洲发展正常的经贸合作感到紧张，抛出所谓的"新殖民主义论"。

"中国威胁论"耸人听闻，不攻自破，西方又提出"中国责任论"，给中国戴不切实际的高帽，如"G2"（两国集团）、"CHIMERICA"（中美国）等，要求中国在世界经济、气候变化、国际发展等问题上承担超出自身能力的责任。这正如鲁迅先生当年所提醒国人的：世上既有"棒杀"，也有"捧杀"。

中西方产生问题的另一个主因是西方不能正确对待中西方的不同。中西方制度不同，这是客观事实，是由各国的历史和国情决定的，本身无可厚非。但西方有种"模式优越论"，即只认为西方的制度才是先进的、放之四海而皆准，只认为西方的"三权分立""一人一票"才是民主。

西方总是以自己的标准衡量别人，总想把自己的一套标准强行推销给别人，因而"一叶障目，不见泰山"，看不到中国的经济、政治全面改革开放，看不到中国人权事业的进步，看不到中国社会的多元及富有活力。我曾经与英国人说，中国人推崇孔子的话，"三人行，必有我师"，但是，你们信奉的却是"三人行，我必为师"。西方对自身弊病也长期疏于检讨，直到这次全球金融危机的爆发并持续演变，西方才认识到自身经济、社会和政治制度中存在的种种缺陷。

如何处理好中西方关系之间的问题，我认为关键是三点。

第一，积极看待中国的发展，减少不必要的担忧。

西方还是有一些有识之士能够正确看待中国发展的。英国前首相托尼·布莱尔多年以前就曾提出："中国的发展是机遇，而不是威胁。"的确，中国的发展不对任何国家构成威胁，中国没有侵略别人一寸领土，中国在海外除了参加联合国维和行动，没有派出一兵一卒。中国对世界经济增长的贡献率近年一直保持在20%以上。中国出口的物优价廉产品满足了世界各地消费者的需求，减缓了当地的通货膨胀。中国过去10年平均每年进口价值6870亿美元的商品，为相关国家和地区创造了1400多万个就业岗位；今后5年，中国有望进口超过8万亿美元的商品。

前几年，西方出版了一本很有影响力的书《当中国统治世界：西方世界的衰落和中国的崛起》，最近又出版了一本书《黯然失色：生活在中国经济主导的阴影下》，有人给这本书取了个别名——《当人民币统治世界》。类似的文章及书籍很多，也很吸引眼球，但是其中不少观点夸大其辞，都在以己度人。中国统治不了世界，中国也没有想过要统治世界。正如邓小平所说，中国永远不争霸、永远不称霸。中国只想走好自己的路，管好自己的事，无意也没有兴趣去输出所谓"中国模式"。西方对中国的担心更多是对自己缺乏信心。

第二，加强民众间的交流与沟通，增进对中国的了解。

一些英国普通民众曾当面告诉我，他们最近去了中国，但发现中国与他们从英国报纸、电视中得到的印象完全不一样，好像来到了另一个国家。中国完全不是西方媒体说的经济快要崩溃，社会封闭，民众怨声载道，而是中国经济很有活力，社会非常开放，人民生活幸福，对未来充满希望。但是，来过中国的人毕竟是少数，绝大多数还不了解中国。只有加强人员往来与交流，更多西方民众才会了解一个真实的中国、现代的中国、进步的中国。

当然，了解中国也不能只到中国东部沿海地区，否则就会以为中国的城市都像上海，中国的农村都如同江浙地区，中国已是发达国家了。我经常与英国人讲，中国的城乡区域发展差距还很大，西部地区还很贫穷落后，并经常以我曾经工作的甘肃省为例，那里一些偏远地方的老百姓饮用水都很困难，有些农村中小学生从来没有用过电脑、上过网。我还告诉他们，中国目前人均GDP只有4000美元左右，仅相当于英国的1/10；按照每人每天1美元收入的联合国标准，中国仍有1.5亿贫困人口，相当于英国人口的2.5倍。

这就是中国的国情，中国还是一个不折不扣的发展中国家。

第三，妥善处理分歧，相互尊重，求同存异。

实际上，一国是很难照学照搬他国的政治、经济和社会制度的，很多发展中国家也采用西方的多党议会制，但并不成功，经济没有发展，社会长期动荡。因此，复制社会制度并不像在电脑上复制一个文件那么简单，只需"复制"和"粘贴"，举手之劳就能搞定。它的复杂性在于要把你的文件复制到我的电脑上，但是你的电脑用的是微软 Windows 7 系统，而我用的是苹果 Mac OS X 系统，两个系统并不兼容。

2011 年 10 月，"苹果之父"乔布斯走完了其传奇一生。许多人在怀念和评价乔布斯时都用了"伟大"一词，我认为，他的伟大既在于不断创新、推陈出新，也在于不断坚持，坚信自己的产品是最好的、最受"苹果迷"欢迎的。正因为如此，尽管苹果与微软是两个系统，但沿着不同的道路发展，各自不断推出最新版本，取得了非凡的成就。今天的中西方难道不也需要这样吗？

要构建更加广阔的中西方关系，我认为需要解放思想，开拓思维。既要顺应人类社会发展的大趋势，也要结合当今的时代潮流；既要吸取人类文明发展的经验教训，也要借鉴中国自身传统思想文化精髓。

2011 年 9 月，中国发表了《中国的和平发展》白皮书，这既是对中国与世界关系的构想，也是中国在新时期对中西方关系的建设性探索。概括起来，我认为新型中西方关系具有三个基本要素。

第一个要素是和平发展。今天"和平发展"的含义不仅是放弃诉诸战争和武力，通过对话与谈判解决争端，也包括中西方彻底抛弃冷战思维这一陈旧观念，实现和平共存、和平共处、和平共富、和平共强。

中国致力于维护和促进世界的和平与稳定，做国际体系的建设者和贡献者。中国不会重复西方国家"国强必霸"的老路，因为中国文化崇尚"以和为贵"，没有侵略扩张的基因；中国在近代历史上饱受外来侵略之苦，深知"己所不欲，勿施于人"；中国在 30 年前就认识到，和平与发展是时代两大主题，世界多极化和经济全球化是两大趋势，不可逆转。因此，中国完全有信心走出所谓"大国兴衰"的"历史循环",打破"国强必霸"的陈旧逻辑,与西方实现和平发展。

第二个要素是合作发展。国与国之间存在分歧和矛盾是正常的,中西方之间也不例外。但这些分歧和矛盾不应成为我们发展关系的障碍。中西方关系的发展并不是一个"零和游戏",我们可以在良性竞争中不断寻找合作机会,拓展合作领域,扩大共同利益,实现共同发展。

1776年,亚当·斯密发表了一本著作《国民财富的性质和原因的研究》,也就是《国富论》,从而开了西方经济学的先河。在书中,他认为人尽管都是自私自利的,只会追求对自己有利的事情,但是很多时候,"经过一双看不见的手的引导""借由追求他个人的利益,往往也使他更为有效地促进了这个社会的利益",换言之,只有合作才能扩大个人利益,实现共同利益。

"看不见的手的引导",这是无意识的被动行为。在今天相互依存、利益交融的世界,中国有意识地主动寻求与世界各国,包括西方国家实现互利共赢。我们在追求自身发展的同时努力实现与他国发展的良性互动,建立和发展不同形式的合作关系,将共同的利益"蛋糕"做大和共享,从而实现共同繁荣。在危机出现时,我们也强调"同舟共济",共渡难关、共迎挑战。

第三个要素是和谐发展。中西方之间怎样才算和谐,"鸡犬之声相闻,民至老死不相往来"的小国寡民思想不是和谐,"井水不犯河水"的江湖规则也不是和谐。我认为,和谐就是孔子说的"和而不同",就是《联合国宪章》里写明的"彼此以善邻之道,和睦相处",就是胡锦涛主席曾指出的"尊重各国自主选择社会制度和发展道路的权利"。中西方应该相互尊重、平等相待,应该相互包容、求同存异,应该相互借鉴、取长补短。

概括起来,要构建新型中西方关系,我认为,和平发展是条件,合作发展是动力,和谐发展是保障,这三者缺一不可。

中国有句古语:"知之非艰,行之惟艰。"构建新型中西方关系"知易行难"。这并非一朝一夕的事情,需要双方树立共同战略目标,长期保持耐心,持之以恒,行之以渐。

构建新型中西方关系是前无古人的事业,没有现成的历史经验可循,也没有现成的理论依据参考，只有靠中西方的这一代人和未来几代人甚至十几代人共同努力创造。这是我们的责任，更是你们的责任！

老师们、同学们，

2010年初，我刚到伦敦，就有缘与贵校前校长高锟先生相见，那是英国皇家工程院为他荣获诺贝尔物理学奖举行的庆祝酒会，我当面向他表示了祝贺，并祝愿他安享晚年。高锟先生是香港中文大学师生的榜样，是中国人的楷模。半个多世纪前，高锟先生年少时从香港赴英国留学，轮船在海上足足航行了30天；而今天，国泰航空公司的班机只需要13个小时；如果使用高锟先生发明的光纤通信技术，香港到伦敦现在最快只需176毫秒即能实现信息传送。

我们的世界变小了，中国和西方曾经相距万里，今天已经近在咫尺、触手可及。那就让中国和西方都伸出双手，握在一起，真正成为合作的伙伴、坦诚的朋友，共同构建新型中西方关系。

谢谢！

Build a New Type of Relationship between China and the West*

Vice-Chancellor Joseph J. Y. Sung,

Teachers and Students,

Let me begin with warm thanks to the Chinese University of Hong Kong (CUHK) for this gracious invitation.

I arrived in the UK nearly two years ago to take up my responsibilities as Ambassador. During that period this is the ninth time I have spoken at a global top 100 university. But today's experience is unique. The reason is that all the other eight universities were British. Today the CUHK offers me the first opportunity to speak to a top world university on Chinese land and in my native language.

On the podium of British universities, I was proud to represent my country as ambassador. Today, standing before students of a prominent Hong Kong university, I have a different feeling of pride. I am proud for Hong Kong to have such a world-class institution of higher learning.

That high ranking has been won in a remarkably short timescale. This is also my first visit to a university younger than me! The CUHK, built in 1963, can justifiably be proud of its achievements. I must congratulate the CUHK on making it into the global top fifty league of universities within only half a century of its birth.

I should congratulate the home base of the CUHK which is Hong Kong. In addition to creating this world class higher education centre, Hong Kong has built an enviable

---

* Speech at the Chinese University of Hong Kong. The Chinese University of Hong Kong, 23 November 2011.

reputation as an international economic and financial hub.

I have had the privilege of serving China as a diplomat for nearly 40 years. This has taken me to North America, Africa and Europe. My experience gave me a front-row seat to witness how China's relationship with the West has evolved for decades. Today, I have increasingly felt this relationship to be at a crossroads of trust and cooperation.

Hong Kong is a well-known meeting point of China and the West. This connecting point is reflected in the core beliefs of CUHK. Your university is committed, "to combine tradition with modernity, and to bring together China and the West." This mission of the CUHK gives me a unique platform to share with you some thoughts on the relations between China and the West.

The engagement between China and the West harks back to a distant past. But it's only from the Opium War of 1840 that deeper exchanges, both positive and negative, began. Since then, our relationship has traveled an extraordinary journey and undergone a vast change.

The most impressive change is the transformation of China's status. One century ago, China was at the mercy of imperial powers and its territory was carved into spheres of foreign influence.

Hong Kong, the oriental Pearl, was ceded to Britain for 155 years. Shanghai's foreign concessions became notorious for their signs warning: "Dogs and Chinese Not Admitted." And China was coerced to accept one unequal treaty after another by Western powers.

China's first senior diplomat posted abroad was the Qing government's minister to Britain called Guo Songtao. He is my earliest predecessor. Instead of being part of the ministerial-level diplomatic relations, his posting resulted from an unequal treaty the Qing government was forced to sign with Britain.

In early 1875, British diplomat Augustus Margary was killed in a conflict with locals in Yunnan. The British government asserted it was an orchestrated assassination by the local authorities and pressured the Qing government to sign the Chefoo Convention. Under this convention, China was required to pay 200,000 silver dollars, open four treaty ports and send a mission of apology to Britain. The Qing government had no alternative but to accept all the demands and, as a face-saving tactic, appointed the head of the mission China's first diplomat stationed abroad. So, the mission of the first

Chinese resident envoy was to beg pardon and the "credential" he handed to the British monarch was a letter of apology! The disgrace surrounding the whole event was a revealing example of the state of China's relations with the West at that point in time.

At the same time, the West labeled China the "Sick Man of the East". Western people used this description to illustrate China is the poverty, weakness and people's poor health. Before the founding of the New China in 1949, the Chinese people's lifespan was only 35 years old. In addition, the Chinese had never won any Olympic gold medal.

Today, China's relationship with the West has been rewritten. China's economy is booming and its national power is on the rise. It's the world's second largest economy, leader in global exports and the biggest holder of foreign currency reserves. China sits on the UN Security Council as one of the five permanent members and is an important player within the G20. We carry considerable weight in world political, security and economic affairs.

Today, both Hong Kong and Macao have returned to the embrace of the motherland. This is my second visit to Hong Kong. This is 14 years on from the historic handover ceremony that witnessed the rise of the five-star national flag and the bauhinia flag at the Hong Kong Convention and Exhibition Centre.

Today, the title of the "Sick Man of the East" has long been thrown into the scrap heap of history. In turn China has advanced in ways unprecedented in the whole of human history.

Chinese people's life expectancy has reached 73 years old and may rise to 74.5 toward the end of the 12th Five-Year Plan period, closing in on the Western average of 76.

The Chinese Mainland's basic medicare system has become the largest of its kind, benefiting 1.25 billion people.

As a measure of its role at the centre stage in world sports, China topped the gold medal count at the 2008 Beijing Olympics.

Next year in the London Olympics, Chinese Olympians are expected to perform with distinction again. I myself will cheer them on in the stadiums, at the poolside and near the finishing lines.

Another enormous change in China-West relations is about the scale of exchange and cooperation.

As recently as 40 years ago China was close to being negligible in the trade and investment pattern of the West. Yet today, China has emerged as Europe and America's most important trade and investment partner. We are Europe's second largest export market and number one source of imports. Looking across the Pacific Ocean, we are America's third largest export market and number one source of imports.

Meanwhile, more Chinese investment is flowing into the West. Britain and other Western countries place a premium on Chinese capital inflow and welcome Chinese investors. Now, China is the 7th largest investor country in Britain and our enterprises have become the third largest investor community in London.

Meanwhile, China and the West have seen their people-to-people contacts reach greater depth than ever. On a daily basis there are at least 13 direct flights between China and Britain. Each day over 9,000 Chinese and American travelers fly over the Pacific. China has 120,000 students in Britain and roughly 130,000 students in America. Britain today hosts 17 Confucius Institutes, and there're another 120 in Europe and 70 in America.

In world affairs, the West's shift of attitude towards China has been profound. The developed countries did not want China to have a voice in the past. Then they began to view China as a regional power. Today, the West has increasingly recognised China's global power status. The consensus view has emerged that many global challenges and crisis issues will fail to find solutions without China's participation and support. Indeed there is broad recognition that world prosperity and stability need China's active participation. That's why China and the West are building closer collaborative ties through consultations in global affairs.

China's relations with the West have gone through great changes over the past century. Today, China's development calls for a good relationship and close cooperation with the whole world and not just the developed countries.

The relationship with the West is a high priority on our foreign policy agenda. The rationale is that strong relations with the West deliver benefits to both China and the West and are critical to world peace and prosperity.

In recent years, China has built a comprehensive strategic partnership with the EU and Britain. We are also building a cooperative partnership based on mutual respect and benefit.

As I have described there has been much positive progress over the past three decades. But there have been many challenges to overcome to secure this advance. China's relations with the West have experienced frequent setbacks and tensions. These can result in dramatic media headlines. Why is that? It seems to me there are two reasons that deserve our attention.

One major reason is the Western mentality. For centuries, the West dealt with a weak China in a condescending way. Today, the West is not so comfortable with a stronger China and is showing increasing unease and anxiety. Their approach is along the lines that, "power means hegemony." Increasingly Western people are concerned about China's competition for global leadership, resources and energy.

In recent years, we have heard so many versions of the "China threat". This manifests itself as China's "military threat", "economic threat", "energy threat", "environmental threat" and "cultural threat".

This year, the temperature is rising on China's "cyber threat". China is billed as a culprit behind hacking activities and cyber spying. The West also tries to demonise China's commercial cooperation with Africa and calls into question China's "neo-colonialism".

Sensational as it is, the case of the "China threat" is self-contradictory. More recently, the West is talking about "China's responsibility" and presenting to China headline grabbing titles such as "G2" and "CHIMERICA".

Often there are demands that China take more than its fair share of responsibility on world economy, climate change and international development.

Mr Lu Xun rightly cautioned the Chinese. He said there are those who "talk you up" and those who "sell you short". China needs to keep a cool head and clear mind about such traps.

The strains on our relations between China and the world also derive from the Western reluctance to recognize China's uniqueness. There shouldn't be any surprise about the different systems of China and the West. This is a reality shaped by our different histories and national circumstances.

The sticking point now is the Western belief in its superior and "one-size-fits-all" model. In this sense, an orthodox form of democracy must be Western. These values reflect a perception that every governing system needs to have such visible attributes as "checks and balances" and "one man, one vote".

The West judges the rest of the world by its own standards. It is at pains to force their standards on others. With that approach comes a failure to see the larger picture, such as China's political reform, economic openness, human rights progress and social diversity.

I explain to my British friends that the Chinese believe in the wisdom of Confucius. I tell them Confucius described how "among any three people, there must be my teacher". But the prevailing belief in the West is the reverse! The Western view is that "among any three people, I must be the teacher". In the Western world there is a continual failure of scrutiny of its own performance and progress. The maelstrom released by the global financial crisis that started three years ago is striking evidence of the failure at the core of the Western model. The crisis is a wake-up call to the West and these events have exposed the failings in its economic, social and political institutions.

To tackle the roots of the Western bias and misconceptions toward China, three things must be done.

First, take a positive view of China and eliminate unnecessary concerns.

The West has no shortage of visionary voices about China's development. Many years ago, former Prime Minister Tony Blair pointed to China as an opportunity, not a threat.

Indeed, China's development is not a threat to anyone. We have never seized one single inch of land abroad and have no boots on foreign soil except under the UN peacekeeping banner.

Economically, China has driven over 20% of world economic growth in recent years. Quality yet reasonably priced Chinese products have met diverse consumer needs and kept inflation low US worldwide.

Over the past ten years, China's annual import of 687 billion US dollars worth of goods has created more than 14 million jobs. The next five years will see China's overall imports rise to 8 trillion US dollars.

China's rise has attracted a great deal of academic interest as well. A couple of years back, a Western writer published an influential book titled *When China Rules the World: The Rise of the Middle Kingdom and the End of the Western World*.

Recently, another book, *Eclipse: Living in the Shadow of China's Economic Dominance*, was out and soon nicknamed "When Renminbi Rules the World". The list goes on and on.

But take a close look at many of these books and you find that they invariably make sensational cases to grab wider attention. China has neither ability nor desire to rule the world. According to Mr Deng Xiaoping, China will never seek hegemony. We believe China's development path fits in well into our national circumstances. It can't be copied everywhere. Therefore, there's no "Chinese model" to speak of and still less the export of a "Chinese model". Indeed there is a case to be made that the Western anxiety about China reflects a lack of confidence in the West.

The second way to demolish misconceptions and misunderstanding is to increase people-to-people contacts and develop a deeper understanding of China.

I was told by some British friends that their recent trips to China had overthrown their previously held perceptions of the country. What they saw was the reality of China today. This is a vibrant, prosperous and open society with happy citizens. This is in stark contrast to the dated clichés repeated endlessly in the Western media and newspapers. This media is filled with opinions about the Chinese collapsing economy, autocratic society and struggling people. The facts about the real China today go unreported.

That said, those Western people who have travelled to and experienced China are in the minority. Most Westerners lack a wide exposure to China. Increased people-to-people contacts is a vital and effective way to build public understanding of the real and modern China.

Of course, a narrow focus on China's eastern seaboard may create an illusion that China has already joined the ranks of developed countries. First-time visitors may easily draw striking parallels between Shanghai and New York, and point to Pudong New Area as China's Manhattan.

But China's story is much more than that. We face a very big regional and urban-rural divide and our western hinterland remains poor and underdeveloped. Take Gansu province where I served as Assistant Governor. Some people in the outlying areas didn't have easy access to drinking water, and some rural students never had access to computers or surfed the internet.

What I always tell my British friends is this. China's annual per capita GDP is only around 4,000 US dollars. That is one tenth the size of Britain. In addition, 150 million Chinese, or two and a half times the size of Britain's population, live below the poverty line as measured by the one dollar per day UN standard.

This is the real picture of China. This is a China that remains a developing country.

The third way to demolish misconceptions and misunderstanding is to manage differences with mutual respect and build broader consensus.

Any open-minded observer of world affairs can see that it is difficult to copy another country's political, economic and social systems. Many developing countries have tried yet failed to borrow the parliamentary system from the West. Adopting that system did not bring widely anticipated growth and stability. Therefore, a social model cannot be transplanted in the real life on a silver platter like "copy and paste" on computer. It runs the danger of a system crash because what's working on Windows 7 is not compatible with MAC OS X.

Last month, the passing of Steve Jobs, father of Apple, brought an end to a legendary life. His mourners and admirers didn't hesitate to describe him a "great" godfather in the technology industry. To me, his greatness is about ingenuity, perseverance and a strong confidence in the ability of his designs to win the hearts of Apple customers.

That's why Apple and Microsoft, though with vastly different computer systems and product lines, have both won success. Shouldn't China and the West use this analogy and do the same?

Building a new era of China-West relations, we need to free our minds and widen our horizon. Most essential is to echo the call of our time with an acute awareness of the general trend of human progress. We need to learn the success stories and lessons from world history and draw on the best of China's traditional philosophy.

In September, China published a white paper on China's "Peaceful Development". It outlines China's vision for its relations with the world and its constructive ideas on building China-West relations. To sum up, the new relations between China and the West need three basic elements.

First, peaceful development.

Today, peaceful development means settling disputes through dialogue and negotiation and rejecting war and force. More important, it means China and the West should rise above the dated Cold War mentality and seek to build peace and prosperity together.

China is committed to promoting world peace and stability and contributing to a sound international system. We don't believe in the logic of "power means hegemony" and won't follow the beaten track of the West.

Instead, we have a culture of peace. Invasion and expansion are not in our genes. China itself was a victim of a whole century of imperial invasion from 1840. We have no intention to do to others what we don't want done to ourselves.

Since thirty years ago, China has come to realize that peace and development were the theme of our time and multipolarity and globalization were the inexorable trends. China has confidence that we will break the "iron law" of the rise and fall of powers and prove the "power means hegemony" wrong. What China opts for is peaceful relations and shared prosperity with the West.

The second point about securing new relations between China and the West is to aim for development through cooperation.

It is natural for countries to have problems and differences among themselves. China and the West are no different. However, differences shouldn't stand in the way of relationship. This relationship between China and the West is not a zero-sum game. We can seek opportunities through healthy competition, expand collaborative areas, widen converging interests and achieve common development.

In 1776, Adam Smith published his book *An Inquiry into the Nature and Causes of the Wealth of Nations*. This is also known as *The Wealth of Nations,* which laid the foundation for the Western economics theories.

Smith pointed out in the book that in many cases, "led by an invisible hand," "by pursuing his own interest he frequently promotes that of the society more effectually than when he really intends to promote it." In other words, only cooperation can expand individual interests and benefit all.

Being "led by an invisible hand" is a passive behavior. By contrast, in today's interconnected and interdependent world, China actively seeks a win-win partnership with the world, including the West. This is a partnership that may take different forms in different areas and that enables more of us to share prosperity. In time of crisis, we call for unity among all countries to rise up to challenges and build a better future.

The third point I want to make about winning new relations between China and the West is to secure a harmonious relationship.

Harmony doesn't mean standing apart in this interdependent global village. Then how can China and the West achieve harmony?

Confucius taught about "harmony in diversity". The United Nations Charter calls for nations "to practice tolerance and live together in peace with one another as good neighbours". In addition, President Hu Jintao pointed to the need to "respect each other's choice of social system and development path". All these three elements offer a guide for the East and the West to accommodate and learn from each other with respect and equality.

In a word, the above three elements are essential to a new partnership between China and the West. Peaceful development is the prerequisite. Cooperation is the driving force. Then harmony provides an effective guarantee.

China has an old saying: "Knowing the challenge is not difficult, but acting on it is." Building a new China-West relationship is easier said than done. It won't happen over night, but instead demands a strategic vision, a strong commitment and a down-to-earth approach from both sides.

Building such a new relationship has no precedent, no ready solution and no existing theories. To chart a path forward, generations of Chinese and Westerners need to work closely together. This is our responsibility. But more importantly, it's your responsibility as teachers and students.

Soon after I began my duty as Ambassador in London, I was pleased to meet Mr Charles Kuen Kao, former Vice-Chancellor of this University. It was at a reception hosted by Britain's Royal Academy of Engineering to celebrate his Nobel Prize for Physics. I congratulated Mr Kao on his great achievement and wished him all the best.

It strikes me that Mr Kao is a role model for the teachers and students of this University and for all the Chinese. Half a century back, it took him 30 days to travel to Britain by ship to pursue studies. Today, a Cathay Pacific flight only needs 13 hours to cover the same distance. If Mr Kao's fiber optics technology is deployed, the time needed to transmit information between the two places will be cut short to just 176 milliseconds.

That's a vivid reminder of our world getting smaller today. Yes, geographically,

China and the West are thousands of miles apart. But modern technology has brought us closer to each other than ever.

We live in a globalized world whose challenges can only be answered through common actions by us all.

For that to happen, China and the West must extend their hands to each other and work side by side to build a new partnership.

Thank you!

弘扬严复精神，加强中西互鉴*

尊敬的英国皇家海军学院旧址基金会主席托尼·海尔斯先生，

女士们、先生们：

我非常高兴出席"严复、帝国留学生与皇家海军学院"展览开幕式。

在137年前的1877年，正值中国晚清内忧外患、国难深重之际，中国历史上的两位著名人物先后来到了伦敦。他们中的一位是我最早的前任，即清王朝首任驻英使节郭嵩焘先生，时年59岁；还有一位就是来英留学、时年23岁的严复先生。

郭嵩焘先生驻节英伦期间，深入工厂学校，钻研政治制度，思想观念发生了根本变化，发出"西洋政教、制造，无一不出于学"的惊呼，向清政府大力介绍西方先进的政治、经济和社会制度，提议效仿学习。郭嵩焘先生的主张为清王朝保守旧势力所不容，最后不得不黯然去职，终老乡野。

年轻的严复先生来到皇家海军学院，不仅学习先进的海军知识和技能，而且系统学习西方近代自然和社会科学思想与理论，努力探求中西方之间的本质差异，探索中国富强之道。

这一老一少在伦敦相识，并结为忘年交。郭嵩焘认为严复谈吐不凡，才华出众，"其言多可听者"，常与严复论述中西学术政制之异同。严复感怀郭嵩焘知遇之恩，后来把郭嵩焘称作"生平第一知己"。

---

* 在"严复、帝国留学生与皇家海军学院"展览开幕式上的讲话。2014年11月13日，英国皇家海军学院旧址，格林尼治，伦敦。

在27年后的1904年，严复因公务再次来到英国。此时，严复已经翻译出版了《天演论》《原富》《法意》等8部著作，将西方的社会学、政治学、政治经济学、哲学和自然科学系统地介绍到中国。他提倡科学民主，主张变法革新，当之无愧地成为中国近代启蒙思想家。1905年，中国历史上又一位著名人物也再次来到伦敦，他就是中国民主革命的先驱孙中山先生。孙中山与严复在伦敦见了面并长时间深谈。严复认为"为今之计，惟急从教育上着手，庶几逐渐更新乎"，即中国的根本问题在于教育，革命非当务之急。孙中山则说："俟河之清，人寿几何？君为思想家，鄙人乃实行家也。"6年之后，严复先生思想启蒙、孙中山先生实践领导的辛亥革命推翻了清朝的统治。但也如严复先生所言，辛亥革命并未从根本上改变当时中国贫穷落后的面貌。

时光荏苒，今天大清帝国没有了，大英帝国也没有了，昔日的皇家海军学院也成了格林尼治大学。但百年前的风云人物并未随时代发展而褪色，他们早已被浓墨重彩地写入汗青，彪炳史册。

今天，我们在这里纪念严复先生，就是要弘扬他开放包容的精神。严复先生是中国传统知识分子，但他摆脱了那个时代中国传统知识分子因循守旧、盲目排外的痼疾，认真学习吸收西方科学和知识，并且在思想和价值领域努力寻找西方强盛之源，这犹如在当时黑暗的中国划亮了一根火柴。毛泽东主席因此评价严复为"向西方寻找真理的代表人物"。今天，西方也有一个如何认识中国的问题：是以开放包容的态度将中国的发展视为机遇，还是以敌视偏见的心态将中国的崛起看作威胁？严复先生一百多年前已经为我们树立了榜样，西方不应再犹豫彷徨，让机遇失之交臂。

我们在这里纪念严复先生，就是要弘扬他首倡变革的精神。在国家民族危亡之际，严复先生敢为天下先，译著西方名著，发表政论文章，抨击封建专制，鼓吹维新自强，提出"物竞天择，适者生存"，为近代中国思想界提供了急需的智慧资源，为中国社会的变革提供了必要的思想基础。习近平主席指出，"时至今日，严复的科学与爱国思想仍不过时"。今天，中国正在继续以大无畏的勇气全面深化改革，激发市场活力，拓宽创新道路，推进依法治国，改革成为推动中国经济社会发展的最大动力。同样，西方面对增长乏力和累积难题，也需要大胆进行改革，不改革难有经济增长，不改革难有社会公平。

我们在这里纪念严复先生，就是要弘扬他甘当沟通和理解的桥梁的精神。严复先生不仅是一位启蒙思想家，也是一位教育家和翻译家。严复任教中国的海军学校，引进西方现代海军管理思想和教学理论，为中国社会培养了许多杰出人才。他提出的"信、达、雅"翻译标准具有划时代意义，对中国后世的翻译理论和实践产生了深远影响。今天，西方的科学、文化、政治、哲学作品被大量翻译成中文并传播，但被翻译成英文、介绍给西方的中国作品则相形见绌，中西方文化交流存在不小逆差。我衷心希望在英国、在西方能涌现更多翻译家，将中国文化、中国思想、"中国梦"更多地以"信、达、雅"标准引进西方，让英国和西方民众更好地了解中国，特别是理解当代中国。

女士们、先生们，

处于 21 世纪的中国早已摆脱了积贫积弱，中国人民正在为实现中华民族伟大复兴的中国梦而努力奋斗。今天的中英关系也与百年前有天壤之别，两国建立了平等互利的合作伙伴关系。我也深感比郭嵩焘先生幸运，因为现在中英之间有着千千万万的"严复"，他们学贯中西，正活跃在经济、教育、文化和科技等各个领域，推动着两国的沟通与合作，促进着双向交流。这正如严复先生在其译著《天演论》中的名言："世道必进，后胜于今。"

在此，我谨感谢皇家海军学院旧址基金会和严复文化教育基金会联合举办这场关于严复生平与成就的展览。我们应当为严复先生歌功与喝采，我们同样期待今天千千万万个"严复"在各自领域为中英关系发展、为中西方交流做出更大贡献，我们也应当为他们鼓掌与加油！

谢谢！

Carry Forward Yan Fu's Spirit *

Chairman Tony Hales,

Ladies and Gentlemen,

It is my great pleasure to attend this opening ceremony.

137 years ago, in 1877, two Chinese came to London. Both of them are famous in modern Chinese history for different reasons.

One of them is my earliest predecessor, Minister Guo Songtao. Fifty-nine years of age, he was the beleaguered Qing Dynasty's first resident envoy overseas.

The other was the 23-year-old. Yan Fu who came onto these shores as a student.

Mr Guo's brief tenure in the UK saw him making extensive visits to factories and schools.

As a keen observer of the British system, Guo found that the Western strength was not limited to its manufacturing power, but more intrinsically lies in the underpinning studies, systems and ways of thinking.

Guo became an avid supporter for the Qing government to learn Western political, economic and social systems. But this made him very unpopular with the still largely conservative bureaucracy at home and led to his dismissal from public office.

The much younger Yan Fu was sent to the UK to study naval expertise. But his studies ranged far further.

He spent most of his time studying Western modern natural and social sciences, and made hard efforts to understand the difference between China and the West, exploring

---

* Speech at the Opening Ceremony of Yan Fu and Chinese Imperial Students at the Royal Naval College. Old Royal Naval College, Greenwich, London, 13 November 2014.

ways towards national prosperity and strength for China.

Despite their generational divide, Guo and Yan built a friendship while they were both living in London. In their conversations they often compared notes on Chinese and Western studies and systems.

Guo was amazed at Yan Fu's talent and insights and the appreciation was returned with gratitude and respect. Yan Fu later referred to Guo Songtao as "the friend who understands me best of all".

27 years later in 1904, Yan Fu returned to London, already an accomplished "enligh tenment"thinker. He had translated and introduced to China *The Evolution and Ethics*, *The Wealth of Nations* and *The Spirit of the Laws* among many other works.

With his translations and commentaries Yan Fu presented the people of China with insights into European natural, social, and political sciences as well as theories of economics and philosophy. He became a preacher of science and democracy and a supporter of reform and modernization.

It was here in London that Yan Fu met Sun Yat-sen, the flag-bearer of China's democratic revolution who came a year later. Yan was of the view that the solution to China's problem was education and reform, not revolution. But Sun disagreed, saying to Yan Fu: "You are a man of thoughts, but I am one of action."

A mere 6 years later, the 1911 Revolution that Yan helped to enlighten and Sun set in motion, put and end to the Qing Dynasty. But as Yan Fu had predicted, the revolution alone did not change China's fortunes for the better.

Here we are in London a century later. Imperial China and British Empire are both no more. Down here in Greenwich much of the Royal Naval College has become the University of Greenwich. But, those larger-than-life figures and their life's work are as relevant and inspiring as ever.

Yan Fu is remembered for his openness and inclusiveness.

As a classically-trained intellectual, Yan Fu stood out among his peers by studying the underlying ideas that made the European countries strong. His efforts to seek answers to China's problems from Europe gave China a glimmer of hope in those dire times.

Chairman Mao Zedong referred to Yan Fu as an icon of seeking answers from the West.

Today for Western countries, the openness and inclusiveness are also relevant when it comes to how to understand China.

Is the rise of China an opportunity or a threat? The answer depends on where one stands. On one side there is openness and inclusiveness; on the other side there is hostility and bias.

On the side of openness Yan Fu set a good example for us over a century ago.

China's rise is an opportunity some may hesitate to embrace, but will definitely hate to miss.

Yan Fu is also remembered for his courage to herald reform. When the Chinese nation's fortune was in its darkest hours, Yan Fu took the initiative to introduce European thinking into China.

He spoke out against the outdated feudal system and argued for reform and modernization. Yan laid the intellectual foundations for the changes that were in desperate need in Chinese society a century ago.

President Xi Jinping once said Yan Fu's understanding of science and his patriotism remain very much relevant today.

That vision and courage still inspires us today in our efforts to reform, to unleash the vigor of the market, to innovate our way forward and to promote the rule of law.

The need to reform is universal if we are to spur growth, unravel structural problems that are decades in the making and strive for a fairer society. It's the same here in this part of the world as well.

Finally, Yan Fu is remembered for his commitment to promoting understanding between cultures and civilizations. Aside from being a remarkable thinker, he was an outstanding educator and translator.

As a teacher and administrator at the naval academy in China, Yan Fu introduced modern teaching theories and practices in his work. Many of his students later played key roles in the course of Chinese history.

As a translator, he gave us the golden rules of truthfulness, expressiveness and elegance which still guides the theory and practice of translation in China.

Today, we have vast troves of Western books translated into Chinese but there is a deficit in the other direction.

It is my hope that we can have more master translators and communicators in the

UK and in the West to introduce Chinese culture, Chinese thinking and Chinese Dream to the public here in a truthful, expressive and elegant way.

That will do great service to the understanding of China, especially modern China, both in the UK and beyond.

Ladies and Gentlemen,

China in the 21st century has far better fortunes that have been hard fought and earned. We are now working for the realization of Chinese Dream of national rejuvenation.

China-UK relations are very different from what they were in Yan Fu's time, too. Today it is a relationship between partners built on equality and mutual benefit.

In such a context I consider myself a much more fortunate diplomat than my predecessor Minister Guo Songtao. Instead of one Yan Fu, we have thousands of them well versed in both cultures and working hard for the betterment of our relations in business, education, culture, science and technology and many other fields. As Yan Fu embodied in his translated version of *The Evolution and Ethics*: "The world gets better as it moves forward."

To conclude, I wish to congratulate the Greenwich Foundation for the Old Royal Naval College and the Yan Fu Foundation for making this exhibition possible.

While we are commemorating the accomplishments of Yan Fu, I believe we should also salute our contemporary Yan Fu's for their efforts in delivering a better tomorrow for East-West ties and a brighter future for China-UK relations.

Thank you!

后　记

我卸任驻英国大使已经三年多，但我一直在关注中英关系的走向。这期间，我曾三次访问英国，与许多英国朋友也保持着联系。看到中英关系持续下滑，英国朋友感到担心，我也十分痛心。回国这三年，我有机会给中央机关、省市、高校、企业、智库做报告，大家都很关心中英关系。其中问得最多的两个问题是：中英关系怎么了？中英关系能否回到从前？关于第一个问题，我的回答是：英国对华认知出了问题。关于第二个问题，我的回答更直截了当：中英关系不会回到从前。

在我出使英国这 11 年里，中英关系也经历过曲折甚至挫折，但总体是向前发展的。一个重要原因是英国始终把中国看作伙伴，把中国发展看作机遇。现在，英国把中国看作对手，把中国发展看作挑战。为什么？英国政客说是中国变了。我说，中国没变，是英国变了。我在 2020 年 7 月 30 日中国驻英国大使馆举行的中外记者会上，从四个方面谈了中英关系的"变与不变"，强调中方坚守初心、始终如一，而英方违背承诺、改变初心，指出英国的变化，以及根源在对华认知出了问题。认知出了问题，对华定位必然出偏差，对华政策必然犯错误，中英关系必然遭挫折。

那么，中英关系为什么不会回到从前？因为英国对华认知不会回到从前。莎士比亚有一句名言："凡是过去，皆为序章。"我们没有必要留恋从前，我们看重的是现在。现在需要回答的问题是：我们需要什么样的中英关系？习近平主席说，中方愿同英方一道努力，以稳定互惠的中英关系更好地造福两国和世界。"稳定互惠"就是我们需要的中英关系。

如何做到"稳定"？首先，要相互尊重，不忘中英建交的初心。中国尊重英国主权，从未做任何干涉英国内政的事。英方也应以同样的态度对待中方，尊重中国主权，停止干涉中国内政。历史告诉我们，只要这些国际法和国际关系基本准则得到遵守，中英关系就向前发展；反之则遭遇挫折，甚至倒退。其次，要求同存异。中英历史文化、社会制度、发展阶段不同，难免存在分歧。70多年前，英国在西方大国中第一个承认新中国。70年来，中英本着求同存异的精神，超越意识形态差异，推动中英关系不断向前发展。历史证明，中英有足够的智慧和能力管控和处理好双方分歧，中英关系可以成为平等相待的伙伴关系，而不是你输我赢的"对手关系"，更不是非此即彼的"敌对关系"。

如何做到"互惠"？首先，要确立正确的对华认知和定位，把中国的发展看作机遇而非挑战，更不是威胁。其次，要正确认识中英经贸关系的互惠互利。中英经济互补性强，利益深度融合，双方从彼此的合作中都获得了巨大收益，不存在谁更依赖谁、谁占谁便宜的问题。所谓"去风险""去依赖"完全是伪命题。英国在"后脱欧时代"要打造"全球化英国"，绕不开、离不开中国。与中国"脱钩"，就是与机遇脱钩，就是与发展脱钩，就是与未来脱钩。

一说到中英关系就总有说不完的话。我要感谢中信出版集团给我这个平台，与广大读者分享我的思考与观点，特别要感谢中信出版集团原董事长王斌和现任董事长陈炜给予我的鼓励和支持，感谢灰犀牛分社总编黄静、特邀译审艾玫子、责任编辑李亚婷和王诗的敬业精神和辛勤付出。我还要感谢陈雯、曾嵘和冯家亮等同志，他们一如既往的支持使本书顺利完成，他们提出的宝贵意见使我受益匪浅。

2024年立夏

Afterword

It has been more than three years since I retired as the Chinese Ambassador to the United Kingdom, but I have continued to follow the development of China-UK relations. I have visited the UK three times during this period and maintain in contact with many British friends. The continuous decline in China-UK relations worries my British friends and deeply saddens me. In the past three years since my return to China, I had the opportunity to give lectures to central government agencies, provincial and municipal authorities, universities, enterprises, and think tanks, and I could see people were concerned about China-UK relations. The two most frequently asked questions are: What has happened to China-UK relations? Can China-UK relations return to what they once were? My response to the first question is: The UK has developed a problematic understanding of China. As for the second question, my answer is more straightforward: China-UK relations will not return to what they once were.

During my 11 years as the Chinese Ambassador to the UK, China-UK relations made overall progress depsite twists and even setbacks. An important reason for this was that the UK consistently viewed China as a partner and China's development as an opportunity. Now, the UK sees China as a competitor and China's development as a challenge. Why? The British politicians say it is because China has changed. I would say, China has not changed; it is the UK that has changed. At the press conference held at the Chinese Embassy in the UK on 30 July 2020, I discussed what has changed and what has not in China-UK relations from four perspectives. I emphasized that China has remained steadfast and consistent, while the UK has violated its commitments and changed its original intentions. I highlighted the changes in the UK and pointed out the root cause being the UK's flawed understanding of China. With a flawed understanding, the UK's definition of China is bound to be skewed, its policy towards China is bound to be wrong, and China-UK relations are bound to suffer setbacks.

So, why cannot China-UK relations return to what they once were? Because the UK's understanding of China will not revert to what it once was. Shakespeare once said, "What's past is prologue." We do not need to yearn for the past; what matters is the present. The question we need to answer now is: What kind of China-UK relationship do we need? President Xi Jinping has stated that China is willing to work with the UK to develop a stable and mutually beneficial China-UK relationship that better serves both countries and the world. "Stable and mutually beneficial" is the kind of China-UK relationship we need.

How can we achieve "stability"? First, we must respect each other and not forget the original intention behind the establishment of diplomatic relations between China and the UK. China respects Britain's sovereignty and has never interfered in the UK's internal affairs. The UK should adopt the same attitude towards China, respect China's sovereignty, and stop interfering in China's internal affairs. History tells us that as long as these basic principles of international law and international relations are observed, China-UK relations will progress; otherwise, they will encounter setbacks or even regress. Second, we must seek common ground while reserving differences. China and the UK have different histories, cultures and social systems, and we are in different stages of development. Differences are inevitable. More than 70 years ago, the UK was the first major Western country to recognize the People's Republic of China. Over the past 70 years, China and the UK, in the spirit of seeking common ground while reserving differences, have transcended ideological differences and continuously advanced China-UK relations. History has proven that China and the UK have enough wisdom and capability to manage and handle their differences well. China-UK relations can become a partnership of equals, not a "competitive relationship" where one side wins and the other loses. They are certainly not an either-or "hostile relationship".

How can we achieve "mutual benefit"? First, we need to establish a right perception and definition of China, viewing China's development as an opportunity rather than a challenge, and certainly not a threat. Second, we need to correctly understand the mutually beneficial nature of China-UK economic and trade relations. China and the UK have strong economic complementarities and deeply integrated interests, from which both sides have gained tremendous benefits. This is not a quesiton of who depends more on whom or who takes advantage of whom. The so-called "de-risking" and "de-coupling" are completely false propositions. In the "post-Brexit era", the UK aims to build a "global Britain", which cannot bypass or detach from China. Decoupling from China means decoupling from opportunities, decoupling from development, and decoupling from the future.

There is always so much to say about China-UK relations. I would like to thank the CITIC Press Group for providing me with this platform to share my thoughts and perspectives with readers. I especially want to thank former Chairman Wang Bin and Chairman Chen Wei of the CITIC Press Group for their encouragement and support, and express my gratitude to the Chief Editor of the Grey Rhino Publishing Division, Huang Jing, Senior Translator Ai Meizi, and Editors Li Yating and Wang Shi for their dedication and hard work. I would also like to thank Chen Wen, Zeng Rong, and Feng Jialiang, whose continued support ensured the smooth completion of this book, and I benefited greatly from their valuable suggestions.

Liu Xiaoming
Summer, 2024